Oceanic Histories

Oceanic Histories is the first comprehensive account of world history focused not on the land but viewed through the 70% of the Earth's surface covered by water. Leading historians trace the history of the Indian, Pacific and Atlantic Oceans and the world's seas from the Arctic and the Baltic to the South China Sea and the Sea of Japan/Korea's East Sea, over the *longue durée*. Individual chapters trace the histories and the historiographies of the various oceanic regions with special attention to the histories of circulation and particularity, the links between human and non-human history and the connections and comparisons between parts of the World Ocean. Showcasing oceanic history as a field with a long past and a vibrant future, these authoritative surveys, original arguments and guides to research make this volume an indispensable resource for students and scholars alike.

David Armitage is the Lloyd C. Blankfein Professor of History at Harvard University, an Honorary Professor of History at the University of Sydney and an Honorary Fellow of St Catharine's College, Cambridge. He is the author or editor of sixteen books, among them *Civil wars: A history in ideas* (2017), *The history manifesto* (co-auth., 2014), *Pacific histories: Ocean, land, people* (co-ed., 2014), *Foundations of modern international thought* (2013), *The British Atlantic world, 1500–1800* (2nd edn, co-ed., 2009), *The declaration of independence: A global history* (2007) and *The ideological origins of the British Empire* (2000).

Alison Bashford is Professor of History at the University of New South Wales. Author and editor of many books on world history, environmental history and the history of science, her most recent are *The new worlds of Thomas Robert Malthus* (2016) with Joyce E. Chaplin and *Quarantine: Local and global histories* (ed., 2016). She is a Fellow of the British Academy and a former Trustee of the National Maritime Museum, Greenwich. From 2013 to 2017, she was the Vere Harmsworth Professor of Imperial and Naval History at the University of Cambridge.

Sujit Sivasundaram is Reader in World History at the University of Cambridge and works on both the Pacific and Indian Oceans, especially in the eighteenth and nineteenth centuries. He is the author of *Islanded: Britain, Sri Lanka and the bounds of an Indian Ocean colony* (2013) and *Nature and the godly empire: Science and evangelical mission in the Pacific, 1795–1850* (2005). In 2012, he won a Philip Leverhulme Prize for History, awarded for outstanding contributions to research by early-career scholars in the UK. He is co-editor of *The Historical Journal* and Fellow and Councillor of the Royal Historical Society.

Cambridge Oceanic Histories

Edited by

David Armitage
Alison Bashford
Sujit Sivasundaram

Across the world, historians have taken an oceanic turn. New maritime histories offer fresh approaches to the study of global regions, and to long-distance and long-term connections. Cambridge Oceanic Histories includes studies across whole oceans (the Pacific, the Indian, the Atlantic) and particular seas (among them, the Mediterranean, the Caribbean, the North Sea, the Black Sea). The series is global in geography, ecumenical in historical method, and wide in temporal coverage, intended as a key repository for the most innovative transnational and world histories over the *longue durée*. It brings maritime history into productive conversation with other strands of historical research, including environmental history, legal history, intellectual history, labour history, cultural history, economic history and the history of science and technology. The editors invite studies that analyse the human and natural history of the world's oceans and seas from anywhere on the globe and from any and all historical periods.

Oceanic Histories

Edited by
David Armitage
Harvard University

Alison Bashford
University of New South Wales

Sujit Sivasundaram
University of Cambridge

Shaftesbury Road, Cambridge CB2 8EA, United Kingdom

One Liberty Plaza, 20th Floor, New York, NY 10006, USA

477 Williamstown Road, Port Melbourne, VIC 3207, Australia

314–321, 3rd Floor, Plot 3, Splendor Forum, Jasola District Centre, New Delhi – 110025, India

103 Penang Road, #05–06/07, Visioncrest Commercial, Singapore 238467

Cambridge University Press is part of Cambridge University Press & Assessment, a department of the University of Cambridge.

We share the University's mission to contribute to society through the pursuit of education, learning and research at the highest international levels of excellence.

www.cambridge.org
Information on this title: www.cambridge.org/9781108423182

DOI: 10.1017/ 9781108399722

© Cambridge University Press & Assessment 2018

This publication is in copyright. Subject to statutory exception and to the provisions of relevant collective licensing agreements, no reproduction of any part may take place without the written permission of Cambridge University Press & Assessment.

First published 2018

A catalogue record for this publication is available from the British Library

ISBN 978-1-108-42318-2 Hardback
ISBN 978-1-108-43482-9 Paperback

Cambridge University Press & Assessment has no responsibility for the persistence or accuracy of URLs for external or third-party internet websites referred to in this publication and does not guarantee that any content on such websites is, or will remain, accurate or appropriate.

Contents

List of Figures and Maps	*page* vii
List of Contributors	viii
Introduction: Writing World Oceanic Histories SUJIT SIVASUNDARAM, ALISON BASHFORD AND DAVID ARMITAGE	1
PART I OCEANS	29
1 The Indian Ocean SUJIT SIVASUNDARAM	31
2 The Pacific Ocean ALISON BASHFORD	62
3 The Atlantic Ocean DAVID ARMITAGE	85
PART II SEAS	111
4 The South China Sea ERIC TAGLIACOZZO	113
5 The Mediterranean Sea MOLLY GREENE	134
6 The Red Sea JONATHAN MIRAN	156
7 The Sea of Japan/Korea's East Sea ALEXIS DUDDEN	182
8 The Baltic Sea MICHAEL NORTH	209

vi   Contents

9 The Black Sea   234
   STELLA GHERVAS

   PART III   POLES   267

10 The Arctic Ocean   269
    SVERKER SÖRLIN

11 The Southern Ocean   296
    ALESSANDRO ANTONELLO

    Index   319

List of Figures and Maps

Figure

8.1 Ship passages through the Sound (Øresund),
1503–1850   *page* 225

Maps

1.1 The Indian Ocean	32
2.1 The Pacific Ocean	64
3.1 The Atlantic Ocean	86
4.1 The South China Sea	114
5.1 The Mediterranean Sea	135
6.1 The Red Sea	157
7.1 The Sea of Japan/Korea's East Sea	183
8.1 The Baltic Sea	210
9.1 The Black Sea	235
10.1 The Arctic Ocean	270
11.1 The Southern Ocean	297

Contributors

ALESSANDRO ANTONELLO is a McKenzie Postdoctoral Fellow in the School of Historical and Philosophical Studies, University of Melbourne. He completed his PhD at the Australian National University and has held a postdoctoral research fellowship at the University of Oregon.

DAVID ARMITAGE is the Lloyd C. Blankfein Professor of History at Harvard University, an Honorary Professor of History at the University of Sydney and an Honorary Fellow of St Catharine's College, Cambridge. He is the author or editor of sixteen books, among them *Civil wars: A history in ideas* (2017), *The history manifesto* (co-auth., 2014), *Pacific histories: Ocean, land, people* (co-ed., 2014), *Foundations of modern international thought* (2013), *The British Atlantic world, 1500–1800* (2nd edn, co-ed., 2009), *The declaration of independence: A global history* (2007) and *The ideological origins of the British Empire* (2000).

ALISON BASHFORD is Professor of History at the University of New South Wales. Author and editor of many books on world history, environmental history and the history of science, her most recent are *The new worlds of Thomas Robert Malthus* (2016) with Joyce E. Chaplin and *Quarantine: Local and global histories* (ed., 2016). She is a Fellow of the British Academy and a former Trustee of the National Maritime Museum, Greenwich. From 2013 to 2017, she was the Vere Harmsworth Professor of Imperial and Naval History at the University of Cambridge.

ALEXIS DUDDEN is Professor of History at the University of Connecticut. Her books include *Troubled apologies among Japan, Korea, and the United States* (2008) and *Japan's colonization of Korea* (2005). Her work frequently appears also in *The Huffington Post*, *Dissent* and *The New York Times*. Dudden is the recipient of the 2015 Manhae Peace Prize. Her current project, *The state of Japan: Islands, empire, nation*, analyses Japan's territorial disputes in light of the internationally changing meaning of islands.

List of Contributors

STELLA GHERVAS is Assistant Professor of History at the University of Alabama Birmingham and an associate of the Department of History at Harvard University. Among her many publications are *Réinventer la tradition: Alexandre Stourdza et l'Europe de la Sainte-Alliance* (2008), which was awarded the Prix Guizot of the Académie Française, and *Conquering peace: From the Enlightenment to the European Union*, which is forthcoming from Harvard University Press. She is now working on a transnational history of the Black Sea Region from the Russian expansion in the eighteenth century to the present day.

MOLLY GREENE is Professor of History in the Department of History at Princeton University, with an appointment at the Seeger Center for Hellenic Studies. Her work centres on the history of the Greeks and the Greek world under Ottoman rule. Her most recent book, *The Edinburgh history of the Greeks, 1454–1768: The Ottoman Empire* (2015), is a general narrative of the Ottoman Empire, with a focus on the sultan's Greek subjects.

JONATHAN MIRAN is Associate Professor of Islamic and African History at Western Washington University. He is interested in the social history of Muslim Northeast Africa and the history of the Red Sea and western Indian Ocean areas. He is the author of *Red Sea citizens: Cosmopolitan society and cultural change in Massawa* (2009). His most recent articles have appeared in *Islamic Law and Society*, *The Journal of African History*, *History Compass* and *Slavery & Abolition*.

MICHAEL NORTH is Professor and Chair of Modern History at Ernst Moritz Arndt University Greifswald. He has previously taught at the Universities of Hamburg, Kiel, Bielefeld and Rostock. He is the author of *From the North Sea to the Baltic: Essays in commercial, monetary and agrarian history, 1500–1800* (2006), *The Baltic: A history* (Eng. trans., 2015) and *Zwischen Hafen und Horizont: Weltgeschichte der Meere* (2016).

SUJIT SIVASUNDARAM is Reader in World History at the University of Cambridge and works on both the Pacific and Indian Oceans, especially in the eighteenth and nineteenth centuries. He is the author of *Islanded: Britain, Sri Lanka and the bounds of an Indian Ocean colony* (2013) and *Nature and the godly empire: Science and evangelical mission in the Pacific, 1795–1850* (2005). In 2012, he won a Philip Leverhulme Prize for History, awarded for outstanding contributions to research by early-career scholars in the UK. He is co-editor of *The Historical Journal* and Fellow and Councillor of the Royal Historical Society.

x   List of Contributors

SVERKER SÖRLIN is Professor of Environmental History in the Division of History of Science, Technology and Environment, KTH Royal Institute of Technology, Stockholm, where he is also a co-founding member of the KTH Environmental Humanities Laboratory. He has published extensively on the historical science and politics of climate change and on the history of the earth and field sciences, with an emphasis on the circumpolar Arctic. *The future of nature: Documents of global change* (2013) and *The environment – a history* (2018) are both outcomes from a longstanding collaboration on the history of environmental expertise with Libby Robin (ANU) and Paul Warde (University of Cambridge). A prize-winning non-fiction author in Sweden, his most recent book is on the history and politics of the Anthropocene (2017).

ERIC TAGLIACOZZO is Professor of History at Cornell University, where he primarily teaches Southeast Asian Studies. He is the author of *The longest journey: Southeast Asians and the pilgrimage to Mecca* (2013) and *Secret trades, porous borders: Smuggling and states along a Southeast Asian frontier, 1865–1915* (2005) and most recently *The Hajj: Pilgrimage in Islam* (2016). He is the Director of the Comparative Muslim Societies Program at Cornell and editor of the journal *INDONESIA*.

Introduction
Writing World Oceanic Histories

*Sujit Sivasundaram, Alison Bashford
and David Armitage*

'World Oceans Day' was first proposed at the 1992 Earth Summit in Rio de Janeiro; the United Nations General Assembly formalised it in 2008. It was proposed with a view to the ocean's status as vital matter for humankind: 'Our rainwater, drinking water, weather, climate, coastlines, much of our food, and even the oxygen in the air we breathe, are all ultimately provided and regulated by the sea.' The oceanic past – indeed a shared oceanic heritage – was also foregrounded in a bid to make World Oceans Day meaningful: throughout history, the UN stated, oceans and seas have linked the peoples of the world through trade and transportation.[1] It is clear from this effort that oceans do all kinds of discursive work for the UN, offering ways to make the world appear to be one. Indeed, UN materials shift constantly and tellingly between the plural oceans of the world and the singular 'world ocean'. On the one hand, for example, World Oceans Day aims to draw attention to how 'the world's oceans – their temperature, chemistry, currents and life – drive global systems that make the Earth habitable for humankind'.[2] On the other, the spin-off network Réseau Océan Mondial, based in Brussels, resolutely posits a single ocean, the world ocean. Its statutes define the key objective of a global network of oceanographers as working 'towards achieving a healthy and productive world ocean and to encourage sustainable use of its resources'.[3] Even more directly, a singular and shared 'world ocean' drives the Intergovernmental Oceanic Commission of the UN Educational, Social and Cultural Organisation (UNESCO) under the slogan 'One Planet, One Ocean'.[4]

---

[1] 'Throughout history, oceans and seas have been vital conduits for trade and transportation'; World Oceans Day – Background, United Nations: www.un.org/en/events/oceans-day/background.shtml (accessed 28 February 2017).

[2] World Oceans Day – Background, United Nations: www.un.org/en/events/oceansday/background.shtml (accessed 28 February 2017).

[3] Constitution, Réseau Océan Mondial, 28 January 2006: www.worldoceannetwork.org/wp-content/uploads/2014/01/WON-STATUT-2006-ENG.pdf (accessed 28 February 2017).

[4] Intergovernmental Oceanic Commission, UNESCO, *One planet, one ocean* (Paris, 2017).

2   S. Sivasundaram, A. Bashford and D. Armitage

Oceanic Histories analyses both the plural oceans of the world and the singular world ocean while bringing both into dialogue, placing oceans and seas within world history and envisaging world history through oceanic and maritime regions. The chapters present assessments of historians' work on the Indian, Pacific and Atlantic Oceans, the Arctic and the Southern Oceans and some of the world's major seas: the Mediterranean, the Black Sea, the Sea of Japan/Korea's East Sea, the Baltic, the Red Sea and the South China Sea. Other chapters might be imagined – for example on the Caribbean, the Java Sea, the North Sea or the Caspian Sea. However, as the first such collective survey by multiple authors, the book's aim is to be extensive more than comprehensive, wide-ranging rather than yet all-encompassing.

Most of the chapters in *Oceanic Histories* have a historiographical objective in the first instance. They seek to chart how the human and natural pasts of these oceans and seas have been framed, written, presented and disputed over time, where they stand now and what might be their prospects for the future. Some seas and oceans – notably, the Pacific, the Atlantic, the Mediterranean and the Indian Ocean – have long, variegated and ramified historiographies; others, such as the Red Sea, the Black Sea and the Southern Ocean, have shorter traditions and therefore demand more historical treatment than historiographical reconstruction at this stage. Every chapter works on the leading edge of its field even if the timelines and terms of discussion differ from sea to sea, ocean to ocean. Yet in every case, we can see that historical scholarship on each oceanic topic was established and influential well before 'World Oceans Day' emerged as a subject of international interest barely a generation ago.

Taken together and read in sequence, the chapters in the volume chart how histories and geographies as modes of knowledge became linked to the sea and its relation with land over the *longue durée*. The move early this century to promote a supposed 'new thalassology' often assumed the primacy of Mediterranean models for oceanic history with frequent reference to Fernand Braudel's work as germinal;[5] more recently, the runaway institutional success of Atlantic history in the early 2000s, spearheaded by Harvard historian Bernard Bailyn, added another influential avatar.[6] However, one running theme of this volume is to critique

---

[5] For consideration and critique, see W. V. Harris, ed., *Rethinking the Mediterranean* (Oxford, 2005); Peregrine Horden and Nicholas Purcell, 'The Mediterranean and "the new thalassology"', *American Historical Review*, 111 (2006): 722–40; Molly Greene, 'The Mediterranean Sea', below.

[6] David Armitage, 'The Atlantic Ocean', below.

Introduction: Writing World Oceanic Histories

and recontextualise this genealogy, by showing how thinkers, narrators and historians have written of the sea beyond the Mediterranean – and, by extension, the Atlantic – over long periods before the rise of US- and Europe-based scholarship on seas. Many of our authors place the historiography of the *Annales* and the Atlantic, of Braudel and Bailyn, within a totally different intellectual ecology often with origins well before the twentieth century. Some also show how inhibiting these prevalent trends have been for generating historiographies for other tracts of water, for instance the Arctic or the Red Sea.[7] And the longer genealogies of, say, the Pacific and Indian Oceans presented here question the claim that they derived, or should draw inspiration, from the Atlantic or Mediterranean, and argue forcefully that they 'should be considered as original model[s] for the historicising of oceans' in their own right.[8]

This recalibration of influence, and resurrection of alternative inspirations, should have effects not only for the specific oceanic histories treated here but also for the future of Mediterranean and Atlantic histories themselves. With these revisions in mind, the authors recognise and take full account of the fact that the accelerated writing of oceanic histories over the 1990s and 2000s paralleled and often intersected with that same environmental and global sensibility that gave rise to such a thing as an 'Earth summit' and a 'World Oceans Day' in the first place. In this regard, the book provides the most comprehensive, comparative and critical mapping now available of the distinct timelines and growth patterns in the historiography of oceanic history.[9] Given the misunderstanding of the origins of ocean histories, it also considers what can be drawn from reading across these separated literatures now.

Oceanic Histories aims, through its various chapters, to answer the question: what is the historical and historiographical relation between world histories, the world's oceans and the world ocean? (This will also be the informing concern of the monographic series, 'Cambridge Oceanic Histories', that this volume inaugurates.) Oceanic historians, especially those rooted in a tradition of maritime scholarship, often claim a particular stake in a world history configured geographically and

---

[7] Sverker Sörlin, 'The Arctic Ocean', and Jonathan Miran, 'The Red Sea', below; also Alexis Wick, *The Red Sea: In search of lost space* (Oakland, CA, 2016).

[8] Sujit Sivasundaram, 'The Indian Ocean', and Alison Bashford, 'The Pacific Ocean' (quoted), below.

[9] For an earlier, less comprehensive, effort see Peter N. Miller, ed., *The sea: Thalassography and historiography* (Ann Arbor, MI, 2013), and for contemporaneous enterprises attempting a *longue durée* sweep, see now Michael North, *Zwischen Hafen und Horizont: Weltgeschichte der Meere* (Munich, 2016), and Christian Buchet, gen. ed., *La mer dans l'histoire/The sea in history*, 4 vols. (Paris and Woodbridge, 2017).

4   S. Sivasundaram, A. Bashford and D. Armitage

economically: that is, in the historical geo-economics of a globe increasingly connected by large waterways and the exchange and commerce they facilitated. This is an approach to oceanic histories in which, broadly speaking, globalisation took place in a maritime world connected forcefully, but certainly not solely, through the European maritime empires and coastal polities in commercial relation with each other, and with regional maritime traders, labourers and navigators in different parts of the world.[10]

While paying attention to the role of European maritime empires as drivers and conduits of world history, *Oceanic Histories* also foregrounds another tradition of world history-writing that concentrates attention on extra-European worlds on their own terms.[11] For example, our authors examine the Middle Kingdom-centred Nanyang, the maritime Malay world, the seafaring traders between Arabia and India and the complex of colonial and Indigenous whalers and sealers in the Southern Ocean.[12] In both of these traditions of world history, some scholarship is squarely maritime while other parts are more oceanic. We suggest below some of the differences as well as the synergies between these proximate and overlapping approaches.

Many recent historians of oceans and seas identify their work within a tradition of transnational history-writing. This is unsurprising, because none of the oceans and seas align with any one polity and the move to their histories represents an 'escape' from the prevailing 'terracentrism' of traditional history-writing.[13] But is 'transnational' the best indicator of the substance and method of oceanic histories? Perhaps not – not least

[10] For example, Philip de Souza, *Seafaring and civilization: Maritime perspectives on world history* (London, 2001); Daniel Finamore, ed., *Maritime history as world history* (Gainesville, FL, 2004); David Cannadine, ed., *Empire, the sea and global history: Britain's maritime world, c. 1760–c. 1840* (Basingstoke, 2007); Maria Fusaro and Amélia Polónia, eds., *Maritime history as global history* (St John's, Newfoundland, 2010); Lincoln Paine, *The sea and civilization: A maritime history of the world* (New York, 2013); Ingo Heidbrink, Lewis R. Fischer, Jari Ojala, Fei Sheng, Stig Tenold and Malcolm Tull, 'Forum: Closing the "blue hole": Maritime history as a core element of historical research', *International Journal of Maritime History*, 29 (2017): 325–66.

[11] For example, K. N. Chaudhuri, *Trade and civilisation in the Indian Ocean: An economic history from the rise of Islam to 1750* (Cambridge, 1985); Wang Gungwu and Ng Chin-keong, eds., *Maritime China in transition, 1750–1850* (Wiesbaden, 2004); Markus P. M. Vink, 'Indian Ocean studies and the "new thalassology"', *Journal of Global History*, 2 (2007): 41–62. Also note Engseng Ho, *The Graves of Tarim: Geneaology and mobility across the Indian Ocean* (Berkeley, CA, 2006).

[12] Eric Tagliacozzo, 'The South China Sea', Sivasundaram, 'The Indian Ocean', Jonathan Miran, 'The Red Sea', and Alessandro Antonello, 'The Southern Ocean', below.

[13] Rila Mukherjee, 'Escape from terracentrism: Writing a water history', *Indian Historical Review*, 41 (2014): 87–101; see also Isabel Hofmeyr, 'The complicating sea: The Indian Ocean as method', *Comparative Studies of South Asia, Africa and the Middle East*, 32 (2012): 584–90.

Introduction: Writing World Oceanic Histories

because, at the heart of the 'transnational', we always find the nation.[14] In many ways it is more useful, or at least as useful, to consider how oceanic histories have been trans-*local* studies.[15] Littoral societies often shared more in common with similar formations across seas and oceans than they did with their own nearby hinterlands.[16] Coastal entrepôts operated in a global geography of connection, not with nations or the capitals of other polities, but primarily, even exclusively, with other local port towns. Many of these were the key urban sites for a converging world history over the long modern period: for instance, Guangzhou, Valparaiso, Cape Town, Manila, Florence or Singapore. These ports hold the trans-local history that constituted world history. Yet at the same time, several authors below highlight how sea-facing cosmopolitans were disowned by their others, necessitating the need for historians to place ports and entrepôts in a broader oceanic context. Ports encompass many divergent histories: for instance, of labourers who travelled through them; of commodities that were transshipped at the site of the port; of technicians, journalists and activists who set up stall in port cities; and of the imperial photographers who roamed across ports to visualise maritime travel and urban development in the nineteenth and twentieth centuries.[17]

Oceanic histories are also perhaps better conceptualised as area or regional (and inter-area and inter-regional) studies, notwithstanding the Cold War scholarly and political connotations of this approach. This is often what is meant by the 'world' or 'worlds' often attributed to oceans: 'the Indian Ocean world', or 'the Pacific world' or 'the Atlantic world', as strategic arenas defined by ideas of political community or even of civilisation. In this respect, it is important to recall that conceptions of an 'Atlantic world' and a 'Pacific world' were products of strategic thinking during the Second World War and diplomatic plans for

---

[14] C. A. Bayly, Sven Beckert, Matthew Connelly, Isabel Hofmeyr, Wendy Kozol and Patricia Seed, '*AHR* conversation: On transnational history', *American Historical Review*, 111 (2006): 1441–64.

[15] Matt Matsuda, *Pacific worlds: A history of seas, peoples, and cultures* (Cambridge, 2012), is an exemplary use of the 'trans-local' within oceanic history.

[16] Michael N. Pearson, 'Littoral society: The concept and the problems', *Journal of World History*, 17 (2006): 353–74.

[17] Arndt Graf and Chua Beng Huat, eds., *Port cities in Asia and Europe* (London, 2009); Haneda Masashi, ed., *Asian port cities, 1600–1800: Local and foreign cultural interactions* (Singapore, 2009); Brad Beaven, Karl Bell and Robert James, eds., *Port towns and urban cultures: International histories of the waterfront, c. 1700–2000* (Basingstoke, 2016); Nile Green, 'Maritime worlds and global history: Comparing the Mediterranean and Indian Ocean through Barcelona and Bombay', *History Compass* 11, 7 (July 2013): 513–23; and C. A. Bayly and Leila Tarazi Fawaz, eds., *Modernity and culture: From the Mediterranean to the Indian Ocean, 1890–1920* (New York, 2002).

6   S. Sivasundaram, A. Bashford and D. Armitage

reconstruction after it.[18] More recently, political and economic concerns have generated parallel designators, such as the 'Indo-Pacific', or given new geopolitical heft to the Baltic and Black Sea as regions of international collaboration.[19] While the nomination of such 'worlds' and areas suggests an underlying bias towards integration, their pluralisation, as a multiplicity of such worlds, reflects division, even competition, among and within them.

The ideological history of oceans and seas is most evident in the continuous geopolitical and epistemological battles over their naming. These can reflect the reactions of outsiders to, say, a South Sea deemed to be relatively calm or 'pacific' or a Black Sea perceived as either threatening (*Axeinos*) or welcoming (*Euxinos*).[20] It can also be an attempt to insert cultural presence: note the debate about renaming the Indian Ocean as the 'Afrasian' Sea.[21] Sometimes the names of bodies of water explicitly signal sovereignty, if controversially so: the Sea of Japan/Korea's East Sea or the South China Sea, for instance.[22] Sometimes, they do so by inference, flagging an orientation and therefore a presumed centre, as in the Nanyang or the Southern Ocean – south, that is, from imperial China's standpoint – the East Sea (east seen from Korea) or the Southern Ocean, north of Antarctica but south of Australia. One history of the naming of the Atlantic Ocean signals a Mediterranean perspective of, and upon, the world; the ocean beyond the pillars of Hercules that enclosed all land, as Atlas supported the heavens. But the Atlantic had a simultaneously diminished and larger function in *longue-durée* world history: from this standpoint, it shifted over the centuries from being the ocean that enclosed all land to the ocean that separated an 'old world' from a 'new

---

[18] For example, in Arnold Ræstad, *Europe and the Atlantic world*, ed. Winthrop W. Case (Princeton, NJ, 1941), and Fairfield Osborn, ed., *The Pacific world* (Washington, DC, 1945).

[19] Rory Medcalf, 'The Indo-Pacific: What's in a name?', *The American Interest*, 9, 2 (November–December 2013): 60–65.

[20] O. H. K. Spate, '"South Sea" to "Pacific Ocean": A note on nomenclature', *Journal of Pacific History*, 12 (1977): 205–11; Mark Peterson, 'Naming the Pacific', *Common-place*, 5, 2 (January 2005): www.common-place-archives.org/vol-05/no-02/peterson/index. shtml (accessed 28 February 2017); François de Blois, 'The name of the Black Sea', in Maria Macuch, Mauro Maggi and Werner Sundermann, eds., *Iranian Languages and Texts from Iran and Turan* (Wiesbaden, 2007), pp. 1–8; Bashford, 'The Pacific Ocean', and Stella Ghervas, 'The Black Sea', below.

[21] See for instance, Michael N. Pearson, *Port cities and intruders: The Swahili coast, India, and Portugal in the early modern era* (Baltimore, MD, 1998) and Michael N. Pearson, *The Indian Ocean* (London, 2013), p. 14.

[22] As well as Tagliacozzo, 'The South China Sea', and Alexis Dudden, 'The Sea of Japan/ Korea's East Sea', below, see Si Jin Oh, 'An identity aspect to the "wars" of maps in East Asia: Focusing on the East Sea/Sea of Japan name debate', *Korea Observer*, 48 (2017): 57–83.

Introduction: Writing World Oceanic Histories

world'. Similarly, the Mediterranean gradually moved from being the centre of the world within the Greco-Roman ecumene to simply one sea among many, with no presumed priority or predominance, flowing into the world ocean itself. And of course it was not the 'Mediterranean' to Arabic and Muslim observers until the term entered Arabic in the nineteenth century by way of European languages.[23]

There is also a curious history in which regional nomination has shifted between watery and territorial spaces, part of the 'terraqueous history' of the globe.[24] For example, 'Australia' became the name for the continent (in part due to its maritime circumnavigation between 1801 and 1803), yet in some early charts it is the ocean to its east that is labelled 'Greater Australia' or sometimes 'Australasia'.[25] This great archipelago of Pacific islands came to be named for the water surrounding them – 'Oceania', now the formal UN regional nomenclature.[26] To take another example, the *Mare Aethiopicum* of Antiquity was still in use as 'the Ethiopic Ocean' on nineteenth-century world maps. Over time it became the South Atlantic and then subsumed by the late nineteenth century into a holistic Atlantic, stretching almost from pole to pole.[27] But modern 'Ethiopia' shifted to the horn of Africa, far closer to the Indian Ocean than the Atlantic: it is, ironically, land-locked. In counterpoint, it is curious to note how our planet is named Earth when 70 per cent of its surface is Ocean. In this regard, it may be exceptional among the known planets, but it is not alone within the solar system and beyond in having oceans, even if these extra-terrestrial 'water worlds' – on Mars or on Saturn's moons, for instance – remain for the moment beyond the reach of historians.[28]

Though divided by oceans and seas, the chapters here indicate clearly the fluid movement between them in the context of the world ocean and how their histories and material forms are entangled. In this way, the history of the Indian Ocean connects with the history of the Red Sea, the

---

[23] Greene, 'The Mediterranean Sea', below.

[24] Alison Bashford, 'Terraqueous histories', *The Historical Journal*, 60 (2017): 253–72; see also Hester Blum, 'Terraqueous planet: The case for oceanic studies', in Amy J. Elias and Christian Moraru, eds., *The planetary turn: Relationality and geoaesthetics in the twenty-first century* (Evanston, IL, 2015), pp. 25–36.

[25] National Library of Australia, *Mapping our world: Terra incognita to Australia* (Canberra, 2013).

[26] Bronwen Douglas, '*Terra Australis* to Oceania: Racial geography in the "fifth part of the world"', *Journal of Pacific History*, 45 (2010): 179–210.

[27] Luiz Felipe de Alencastro, 'The Ethiopic Ocean – History and historiography, 1600–1975', *Portuguese Literary & Cultural Studies*, 27 (2015): 1–79.

[28] Jan Zalasiewicz and Mark Williams, *Ocean worlds: The story of seas on Earth and other planets* (Oxford, 2014), ch. 9, 'Oceans of the solar system'.

8   S. Sivasundaram, A. Bashford and D. Armitage

history of the Red Sea to the history of the Mediterranean, the history of the Mediterranean becomes the history of the Atlantic, the Atlantic of the Pacific, the Pacific of the Southern Ocean, and so forth. Strangely, though, the two oceans most physically distant from one another – the Arctic Ocean and the Southern Ocean – are closely combined, institutionally and historiographically, under 'polar history' and 'polar studies', as in the *Journal of Polar Studies*, for example, or at the Scott Polar Research Institute in Cambridge; accordingly, we have linked them here.[29]

As maritime historians have shown, it was circumnavigators and merchant mariners, whalers and navies in peace and war, who directly experienced the world ocean: the waters of the eastern and western, northern and southern hemispheres. And as environmental historians discuss, the world ocean also belonged to the mammals and fishes who swam, fed and migrated beneath it.[30] As a research enterprise for hydrographers, the 'world ocean' has been essential to oceanography since the 1960s.[31] It has also become a highly politicised entity, linked both to an environmentalist global ecology and to the global history of capitalism. The world ocean, some argue, was the natural entity that facilitated the world system of commercial globalisation.[32] And the world history of that globalisation depended on diverse human ingenuity and capacity to pass over the sea and to live upon it.

The Naval and the Oceanic

The challenge of making the sea a home has been a perennial human quest. Its persistence comes from how the ocean is seen to teem with life but is still unfit for our species. To venture onto the ocean has long been seen as somehow unnatural, with shipwreck and drowning the fitting rewards for hubris in contravening our terrestrial destiny.[33] Humans can swim, but only just. Swimming itself has a cross-cultural history including how European explorers of the sixteenth century such as Francis Drake attempted to frighten off Pacific islander swimmers who attacked

---

[29] Sörlin, 'The Arctic Ocean', and Antonello, 'The Southern Ocean', below.

[30] Ryan Tucker Jones, 'Running into whales: The history of the north Pacific from below the waves', *American Historical Review*, 118 (2013): 349–77.

[31] Richard Carrington, *A biography of the sea: The story of the world ocean, its animal and plant populations, and its influence on human history* (New York, 1960); William A. Anikouchine and Richard W. Sternberg, *The world ocean: An introduction to oceanography* (London, 1981).

[32] For example, Peter Jacques, *Globalization and the world ocean* (Oxford, 2006).

[33] Hans Blumenberg, *Shipwreck with spectator: Paradigm of a metaphor for existence*, trans. Steven Rendall (Cambridge, MA, 1997).

Introduction: Writing World Oceanic Histories

them.[34] In much of the West, from the fall of Rome to the nineteenth century, there was an active prejudice against swimming. The quest to be with the sea means that those who cross the vast swathes of the world ocean have been cast as heroes. The challenge now combines with the prediction of a watery human future. As one set of authors notes, conceiving the sea in this way has been gendered: 'Could the ocean then, be thought of as a source of all things, a kind of maternal sublime?'[35]

If such is the tension in human engagements with the sea, the ship has served as a vehicle for experiments in habitation: how to live on board ship; how to create, distil or transform social and cultural norms in such spaces; how to govern and legislate on a ship over prisoners, sailors or 'natives'; how to control a ship so that it transfers materials, ideas, nature and people across locales; and, how to proclaim and dramatise a culture from the deck and 'across the beach' to a newfound land or indeed to go to war with other nations on the water. It is as if the ship becomes a floating piece of land, practically, socially and often legally.[36] As the ship is given a name and biography, also a launch and decommissioning, along with flags, papers and nationality, it becomes akin to a person on the sea. On the casting of ships as alive, tales of Indigenous people who mistook European ships as birds or islands are many; they reveal as much about Euro-American projections and self-mythology as about indigenous cosmologies. When placed together with the difficulties of being at home with the sea, and the Foucauldian labelling of ships as classic 'heterotopias', it is unsurprising that epic moments of shipping have been commemorated with grandeur as alleged turning points in the human past.[37]

Take for instance, the over-confident ship-shaped memorial to Portuguese early modern 'discoveries', the Padrão dos Descobrimentos, at one of the most westward points of Europe, on the River Tagus as it flows into the Atlantic in Lisbon. The memorial originated in 1940 from an exhibition of the Portuguese World held to celebrate the birth of the Portuguese nation in 1140, a celebration which chimed with the country's authoritarian Estado Novo.[38] It was built in permanent form in 1960 to coincide with the death anniversary of Henry the Navigator. Set

---

[34] Nicholas Orme, *Early British swimming, 55 BC–AD 1719* (Exeter, 1983), p. 49.

[35] David Lambert, Luciana Martins and Miles Ogborn, eds. 'Currents, visions and voyages: Historical geographies of the sea', *Journal of Historical Geography*, 32 (2006): 484.

[36] Lauren Benton, *A search for sovereignty: Law and geography in European empires, 1400–1800* (Cambridge, 2010).

[37] Michel Foucault, 'Of other spaces', *Diacritics*, 16 (1986): 27.

[38] Ellen W. Sapega, 'Image and counter-image: The place of Salazarist images of national identity in contemporary Portuguese visual culture', *Luso-Brazilian Review*, 39, 2 (Winter 2002): 48–50.

in rose-tinted stone and cement and shaped like a Portuguese caravel, it depicts men, following Henry the Navigator who is at the prow, reaching in fervent pose for the sea. The monument itself is firmly rooted on the shore, and yet it stretches from the land to the water. If this ship takes its meaning from its physical setting as such a bridge, then a similar reading is open for another ship-shaped monument to epic 'discovery', the so-called 'Singing Ship' monument in Emu Park in Queensland, Australia, which marked the Cook bicentenary in 1970. Here the element that plays a role is the wind: the ship is designed to 'sing' as the wind blows through it.[39] If successful navigation is about rising above the elements and taming them so as to live at sea and to cross the sea, it is curious that ship monuments like these are still environmental signs.

Indeed, such monuments serve as evidence of the multiply conflicted roles played by ships. For ship memorials are also found which are tokens not of achievement but of death on a vast scale. One example is the National Famine Monument or 'Coffin Ship' in Murrisk, County Mayo, Ireland.[40] A bronze sculpture with skeleton bodies in the riggings, it commemorates those who left Ireland for the New World. It was built by the Irish government for the 150th anniversary of the Great Famine. In popular telling, sharks followed the 'coffin ships' for the number of dead who were thrown overboard.[41] Memorials to the Middle Passage also point to the ship as a bearer of memories of enslavement, violence, dehumanisation and death. One instance of this is the slave ship which is a part of the African American Monument in the South Carolina State House. If such is the memory of ships, this volume asks: how should historians return to the ship from the perspective of the world ocean?

To begin such an enterprise, it is important to contend with the variegated dimensions of human engagement with ships. Ships have served as experimental sites for life at sea as much as spaces of death, and watery tombs beneath the waves continue to fascinate the public as well as archaeologists. Modernity could quite literally be shipped as much as shipwrecked.[42] Ships are, as revealed even by their monuments, environmental projects. They are also legal personalities and even cast as figures, as is evident from the elaborate figureheads kept in many maritime

---

[39] Ros Bandt, 'Taming the wind: Aeolian sound practices in Australasia', *Organised Sound*, 8 (2003): 198–99.

[40] Emily Mark-Fitzgerald, *Commemorating the Irish famine: Memory and the monument* (Liverpool, 2013).

[41] Marcus Rediker, 'History from below the water line: Sharks and the Atlantic slave trade', *Atlantic Studies*, 5 (2008): 285–97.

[42] Steve Mentz, *Shipwreck modernity: Ecologies of globalization, 1550–1719* (Minneapolis, MN, 2015).

Introduction: Writing World Oceanic Histories

museums around the world. Ships are material and artefactual and as some new scholarship reminds us they can be traded and exchanged, even shifting cultural signification in the process: Japanese sampans could become American Hawai'ian vessels.[43] As things, they are composites requiring labour to produce and maintain; Indigenous communities could raid a wrecked ship on their shores for precisely this reason, only taking what they valued and what they wished to recycle. The passage from sail to steam, and increasing containerisation has made shipping so successful that, though it is the main conduit of global trade, it has taken on an invisible life when compared with air or land travel.[44] However, this should not allow historians to forget how ships still fail and spill (oil and garbage for instance). In addition, the ship has been the vector of a 'world hunt'.[45] In the Southern Ocean, for instance, this began with a trade in seals and whales. That world hunt started from a human desire to exploit the seas' resources and that desire in turn fed into, as is argued below, scientific, commercial and diplomatic concerns and programmes of order.[46]

The social, political, legislative, economic and social and cultural histories of navigation are thus connected here with environmental history: it is important to insist on the mutually constitutive force of these historiographies. Otherwise the history of the ship is taken to mean the history of shipping techniques and technologies alone or simply the history of war; this does not get to the complexity of how the ship intervenes between humans and the sea or how it serves as an intensive site for working out power and submission. As one recent argument puts it, the ship is the perfect object which with to consider 'transit' and global connections and disconnection, and it serves as a topic of global microhistory.[47] If so, the 'transit' is between places and terrains and among mediums. This transition is also evident in how ships can speak to nationalist idealisation as much as to the fragility of the human condition and how they can stand for some achievements cast as the greatest human triumphs as much as terrible calamity. The Indian state can thus glorify its boat-building culture as a bulwark of nationalism as much as Portugal has in

---

[43] See Hans Konrad Van Tilburg, 'Vessels of exchange: The global shipwright in the Pacific', in Jerry H. Bentley, Renate Bridenthal and Kären Wigen, eds. *Seascapes: Maritime histories, littoral cultures and transoceanic exchanges* (Honolulu, HI, 2007), pp. 38–52.

[44] Marc Levinson, *The box: How the shipping container made the world smaller and the world economy bigger* (Princeton, NJ, 2006).

[45] John F. Richards, *The world hunt: An environmental history of the commodification of animals* (Berkeley, CA, 2014).

[46] Antonello, 'The Southern Ocean', below.

[47] Martin Dusinberre and Roland Wenzlhuemer, eds., 'Special issue: Being in transit: Ships and global incompatibilities', *Journal of Global History*, 11, 2 (July 2016).

12   S. Sivasundaram, A. Bashford and D. Armitage

the past. Meanwhile, in the Sea of Japan, what are called 'ghost ships' can continue to arrive on the coast of Japan with North Korean refugees, while another ship, the SS *Meredith Victory*, has been memorialised as a 'Ship of Miracles' for its humanitarian rescue of refugees in the midst of the Korean War.[48]

To undercut the imperial, military and national inclinations of much maritime historiography, it is important to highlight how many different cultures of navigation and boat-making have intersected in world history. While past historians have denied or ornamentalised the maritime culture of non-Western societies, or used assessments of boats as a stadial measure of advancement, our authors instead highlight the fact that encounter was often from ship to ship rather than ship to beach. Pacific double-hulled canoes were not insignificant in size and capacity when placed next to the sailing vessels they met; they were comparable to European ships. Riverine Burmese war-boats meanwhile outstripped the *Diana*, the first steamship used in war, during the first Anglo-Burmese war (1824–26).[49] Further, our authors deconstruct such stereotypes as the Muslim fear of the sea or the classificatory labelling of the Chinese 'junks' and Indian Ocean 'dhows', showing how such classifications were colonial products beneath which lay a dizzying range of traditions of manufacture and boat-making.[50] Engagements with the sea have been surprisingly wide-ranging and even those empires which were once cast as landlubbers – for example, the Austro-Hungarian and Russian empires – are now being seen as maritime.[51]

The site of the shipyard is fast emerging as a key topic for world historiography, drawing in questions about modernisation, scientific exchange, migration, labour and capitalism. Until the early nineteenth century, shipyards like the Arsenal in Venice comprised the world's largest industrial plants:[52] a single ship of the line, like Nelson's flagship *Victory*, could command a greater investment of capital than a contemporary factory. Indeed, tracking ships through cycles of making and

[48] Dudden, 'The Sea of Japan/Korea's East Sea', below.
[49] Compare with Satpal Sangwan, 'Technology and imperialism in the Indian context: The case of steamboats, 1819–1839', in Teresa A. Meade and Mark Walker, eds., *Science, medicine and cultural imperialism* (London, 1991), pp. 61–64.
[50] Greene, 'The Mediterannean Sea', and Sivasundaram, 'The Indian Ocean', below.
[51] Alison Frank, 'Continental and maritime empires in an age of global commerce', *East European Politics and Societies*, 25 (2011): 779–84; Julia Leikin, 'Across the seven seas: Is Russian maritime history more than regional history?', *Kritika: Explorations in Russian and Eurasian History*, 17 (2016): 631–46.
[52] Frederic Chapin Lane, *Venetian ships and shipbuilders of the Renaissance* (Baltimore, MD, 1934); Robert C. Davis, *Shipbuilders of the Venetian arsenal: Workers and workplace in the preindustrial city* (Baltimore, MD, 1991).

Introduction: Writing World Oceanic Histories

unmaking, in turn, has been a way of following a long-distance trade in wood, between South Asia and Arabia for instance; and research on wood carries on to the present in order to determine the provenance and histories of ship parts in museums. In this way too, the history of the ship does not now assume that the ship is a stable subject of research.[53] In the South China Sea, techniques of ship-making have a long history, taking in the important Sung period, propelling Chinese engagements with Southeast Asia. In the Southern Ocean, the ship-building of sealers from America and France was seen as an affront to the settled sovereignty of the British Empire. The ability to make a ship was in both these cases a means of state-making and, curiously, it was also a token of settlement and of power over land, even a claim to that land.

Oceanic Environments and Ecologies

The study of humans and their sea-going vessels has long defined maritime history. But what is the relationship between this field and oceanic history? While they overlap in clear and important ways, we suggest that it is an environmental approach that is the distinguishing point. Environmental history has helped turn a longstanding historiography of humans, vessels and exploration, toward analysis of complex relations between elements (winds, tides, currents), ocean life (mammals, fish, crustaceans, birds, plants), and human activity in and on the seas. Put another way, oceanic histories require the equivalent consideration of marine and maritime actors in all their complex relations with each other.

This approach is ecological in both substance and method, and inquires into past conjunctions of human and non-human life. Oceans are full of organisms, some still as strange to humans as the fantastic monsters of the sea on medieval and early modern maps. While maritime and economic histories have documented mariners' and researchers' interest in, and often dependence on, sea mammals, birds and fish, environmental historians have documented the human impact on marine ecologies.[54] Whaling and fishing histories are especially significant, often

---

[53] See Alastair J. Reid, *The tide of democracy: Shipyard workers and social relations in Britain, 1870–1950* (Manchester, 2010); for the Bombay shipyard, see Frank Broeze, 'Underdevelopment and dependency: Maritime India during the Raj', *Modern Asian Studies*, 18 (1984): 429–57; for shipyards in China, see Benjamin A. Elman, *On their own terms: Science in China, 1550–1900* (Cambridge, MA, 2009), pp. 370–86.

[54] Paul Holm, Tim D. Smith and David J. Starkey, eds., *The exploited seas: New directions for marine environmental history* (Liverpool, 2001); W. Jeffrey Bolster, 'Opportunities in marine environmental history', *Environmental History*, 11 (2006): 567–97; Kathleen Schwerdtner Máñez and Bo Poulsen, eds., *Perspectives on oceans past: A handbook of marine environmental history* (Dordrecht, 2016).

14   S. Sivasundaram, A. Bashford and D. Armitage

foreshadowing the project of world history; these histories track the whalers who themselves tracked the whales across the world ocean.[55] Indeed whaling history *is* world history over time and place, from early modern Basque whaling in Labrador to Japanese whalers in Antarctic waters – the whales in their own habitat, the humans far from home. Whaling as an environmentalist issue has prompted a specifically international history as well; that is, a history of the intergovernmental regulation of the industry and of its scientific foundations.[56] Sometimes troubling international treaties and agreement is longstanding Indigenous and Aboriginal whaling practice, and both historical and anthropological studies have had particular impact in terms of establishing continuing rights to hunt, and sometimes renewed rights to hunt. The Makahs of America's northwest coast, for example, harpooned and brought ashore a female grey whale in 1999, the first for seventy years. It was a highly publicised event, the outcome of a successful negotiation with the International Whaling Commission and based on evidence and history of customary hunts.[57]

Environmental history, then, has helped broaden the scope of maritime history. It is also the case that the study of oceans has lifted and expanded environmental history from its traditional soil-based concerns. While geographical and historical scholarship between the 1920s and 1960s plainly incorporated seas and oceans, the first generation of self-nominated 'environmental historians' tended to privilege land over sea, *terra* over *aqua*. Historical analyses focused on over-cultivation, forest-clearing, land-based species extinctions, 'wilderness' and the exchange of old world and new world biota, microbes and crops. When it came to water, fresh waters generally trumped salt waters. Rivers were certainly investigated early within the environmental history corpus,[58] and to some extent lakes, a focus that perhaps signalled the influence of canonical Great Lakes ecological studies. But environmental history slowly turned toward the sea, a re-orientation strongly directed by interest in the inverse of territorially surrounded lakes: that is, ocean-surrounded islands.[59] By

---

[55] See the analysis of global whaling in J. N. Tønnessen and A. O. Johnsen, *The history of modern whaling*, trans. R. I. Christophersen (Berkeley, CA, 1982), and Richard Ellis, *Men and whales* (New York, 1991).

[56] For example, Ray Gambell, 'International management of whales and whaling: An historical review of the regulation of commercial and Aboriginal subsistence whaling', *Arctic*, 46 (1993): 97–107; D. Graham Burnett, *The sounding of the whale: Science and cetaceans in the twentieth century* (Chicago, IL, 2012).

[57] Joshua L. Reid, *The sea is my country: The maritime world of the Makahs, an indigenous borderlands people* (New Haven, CT, 2015), pp. 271–79.

[58] For example, Richard White, *The organic machine: The remaking of the Columbia river* (New York, 1995).

[59] Richard H. Grove, *Green imperialism: Colonial expansion, tropical island Edens, and the origins of environmentalism, 1600–1860* (Cambridge, 1995); John R. McNeill, 'Of rats and

Introduction: Writing World Oceanic Histories

the late 1990s, a sub-field of environmental history was identifiable that recognised oceans as themselves objects of inquiry, as historians more generally claimed that the spaces and scales of world history might be re-ordered on the basis of natural boundaries of oceans.[60] Yet it was only in the twenty-first century that scholars put the ocean into history, revealing changes in the sea as earlier pioneers in the field had mapped changes in the land.[61]

The oceanic turn in environmental history indicates a larger cultural and political shift in which 'blue' has, to some extent, succeeded 'green'. The 'blue humanities' have engaged scholars in adjacent fields – literary studies and cultural studies – to create a rich conversation focussing on the sea, imagination and cultural production in the past and present.[62] There is already an emergent 'sociology of the oceans',[63] while oceanic histories might collectively present a blue history of the world, drawing inspiration from green histories of the world.[64] In this vein, there is a Pacific-centred 'Blue Revolution', focused on the management of fish stocks, to stand alongside the agricultural 'Green Revolution'.[65] More broadly, the idea of a 'blue planet' has gained real purchase, an image that can more readily unify (and simplify) a deeply divided world polity than the continental distance and disparity of soil-based 'green' politics.

---

men: A synoptic environmental history of the island Pacific', *Journal of World History*, 5 (1994): 299–349; Lill-Ann Körber, Scott MacKenzie and Anna Westerståhl Stenport, eds., *Arctic environmental modernities: From the age of polar exploration to the era of the Anthropocene* (Basingstoke, 2017).

[60] Jerry H. Bentley, 'Sea and ocean basins as frameworks of historical analysis', *Geographical Review*, 89 (1999), 215–24; Martin Lewis and Kären E. Wigen, *The myth of continents: A critique of metageography* (Berkeley, CA, 1997).

[61] For example, Jeffrey Bolster, 'Putting the ocean in Atlantic history: Maritime communities and marine ecology in the Northwest Atlantic, 1500–1800', *American Historical Review*, 113 (2008): 19–47; Bolster, *The mortal sea: Fishing the Atlantic in the age of sail* (Cambridge, MA, 2012).

[62] Steven Mentz, 'Toward a blue cultural studies: The sea, maritime culture and early modern English literature', *Literature Compass*, 6, 5 (September 2009): 997–1013; Hester Blum, 'The prospect of oceanic studies', *PMLA*, 125 (2010): 770–79; Susan Gillman, 'Oceans of *longue durées*', *PMLA*, 127 (2012): 328–34; Blum, ed., 'Special issue: Oceanic studies', *Atlantic Studies*, 10, 2 (April 2013): 151–227; John Gillis, 'The blue humanities', *Humanities*, 34, 3 (May/June 2013): 10–13; Tricia Cusack, ed., *Framing the ocean, 1700 to the present: Envisaging the sea as social space* (Farnham, 2014); Kerry Bystrom, Ashley L. Cohen, Elizabeth DeLoughrey, Isobel Hofmeyr, Rachel Price, Meg Samuelson and Alice Te Punga Somerville, 'ACLA Forum: Oceanic routes', *Comparative Literature*, 69 (2017): 1–31.

[63] John Hannigan, 'Toward a sociology of oceans', *Canadian Review of Sociology*, 54 (2017): 8–27.

[64] For example, Clive Ponting, *A green history of the world: Environments and the collapse of great civilizations* (London, 1991).

[65] As proposed by Gregory T. Cushman, *Guano and the opening of the Pacific world: A global ecological history* (Cambridge, 2013), pp. 289–96 and Md Saidul Islam, *Confronting the blue revolution: Industrial aquaculture and sustainability in the Global South* (Toronto, 2014), among others.

16 S. Sivasundaram, A. Bashford and D. Armitage

This is largely because a blue, ocean-oriented environmentalism has the fact of the world ocean at its disposal, singular and shared: 'Acting together for the Future of the Blue Planet.'[66] Such UN-oriented usage derives from and conflates the 'one world' idea from the political realm and the 'one planet' idea from the environmental realm. There is a long-standing history of the United Nations deploying and advancing both – hence, 'World Oceans Day'.

Watery Spaces

Oceans, then, have served as critical spaces in world history, for all kinds of projects of the imagination, governance and material exchange. Indeed, the waves which link the world's oceans can stand for the diversity of these spatial endeavours. For scientists, waves can be described as populations, systems, events, rogues, tsunamis and formations which eat away at coasts or which are malleable and controllable. They are depicted as both male and as female. For writers, they are a source of terror and inspiration. As one scholar notes: 'waves are phenomenological-technical-mathematical-political-legal objects'.[67] They are now taken as indicators of climate change (will climate change generate more significant wave heights?) and there is even scepticism about applying northern science to the southern hemisphere of waves, which are exposed to more solar radiation than in the north, more oceanic connectivity and thus more swell. Waves have also been central to the way humans conceive of the sea as a boundary. They are a frontier to the undersea and crash upon the crossing point of the beach. As surfers know well, the surfed wave is a 'convergence' or 'assemblage', between mind, body and sea.[68] The difficulty of theorising a wave as a space, given how it is always in an act of becoming, and as an object, because of its entanglement with a whole series of human framings, predictive models and intensive experiences, is a telling fact for a book about the comparative histories of oceans.

The seas located in this volume, like the waves which run across them, oscillate between objecthood and fragmentation, internal coherence and trans-oceanic connection, openness and closure. From Braudel in the 1940s to Bailyn in the early 2000s, many oceanic historians, especially

---

[66] UNESCO, *One planet, one ocean.*

[67] This paragraph follows Stephen Helmreich, 'Waves: An anthropology of scientific things (The 2014 Lewis Henry Morgan lecture)', *HAU: Journal of Ethnographic Theory*, 4 (2014): 273.

[68] See for instance, Jon Anderson, 'Merging with the medium: Knowing the place of the surfed wave', in Anderson and Kimberley Peters, eds., *Water worlds: Human geographies of the ocean* (Farnham, 2014), pp. 73–88.

Introduction: Writing World Oceanic Histories

of the Mediterranean and the Atlantic, had stressed oceans as connectors among lands, peoples, cultures and environments. In more recent years, oceanic historians have focused instead on disaggregation, from the multiple micro-environments composing the natural history of the Mediterranean to the 'hundred horizons' imagined in the Indian Ocean.[69] Many of the chapters collected here follow this approach of 'revisionist pluralism – across space and time', as Sujit Sivasundaram calls it in his chapter on the Indian Ocean, while others emphasise in parallel the geopolitics of oceanic spaces, especially those like the Red Sea, the Black Sea or the Baltic, whose shores were more susceptible to capture by imperial powers, leading to periods of relative closedness as seas became 'lakes', under the temporary dominance of hegemonic powers such as the Ottomans, Dutch, Swedes or Russians, or the South China Sea, where in the twentieth century 'spheres of influence were carved into what had formerly been a freewheeling, liquid space'.[70]

Oceanic Histories does not for this reason essentialise or classify the seas of the world as spaces set apart from each other, nor does it prioritise the spatial scale of the global over the micro-regional, the whole ocean over the little sea, the ship over the port, the interior sea over the open ocean. Instead, it follows and collects an eclectic body of work by historians who are all interested in the different scales and optics appropriate for their subjects. Although all approach their subjects holistically, their arguments are in dialogue with those of other scholars who study infra- and inter-oceanic regions such as the Singapore and Malacca Straits, the Persian Gulf, the Tasman Sea and the Bay of Bengal or the English Channel/La Manche and the Suez Canal.[71] Indeed, we expect that histories of such 'narrow seas' – bays and straits, channels and deltas, as well as other enclosed, borderland, connective and intermediary bodies of water – will attract increasing historical attention in future. Like watery

---

[69] Nicholas Purcell and Peregrine Horden, *The corrupting sea: A study of Mediterranean history* (Oxford, 2000); Sugata Bose, *A hundred horizons: The Indian Ocean in the age of global empire* (Cambridge, MA, 2006).

[70] Sivasundaram, 'The Indian Ocean', Miran, 'The Red Sea', Ghervas, 'The Black Sea', Michael North, 'The Baltic Sea', and Tagliacozzo, 'The South China Sea' (quoted), p. 115 below.

[71] For example, Peter Borschberg, *The Singapore and Melaka Straits: Violence, security and diplomacy in the 17th century* (Singapore, 2010); Lawrence G. Potter, ed., *The Persian Gulf in history* (Basingstoke, 2009); Neville Peat, *The Tasman: Biography of an ocean* (North Shore, NZ, 2010); Sunil Amrith, *Crossing the Bay of Bengal: The furies of nature and the fortunes of migrants* (Cambridge, MA, 2013); Renaud Morieux, *The Channel: England, France and the construction of a maritime border in the eighteenth century* (Cambridge, 2016); Valeska Huber, *Channelling mobilities: Migration and globalisation in the Suez canal region and beyond, 1869–1914* (Cambridge, 2013).

18 S. Sivasundaram, A. Bashford and D. Armitage

undulations, spaces and scales continuously emerge and then merge with each other.

Though entangled in history, there are certainly different historiographical tenors in each of these seas, for instance, the anthropologised Pacific or the frontiered Southern Ocean, cast as the 'last ocean'. They even present in different colours: from the white ice of the Arctic to the medieval mapping which gave rise to the Red Sea as a name. The waters of these seas change in salinity; from the high salinity of the Mediterranean, arising as it does from a high ratio of evaporation compared with the extent to which freshwater is added through rivers and rains, to the low salinity of the waters of the Antarctic as icebergs melt or the brackish waters of the Baltic Sea with its many emptying rivers. Regardless, in thinking of these spaces of the world ocean and their inter-relations, it is helpful to adopt what has recently been called a 'fluid ontology', where coastal frontiers are margins constituted by land and fresh and salty water and amongst the most fertile regions of the world in terms of biodiversity and for the co-constitution of the human and the non-human.[72] By symmetry, a fluid ontology should be applied to think not just of the coast, but the series of spaces – from ship to world ocean – over which the terraqueous realm extends.

Approached in this way, oceanic histories revise traditional spatial considerations in world historiography. Take this classic question: is global history in danger of taking the view from outer space? Such a question, with its suggestion of the vertical as methodologically imperial, looks utterly different when considered from the undersea. Maritime histories have too often ignored the seabed as ground. In this vein, maritime histories are cast as horizontal motion across a flat wave-less sea – a literally superficial view that does not penetrate beneath the surface. From the viewpoint of undersea historians, as with recent histories of mountainous and elevated zones, the vertical axis should be reinserted rather than dismissed and the surface of the sea should be seen as spatially changeable and rugged even as undersea currents and turbulences are brought

---

[72] John Gillis and Franziska Torma, 'Introduction', in Gillis and Torma, eds. *Fluid frontiers: New currents in marine environmental history* (Cambridge, 2015), p. 9, and Jon Anderson and Kimberley Peters, ' "A perfect and absolute blank": Human geographies of water worlds', in Anderson and Peters, eds., *Water worlds*, pp. 3–19 (p. 12 quoted). See also, for work in the historical and political geography of the sea, Philip Steinberg, *The social construction of the ocean* (Cambridge, 2001), and David Lambert, Luciana Martins and Miles Ogborn, eds., 'Currents, visions and voyages: Historical geographies of the sea', *Journal of Historical Geography*, 32 (2006): 479–93.

Introduction: Writing World Oceanic Histories

to view.[73] Oceanic histories of the submarine and subaquatic realm are thus a new way to write a history 'from below'.[74]

From another perspective, a focus on the sea also critiques how area studies collapses into the history of subcontinents and large landmasses, ignoring their watery margins and in turn losing how forms of law, government, or racial and cosmopolitan thought and practice are crystallised at the water's edge in the modern era, in the Qing empire, or in South Asian successor states in the eighteenth century for instance. This is relevant in considering how a sea like the Red Sea only becomes a passageway of transit between two regions studied separately by area studies scholars.[75]

To think of seas is thus to add several more dimensions, planes and viewing points to the present global turn in historiography and at once to consider spaces as concatenations of the human and non-human. A specific theme which has generated great debate in world history is the nature of connection. On this score, the rise of oceanic histories intersected with postcoloniality, a critique of empires and nations which led into attempts to find a common ground of exchange between the dominated. This is apparent is such elaborations as the 'Black Atlantic', the Pacific as a 'sea of islands', or the 'subaltern' Indian Ocean.[76] Yet an emphasis on such connectivity can achieve an end opposite to its aim, by privileging the cosmopolitan and the mobile in motion rather than the enslaved or the labouring *lascar* in place. It can naturalise a space of exchange and interaction which is disconnected from hinterlands, the confined, the subjugated and the particular.

One response to this critique is to track the evolution of fluid frontiers to more discrete edges, as the law and the state established their protocols over the oceans and as cartographers went about delineating the ocean with their compasses and sounding devices. As one set of authors write: 'Coasts lost the quality of a margin and became an edge.'[77] In such

---

[73] Michael S. Reidy, 'From oceans to mountains: Constructing space in the imperial mind', in Jeremy Vetter, ed., *Knowing global environments: New historical perspectives on the field sciences* (New Brunswick, NJ, 2010), pp. 17–38.

[74] For the European discovery of the undersea, see Rebekka von Mallinckrodt, 'Taucherglocken, U-Boote und Aquanauten—Die Erschließung der Meere im 17. Jahrhundert zwischen Utopie und Experiment', in Karin Friedrich, ed., *Die Erschließung des Raumes: Konstruktion, Imagination und Darstellung von Räumen und Grenzen im Barockzeitalter* (Wiesbaden, 2014), pp. 337–54; Helen Rozwadowski, *Fathoming the ocean: The discovery and exploration of the deep sea* (Cambridge, MA, 2008).

[75] Miran, 'The Red Sea', below.

[76] Paul Gilroy, *The black Atlantic: Modernity and double consciousness* (Cambridge, MA, 1993); Epeli Hau'ofa, 'Our sea of islands', *The Contemporary Pacific*, 6 (1994): 147–61; Clare Anderson, *Subaltern lives: Biographies of colonialism in the Indian Ocean world, 1790–1820* (Cambridge, 2012).

[77] Gillis and Torma, 'Introduction', in Gillis and Torma, eds., *Fluid frontiers*, p. 9.

20   S. Sivasundaram, A. Bashford and D. Armitage

a narrative, connection veered into its opposite (and back again too) and this was very much in keeping with the spatiality of the ocean and its clashing and crashing waves. For terraqueous zones are changeable in their relationality and embeddedness. How to conceive of the boundaries and endings of connectedness, a key concern of the newest world historiography as it responds to its critics, is thus at the heart of oceanic histories too.[78] In what follows, it is striking to see the Mediterranean undergoing repeated integration and disintegration and even 'vanishing' with modernity, or the Indian Ocean as a space over which narrators have sought to create unity despite their efforts being constantly challenged by plurality.[79] Further, theories of the 'Ming Gap', though critiqued are said still to hold in pointing to the mutable rhythms of Sino–Southeast Asian relations.[80]

For too long the oceans have been conceived simply either as dead and without history or as inescapably other to the landlocked gaze. Indeed this tradition has played a particular role in an ocean like the Arctic.[81] This emptying of the ocean is often said to be a Western and European tradition. Yet note what the Qianlong Emperor wrote to George III in 1793: 'I do not forget the lonely remoteness of your island, cut off from the world by intervening wastes of sea.'[82] If the creation of edges between land and sea was tied to the positing of the sea as placeless and wasted, this was not a trope that was necessarily shared by all cultures. For instance, the genealogical tradition of Pacific islanders cast their islands as alive, arising out of the seas. For the Ainu, the chapter on the Sea of Japan/Korea's East Sea, below attends to Repun, the god of the Sea.[83] But rather than taking the imposition of human frames such as the law, the state and metaphor, for granted, the task of oceanic histories is to trace how the emerging spatiality in fluid zones still bears the interruptions of the waves. The world ocean is not a set of spaces which is easily habitable, readily researchable or smoothly narrated. In this sense, the

---

[78] See for instance, Sujit Sivasundaram, 'Towards a critical history of connection: The port of Colombo, the geographical "circuit" and the visual politics of new imperialism, ca. 1880–1914', *Comparative Studies in Society and History*, 59 (2017): 346–84.

[79] Greene, 'The Mediterranean Sea', and Sivasundaram, 'The Indian Ocean', below.

[80] Tagliacozzo, 'The South China Sea', below; Roxanna M. Brown, *The Ming gap and shipwreck ceramics in Southeast Asia: Towards a chronology of Thai trade ware* (Bangkok, 2009).

[81] Sörlin, 'The Arctic Ocean', below.

[82] The Qianlong Emperor to King George III (1793), in Edmund Backhouse and J. O. P. Bland, *Annals and memoirs of the court of Peking* (London, 1914), pp. 322–31, on which see Henrietta Harrison, 'The Qianlong Emperor's letter to George III and the early-twentieth-century origins of ideas about traditional China's foreign relations', *American Historical Review*, 122 (2017): 680–701.

[83] Dudden, 'The Sea of Japan/Korea's East Sea', below.

Introduction: Writing World Oceanic Histories

elusive quality of the sea as itself an agent of history should still be kept in view, even as modernisation led to boundary-making in watery zones.

Oceanic cartography was a key mechanism of such boundary-making and sought to impose stillness on to the changeable medium of water. The success of oceanic maps depended on geographical points and features that could be assumed to be changeless. Many of the chapters in this volume trace the rolling out of scientific cartography in precisely this manner. For instance, the South China Sea moved, it is said, from *mare liberum* to a closed sea by the nineteenth and twentieth centuries.[84] Yet despite the rise of a still view of the wavy ocean, mapping was tied to the paths of mobile ships. Recent work shows how the nature of the ships affected the resulting traces; ships themselves were scientific instruments of cartography.[85] At the same time, oceanic mapping was also about tracking Pacific migrations and dealing with sea-borne ethnological puzzles.[86] If this is so and ship-based scientific mapping was performative as well as evacuative, about human absence as much as human movement, the maps generated by European mariners need to placed alongside the equally embodied sailing instructions, charts and tablets which are also discussed below, used and left by Chinese explorers, Arab mariners or Roman cartographers.

The spread of Western cartography over the seas never had the capability to set itself free from extant traditions, neither has it yet become universal in its reach, notwithstanding Greenwich Mean Time. For international debates carry on with respect to the legal regimes of seas stretching from the South China Sea to the poles and historic maps and evidence of contact are still used as evidence of presence, claims and sovereignty. In other words, oceanic histories, especially as they respond to the critique that it was European imperialists and later nationalists who named many of the world's seas, includes important new work that stretches the category of mapping out to include diverse ways of knowing maritime space. In this sense, the chapters below also fit oceanic mapping together with other oceanic knowledges, ranging from knowledge of weather and the sky to tellings of natural history and natural calamity, such as debates over the mythical sunken continents of Lemuria and Atlantis. In all of these spheres, there was a braiding of ways of knowing.

---

[84] Tagliacozzo, 'The South China Sea', below.

[85] The classic article on this is Richard Sorrensen, 'The ship as a scientific instrument in the eighteenth century', *Osiris*, 11 (1996): 221–36.

[86] Bronwen Douglas, *Science, voyages and encounters in Oceania, 1511–1850* (Basingstoke, 2014).

22   S. Sivasundaram, A. Bashford and D. Armitage

Historical Temporalities of the Sea

Finally, how is historical periodisation affected by oceanic histories, and conversely how do we periodise oceanic histories? Notwithstanding historians' lament over the dominance of national frameworks, it is a curious fact that historic 'ages' have sometimes been identified by oceans or the progression of world history through its basins, in a Hegelian circuit from a 'Mediterranean Age' to a 'Pacific Age' via an Atlantic era. 'The Pacific Age' or 'Pacific Century' is the most prominent example in which periodisation has accrued to an ocean, and new kinds and intensities of human activity on it.[87] Atlantic historians similarly identified an Atlantic age, between the late fifteenth and early nineteenth centuries, with modernity itself. In other instances, canonical periodisation in world history has been called into sharp question by historians of the seas. For example, Kirti Chaudhuri's *Trade and Civilisation in the Indian Ocean* (1985) challenged a world historiography of maritime commerce and traffic dominated by European expansion after 1500, by periodising his study 'from the rise of Islam' in the mid-seventh century.[88] Conventional historical markers, often drawn from dynasties and diplomacy, rarely map comfortably onto the fluid histories of oceans and seas. Historical periodisation has often followed the determinations of territoriality and sovereignty:[89] by evading such logics, oceanic histories can be not only transnational but also transtemporal in scope. As a result, they may be productively disruptive, especially as defences against the capture of oceanic regions by national interests or attempts to carve out geopolitical spheres of influence, whether in the post-Soviet arena or in the regional competition among Asian powers for instance in the Indian Ocean.

Before most of these watery regions had historians, they had histories, in the plural, most extending back millennia rather than centuries, as shown by the continuity of human migration and mobility in the Pacific, the Red Sea, the South China Sea and the Black Sea, among others. As many of the chapters below demonstrate, the deep histories of oceans and seas provide better frameworks for historical understanding than Eurocentric categories like modernity and Enlightenment. From such a terrestrial standpoint, 'the sea which will permit no records' could appear to be outside history and beyond time.[90] This was the implicit

---

[87] Pekka Korhonen, 'The Pacific Age in world history', *Journal of World History*, 7 (1996): 41–70.

[88] Chaudhuri, *Trade and civilisation in the Indian Ocean*.

[89] Kathleen Davis, *Periodization and sovereignty: How ideas of feudalism and secularization govern the politics of time* (Philadelphia, PA, 2008).

[90] Herman Melville, *Moby-Dick* (1851), quoted in Blum, 'Terraqueous planet', p. 25.

Introduction: Writing World Oceanic Histories

claim behind a long series of attempts to place the prime meridian off-shore, in the eastern Atlantic or through the Bering Strait, before it was finally planted at Greenwich in the late nineteenth century.[91] Even then, the oceans slipped the bonds of modernist webs of universal time. It has been hardly a century since time-zones were extended from land to sea: 'Until 1920, oceans and seas remained timeless.'[92]

Oceans may have been formally timeless, until recently, but they were enmeshed in multiple temporalities. Many students of oceans and seas claim *longue durée* ambitions for their studies, picking up the traditions of narration of Arab cosmographers, or explicitly and implicitly recalling Braudel. This is with good reason and application for some oceanic spaces, but for others plainly fails to encompass the incommensurable temporalities of non-Western cultures.[93] Human history in the Pacific, for example, challenges historians to think in different temporal terms altogether: simultaneously tens of thousands of years (human movement into Papua New Guinea and the Australian continent), seven to eight centuries (human movement across Polynesia), five centuries (European maritime traffic) and two centuries (European colonisation). Just as significantly, comprehension of time past and passed across the sea is recounted generationally and genealogically by some Islanders, a productive challenge to historians considering oceanic pasts. Even in the Atlantic, that most time-bound of oceans, enslaved Africans experienced time quite differently from their masters and those who profited from their labour: the Atlantic, like parallel regions, was a sea of histories, not an ocean with a single history.[94] Oceans were therefore arenas for the competition of time-scales and the negotiation of histories. Artificial efforts to demarcate and define them, whether by inscribing territorial limits, slicing them longitudinally with treaty zones or date-lines or bisecting them across the equator, were only writ in water.

It is also striking that oceans have served as sites for telling futures. The contemplation of rising levels of sea is not simply a recent phenomenon. Scientific debate around the long-term relation between land and sea, drawing on catastrophist and evolutionist geological models, attracted

---

[91] Charles W. J. Withers, *Zero degrees: Geographies of the prime meridian* (Cambridge, MA, 2017), pp. 29–37, 159–67.

[92] Vanessa Ogle, *The global transformation of time, 1870–1950* (Cambridge, MA, 2015), pp. 87–88.

[93] See, for example, Damon Salesa, 'The Pacific in indigenous time', in David Armitage and Alison Bashford, eds., *Pacific histories: Ocean, land, people* (Basingstoke, 2014), pp. 31–52.

[94] Walter Johnson, 'Possible pasts: Some speculations on time, temporality, and the history of the Atlantic slave trade', *Amerikastudien/American Studies*, 45 (2000): 485–99.

24   S. Sivasundaram, A. Bashford and D. Armitage

controversy because they were also a claim on the future.[95] Meanwhile, the clash of futures told over the sea is especially obvious across the axis of coloniser/colonised; Indigenous peoples have used the sea as a horizon of expectation and a space of the imagination in the face of terrestrial political threat and at times of decolonisation or when faced with colonial narratives of progress and improvement.[96] The arrival of new and future-facing technologies that have bypassed the sea – from air travel to space travel, have often returned by way of metaphor, comparison, naming or routes, or even by the new images they provide of the sea, to the maritime.[97] Present concerns about climate refugees and extreme weather events and debates about the way ahead after the proposal of the Anthropocene, as also the unfolding intersection of climate studies and postcolonialism, will feed into oceanic histories.[98] Thinking with the oceans therefore opens up the possibility of a wide-scale recalibration of our senses of historical temporality and human and terrestrial subjectivities, while at the same time prising open vistas on time's future, in historiography and beyond.

Conclusions

Oceanic Histories takes to the sea, in order to compare and place alongside each other a series of terraqueous zones which have not previously been brought together. This is not an exercise in comparativism for the sake of comparison; rather, it is motivated by the aim of engaging what have been vastly separated historiographies of water, distanced from each other despite their undoubted inter-relation, spatial entanglement and human and non-human connectivity. That distancing has occurred because of the politics of empires, nations, area studies, indigeneity and internationalism. It has also happened because of the way historiographies easily operate as worlds – oceanic and otherwise – unto themselves.

The ordering of the chapters that follows highlights a new route through oceanic historiography; we have prevented ourselves from starting with the Mediterranean, thus enabling a new historiographic cartography,

---

[95] Sujit Sivasundaram, 'Science', in Armitage and Bashford, eds., *Pacific histories*, pp. 237–60.

[96] See for instance, Tracey Banivanua Mar, *Decolonisation and the Pacific: Indigenous globalisation and the ends of empire* (Cambridge, 2016).

[97] Frances Steele, 'Maritime mobilities in Pacific history: Towards a scholarship of betweenness', in Gijs Mom, Gordon Pirie and Laurent Tissot, eds., *Mobility in history: Themes in transport* (Neuchatel, 2010), pp. 199–204.

[98] Dipesh Chakrabarty, 'The climate of history: Four theses', *Critical Inquiry*, 35 (2009): 197–222.

Introduction: Writing World Oceanic Histories 25

and begin instead with three oceans – the Indian, Pacific and Atlantic – in rough order of the histories of attempts to integrate them, but also to displace the Atlantic in favour of other oceanic models. Then, the book proceeds through pairings of seas also with the goal of avoiding geographical determinism and narratives that spread outward from the false universal of Europe or of the Mediterranean. The novel juxtapositions in this section – for instance, the South China Sea with the Mediterranean, the Red Sea and the Sea of Japan – are designed to highlight historiographical similarities even across geographical expanses, while the more conventional pairing of the Black Sea and the Baltic should facilitate comparison between two regions which have recently experienced political efforts to reintegrate them after a century or more of historical division. Finally, the closing dialogue between the Arctic and Southern Oceans returns the book to two seas more often linked institutionally and intellectually despite their separation at greatest distance from each other. Readers and teachers using the volume can, of course, rearrange the chapters for their own purposes. Nonetheless, we hope our oceanic reshuffling will divert them from conventional tracks and suggest new visions of their oceans and their histories.

The seas that are narrated below are connected and disconnected, spatially interwoven with micro-ecologies and micro-geographies as much as the global plane. In a similar way, we expect that the series that this volume inaugurates will attend to a further cluster of spaces: ports and ships, straits, bays and islands and the undersea realm. All of these travel across, above and below the seas of this volume: ships and airplanes, telegraph lines and missiles, refugees and migrants, trepang and whales, monsoonal winds and El Niño, currents and underwater storms. Taken together, these seas constitute the watery horizons of our planet and a historiographical horizon too.

Our project is inter-disciplinary and methodologically capacious in historical terms. This is evident in how history itself is stretched out over time in what follows, in making the case that the origins of oceanic historiography are long and multicentred and that it overlaps with geographies, cartographies, astronomies, ethnographies, climatic studies and natural histories. Though each of the sub-fields of oceanic historiography surveyed below has developed with a critical sense of its own distinctive flavour, there has been and continues to be a borrowing of concepts and methods. This borrowing at times has been detrimental to the emergence of original questions; and yet at other times the inability to talk beyond the divides of Atlantic, Indian Ocean, Pacific and Mediterranean history for instance, has closed down subjects and areas. To think critically about the relatedness and becoming of each of these seas is thus an

26 S. Sivasundaram, A. Bashford and D. Armitage

urgent concern, moving beyond the simplistic and dichotomous impasse which questions whether world historiography collapses everything into one or creates new grids of imperial, regional and national difference. To consider the world historiography of oceans in this way is also to take account of the environmental politics of our age and its implication of the need to think of the world ocean as a whole and as a commons. In keeping with the avowed spirit of 'World Oceans Day', it represents a historiographical commitment to plural seas and oceans as well as to the singular ocean itself.

Further Reading

While naval, maritime and ocean histories were written throughout the twentieth century, and indeed earlier, historiographical reflection on, and meta-histories of these fields appeared in the 1990s, led by Indian Ocean historians; see K. N. Chaudhuri, 'The unity and disunity of Indian Ocean history from the rise of Islam to 1750: The outline of a theory and historical discourse', *Journal of World History*, 1 (1993): 1–21. Considerations of the potential of oceans to reframe world historical scholarship suddenly flourished in the first decade of the twenty-first century: Bernard Klein and Gesa Mackenthun, eds., *Sea changes: Historicizing the ocean* (New York, 2004); Rainer F. Buschmann, 'Oceans of world history: Delineating aquacentric notions in the global past', *History Compass*, 2 (2004): 1–10. And for early links between environmental history and marine worlds, see W. Jeffrey Bolster, 'Opportunities in marine environmental history', *Environmental History*, 11 (2006): 567–97. Kären Wigen convened and edited the much-cited forum in *American Historical Review*, 111 (2006): 717–80, 'Oceans of history', considering the Mediterranean (Peregrine Horden and Nicholas Purcell), the Pacific (Matt Matsuda) and the Atlantic (Alison Games). See also Gelina Harlaftis, 'Maritime history, or the history of *Thalassa*', in Harlaftis, Nikos Karapidakis, Kostas Sbonias and Vaios Vaipoulos, eds., *The new ways of history: Developments in historiography* (London, 2010), pp. 211–38; Rila Mukherjee, 'Escape from terracentrism: Writing a water history', *Indian Historical Review*, 41 (2014): 87–101; and Michael Pearson, 'Oceanic history', in Prasenjit Duara, Viren Murthy and Andrew Sartori, eds., *A companion to global historical thought* (Chichester, 2014), pp. 337–50. Meanwhile, historians of the Indian Ocean and of the Malay maritime world provided important collected statements about substance and methodology, including Rila Mukherjee, ed., *Oceans connect: Reflections on water worlds across space and time* (Delhi, 2013), and Antoinette Burton,

Madhavi Kale, Isabel Hofmeyr, Clare Anderson, Christopher J. Lee and Nile Green, 'Sea tracks and trails: Indian Ocean worlds as method', *History Compass*, 11, 7 (July 2013): 497–535. Throughout, two key journals have consistently presented and challenged the bounds of maritime history: *The Journal for Maritime Research*, established by the National Maritime Museum at Greenwich in 1999, and the *International Journal of Maritime History*, originally the organ of the International Maritime Economic History Association. A special issue of the former has recently brought a gendered analysis to maritime and oceanic history: Quintin Colville, Elin Jones and Katherine Parker, eds., 'Gendering the maritime world', *Journal for Maritime Research*, 17 (2015): 97–181. Cultural, political and human geographers have contributed significant historical work, including Philip Steinberg, *The social construction of the ocean* (London, 2001), who investigates a geography of law of the sea. See also Jon Anderson and Kimberly Peters, eds., *Water worlds: human geographies of the ocean* (Farnham, 2014). On land/sea connections, see Alison Bashford, 'Terraqueous histories', *The Historical Journal*, 60 (2017): 253–72; Michael N. Pearson, 'Littoral society: The concept and the problems', *Journal of World History*, 17 (2006): 353–73; Jerry H. Bentley, Renate Bridenthal and Kären Wigen, eds., *Seascapes: Maritime histories, littoral cultures and transoceanic exchanges* (Honolulu, HI, 2007); and Donna Gabaccía and Dirk Hoerder, eds., *Connecting seas and connected ocean rims: Indian, Atlantic, and Pacific Oceans and China Seas migrations from the 1830s to the 1930s* (Leiden, 2011). Coastlines have received particular treatment in John R. Gillis, *The human shore: Seacoasts in history* (Chicago, IL, 2012) and with a focus on fishing and fishers in Charu Gupta and Mukul Sharma, *Contested coastlines: Fisherfolk, nations and borders in South Asia* (New Delhi, 2008). For recent studies of the connections between world history and oceanic histories, including comparative methods, see Nile Green, 'Maritime worlds and global history: Comparing the Mediterranean and Indian Ocean through Barcelona and Bombay', *History Compass*, 11, 7 (July 2013): 513–23; Michael N. Pearson, 'Notes on world history and maritime history', *Asian Review of World History*, 3 (2015): 137–51. There is a growing cultural history of oceans, including calls for a new 'blue humanities': for example, Steven Mentz, 'Toward a blue cultural studies: The sea, maritime culture and early modern English literature', *Literature Compass*, 6, 5 (September 2009): 997–1013; Hester Blum, 'The prospect of oceanic studies', *PMLA*, 125 (2010): 770–79; and Charlotte Mathieson, ed., *Sea narratives: Cultural responses to the sea, 1600–present* (London, 2016).

Part I

Oceans

1   The Indian Ocean

Sujit Sivasundaram

The Indian Ocean ranks among the most long-lived spaces of historical memory and the present burst of historiographical attention to this ocean should be interpreted in this context. The key terms driving recent histories of the Indian Ocean are said to be: 'porousness, permeability, connectedness, flexibility, and the openness of spatial and temporal boundaries and borders'.[1] Such terms reflect how present-day Indian Ocean historians like crossing the boundaries of national and regional units (especially, Africa, the Middle East and Asia, which arose out of nationalist or Cold War politics in the twentieth century), replacing them with the Indian Ocean as a more resonant cartography. They also reflect how recent histories of the Indian Ocean have crossed temporal thresholds, inherent in such labels which were once applied to this sea: 'Islamic Sea', 'The Early Modern Indian Ocean' and 'British Lake'. However, this revisionist pluralism – across space and time – in histories of the Indian Ocean is in keeping with this sea's narration over the *longue durée*.

Over the centuries, narrators of the Indian Ocean have come from myriad cultural perspectives, East and West. The chapter begins with the claim that this historiography of the Indian Ocean has no clear beginning, nor has it operated in a linear track, by way of geography, temporality or method. Despite this long-term fluidity, over the centuries and now once again, there have been those who have sought to define and contain the Indian Ocean as a whole. Yet as this chapter demonstrates, their efforts have had to come to terms with layered inheritances and forgotten histories, disconnected locales and the pull of adjoining waters. In other words, despite attempts to move towards structuralism or an 'Indian Ocean history school', such endeavours have not stood in these

---

[1] Marcus Vink, 'Indian Ocean studies and the "new thalassology"', *Journal of Global History*, 2 (2007): 52. Other useful reviews: Isabel Hofmeyr, 'The complicating sea: The Indian Ocean as method', *Comparative Studies of South Asia, Africa and the Middle East*, 32 (2012): 584–90, and Sebastian Prange, 'Scholars and the sea: A historiography of the Indian Ocean', *History Compass*, 6, 5 (2008): 1382–93.

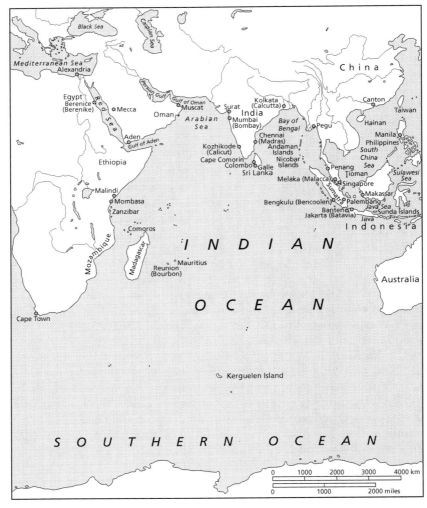

Map 1.1 The Indian Ocean

waters, as is shown in sections below, on trades and labourers, environments and knowledges, and modern formations.

As historians shift between finding a singular Indian Ocean 'system', environmental pattern or social formation and breaking all of these up into competing Islams or distinct environmental belts, or indeed, moving beyond slavery versus indenture, relinking this sea to the Atlantic and

The Indian Ocean   33

Pacific, and reinserting race, legality, and state-making, the way ahead must surely lie in embracing the many historiographical Indian Oceans. To the key terms cited above might then be added their opposites. The chapter attends then to this question: why has the Indian Ocean seen structures, peoples, ideas and things shifting between porous and bounded incarnations in historical time as well as in historical tellings of this sea? It begins with the history of histories and geographies of the Indian ocean.

Narrators of the Indian Ocean

By 2000 BCE, there was contact between the coastal communities of the Red Sea, the Gulf and the Indus Valley. At the other end of the Indian Ocean, from around 3000 BCE, there was a migration from Taiwan to the Philippines and down to Southeast Asia, and on to Micronesia and Polynesia with the Sulawesi Sea as a major point of transit from about 1500 BCE. South Asian merchants, Malay mariners, Buddhist monks, and the eventual emergence of states such as the Sassanians in Persia, the Guptas in India and Funan in Southeast Asia, who were interested in oceanic trade, set a template for the Indian Ocean in the first centuries of the common era, prior to the increasing spread of Islam, south and east from the Middle East. Contact between the Middle East and China by way of the Indian Ocean is evident in the establishment of settlements: a Persian settlement on the island of Hainan in 748 and a mixed Arab-Persian colony at Canton around the same time. Chinese ships were also visiting the Persian Gulf in the ninth century.[2]

For Sugata Bose, the Indian Ocean has never been a 'system' as much as an 'arena' of 'a hundred horizons', which are economic, political and cultural, and where both space and time was crossed.[3] This surely applies to the history of histories of the Indian Ocean too. Even the earliest histories of trade and migration explode the Indian Ocean's boundaries in geographical terms, linking it to the Mediterranean and the Pacific. Among sources which link the ocean west are those connected to the Roman Empire, for instance *Periplus Marae Erythraensis* or 'Sailor's Guide to the Indian Ocean', whose author was probably a Greek who lived in the mid-first century, based in the port of Bernice on the Red Sea coast of Egypt and who had travelled to the Pandya kingdom of South India, which in turn had sent a mission to Rome to encourage traders to visit it.

---

[2] For more details on the early history of the Indian Ocean, see the excellent survey by Edward Alpers, *The Indian Ocean in world history* (Oxford, 2014).
[3] Sugata Bose, *A hundred horizons: The Indian Ocean in the age of global empire* (Cambridge, MA, 2009).

34   S. Sivasundaram

Or indeed, there is *Hyphegesis Geographike*, 'Guide to Geography', written around 150 CE, by the astronomer Claudius Ptolemy, based in Alexandria, showing especial interest in Southeast Asia, recording accurate information as far as the borderlands of China. The Indian Ocean's indefinition is certainly evident in these early sources: should they be classed as Greco-Roman, Alexandrian or, as one important Southeast Asianist writes, reliant 'on a whole series of stories heard in the ports of India and Sri Lanka?'[4]

Yet despite this undoubted multi-dimensionality, people who faced this ocean sought to encompass it as a unit. One marvellous recent find that bears this out is an eleventh-century Egyptian cosmographic treatise, in Arabic manuscript, *The Book of Curiosities of the Sciences and Marvels for the Eyes*. While the author is unknown it is likely to have arisen from the Fatimid caliphate. The second book or *maqalat* relies heavily on Ptolemy and includes a map of the Indian Ocean, alongside one of the Mediterranean and the Caspian Sea; maps of Sicily and Cyprus and ports in North Africa and five maps of rivers, including the Nile, the Euphrates, the Tigris, the Oxus and the Indus. Intriguingly, the Indian Ocean is presented as an enclosed, symmetric and oblong green oval with mountains sprouting almost tree-like from it. This is containment *par excellence*. As two authorities on this find write: 'The concept of an enclosed Indian Ocean may have derived directly from Ptolemy, who surmised that the Chinese coast extends southwards and the African coast eastwards, so that they eventually join up.'[5]

The Indian Ocean is drawn here in two halves, east and west.[6] There is specific attention to islands of transit – such as Pulau Tioman and the Nicobar islands, which are stopping places on the way to China, or Zanzibar which appears as Unjuwa, a corruption of the Swahili, Unguja, as a rectangular box in the sea. Protruding into the sea and out of it are ports – such as Aden and a volcano, 'in which there is fire night and day', possibly Krakatau in Indonesia. While this demonstrates an understanding of the Indian Ocean as an integrated space, that space is already plural and it is historicised, for knowledge of it already comes from prior classical sources and Muslim sailors and merchants served as informants in the making of this map. Thinking with this source, as with *Periplus* or

---

[4] For a Southeast Asian reading of these texts, see John N. Miksic, *Singapore & the silk road of the sea, 1300–1800* (Singapore, 2013), pp. 34–37.

[5] Yossef Rapoport and Emilie Savage-Smith, 'Medieval Islamic view of the cosmos: The newly discovered Book of Curiosities', *The Cartographic Journal*, 41 (2004): 256.

[6] For the map and annotations, see *An eleventh-century Egyptian guide to the universe*, ed. and trans. Yossef Rapoport and Emilie Savage-Smith (Leiden, 2014), pp. 156–60, 443–46.

The Indian Ocean 35

Hyphegesis, the enclosure of the Indian Ocean hides a more complicated history of intellectual inheritance.

One fabled island of transit in the middle of the Indian Ocean which was listed in the *Book of Curiosities* under 'islands of the infidels' was 'Sarandib', present-day Sri Lanka, which is called 'Taprobane' in maps attributed to Ptolemy and exaggerated to fourteen times its size today:

> It is ruled by two kings and is inhabited by members of every nation. There is the Mountain al-Rahūn, which is the place where Adam, may the Blessings of God be upon him, fell [from Heaven]. . . No other country on the face of the Earth equals the wealth of Sarandīb. Its people sail the seas. . .[7]

By the early fifteenth century, Zheng He, the Muslim eunuch appointed to 'display [Ming] soldiers in strange lands in order to make manifest the wealth and power of the Middle Kingdom' arrived on Sri Lanka for the third time. At the southern port of Galle he held a fair to display Chinese products: candlesticks, lacquer ware, silks, porcelain, textiles, and Buddhist sutras and incense burners.[8] A commemorative tablet was installed at Galle, which referred to the holy Lankan mountain, noted above. Critically, and in keeping with the plurality of the Indian ocean, it was inscribed in three languages, Persian, Tamil and Chinese, bestowing offerings to Buddha, Vishnu and the Light of Islam. The Chinese inscription included the alms bestowed to the Temple of the Mountain, including 1,000 pieces of gold, 5,000 pieces of silver and fifty rolls of silk. In praise of Buddha, it noted: 'Of late we have despatched missions to announce our mandate to foreign nations, and during their journey over the ocean they have been favoured with the blessing of your beneficent protection.'[9]

Zheng He's seven voyages, from 1405 to 1433, sponsored by the third Ming Emperor, Yongle, are perhaps the best example of a view of the Indian Ocean from the East, to counterbalance that provided by the Arab cosmographies of the West. They exemplify a Chinese bid for a Silk Road of the Sea, evident in the description of his vessels as 'jewel-ships'.[10] They also demonstrated the Ming dominion over Chinese 'pirates', for instance in Palembang, where 5,000 local Chinese were killed on the Zheng He's first mission. Though Zheng He's are the best known, twelve

---

[7] *An eleventh-century Egyptian guide*, eds. Rapoport and Savage-Smith, p. 481.

[8] See Edward L. Dreyer, *Zheng He: China and the oceans in the Early Ming Dynasty, 1405–1433* (New York, 2007), p. 33. See also Sally K. Church, 'Zheng He: An investigation into the plausibility of 450-ft treasure ships', *Monumenta Serica*, 53 (2005): 1–43.

[9] Lorna Dewaraja, 'Cheng Ho's visits to Sri Lanka and the Galle trilingual inscription in the National Museum in Colombo', *Journal of the Royal Asiatic Society of Sri Lanka*, 52 (2006): 64.

[10] Miksic, *Singapore*, p. 193.

36   S. Sivasundaram

other Chinese admirals headed up similar enterprises into the Indian Ocean. While the Galle inscription denotes the plurality of this view of the Indian Ocean, it was still an attempt, like that in the *Book of Curiosities*, to contain this vast sea and frame it as a unit, and to exercise tributary relations over it.[11] Although he is often analysed as a maritime pioneer, Zheng He did not discover anything new. He relied on what had been known 'to Indonesians, Indians, or Arabs, for over a thousand years' and indeed to the Chinese too.[12] This was no conceptual beginning.

In as much as these pre-1500 cartographies and histories roam across the ocean, borrowing from their predecessors, the recurrence of the ocean as a space of historical consciousness and geographical thought is apparent into the late modern period. For instance, in the early-twentieth century, Tamil scholars looked back to an undated past when their homeland stretched across the Indian Ocean.[13] The biogeographer Philip Sclater (1829–1913) recast Lemuria as 'Ilemuria', or as Kumari's territory or continent. Kumari was a virgin and her sunken continent was for some writers characterised by the rule of queens. In 1903, for Suryanarayana Sastri, the author of a history of the Tamil language, this land extended from Cape Comorin to Kerguelen Island and from Madagascar to the Sunda Islands, including Sumatra and Java.[14] In the literary rendition of R. P. Sethu Pillai, professor of Tamil at the University of Madras, the sage Ilango Adigal speaks to the ocean thus: 'O mischievous ocean! . . . Alas! You ate up our land! You drank our rivers! You consumed our mountains.' Tamil scholars wrote of this event as *katarkol* indicating 'seizure by the sea'.[15] In these Tamil renditions of Lemuria, time itself collapses, as the Pandya past becomes interwoven with a modern conception of the Tamil nation. As Lemuria moved from Europe to India and across the ocean, this is a fluid story in many senses, but it is one of asserted sovereignty, longing and ownership, arising out of the waves. It does not stand alone: for instance, in Sri Lanka, the Ptolemaic conception of Taprobane, noted above as a much-enlarged island, was discussed in the aftermath of the 2004 Indian Ocean tsunami and placed alongside Buddhist chronicles to prompt the following question: did unrighteous government periodically give rise to tidal waves which resized Sri Lanka?[16]

---

[11] For the tributary system, see Dreyer, *Zheng He*, ch. 3.

[12] Dreyer, *Zheng He*, p. 30.

[13] This paragraph is based on Sumathi Ramaswamy, *The lost land of Lemuria: Fabulous geographies, catastrophic histories* (Berkeley, CA, 2004).

[14] Ramaswamy, *The lost land*, p. 130.

[15] Ramaswamy, *The lost land*, pp. 142–43.

[16] See Chanuka Wattegama, 'Seven historical tsunamis', reprinted at: http://indi.ca/2005/01/seven-historical-tsunamis/footnote (accessed 24 January 2017).

The Indian Ocean

If these engagements from South Asia, China and the Middle East demonstrate the longevity and chronological resonance of meanings attached to the Indian Ocean, and how the making of a singular space of meaning and a plural terrain of inheritance wrestle with each other, it is problematic that the origin of Indian Ocean historiography is dated to the midtwentieth century. Accordingly, the first wave of Indian Ocean histories came in the 1950s and 1960s, followed by a cross-fertilisation between the *Annales*-school and world-systems analysis in the 1980s. Among the first wave are said to be the Mauritius archivist Auguste Toussaint, and the Australian mariner, photographer, author and circumnavigator, Alan Villiers; among the second wave were Kirti Chaudhuri, Michael Pearson and Kenneth McPherson.[17] While Toussaint critiques Villiers for not being a historian, both Villiers and Toussaint's texts share a similar narrative arc. Toussaint puts to one side 'the obscure ages of Lemuria', and begins 'about 2300 BC' in Egypt and ends with the Second World War.[18] There is in both a marked romanticisation of the Indian Ocean.[19] Toussaint ends urging 'a new balance' in the global order, inspired by the Indian Ocean as a space that would tie East to West. The book ends with a quotation from Sri Aurobindo, 'among the classics of the Indian Ocean' and posits a world moving more and more towards the 'mixture of races'. 'White Australia' and apartheid South Africa are things of the past. Rather there should be 'the formation of an Indian Ocean community and an understanding among the peoples of the oceanic world without further delay'.[20]

Histories such as these are travel texts, prognostics and prophecies, technical digests and geographical surveys of location, islands and routes. While surely affected by new technologies of steam and even air, they are mythic imaginaries; attempts to create a new future through the definition of the Indian Ocean's history at a moment when the world of old empires was fading. Take this paragraph from Villiers:

In my mind's eye, flying over the Indian Ocean – as once I had to do during the war – I see something of the great array of the illustrious past across those blue and sunlit waters. I see the curious ships of Egypt putting out for the land of Punt. I see the Chinese junks; the Arab, the Indian, the Persian dhows in their thousands; the *praus* of the East and the sewn boats of Shihr, and Lamu . . . It

---

[17] Vink, 'Indian Ocean studies', 42–43, for a chronology of works.

[18] Auguste Toussaint, *History of the Indian Ocean*, trans. June Guicharnaud (London, 1961), p. 12.

[19] Alan Villiers, *The Indian Ocean* (London, 1952), pp. 13–15. Villiers casts the Indian Ocean, next to the other two great oceans: it is 'upon the whole the most kindly to sailing-ships', 'the most interesting' and especially calm due to being 'embayed'.

[20] Toussaint, *History of the Indian Ocean*, pp. 243–44, 248, 246.

38   S. Sivasundaram

is a swansong, for already the belch of smoke shows upon the western horizon and, far away, a score thousand lean brown hands are scraping at the sands of Suez. The vision fades. Far below me, a great steamer, a 20,000-tonner with an enormous, bolt-upright and curiously ugly stack, is belting at the gentle mounds of rippling water at her heedless bows. The year now is 1951, and the radio at my side is telling, in a toneless and affected voice, of warfare in Korea, dock strikes in Australia, New Zealand, London, a festival in Britain, an immense armament drive in the United States.[21]

Such a flight across the ocean – despite the new vista provided by air travel – is totally aligned with the potentiality of the Indian Ocean across the centuries, to rethink space, time and civilisation. The late beginning of a more 'professional' historiography of the Indian Ocean might then be dissolved within the story told here of the ocean as a fluid space of meaning, and yet one over which ownership has been attempted from multiple starting points without full success. The Indian Ocean evaded the historical mastery of a singular culture or a privileged set of narrators into the twentieth century.

Traders and Labourers

If there was a concentration of focus in mid-twentieth-century professional histories of the Indian Ocean it lay in debates about how to characterise the trading world of this sea. The rival traditions are best illustrated in the differing emphases of two India-focussed historians: Kirti Chaudhuri and Ashin Das Gupta. Chaudhuri turned to the Indian Ocean after writing on the East India Company as an economically logical institution.[22] He repeatedly paid homage to Fernand Braudel. Das Gupta, however, began not with the European expansion but with a focus on Asian maritime merchants based on the Malabar coast as they encountered the Portuguese and the Dutch.

For Das Gupta, the impact of Europe was said at first to be minimal. Rather the resurgence of ports and communities was tied to the restructuring of inter-Asian trade with the rise of newly centralised polities – such as Travancore. Accordingly, 'the maritime empire of Portugal gradually became a part of the structure of medieval Asian trade' and the Dutch who followed, 'carried on trade much as any Asian merchant with a substantial capital to invest would have done'.[23] For Das Gupta, though the British played a role in explaining the end of this story, he

---

[21] Villiers, *The Indian Ocean*, pp. 239–40.
[22] Kirti N. Chaudhuri, *The English East India Company: The study of an early joint-stock company 1600–1640* (London, 1965).
[23] Ashin Das Gupta, *Malabar in Asian trade, 1740–1800* (Cambridge, 1967), pp. 11, 18.

The Indian Ocean   39

was as keen to trace, for instance in his work on Surat, the breakdown of Indian polities, the changing profitability of trade and the impoverishment of merchant communities. In locating local agency, in contrast to Chaudhuri's quantification and systematisation, Das Gupta turned to the human face of trade. In the case of Surat, Mulla Abdul Ghafur stood as a gauge of the whole: a ship-owner, merchant and Bhora, who might be compared in worth to a European company and who turned against the Dutch in the late seventeenth century by declaring a crusade against the *firangis* for the piracy and plunder of Indian ships, including his own and pilgrim ships too.[24]

As he stretched back in time and filled out his schema, Chaudhuri took up the impact of Vasco da Gama and wrote of the Portuguese desire for systematic control of the spice trade, connected to the *cartaz* system of passes issued to Indian ships and 'redistributive enterprise', which was then followed by the Dutch who were drawn to South Asia for its cottons and also indigo, saltpetre, silk, cinnamon and pepper. The innovation brought about by the Dutch and the English rested in a common structural form. This was the world-spanning joint-stock company, and in India it was manifest in 'a head settlement or factory situated at or near some major Indian port with subordinate stations in the interior where many of the export goods were produced'. Some Dutch bases lay at Surat, Cochin, Pulicut, Negapatam, Musilipatam and Hugli and the English of course set up what became their key bases, in Madras, Bombay and Calcutta, as part of a 'general plan to make the Company's trade independent of the political power of the indigenous rulers'. If there was a resurgence of trade, in Chaudhuri's view this came about not because of indigenous political changes but because of the participation of Europeans in the eighteenth century, lubricated by Latin American silver. The emphasis on control of quality and regular delivery marked this moment off as novel. All of this led to the crescendo of the Battle of Plassey in 1757, which Chaudhuri saw as a 'revolution'.[25]

Despite their differences over the dynamic of transition to European rule and the reasons for a resurgence in trade at the advent of the Europeans, both these scholars shared a commitment to the Indian Ocean world as a unit. Drawing on world-systems theorist Immanuel Wallerstein,

---

[24] See Rudrangshu Mukherjee, 'Ashin Das Gupta: Some memories and reflections', in Rudrangshu Mukherjee and Lakshmi Subramaniam, eds., *Politics and trade in the Indian Ocean: Essays in honour of Ashin Das Gupta* (Delhi, 1998), pp. 6–18.

[25] Kirti Chaudhuri, 'European trade with India', in Tapan Raychaudhuri and Irfan Habib, eds., *The Cambridge economic history of India*, Vol. 1 (Cambridge, 2010), pp. 391, 392, 395.

40   S. Sivasundaram

and allegedly going beyond Braudel to a purer kind of structuralism, Chaudhuri wrote of a 'life cycle' in the capitalist world economy from the 'rise of Islam to 1750' linking 'Indian ocean civilisations'. The equation here pivoted on the spread of Islam from Alexandria to Canton, but also the migration of 'nomads from Central Asia' who founded Eurasian empires and the extending reach of China to the Indian Ocean.[26] It was summarised as the combination of 'Islam, Sanskritic India, the societies of southeast Asia, and finally Confucian China'.[27] Meanwhile, Das Gupta wrote of a 'high medieval' Indian Ocean. Picking up the resilient role played by merchants, he cast the period from 1500 to 1800 as an 'age of partnership'.[28] Relatedly, Southeast Asian historiography has presented the region as experiencing an 'age of commerce' from 1400 to 1650 followed by de-commercialisation, while others have looked to 1400 to 1800 as an 'Asian age', where global trade pivoted on the Indian ocean.[29]

If the classification of the Indian Ocean as a terrain of globalisation, grew out of work on India, recent approaches seek to break it down into granular detail, moving away from the 'system' of the Indian Ocean. One way to do this is to stretch the chronology into the twentieth century, bypassing the question of the impact of European empires: 'from about 1800 to 1930 pre-existing interregional networks were utilized, moulded, reordered, and rendered subservient by Western capital and the more powerful colonial states, but never torn apart'.[30] To argue this is to trace the world of migrant merchants, moneylenders, soldiers and labourers, working beneath and beyond the radar of formal empires. In one well-worked recent case study, from the middle of the eighteenth century and into the early nineteenth century, Gujarati merchants expanded their connection to Mozambique, finding African consumers for their woven cloths and ably predicting changes in taste for styles and patterns and thus overtaking European traders. In return for cloth these merchants traded in ivory, but also in slaves.[31]

---

[26] Kirti N. Chaudhuri, *Asia before Europe: Economy and civilisation in the Indian Ocean from the rise of Islam to 1750* (Cambridge, 1991), p. 382 and *Trade and civilisation in the Indian Ocean* (Cambridge, 1985), pp. 3–4.

[27] Kirti N. Chaudhuri, 'The unity and disunity of Indian Ocean history from the rise of Islam to 1750', *Journal of World History*, 4 (1993): 1–21, 8.

[28] Subrahmanyam, 'Introduction', 9.

[29] See Prange, 'Scholars and the sea'.

[30] Bose, *A Hundred Horizons*, p. 14.

[31] Pedro Machado, *Ocean of trade: South Asian merchants, Africa and the Indian Ocean c.1750–1850* (Cambridge, 2015). For Africa in the Indian Ocean economy, see also Jeremy Prestholdt, *Domesticating the world: African consumerism and the genealogies of globalization* (Berkeley, CA, 2008).

The Indian Ocean 41

Yet stretching chronology is not the only route. Another related method comes from shifting to new geographies and smaller seas. In the Bay of Bengal, for instance, prior connections were transformed but not in a singular fashion in the period after the 'age of commerce'. For the second half of the seventeenth century saw an intensification of commercial relations with China, arising out of agricultural expansion in Southeast Asia.[32] This intensification went together with a disconnection of the Malay courts from northern Indian Mughal ports as a result of the encroachment of European corporations. But Muslims from Southern India, such as the Maraikkayar, or indeed Afghans, connected the subcontinent to southeast Asia. At the northern end of the Bay of Bengal, Arakan and Pegu ceased to be points of transit between India and Southeast Asia turning to their hinterlands. The Dutch made inroads by taking Makassar or Banten, at the end of the seventeenth century, but further to the west their control continued to be less pronounced. Eric Tagliacozzo takes the story forward: 'Well into the seventeenth century Southeast Asian rulers on the whole had to be much more concerned with their own internecine struggles than with European rivalry, but by the 1760s Anglo-Dutch competition in the region (punctuated by British demands for free trade) launched a new spectre of territorial conquest.'[33]

A similarly layered story is now emerging out of the Persian Gulf. Here, longstanding connections between Arab and Indian commerce, tied to the need for timber, cotton and rice, for instance in the Gulf, and horses, silk and dates in India, were reconfigured, but not without leaving space for new successor regimes, perhaps most notably the Omani sultanate, which rode the waves of European commerce into the nineteenth century. The surge in commerce in the Persian Gulf came about at the crossroads of two declining empires – the Safavids, who gave way to the Qajars, and the Ottomans. By the end of the eighteenth century this surge included such sea-based trades as pearls, wool and opium. It relied on increasing numbers of Indian merchant communities and moneylenders in Muscat and Mutrah in Oman.[34] This trade required labour – which also came via the ocean – primarily slaves from East Africa. The slave trade benefitted from the growing political alliance between Oman

---

[32] Jos Gommans, 'Trade and civilization around the Bay of Bengal, c. 1650–1800', *Itinerario*, 19 (1995): 82–108.

[33] Eric Tagliacozzo, 'Trade, production and incorporation: The Indian Ocean in flux, 1600–1900', *Intinerario*, 26 (2002): 81.

[34] See for instance, Patricia Risso, 'India and the Gulf: Encounters from the mid-sixteenth to the mid-twentieth centuries', in Lawrence Potter, ed., *The Persian Gulf in history* (Basingstoke, 2009), pp. 189–203.

and Zanzibar.[35] Slavery itself was reconstituted as a result of the rise of these maritime trades in the Gulf: it shifted from being primarily domestic and agricultural to being connected for example, with pearling, with loading and unloading at port and with work aboard *dhows* or other ocean-going craft.

Slaving in the Gulf takes us neatly to a related theme of debate in Indian Ocean studies. If Chaudhuri and Das Gupta were operating in the shadow of Mediterranean historiography, the push and pull of the Atlantic is evident in the contest over characterisations of labour in the Indian Ocean. The field began with an insistence that Indian Ocean slavery was distinct in form and character to the Atlantic. Accordingly, the difference between freedom and unfreedom was blurred in the Indian Ocean, and most labourers entered slavery through indebtedness. The range of work undertaken by slaves was said to be wider than in the Atlantic and often non-agricultural: 'porters in Imperial Madagascar could sometimes earn an income that made them the envy of ordinary non-slaves'.[36] This meant that major rebellions were exceptions and sought to reform rather than overthrow bondage. In this framework, slavery in the Indian Ocean could not be 'understood fully in terms of "open" and "closed" systems, characterised respectively by slave assimilation into the dominant society and exclusion from it'. Indeed women slaves could have exalted status in the Indian Ocean world as concubines and wives, superior to female peasants. The chronology and geography of Indian Ocean slavery was different. It linked maritime and overland routes and ran from 'before the Common Era' into the twentieth century and even to the present. It expanded in numerical terms in the nineteenth century at a time of colonial abolitionism, because of the expansion of the Omani, Merina, Ethiopian and Egyptian states.[37] Even though the intent of this argument was to release the Indian Ocean from the Atlantic model and to attend to plurality – in practice it also flattened the differences within the Indian Ocean in generalisations such as this: 'for most IOA [Indian Ocean Africa] and Asian populations, security, food and shelter rather than an abstract concept of liberty, were the primary

---

[35] See Robert Carter, 'The history and prehistory of pearling in the Persian Gulf', *Journal of the Economic and Social History of the Orient*, 48 (2006): 151. See also William Gervase Clarence-Smith, ed., *The economics of the Indian Ocean slave trade in the nineteenth century* (New York, 1989).

[36] Gwyn Campbell, 'Introduction: Slavery and other forms of unfree labour in the Indian Ocean world', in G. Campbell, ed., *The structure of slavery* (London, 2004), pp. xi, and material below from ibid., pp. xxiv, xi, ix.

[37] William Gervase Clarence-Smith, 'The economics of the Indian Ocean and Red Sea slave trades in the nineteenth century: An overview', *Slavery and Abolition*, 9 (2008): 3.

The Indian Ocean

aims'.[38] In other words, it borrowed from the structuralism of the likes of Chaudhuri.[39]

Different work seeks to multiply the kinds of slavery in particular locales. Take for instance the Cape Colony. In the seventeenth- and eighteenth-century Cape, the rise of a capitalist order under the Dutch East India Company depended on large numbers of slaves brought from across the Indian Ocean, from Madagascar and Mozambique, Southeast Asia, South Asia and East Africa. Yet in popular memory this diversity was often lost, with the application of unitary labels such as 'coloured' or the essentialisation of 'Cape Malay', effacing the variety of people that lay beneath such categories. Contrary to the view of those who wish to qualify the extent of coercion experienced by slaves in the Indian Ocean: 'the isolation of many farmsteads in a society in which male slaves greatly outnumbered male colonists led to a level of control and coercion which at local levels could be violent and extreme'. This generated resistance, sometimes drawing on Islam and often including escape. In turn the culture of slavery was expanded in rural contexts to include Khoisan labourers and took on a politics of race.[40] Dutch Cape Town saw an especial concentration of slaves, which was in line with the demography of Dutch ports like Batavia or Colombo. In the eighteenth century, intriguingly, slaves from South and later Southeast Asia outnumbered those from Madagascar in Cape Town.[41] Further new work on the history of the slave trade at Cape Town at the end of the eighteenth century places it within a network stretching from the southwest Indian Ocean to Brazil and Europe. Portuguese traders, as well as French and Spanish operatives, supplied slaves to Cape settlers, and this trade operated beyond the control of British colonial surveillance and abolitionist ideology into the nineteenth century. Strikingly, given earlier anti-Atlanticism in this field, Patrick Harries uses an Atlantic concept to describe it: a 'trans-Atlantic Middle Passage'.[42]

---

[38] Campbell, 'Introduction', p. xvi.

[39] See the line of influence at the start of Campbell, 'Introduction'.

[40] Nigel Worden, *Slavery in Dutch South Africa* (Cambridge, 1985), p. 4; see also Worden and James Armstrong, 'The slaves', in Richard Elphick and Hermann Gilliomee, eds., *The shaping of South African society, 1652–1840* (Middletown, CT, 1989), pp. 107–83. More recently, Markus Vink, '"The world's oldest trade": Dutch slavery and slave trade in the Indian Ocean in the seventeenth century', *Journal of World History*, 14 (2003): 131–77.

[41] Nigel Worden, 'Indian Ocean slaves in Cape Town, 1695–1807', *Journal of Southern African Studies*, 42 (2016): 1695–807.

[42] Patrick Harries, 'Middle passages of the Southwest Indian Ocean: A century of forced immigration from Africa to the Cape of Good Hope', *Journal of African History*, 55 (2014): 173–90.

44   S. Sivasundaram

Thinking with the 1830s, allows another lineage for debates about slavery in the Indian Ocean and one which precedes the push and pull of Mediterranean and Atlantic historiography. In this period, humanitarians questioned whether Indian indentured labour constituted a new kind of slavery. More than one million Indian indentured labourers serviced plantations such as sugar, coffee, cocoa, rubber and tea in the period between 1826 and 1920. The comparison with slavery echoed in historiographical terms down into the 1970s, most notably in Hugh Tinker's *A new system of slavery* (1974), generating 'a degree of conceptual complacency'.[43] In this framework labourers were victimised like slaves and they filled the gap left by slavery in the Caribbean, and a further revision urged that the model of their contracts paralleled the use of European indentured servants in the Americas in the seventeenth and eighteenth centuries and saw rather the exercise of some consent.[44] Yet it is now clear that the test case for indentured labour was not in the Atlantic, but Mauritius, the colony that received the largest number of indentured labourers through the entire period: Mauritius has seen a concentration of historical scholarship on indenture.[45] Here South Asian models of slavery, caste and agricultural bondage fed into indenture. In addition, emerging work shows how the East India Company had experimented with the use of Chinese labour in the late eighteenth and early nineteenth century, via Penang and Canton and stretching to St Helena and Trinidad, establishing a template for South Asian indenture. This once again stretches the history of labour practice in the Indian Ocean further east rather than into the Atlantic.

Instead of comparing and contrasting Atlantic slavery and indenture, newer work brings to light the intermediate spaces between types of labour: recovering freed slaves and apprentices, the migratory patterns, ship-board journeys, gendered lives and 'subaltern voices' of indentured labourers and lascars and convicts.[46] The turn away from discussions of consent, rights and victimhood towards discourse, governance, experience and culture has allowed the intriguing argument that convicthood and indenture operated in a shared mental world for Indians: the ocean

---

[43] Hugh Tinker, *A new system of slavery: The export of Indian labour overseas, 1830–1920* (London, 1974); Richard Allen, 'Re-conceptualizing the "new system of slavery"', *Man in India*, 92 (2012): 226.

[44] See David Northrup, *Indentured labour in the age of imperialism, 1834–1922* (Cambridge, 1995).

[45] Richard Allen, *Slaves, freedman and indentured laborers in colonial Mauritius* (Cambridge, 1999) and Marina Carter, *Servants, sirdars and settlers: Indians in Mauritius, 1834–1874* (Oxford, 1995).

[46] See for instance work emerging from 'Becoming Coolies' a research project at the University of Edinburgh, www.coolitude.shca.ed.ac.uk/ (accessed 24 January 2017).

The Indian Ocean 45

journey was *kala pani* or black water, denoting caste pollution, through the necessity for shared eating and living on ships. The use of this term to describe indentured journeys out of India came via its currency as a descriptor of Indian convict transportation.[47] From a different perspective, seeking not to blur categories but to work beyond the slavery/indenture dichotomy, Megan Vaughan's history of labour in eighteenth-century Mauritius ends with a recovery of apprenticeship, where slaves were tied to their masters after abolition in 1834 for six years and then became small-holders of land, before becoming a marginalised or 'creolised' community, in the midst of the surge of numbers of Indian indentured labourers and the forgetting of African and Malagasy pasts. Just as with work on the Cape, this is an attempt then to pluralise the cultural spaces of labour – in a landscape where indentured historiography can easily cover too much ground or be taken to stand for everything.[48]

In place of a concern with quantification, and reminiscent of how Das Gupta focussed on individuals in the history of trade, these approaches recover what has recently been termed 'subaltern biography' critically set in maritime context. The ability of workers to move between categories and to exercise creative agency, shifting from docks to ships and from farms to ports is now of interest.[49] Spatial and cultural geography is being turned inside out. Historians are both breaking away from or moving towards the Atlantic or shifting histories of connection by swapping nodal points in the network, replacing India with China, or emphasising South Asia instead of Southeast Asia, or re-centring Africa instead of South Asia as a cultural resource for labourers' memory. The plantation is seen less as a singular complex, while the sea is coming into closer view as a scape of labour. Across the Indian Ocean and elsewhere *lascar* sea-men manned ships, ranging from Pacific whalers to convict transportation ships to Bengkulu, Penang and the Andaman islands or ships of war in the Napoleonic wars. In the age of sail, this included vessels which were East Indiamen and 'country' or India-built ships. In the age of steam and into the world wars, the Indian maritime worker, recently described as 'India's earliest global workers' travelled across the world, navigating and defining race, nation and empire and interrogating

---

[47] Clare Anderson, 'Convicts and coolies: Rethinking indentured labour in the nineteenth century', *Slavery and Abolition*, 30 (2009): 101.

[48] Megan Vaughan, *Creating the creole island: Slavery in eighteenth-century Mauritius* (Durham, NC, 2005), ch. 10.

[49] See for instance, Janet Ewald, 'Crossers of the sea: Slaves, freedmen and other migrants in the northwestern Indian Ocean, c. 1750–1914', *American Historical Review*, 105 (2000): 69–91.

46 S. Sivasundaram

the terms of globalisation.[50] It is their political voice and protest which is proving to be of recent interest: between the 1780s and the Indian Rebellion there were about thirty serious disturbances aboard merchant vessels which could be classed as *lascar* mutinies.[51] More spectacular in turn was the sight of ships burning in Indian ports as the reported result of *lascar* action in the first half of the nineteenth century. In 1847, in a list of burnt ships appeared this entry:

> *The ship Bombay Castle*, Capt. Frazer, burnt off Sangor Island, 27th May 1846, burnt till daylight, captain, passengers, and most of the crew saved by vessels in company. – Bound to China; cargo cotton, fire discovered about midnight; every reason to believe the loss of this fine ship was owing to the diabolical conduct of some the crew. Several lives lost – Lascars took a raft.[52]

To summarise, those who write the economic history of commodities such as Indian cloth or Persian Gulf pearls or labourers on the move, have sought at times to unite the Indian Ocean as a system, or to unify the trades and labourers of this ocean, but others have pulled the ocean apart, dividing it and its peoples, insisting on the need to decentre particular networks, to return to a focus on violence and rebellion, or in turn to look out from the Indian Ocean to newer routes. The excitement of interpreting a source like that above could stand for the broader questions in Indian Ocean histories of trade or labour: colonial vision and impact or plural geographies, agencies and times? There is in accounts of trade and labour, a characteristic restlessness, evident elsewhere too in Indian ocean histories.

Knowledges and Environments

The conflict between bounding and unbounding the Indian Ocean in historiographical terms may be read from its environmental history. The monsoon, which the lascars knew well, tugged the sea apart while linking its further corners, and this fact explains the difficulty of mounting a total view of the Indian Ocean. The monsoon was named across the Indian Ocean world – as *mawsim* in Arabic, *mosum* in Hindi and *msimu* in Swahili. It described the change of winds over the Indian Ocean in two periods, connected to the differential heating of land and sea, and the arrival of the rains. The southwest monsoon from April to August

---

[50] G. Balachandran, *Globalizing labour? Indian seafarers and world shipping, c.1870–1945* (Oxford, 2012), p. 8.

[51] Aaron Jaffer, *Lascars and Indian Ocean seafaring, 1780–1860* (Woodbridge, 2015), p. 18.

[52] 'Ships and Vessels Burnt', *The Nautical Magazine and Naval Chronicle* (London, 1847), p. 590.

The Indian Ocean 47

sees winds blowing towards the north, inundating South and Southeast Asia, while the northeast monsoon does the reverse, accelerating vessels journeying south. Two important historians of the Indian Ocean, of the supposed second wave, describe the monsoon in slightly different ways. For Michael Pearson, it is part of the 'deep structure', of the Indian Ocean, 'which constrained movement' in predictable patterns.[53] However, for Kenneth McPherson: 'there are vast tracts of territory in the Middle East, East Africa and Australia, where the monsoon system has no impact'. Rather the monsoon divides the Indian Ocean world into quite different landscapes, climates and animal and vegetable life.[54] These in turn generated distinct patterns of early settlement, nomadism and hunter-gathering. With the arrival of Europeans, it generated the need for oceanic bases and footholds for ships to refit themselves and face the next phase of the fury of the winds.

On the sea itself, navigational knowledge focussed on the puzzle of the monsoon. A key early navigational authority from the Arab side was Ahmad ibn Majid of Julfar in Oman, who died around 1504. Ibn Majid's navigation manuals, in verse and prose were designed for memorisation. His father and grandfather were maritime pilots, *mu'allim*, by profession and in one (probably erroneous) rendition it was Ibn Majid who guided Vasco da Gama from Malindi to Calicut in 1498. Regardless, Ibn Majid provides a rich instance of the achievements of Arab nautical science, which ran ahead of European scientific breakthroughs. For Ibn Majid, *mawsim* indicated not a system of winds, but the date or time on which to sail from port to port.[55] Navigators such as Ibn Majid used a 365-day solar year devised around the Persian new year, celebrated at the spring equinox: accordingly, Ibn Majid's advised departure from Aden to East Africa between the 320th and 330th days.[56] Increasing prowess with instrumentation was critical to this navigation – for instance, the Islamic compass, *qiyas* for star measurement, *khashabat* for latitude measurement, and the *kamal*, a rectangle made of horn or wood with a string through the middle, held to the horizon. By interpreting winds and geography and the sighting of land, and with the guidance of the Polar Star which indicated latitude, the *mu'allim* determined his course and

---

[53] Michael Pearson, *The Indian Ocean* (Abingdon, 2003), p. 19.
[54] Kenneth McPherson, *The Indian Ocean: A history of people and the sea* (Delhi, 1993), p. 9.
[55] G. R. Tibbetts, *Arab navigation in the Indian Ocean before the coming of the Portuguese* (London, 1971), pp. 361–62.
[56] Abdul Sheriff, 'Navigational methods in the Indian Ocean', in David Parkin and Ruth Barnes, eds., *Ships and the development of maritime technology in the Indian Ocean* (London, 2002), pp. 212–13.

48 S. Sivasundaram

made necessary corrections along the way. Ibn Majid, wrote, laying out some of the signs that were critical for finding the way:

Know, oh reader, that sailing the sea has many principles. Understand them: The first is the knowledge of lunar mansions and rhumbs and routes, distances, *bāshīyat*, latitude measuring, signs (of land), the courses of the sun and moon, the winds and their seasons, and the seasons of the sea, the instruments of the ship. . . It is also desirable that you should know all the coasts and their landfalls and their various guides such as mud, or grass, animals or fish, sea-snakes and winds. You should consider the tides, and the sea currents and the islands on every route, make sure all the instruments are in order.[57]

One of the central historiographical debates about nautical knowledge, and by extension other kinds of natural knowledge, is the extent to which Europe changed what was known. For too long, it was believed that the workings of the monsoon were cracked by Europeans – starting with the Greeks – and that the arrival of the Portuguese saw the wiping out of whatever existed of Indian Ocean nautical knowledge. Yet the claim is now made that knowledge passed in multiple directions generating 'syncretism':[58] Marco Polo's return journey in the late thirteenth century was aided by Arab craft; Vasco da Gama took a *kamal* back to Portugal in 1499; sixteenth-century Portuguese maps show Arab influence; and there is evidence of the passage of knowledge across the Indian Ocean itself between the Arabs and the Chinese. In India, there has been an attempt to recover a forgotten history of navigation, for instance the glorification of ship-building in the 'Maritime Heritage Gallery' at the National Museum of India, in Delhi. Here one sees not a commitment to syncretism but to the allegedly originary maritime knowledge of the subcontinent as a bulwark to contemporary nationalism. The gallery introduces the nation's 'maritime history dating back to nearly 4000 years' as a 'kaleidoscope of – mythology, ancient text; archaeological findings', making an argument that 'the influence of Europeans on the maritime science in historical terms has been a relatively recent one'.[59] It dates Indian's 'first known boat' to the Harappa culture of 3000 BCE. It includes an account of Maratha naval tactics and a diorama of Shivaji's fleet under Admiral Daulat Khan attacking the British. The gallery feeds an account of the consolidation of the Indian Navy.

From a more secure scholarly footing, as with nautical knowledge, historians see ship-building generating convergence and divergence between various Indian Ocean cultures. Despite the fact that there were

[57] Tibbetts, *Arab navigation*, p. 77.
[58] Sheriff, 'Navigational methods', pp. 207, 223.
[59] This is based on notes made at the gallery in December 2015.

The Indian Ocean

49

a multitude of different types of vessels built across the Indian Ocean world, one has come to stand for all. This is the *dhow*. Europeans used '*dhow*' as a blanket category, typifying this set of vessels as Arab; however, Arabs themselves named their sea-going vessels for the shape of their hull and in turn their size, nominating a range of vessels and *dhows* could also come from India and the Swahili coast.[60] In the Arab world and many parts of the Indian Ocean, teak or coconut wood was used for the making of hulls, giving rise to an important trade in teak out of India. In building a vessel, wood was stitched together using coir or reed rope, with no iron or bolting. Arab ships displayed lateen sails, woven out of palm leaves, likened in Arab literature to a whale's fin or spout.[61] While it is easy to visualise the Indian Ocean as the domain of the *dhow*, Chinese junks, South and Southeast Asian outrigger canoes, sometimes classed together as *perahu*, and the Indonesian *jong*, also plied the waterways. Looking beyond the physical craft to temple murals, art, graffiti, memorial stones, coins and sealings reveals a dizzying range of traditions of representing ships.[62] Shipping proved a rich stream of meaning for littoral societies: in Indonesia, for instance, as Barbara Watson Andaya beautifully illustrates, household relationships were expressed in terms of shipboard life, and in Sulawesi, 'the construction of the boat mirrors the union of men and women and it is understood that an owner and his wife should have sexual relations before the keel is joined to ensure good fortune'.[63]

The passage of the winds of the monsoon and its navigation involved the watching of nature's cycles, even as Ibn Majid's nautical science touched on everything from fish to stars. If this was so, historiographical debate about European impact has also stretched to accounts of coastal environments. Using archaeobotany, ethnobotany and climatic studies, scholars now hold that the Indian Ocean was a terrain of plural plant and agricultural exchanges from the third millennium onwards, prior to European botany. Coastal sites in Arabia and India served as centres of agricultural experimentation and the diffusion of plants. It is proposed that sorghum, pearl millet, finger millet, cowpea and hyacinth bean moved from Africa to the Indian subcontinent around or after a 'dry event' at 2200 BCE, which weakened the monsoon. In another pathway, taro, yams and banana may have constituted another package of transfers

---

[60] George F. Hourani, *Arab seafaring in the Indian Ocean in ancient and early medieval times*, rev. John Carswell (Princeton, NJ, 1995), ch. 3.

[61] Hourani, *Arab seafaring*, p. 103.

[62] H. P. Ray, 'Shipping in the Indian Ocean: An overview', in Parkin and Barnes, eds., *Ships*, pp. 1–27.

[63] Barbara Watson Andaya, 'Oceans unbounded: Transversing Asia across "area studies"', *The Journal of Asian Studies,* 65 (2006): 681.

50   S. Sivasundaram

from Island Southeast Asia to Africa.[64] Mastering the monsoon allowed the transportation of specimens to gather pace and focus.

By the time of the Portuguese and the Dutch, the coast of India became a testing ground once more. Two of the major works of European botany undertaken in coastal India were Garcia d'Orta's *Coloquios dos simples e drogas a cousas medicinas da India*, published in Goa in 1565 and the midshipman turned Dutch commander, Hendrik van Rede tot Drakenstein's twelve-volumed *Hortus Malabaricus* which appeared between 1678 and 1693. As Richard Grove argues these two classics were fundamentally 'indigenous texts': '[f]ar from being inherently European works they are actually compilations of Middle Eastern and Asian ethnobotany, organised largely according to non-European precepts'.[65] Furthermore, the Indian Ocean's islands, became experimental sites to collect, improve and pass on the natural finds of Europeans, so much so that Grove contends that it was on Mauritius that 'the early environmental debate acquired its most comprehensive form'.[66] For a band of physiocratic and Romantic French and later English naturalists, the limits of the Indian Ocean island of Mauritius, provided the setting for a controlled experiment to document the impact of deforestation and European colonisation.

These naturalists stood in an intriguing intellectual heritage. In the broader region, the idea of the botanical garden, a central site of expertise for the plantation regime, descended from 'ancient Iranian, Babylonian, Islamic, Central Asian, Mughal and European traditions'.[67] On another island testing ground, Sri Lanka, the British botanical garden in Peradeniya, founded in 1821 by Alexander Moon, shortly following the fall of the interior kingdom of Kandy, was set up on the site of a Buddhist temple garden.[68] Of particular interest for Indian Ocean histories of botany is the role of the intermediary – a figure who crossed oceanic locales and linked rival regimes of knowledge. In one colourful recent telling, which covers the less well-known seventeenth-century world of the English East India Company, Madras served as a hub

---

[64] Haripriya Rangan, Judith Carney and Tim Denham, 'Environmental history of botanical exchanges in the Indian Ocean world', *Environment and History*, 18 (2012): 311–42.

[65] Richard H. Grove, 'Indigenous knowledge and the significance of South-west India for Portuguese and Dutch constructions of tropical nature', in Richard H. Grove, Vinita Damodaran and Satpal Sangwan, eds., *Nature and the Orient: The environmental history of South and Southeast Asia* (Delhi, 2000), p. 192.

[66] Richard Grove, *Green imperialism: Colonial expansion, tropical island Edens and the origins of environmentalism* (Cambridge, 1995), p. 9.

[67] Grove, *Green imperialism*, p. 13.

[68] Sujit Sivasundaram, 'Islanded: Natural history in the British colonization of Ceylon', in David Livingstone and Charles W. J. Withers, eds., *Geographies of nineteenth-century science* (Chicago, IL, 2011), pp. 123–48.

The Indian Ocean 51

for botany and medicine: resident surgeons acquired specimens from Company ships and sent instructions to collectors spread across the ocean, keeping up exchanges with Manila, Cape Town and Batavia. The connective tissue was provided by a figure such as the surgeon Samuel Browne who worked both for the Mughal and Company establishment, collecting plants while on tour, with the help of a Tamil physician. His specimens are now in the Hans Sloane Herbarium – with the Tamil name pasted in and written on a strip of palm leaf.[69]

'Syncretism' and 'hybridity' are alluring words to describe sources such as these; yet, these words have been challenged for displacing the relations of power in the making of modern knowledge. One alternative is to work with contemporary sensibilities so as to evaluate how observers moved between concepts of cooperation and resistance. Another is to sketch the constantly evolving and mutating form of colonial knowledge – tied to cycles of militarised plunder and warfare, changing notions of statehood connected to corporations and crowns and, changing styles of intermediaries from *pandits* and *munshis* to monks and Anglicised elites or the descendants of the Portuguese and the Dutch in the British complex of knowledge across the Indian Ocean. From an oceanic perspective, the relations of knowledge and colonialism are well tested at the moment of the advent of steam-shipping. Take Stamford Raffles's scribe, Abdullah Bin Abdul Kadir (1797–1854), who worked as a language teacher alongside missionaries and other foreigners in Singapore and who is sometimes valorised as one of the earliest Malay writers of the modern age. This is despite Abdullah's own Indian Ocean heritage as the son of a Tamil from Nagore in South India, who had ancestors from Yemen.[70] Abdullah travelled constantly between Singapore and Melaka, to visit his family, and died in Mecca in 1854, while undertaking the *hajj*. Abdullah visited a steamship in 1841, the *Sesostris* which was involved in the Opium Wars in China. In writing a Malay text on it, he used what he already knew to comprehend the novel. He wrote for instance that the fire on the steamship does not arise from wood, like that used by Malays for fire: 'The coal looks like a rock or a stone, shiny, hard, and as if it were removed from the ground or from the mountains.' The ship itself seemed to have a speed like that pulled by six to seven hundred horses on land.

---

[69] Anna Winterbottom, *Hybrid knowledge in the early East India Company world* (Basingstoke, 2016), p. 119.

[70] Abdullah Bin Abdul Kadir, *The Hikayat Abdullah*, annotated and trans. A. H. Hill (Kuala Lumpur, 2009). For more on Abdullah, see for instance, Diana Carroll, 'The "Hikayat Abdullah": Discourse of dissent', *Journal of the Malaysian Branch of the Royal Asiatic Society*, 72 (1999): 91–129; and Amin Sweeney, 'Abdullah Bin Abdul Kadir Munsyi: A man of bananas and thorns', *Indonesia and the Malay World*, 34 (2006): 223–45.

52   S. Sivasundaram

He noted that its cannon balls were as big as his head. In perhaps the ultimate indicator of how he placed new machines in the light of extant ways of thought, he described the *Sesotris* as 'a gift bestowed by Allah upon man for his thought and enterprise'.[71]

The power of new technologies changed the speed and intensity of globalisation across the Indian Ocean, and yet these technologies were appropriated by maritime peoples on the rim of this sea for their own purposes and within their own mental universes. This is not an argument for full European impact or for syncretism and hybridity but for analysis that shows how historical actors appreciated the differences between intellectual traditions and even the materiality of different ships. They understood the acceleration of the modern and evinced the ability to move between alternatives, while stitching together cohesive natural knowledge.

If there was a seaborne knowledge which was accelerated as a result of steam it was Islam. The arrival of Islam in Southeast Asia is difficult to date, but there was an Islamic presence from the mid-seventh century. Arab envoys visited the Sumatran court of Srivijaya between the tenth and twelfth centuries, and Melaka became an Islamic trading state, with the conversion of its ruler Paramesvara, from the fifteenth century until its fall to the Portuguese.[72] Further to the east, Islam reached China during the Tang dynasty. Its spread in coastal South Asia came out of settlements of Muslim traders, who were sometimes also ship-owners, who made alliances with ruling authorities, such as the Caulukya dynasty of Gujarat (941–1297). Yet the arrival of modern steam accelerated this old template, most notably the *hajj*. Abdullah was amongst hundreds of thousands of Southeast Asians who made the journey in the nineteenth and twentieth centuries. If Portuguese and Dutch botanical texts could be 'indigenous', it is curious that the *hajj* became 'colonial' on one reading, state-sponsored and regulated by the British, the Dutch and others, for the fear of anti-colonialism and cholera in turn, while European shipping companies controlled the main pilgrim routes as a business, by deploying fleets of ships, and enabled a wider class of people to make the pilgrimage at lower cost till the arrival of air travel.[73] Yet as with the history of botany, the individual pilgrim, in *hajj* memoirs, a key source for

---

[71] 'Teks Ceretera Kapal Asap', in Amin Sweeney, ed., *Karya Lengkap Abdullah bin Abdul Kadir* (Jakarta, 2006), Jilid 2, pp. 275, 278.

[72] For some orientation, see Alpers, *The Indian Ocean*, ch. 3; also M. C. Ricklefs, *Mystic synthesis in Java: A history of Islamization from the fourteenth to the early nineteenth centuries* (Norwalk, CT, 2006).

[73] Eric Tagliacozzo, *The longest journey: Southeast Asians and the pilgrimage to Mecca* (Oxford, 2013); John Slight, *The British Empire and the Hajj 1865–1956* (Cambridge, MA, 2015).

The Indian Ocean

historians of pilgrimage, emerges with the ability to straddle concepts, to articulate their own narrative of self-fashioning and to move beyond the panopticon control of the colonial state.

If religious knowledge, like natural knowledge, was made modern by the recasting of the old in the context of new technologies, some of the best scholarship on early modern and modern Islam in the Indian Ocean approaches it as text, language and print, seeking to trace the emergence of an *ecumene*. Islamic literary networks are said to include stories, poems, genealogies, histories and treaties, together with the patrons, authors and audiences who supported such activity, linking the oral to the printed, the textual to the performative and allowing Arabic to be translated into a series of vernaculars and vice versa. Borrowing from Sheldon Pollock's 'Sanskrit cosmopolis', Ronit Ricci has recently located an 'Arabic cosmopolis' by tracking the *Book of One Thousand Questions*, which narrates the conversion of Abdullah Ibnu Salam from Judaism to Islam, and which was multiply translated from the tenth century into Persian, Urdu, Tamil, Malay, Javanese, Sudanese and Buginese.[74] In a later period, Nile Green locates Islam in the marketplace of the burgeoning late nineteenth-century port of Bombay, arguing that Bombay was to steam travel what Dubai is to today's air travel, 'its iron printing-presses produced books in Persian and Arabic, English and Urdu, Malay and Swahili ... its sheer size allowed Muslims to alternatively discover the collective unity of the *umma* or to learn instead that they were above all "Indian"'.[75] Yet intriguingly, the salient lesson is that steam produced myriad competing forms of reformist and customary Islam in Bombay rather than a standard, and these faiths were part of a religious economy fed by a bewildering range of family firms, entrepreneurs and writers, generating individual re-enchantment as a commodity rather than technological disenchantment on a global scale. From a totally different geographical vantage point, what is called the 'ocean of letters' appears to view in how Malagasy encountered Christianity, in the creation of a sphere of vernacular literacy among converts between Madagascar, Mauritius and Bourbon, and also the Comoros archipelago and the Cape.[76] Critically, this linguistic space was not simply 'creole'; creolisation existed side by

---

[74] Ronit Ricci, *Islam translated: Literature, conversion, and the Arabic cosmopolis of South and Southeast Asia* (Delhi, 2011). See also the important work by Engseng Ho, *The graves of Tarim: Genealogy and mobility across the Indian Ocean* (Berkeley, CA, 2006).

[75] Nile Green, *The religious economy of the West Indian Ocean, 1840–1915* (Cambridge, 2011), p. 3.

[76] Pier Larson, *Ocean of letters: Language and creolization in the Indian Ocean diaspora* (Cambridge, 2009).

54   S. Sivasundaram

side with the continued nourishment of practices from the homeland, the Big Island of Madagascar.

Knowledges and environments were interlaced in the Indian Ocean, by the winds and waves, by technological changes that contorted their relationship, and by the speeding up of encounter, the rapid serialisation of what was known across the waters. Yet the old did not disappear, nor did the new not hold power. There were unexpected contradictions in the relatedness of nativeness and coloniality; not all was mixed up into the syncretic, hybrid or the creole, but woven knowledge could encompass alternative strands and formats in a tense and competitive embrace.

Modern Formations

If historians of knowledge and religion debate long-term continuity versus modernisation and mixing versus differentiation, cosmopolitanism is a key route for social historians wishing to engage with the modern Indian Ocean. Port cities are cast as 'the quintessential sites of Asian cosmopolitanism'.[77] One way of defining cosmopolitanism is to sketch 'boundary crossing' or local or transnational attempts of conceiving a whole beyond ethnicity, denomination, nationality and social diversity.[78] In Indian Ocean port cities, it is said that a globalised public sphere came to its height before the impact of the First World War, while newer work pushes this story into the interwar period.[79] Southeast Asianists claim that such public spheres depended on the co-option of local elites into governing bodies, the spread of the press, the relay of news and a fetish for translation. They were evident in reforming and voluntary societies and campaigns for instance related to opium, indenture or the status of women. They stretched to encompass Chinese opera, Hindi drama and jazz. The result was 'universal neighbourliness' and the lineaments of civil society which arose out of the waters.[80]

On the Arabian and East African coast three ports may illustrate maritime cosmopolitanism: Zanzibar, Mombasa and Aden. In each case, the port became a thickening link between the hinterland and the ocean. As

[77] Tim Harper and Sunil Amrith, 'Sites of Asian interaction: An introduction', *Modern Asian Studies*, 46 (2012): 250.

[78] For some help on definitions, see Sugata Bose and Kris Manjapra, eds., *Cosmopolitan thought zones: South Asia and the global circulation of ideas* (Basingstoke, 2011), Introduction.

[79] For this argument, see Tim Harper, 'Empire, diaspora and the languages of globalism, 1850–1914', in A. G. Hopkins, ed., *Globalization in world history* (London, 2002), pp. 141–66; for new work that stretches it forward to the interwar period, see Su Lin Lewis, *Cities in motion: Urban life and cosmopolitanism in Southeast Asia, 1920–1940* (Cambridge, 2016).

[80] Harper, 'Empire, diaspore and the languages of globalism', p. 157.

The Indian Ocean 55

a servicing point for plantations and trades such as ivory, copal, hides and labour, through the moment it was taken as a British protectorate in 1890, with uncontrolled immigration into the First World War, Zanzibar attracted to itself Omani Arab settlers and political elites; Indian moneylenders and traders; fishermen and traders, from Hadhramaut, the Comoros and Madagascar; various slaves and ex-slaves from East Africa and elsewhere, and a European and American merchant class.[81] In 1890 it boasted fifty mosques ranging in theology from Sunni-Shafi'i to Ibadi and Shi'a.[82] Aden's story is as eclectic: Janet Ewald sketches dizzying 'crossers of the sea', originally from South Asia, East Africa or the Arab highlands, who crossed the boundaries of free and unfree, ship and dock, and social rank, and at times travelled the world, through Aden.[83] Meanwhile, Mombasa was transformed from a hinge between caravan porters and Indian Ocean craft to the terminus of the Kenya–Uganda railway by the start of the twentieth century, with numbers of steamers arriving in it doubling between 1903 and 1913. It drew to itself from the collapsing agricultural sector of the hinterland, labourers who served on the docks, and new arrivals gave rise to the repeated redefinition of self and other in Islamic communities into the late twentieth century.[84] Yet in the midst of these transformations is a story that present-day scholars cannot celebrate, the continued legacy of racial understandings, reasserted in colonial bureaucratic structures and public ceremonies. In Zanzibar, longstanding Arabocentricism continued to be potent, authorised by British indirect rule through Omani elites, leading to ethnic tensions which reverberated through the 1964 revolution, when Zanzibar lost, as a result of death or flight, a quarter or more of its Arab population as its African majority rose against the sultan.[85]

At the heart of the Indian Ocean is the port of Colombo, another site at the rim of the waters that witnessed an explosion of ethnic tension, for instance in the 1983 riot which is taken to mark the start of the island's civil war. The early twentieth-century port is a telling lens

---

[81] See Abdul Sheriff, ed., *The history and conservation of Zanzibar Stone Town* (London, 1992); esp. Garth Andrew Myers, 'The early history of the "other side" of Zanzibar Town', pp. 30–45.

[82] See for instance, Anne Bang, 'Cosmopolitanism colonised: Three cases from Zanzibar, 1890–1920', in Edward Simpson and Kai Kresse, eds., *Struggling with history: Islam and cosmopolitanism in the Western Indian Ocean* (London, 2007), pp. 167–88.

[83] Ewald, 'Crossers of the sea', pp. 69–91.

[84] See for instance, Fred Cooper, *On the African waterfront: Urban disorder and the transformation of work in colonial Mombasa* (New Haven, CT, 1987).

[85] Jonathon Glassman, *War of words, war of stones: Racial thought and violence in colonial Zanzibar* (Bloomington, IN, 2011).

56 S. Sivasundaram

from which to view this later history. At one level it was cosmopolitan.[86] Colombo's intelligentsia combined Western modes and customs with religious revivalism, temperance and an interest in the vernacular. This kept narrower communal nationalism at bay.[87] Yet when such a social history is approached from the infrastructure of the port, the first decades of the twentieth century look rather different.[88] The growth of the port led to a reorganisation of the capital: a significant segment of the fort and the area north of Colombo became unbearable to its middle-class and Burgher residents. They moved their pretty mansions south to escape the coal, the noise and the shops that sprung up to cater to the traffic through the port. In their place arose the slums or 'tenement gardens'. Thus developed a differentiated city: on one hand, the richer and greener south and its prized district of Cinnamon Gardens (today's wealthy Colombo 7), and on the other, the poorer north. Port workers were central agents to the working-class strikes that began to occur by the 1920s: in 1919 the workers of the Harbour Engineers' Department petitioned for an eight-hour day, and the next year 5,000 coal 'coolies' struck. In 1927, 13,000 harbour workers followed suit, 5,000 of them coalers.[89] The divided history of the port becomes here a mirror to the history of the segregated city and the history of class and identity more generally.

Indian Ocean social formations moved therefore between alternative presentations: peaceable and neighbourly and violent and segregated. Cosmopolitanism did not stand alone. The combination of these slightly different historiographical impulses falls in line with recent breakthroughs in Indian Ocean intellectual histories. In one now-familiar story, Mahatma Gandhi's thinking in South Africa grew out of a commitment to imperial 'citizenship', tied to the plight of Indian merchants whom he represented as a lawyer, and who wished to keep their status in the local hierarchy. In place of 'citizenship', came the template of the Indian 'nation' outside empire, encompassing overseas Indians within a 'Greater India'.[90] In other words, Gandhi calibrated a conception of

[86] Michael Roberts, Ismeth Raheem and Percy Colin-Thomé, *People in between* (Ratmalana, Sri Lanka, 1989), p. 108.

[87] Mark Frost, '"Wider opportunities": Religious revival, nationalist awakening and the global dimension in Colombo, 1870–1920', *Modern Asian Studies*, 36 (2002): 937–67.

[88] Sujit Sivasundaram, 'Towards a critical history of connection: The port of Colombo, the geographical "circuit" and the visual politics of new imperialism, 1880–1914', *Comparative Studies in Society and History*, 59 (2017): 346–84.

[89] Kumari Jayawardena, *The rise of the labor movement in Ceylon* (Durham, NC, 1972), pp. 218–19, 286ff.

[90] See for instance, Isabel Hofmeyr, *Gandhi's printing press: Experiments in slow reading* (Cambridge, MA, 2013) and Claude Markovits, *The Un-Gandhian Gandhi: The life and afterlife of the Mahatma* (London, 2004).

The Indian Ocean   57

Indianness and Indian sovereignty with respect to Africa (and the status of African 'natives' specifically, who he excluded) and events on the ground in South Africa, such as *satyagraha* protest between 1906 and 1914, imprisonment, the 'Boer' war which led to his mobilisation of ambulance brigades in support of the British, and his social relations with other communities, such as the Chinese. It is important not to fixate on Gandhi – for this type of oceanic and diasporic thinking was evident among other Indians on the African coast. Yet, there were limits to such intellectual prospecting. According to one recent argument, cosmopolitan thought zones need to be brought back to particular 'religious, philosophical, and ethical traditions', without being read from today's liberal universalism, arising out of Europe. This specific critique rests on the career of Abul Kalam Azad (1888–1958), the scholar, journalist and Khilafat activist, who had studied both Islamic law and Western philosophy and mastered many languages. On the one hand, he was committed to the India National Congress's vision of Indian democracy and anti-colonial politics across Eurasia; on the other hand, he supported Sa'udi conquest of the Hijaz in 1925.[91]

Attention to governance and the law is vital in understanding the malleability of self, sovereignty and the social, between the cosmopolitan and more rooted and territorial forms. As early modern historians have demonstrated, the Indian Ocean was a contested space for the law, given clashes between land-based polities and maritime European empires.[92] Recent work on piracy reveals this tussle in rich detail. In the nineteenth-century Indian Ocean, violence directed towards 'pirates' through steam and firepower, emerged from and authorised liberal commitments to the law, free trade and mercantile and civil port society.[93] Militarised regimes of law-keeping were particularly evident in island locations in this sea and 'islanding' was a scheme of government, connected to repatriation, exile or confinement. One string of islands which demonstrates this story, now in compelling inter-disciplinary hues, is the Andamans. The colonial phase began with a characterisation of these islands as inhabited by cannibals or as a place where piracy was rife. Into the 1850s, the East India Company saw piracy orchestrated from the islands as a threat to its sovereignty. Malays and Chinese operating

---

[91] John M. Willis, 'Azad's Mecca: On the limits of Indian Ocean cosmopolitanism', *Comparative Studies of South Asia, Africa and the Middle East*, 34 (2014): 574–81.

[92] Lauren Benton, *A search for sovereignty: Law and geography in European Empires, 1400–1900* (Cambridge, 2010), pp. 137 ff.

[93] S. H. Layton, 'Hydras and Leviathans in the Indian Ocean world', *International Journal of Maritime History*, 25 (2013): 213–55.

58   S. Sivasundaram

in the Bay of Bengal, possibly in search of birds' nests as a culinary delicacy, were classed as 'perfidious'.[94]

The Andamans' alignment with cannibalism and piracy made this the perfect location for a penal colony. After the Indian Rebellion, in 1858, 200 convicted mutineers and rebels arrived; some 80,000 criminal convicts were transported to the islands up to the 1930s and 1,000 political prisoners.[95] The notorious Cellular Jail in Port Blair can easily open up Foucauldian approaches to imprisonment, yet the recent literature has instead drawn attention to the variety of communities on these islands. Beyond the convicts, the indigenous community was decimated; and non-convict settlers arrived as agriculturalists and labourers. The story becomes more complex by the Second World War, when the Andamans were occupied by the Japanese and visited by Subhas Chandra Bose in 1943. 'The Andaman Islands, then, have a complex and entangled history, they constitute and remain a place at the centre of networks of governance, coercion and mobility.' In other words, migration and linkage is important, but it doesn't capture the whole, for forms of classification, settlement and differentiation continue to play a role in the islands to the present as arrivals from elsewhere encroach on the lands of indigenous peoples. When Bose visited, he exulted in standing in 'Free India' and seeing the tricolour Indian flag. Yet the question of whether he was aware of the violence committed by the Japanese against islanders, including torture and rape, continues to be debated. These charged histories, which are directed across various axes, island–mainland, colonised–coloniser, settler–indigenous, are ever present, neither totally Foucauldian nor cosmopolitan.

In closing this section on modern formations – stretching over society, ideas, law and government – the Andamans is the perfect site at which to observe another set of sources. Indian Ocean locales are proving excellent places to debate the grammar of the visual and to write 'object biographies', utilising material culture as a means of getting to histories which are absent in textual remains. This is because they served as hunting grounds for collectors in the modern era, including tourists, and also photographers, scientists and anthropologists motivated by commitments to cultural salvage and the utility of islands as laboratories. On the Andamans, between 1906 and 1908, A. R. Radcliffe-Browne,

---

[94] Aparna Vaidik, *Imperial Andamans: Colonial encounter and island history* (Basingstoke, 2014), pp. 47 ff.

[95] This relies on Clare Anderson, Madhumita Mazumdar and Vishvajit Pandya, eds., *New histories of the Andaman Islands: Landscape, place and identity in the Bay of Bengal, 1790–2012* (Cambridge, 2016), p. 4, citation below from p. 8, and also Clare Anderson, 'Entangled struggles, contested histories: the Second World War and after', pp. 62–94.

The Indian Ocean

the social anthropologist and supposed originator of structural functionalism, conducted his doctoral work and collected objects. Expert collecting sat together with the production of curios for sale by various Andamanese in colonial 'homes' formed for civilisation.[96] In this context, focusing on material culture has also allowed reflection on gender and sexuality. Take the large corpus of homoeroticised photographs of the Andamanese, mostly taken between 1890 and 1895, by colonial administrator and former officer of the Indian Marine, Maurice Vidal Portman. For Portman, 'the colonizer's assertions of control and delinquent fantasies of losing control came together in the aesthetics and measurements of the eroticised aboriginal body'.[97] Debating cosmopolitanism and its limits should include the intersection between sexuality and modes of self formation too.

No Single Line Across the Ocean

As a closing vista of the effect of the waters of the Indian Ocean, I turn to the island of Mauritius, which was unpopulated before the arrival of colonists and labourers. Yet the Grand Bassin crater lake is now taken to be a sacred site, to which hundreds of thousands of Hindus throng. In a tradition which began in the 1890s, they hold that the lake is connected – across the ocean – with the River Ganges in India and call it 'Ganga Talao', the lake of the Ganges. In popular telling, Shiva, the Hindu deity and his wife Parvati, when flying around the world in a ship, stopped in Mauritius. Shiva was carrying the River Ganges and accidently spilt some holy water into the crater giving rise to Grand Bassin. In 1972, water from the Ganges was poured into the lake. Grand Bassin illustrates the continuing work that goes into making the Indian Ocean: through imagination, religion and knowledge, through the dispersal of labour and trade and through the constitution of diasporic communities, such as those who have descended from indentured South Asians on Mauritius. Grand Bassin links the timeless past with the rapid changes of modernity. Today, large statues, pilgrims and tourists jostle with each other on the banks of the lake.[98]

In the spirit of the elements that make up the pilgrimage to Grand Bassin, this chapter has surveyed the historiography of the Indian Ocean under three broad headings: trades and labourers; environments and

[96] See for instance, Claire Wintle, *Colonial collecting and display: Encounters with material culture from the Andaman and Nicobar Islands* (New York, 2013).

[97] Satadru Sen, 'Savage bodies, civilised pleasures: M. V. Portman and the Andamanese', *American Ethnologist*, 36 (2009): 207.

[98] For some of the details, see V. Govinden, 'Subjects of history: Gokoola and Jhumun Giri Gosye, indentured migrants to Mauritius', *Man in India*, 92 (2012): 333–52.

60 S. Sivasundaram

knowledges; and, modern social, intellectual and material formations. In each case the Indian Ocean appears to view in the tussle between systematisation and plurality; foreign invaders and long-term legacies; cosmopolitan strivings and commitments to place, self, race and identity; and control and the lack of it. It is the longevity of consciousness about the Indian Ocean which is noteworthy. It is impossible to point to a single moment which birthed Indian Ocean historiography or served as a conceptual beginning for the meaning of the Indian Ocean. Throughout this historiography, regardless of method or vantage point, or indeed, Arab navigators, South Asian merchants or Chinese explorers, is the ever present problem: does this ocean bring to mind a structure or many horizons, one big ocean or ships passing in the night, enmeshed networks or disconnections and forgotten heritages?

It would be facile to insist on presenting the Indian Ocean as simply a story of one of the following: syncretic knowledge, cosmopolitan sociability, long-term migration and trade, or European imperial impact. If there is one lesson from this survey of its historians, it is that no singular mode of writing this ocean will survive these waves and its navigators. The pull of others waters, the Mediterranean, the Pacific and the Atlantic, though problematic, has prevented a divorce of the Indian Ocean from its neighbours. In turn the Indian Ocean has given rise to histories of islands, bays and passages, exemplifying more granular approaches. The Indian Ocean teases its narrators by dissolving and cohering in turn, never appearing as an easily isolatable or standardised subject. It has served as a space for exercises of power in as much as mythic imaginaries of resistance, self-making, intellectual prospecting and future prognosis. If the historians of this sea over the centuries are a guide to the future, there can be no doubt that Indian Ocean historiography will continue to be lively.

Further Reading

For an excellent starting point to the long-term history of the Indian Ocean, see Edward Alpers, *The Indian Ocean in world history* (Oxford, 2014); and the earlier Michael Pearson, *The Indian Ocean* (New York, 2003). For an important intervention for the modern period, see Sugata Bose, *A hundred horizons: The Indian Ocean in the age of global empire* (Cambridge, MA, 2009). For a long-term history of a smaller sea, see Sunil Amrith, *Crossing the Bay of Bengal: The furies of nature and the fortunes of migrants* (Cambridge, MA, 2013). For recent approaches which adopt more granular modes; on biography, see Clare Anderson, *Subaltern lives: Biographies of colonialism in the Indian*

The Indian Ocean 61

Ocean world, 1790–1820 (Cambridge, 2012); for islands, see Sujit Sivasundaram, *Islanded: Britain, Sri Lanka and the bounds of an Indian Ocean colony* (Chicago, IL, 2013); for literacy, see Ronit Ricci, *Islam translated: Literature and conversion and the Arabic cosmopolis of South and Southeast Asia* (Delhi, 2011) and also Pier Larson, *Ocean of letters: Language and creolization in the Indian Ocean diaspora* (Cambridge, 2009) and Isabel Hofmeyr, *Gandhi's printing press: Experiments in slow reading* (Cambridge, MA, 2013). For entry points to the history of Islam and the Indian Ocean from South and Southeast Asian in turn, see Nile Green, *Bombay Islam: The religious economy of the West Indian Ocean, 1840–1915* (Cambridge, 2011) and Eric Tagliacozzo, *The longest journey: Southeast Asians and the pilgrimage to Mecca* (Oxford, 2013); also the very influential, Engseng Ho, *The graves of Tarim: Genealogy and mobility across the Indian Ocean* (Berkeley, CA, 2006). For imperial histories of the Indian Ocean, see, Kerry Ward, *Networks of empire: Forced migration in the Dutch East India Company* (Cambridge, 2009) and Thomas Metcalf, *Imperial connections: India in the Indian Ocean arena, 1860–1920* (Berkeley, CA, 2007). For Indian Ocean diaspora, as a starting point, see Sana Aiyar, *Indians in Kenya* (Cambridge, MA, 2015). For the key debate on the trading world of the Indian Ocean, see, for instance, Kirti N. Chaudhuri, *Asia before Europe: Economy and civilisation in the Indian Ocean from the rise of Islam to 1750* (Cambridge, 1991); Ashin das Gupta, *The world of the Indian Ocean merchant 1500–1800: Collected essays* (Delhi, 2001); Jeremy Prestholdt, *Domesticating the world: African consumerism and the genealogies of globalization* (Berkeley, CA, 2008); and Pedro Machado, *Ocean of trade: South Asian merchants, Africa and the Indian Ocean c.1750–1850* (Cambridge, 2015). For environmental history and history of science, see Richard Grove, *Green Imperialism: Colonial expansion, tropical island Edens and the origins of environmentalism* (Cambridge, 1995) and Anna Winterbottom, *Hybrid knowledge in the early East Indian Company world* (Basingstoke, 2016). For the history of labour, see Richard Allen, *Slaves, freedman and indentured laborers in colonial Mauritius* (Cambridge, 1999); Megan Vaughan, *Creating the Creole island: Slavery in eighteenth-century Mauritius* (Durham, NC, 2005), G. Balchandran, *Globalizing labour? Indian seafarers and world shipping, c.1870–1945* (Oxford, 2012) and Aaron Jaffer, *Lascars and Indian Ocean seafaring, 1780–1860* (Woodbridge, 2015). For the social history of the Indian Ocean, see Abdul Sheriff and Engseng Ho, eds., *The Indian Ocean: Oceanic connections and the creation of new societies* (London, 2014) and H. P. Ray and E. A. Alpers, *Cross currents and community networks: The history of the Indian Ocean World* (Oxford, 2007).

2 The Pacific Ocean

Alison Bashford

Atlantic historians have a habit of characterising the study of the Pacific Ocean as belated, a field that took shape after *Annales*-based Mediterranean scholarship, and after Braudel-inspired analysis of the Atlantic world. Yet this historiographical sequence is inaccurate and usually signals historians' own belated reading in, around and about the Pacific. On one measure, the Pacific was historicised within late nineteenth- and early twentieth-century geopolitics by Japanese, German, and Anglophone scholars alike.[1] Latin American histories of the Pacific were also available in the early twentieth century, some in translation and taken up by North American scholars.[2] On another measure, from the 1920s the Pacific emerged as central to the professionalisation of history departments within the region itself. Ralph S. Kuykendall published extensively on Hawai'i and the Pacific North West, for example, from his base in Manoa.[3] And New Zealand-based John Beaglehole wrote *Exploration of the Pacific* (1934) which detailed Spanish, Dutch, French, and British expeditions, from Magellan's to Cook's circumnavigations.[4] Beaglehole's book was reviewed at the time (ironically by a Hawaiian-based antiquarian) as

---

[1] Manjiro Inagaki, *Japan and the Pacific, and a Japanese view of the Eastern question* (London, 1890); H. Morse Stephens and Herbert E. Bolton, eds., *The Pacific Ocean in history: Papers and addresses presented at the Panama-Pacific Historical Congress, held at San Francisco, Berkeley and Palo Alto, California, July 19–23, 1915* (New York, 1917); E. W. Dahlgren, *Were the Hawaiian Islands visited by the Spaniards before their discovery by Captain Cook in 1778?: A contribution to the geographical history of the North Pacific Ocean especially of the relations between America and Asia in the Spanish period* (Stockholm, 1916); Guy H. Scholefield, *The Pacific its past and future, and the policy of the great powers from the eighteenth century* (London, 1919); Karl Haushofer, *Geopolitik des Pazifischen Ozeans* (Berlin, 1924).

[2] Altamira y Crevea, 'The share of Spain in the history of the Pacific Ocean', in Morse Stephens and Bolton, eds., *The Pacific Ocean in history*; Roland Dennis Hussy, 'Pacific history in Latin American periodicals', *Pacific Historical Review*, 1 (1932): 470–76; William Lytle Schurz, 'The Spanish Lake', *Hispanic American Historical Review*, 5 (1922): 181–94.

[3] Ralph S. Kuykendall, *A history of Hawaii* (New York, 1926); Kuykendall, *The Hawaiian kingdom: 1778–1854: Foundation and transformation* (Honolulu, HI, 1938).

[4] John Beaglehole, *The exploration of the Pacific* (London, 1934).

The Pacific Ocean

comprehensive in its 400-plus pages, but insufficiently interested in the Polynesian perspective.[5] This is as we might expect, but such histories are not to be sidelined. In the same way that we read early *Annales* historical geographies as both period pieces *and* still-useful secondary scholarship, many of the Pacific geographical histories of the 1920s and 1930s repay close reading.[6] Thus, to understand Pacific oceanic history as a latecomer, or as derivative of the *Annales* school is to fail to understand that the *Annales* tradition was part of a much wider historical geography, inclusive of oceans. In short, the Pacific Ocean was being historicised as part of the same early twentieth-century geographical trend as Braudel's Mediterranean.

Yet there was a tenor to Pacific scholarship that was quite particular. Early historical geography and maritime history intersected with an adjacent burgeoning field: the anthropology of Oceania. The cultural analyses of Malinowski and Mead in the South Pacific and of Boas and Hunt in the North Pacific were just then revolutionising anthropology itself, methodologically speaking. Their inquiries built on earlier studies in which ethnography met history, featuring the celebrated Polynesian canoe journeys from Samoa and Tonga to Hawai'i, Rapanui and Aotearoa/New Zealand.[7] For example, Alfred Cort Haddon's 'the cultural history of the Pacific' (1924), leading to his *Canoes of Oceania* (1936–38), must surely be seen as early Pacific history-writing, part of a scholarly tradition that rendered these oceanic journeys almost canonical.[8] Or, to take another example, the work of Te Rangi Hiroa (Sir Peter Buck), beginning in the late 1930s, who in his own words recounted history 'from the evidence in Polynesian myths regarding the creation of man and of islands, and in legends and traditions of the great seafaring ancestors and their voyages'.[9] In such work, the anthropology of Oceania *was* history because Polynesian genealogies ordered and systematised the past, and because the transfer of culture and language over large ocean

---

[5] Reviewed by H. H. Gowan, *The Washington Historical Quarterly*, 26 (1935): 302.

[6] N. E. Coad, *A history of the Pacific* (Wellington, NZ, 1926); Stephen Roberts, *Population problems in the Pacific* (London, 1927); Thomas Dunbabin, *The making of Australasia, a brief history of the origin and development of the British dominions in the South Pacific* (London, 1922); R. M. Crawford, *Ourselves and the Pacific* (Melbourne, 1941). And, interestingly, J. B. Condliffe, *The third Mediterranean in history: An introduction to Pacific problems* (Christchurch, NZ, 1926).

[7] J. Macmillan Brown, *Maori and Polynesian, their origin, history, and culture* (London, 1907).

[8] A. C. Haddon, 'The cultural history of the Pacific', *New Zealand Journal of Science and Technology*, 7 (1925): 101; A. C. Haddon and James Hornell, *Canoes of Oceania* (Honolulu, HI, 1936–38).

[9] Te Rangi Hiroa [Peter Buck], *Vikings of the sunrise* (New York, 1938), preface; Te Rangi Hiroa, *The evolution of Maori clothing* (New Plymouth, NZ, 1926); Peter Buck, *Anthropology and religion* (New Haven, CT, 1939).

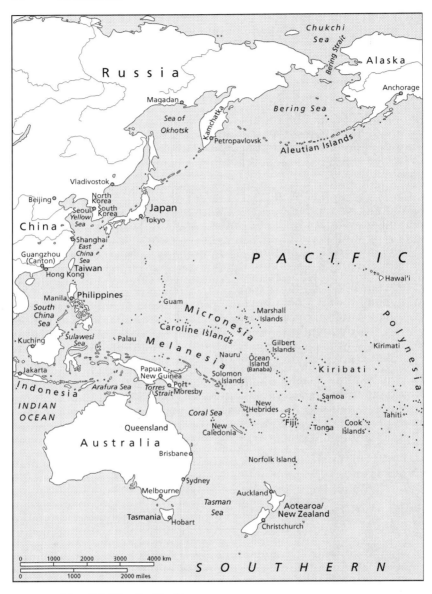

Map 2.1 The Pacific Ocean

The Pacific Ocean 65

Map 2.1 (*cont.*)

66   A. Bashford

spaces implied transfer of culture over changing times, over generations. And historical work based on thousands of seventeenth-, eighteenth- and nineteenth-century accounts of maritime expeditions was often anthropologically oriented because the sources themselves were: more than anything else they detailed relations between European outsiders and Pacific people across the ocean.

This early scholarly corpus tuned Pacific history-writing in a particular key, deeply inflected by geography on the one hand and anthropology on the other. It is no coincidence that so many of the great historians of Oceania were (and perhaps still are) trained and practised in adjacent disciplines: in the 1960s, art historian Bernard Smith, in the 1970s, geographer O. H. K. Spate, in the 1980s, ethnohistorian Greg Dening, and from 1990s onwards, any number of distinguished anthropologists trained in these schools, and their work still makes up a large part of the field. Historical work on Oceania is hardly belated, then, and we can scarcely see this rich tradition as anything but the core of wider Pacific history that includes the continental rim. Far from being a follow-on, Pacific historiography should be considered an original model for the historicising of oceans.

Pacific Chronologies

Oceans and sea-crossings figure centrally both in Polynesian histories and in the deep history of the region. Indeed what is likely *homo sapiens'* first major sea-crossing took place from the landmass called Sunda, starting at least 50,000 years ago, into Sahul, the landmass that then linked present-day New Guinea, Australia and Tasmania. About 8,000 years ago, sea levels rose separating New Guinea, Australia and Tasmania from each other, creating different kinds of isolation in the three islands. The rising and falling of seas, the joining and separating of water and land, are sometimes taken to be key events in this region's human as well as natural history.[10] It is but one of the ways in which Pacific historiography foregrounds not just geographical but geological and oceanographic phenomena. And yet the ancient migration that accounts for Australian Aboriginal people's past is often separated out – historiographically speaking – from the much more recent Pacific migrations of the so-called 'Austronesians' from present-day Taiwan to Micronesia, Melanesia and Polynesia, beginning perhaps 6,000 years

---

[10] 'It is now my view that the great rising of the seas . . . is the most important event in the human history of Australia': Geoffrey Blainey, *The story of Australia's people: The rise and fall of ancient Australia* (Melbourne, 2015), p. x.

The Pacific Ocean   67

ago. The Polynesian descendants of 'Lapita' societies explored waters and islands along winds to the south-east, migrating to Tonga and Samoa and eventually to the distant points of Rapa Nui (3–400 CE) and, in a different direction, Aotearoa/New Zealand (perhaps 1300 CE). The vast Polynesian voyages in double-hulled canoes have, for generations now, sat at the heart of the Pacific's oceanic and maritime history.[11] It is known that the long journeys diminished and then ceased around 1300 and it was only several centuries later that the Spanish and Portuguese would begin to explore and trade in the Pacific Ocean. It was not they, but the French and British – another century on again – whose journeying facilitated re-connections between Polynesians and, so far as we know, new connections between Aboriginal people and Māori.

Claims about connection and reconnection over the island Pacific are made through genealogical, linguistic, archaeological and increasingly genetic evidence.[12] The 'Austronesian' designation is primarily linguistic, while the related 'Lapita' culture is archaeological, based on distinctive pottery found from Near to Remote Oceania.[13] Connections have long been tracked and debated through Islanders' genealogies and origin stories as well. In such studies, genealogies are sometimes treated as evidence – as a kind of primary source – and sometimes as history, a secondary source, a systematic ordering of the past through generational re/counting. Te Rangi Hiroa detailed histories of Hawaiki, the place of origin over the seas, for example. Oral accounts were told and retold within Polynesian societies as history, and, when first presented in written translation, were unequivocally presented as history, as in John White's multivolume *Ancient history of the Maori* (1887–91).[14] In the Pacific region, then, we find pioneering methodological work on how oral accounts, memory and conventional text-based sources have been, and can be, productively aligned.[15] This tantalising mix of genres, along with diverse approaches to

---

[11] Andrew Sharp, *Ancient voyagers in Polynesia* (Berkeley, CA, 1964); David Lewis, *We, the Navigators: The ancient art of landfinding in the Pacific* (Honolulu, HI, 1972); K. R. Howe, *Waka Moana: Voyages of the Ancestors: The discovery and settlement of the Pacific* (Honolulu, HI, 2007); K. L. Nālani Wilson, '*Nā Wāhine Kanaka Maoli Holowa'a*: Native Hawaiian Women Voyagers', *International Journal of Maritime History*, 20 (2008): 307–24.

[12] Jonathan Scott Friedlaender, ed., *Genes, language, and culture history in the Southwest Pacific* (Oxford, 2007).

[13] On near and remote Oceania, see Ben Finney, 'The other one-third of the globe', *Journal of World History*, 5 (1994): 274.

[14] John White, *The ancient history of the Maori, his mythology and traditions* (Wellington, NZ, 1887–91).

[15] See Jocelyn Linnekin, 'Contending approaches', in Donald Denoon, ed., *Cambridge history of the Pacific Islanders*, pp. 9–14 ('History and ethnohistory'); Niel Gunson, 'Understanding Polynesian traditional history', *Journal of Pacific History*, 28 (1993): 139–58.

68   A. Bashford

the past, has made Pacific history a rich domain for thinking through just what history is. It is unsurprising that when the *Journal of Pacific History* was established (1966), its opening articles dealt with the periodisation of history on the one hand, and historical method on the other.[16]

Inquiry into human migration over the Pacific Ocean has challenged – perhaps even confounded – conventional world history chronologies. Privileging a 'first agricultural revolution' from hunter-gathering to cultivation around 10,000 BCE, and written language as requisite for 'civilisation', implies that oral-based societies and hunter-gathering economies were unchanging, and had either a lesser history, or even no history. Yet the so-called prehistory of Australian Aboriginal people is both at least a 50,000-year history and a modern one of connection with Macassan fishers across the Torres Strait to the north (from c. 1500 CE), and with British and French expeditions along the Pacific Ocean coast (from c. 1770 CE). And the so-called ancient history of Polynesians included settlement of New Zealand from a relatively recent 1300 CE. Indeed White's 'ancient' history was based on contemporary evidence from the 1860s and 1870s.[17] When the Pacific region is the reference point, then, 'prehistory' as conventionally defined has both a comparatively recent past, as well as a remote one. Thus 'deep history', 'prehistory' and 'ancient' history are drawn forward and folded into modern history in the Pacific, producing unconventional questions and problems.[18]

Pacific Geographies

Between its long temporality and its massive geography, the Pacific has attracted historians interested in large scales, and the possibility of synthetic histories organised regionally and geographically rather than nationally or politically. As geographer Donald Freeman states in one such study, the scope of the Pacific is formidable. It is also, of late, fashionable.[19] One of the tasks facing Pacific historians is to recognise and navigate the many orientations of human activity in the region's seascapes and landscapes. The plural cartographies of the Pacific, including its suite of names – *Te moana nui a Kiwa* (the great ocean of Kiwa), *Océanie, Mar del Sur, El Oceano Pacifico*, the Great Ocean, *Stille Ocean*,

---

[16] J. W. Davidson, 'The problem of Pacific history', *Journal of Pacific History*, 1 (1966): 5–21; Greg Dening, 'Ethnohistory in Polynesia: The value of ethnohistorical evidence', *Journal of Pacific History*, 1 (1966): 23–42.

[17] White, *The ancient history of the Maori*.

[18] Jesse Jennings, ed., *The prehistory of Polynesia* (Cambridge, MA, 1979).

[19] Donald B. Freeman, *The Pacific* (London, 2010); Patrick Kirch, review of Freeman, *The Pacific*, *International Journal of Maritime History*, 22 (2010): 292.

The Pacific Ocean

the South Sea – signal multiple vantage points, each with an accompanying epistemology. Indeed the Pacific is so big that the four cardinal directions that historical actors and their historians have used to locate their business – like navigators – can be as confusing as they are useful. The American-oriented 'Pacific North West', for example, is in fact the Pacific North East, if we orient by the ocean's centre (let's say Hawai'i). Many a student has tried in vain to reconcile the Southwest Pacific with the Pacific North West. Likewise, Balboa's *mar del sur* stretched for its great navigator, James Cook, from icebergs in the far Arctic north to icebergs in the Antarctic circle at 67 degrees south.[20] And yet such confusions in orientation in effect signal something much more meaningful: the literally different orientations, standpoints and ontologies of Pacific knowledge. There are as many axes across the Pacific as there are degrees in the compass or celestial markers. Six are particularly recognisable, and serve here to fix us in what is a very large historiographical ocean.

First, for Pacific Islanders, the ocean stretches from Hawai'i in the north to New Zealand in the south, Micronesian Palau and Guam in the west to Polynesian Rapanui in the east. For a Polynesian navigator such as Tupaia, the celebrated Rai'iatean who accompanied Cook on his first journey, the Pacific Ocean circled concentrically out from his central island home. Latterly, this was figured as 'the Polynesian triangle'. Second, there is an historical and historiographical west–east axis across the middle of the ocean, from Acapulco to Manila. The so-called Manila or Spanish galleons sailed several times a year between 1565 and 1815, exchanging silver mined in Mexico for silk, porcelain and spices traded by Chinese merchants in the Philippines. The oceans and coastal economies of the world became meaningfully linked less with the Magellan–Elcano first circumnavigation (1519–22), than with this Spanish–Chinese trade. Manila was a critical entrepôt of the early modern world.[21]

And yet, remarkably, the Spanish galleons missed or avoided all the islands that Tupaia later mapped. These were connected in a third Pacific axis when eighteenth-century European mariners – whalers, British and French naval expeditions, commercial shipping companies – linked maritime South East Asia (the Netherlands East Indies and the Malay world), the coasts of New Holland and New Zealand with the South Pacific islands and coastal South America. We can see this vast South Pacific axis in Cook's 'Chart of the Great South Sea or Pacifick Ocean'.[22]

---

[20] James K. Barnett and David L. Nicandri, eds., *Arctic ambitions: Captain Cook and the Northwest Passage* (Seattle, WA, 2015).

[21] Arturo Giráldez, *The Age of Trade: Manila galleons and the dawn of the global economy* (Lanham, MD, 2015).

[22] www.captcook-ne.co.uk/ccne/exhibits/10001/index.htm (accessed 31 March 2017)

70 A. Bashford

In the process of navigating this domain, Cook became aware of the cultural polity at the centre of the South Sea: 'how shall we account for this nation spreading itself so far over this Vast ocean?'.[23] He perceived, and was awed by, a vast Polynesian geography and history, even as his own navigations facilitated a reconnection between the islands that became Oceania.[24]

Océanie was first designated in 1812 and endures as a geopolitical and scholarly region. But it took some time to settle on mental maps, as on charts. Oceania often included Australia, New Guinea and Tasmania, as well as Polynesia, Melanesia and Micronesia, a geopolitical definition still deployed by the United Nations. In the nineteenth century, regionally based geographers (also writing histories) included some Antarctic waters and islands as well, as did Hobart-based Alexander Ireland in *The geography and history of Oceania abridged, or, A concise account of Australasia, Malaysia, Polynesia, and Antarctica* (1863).[25] And curiously, in other nineteenth-century maps, what came to be called Near and Remote Oceania was charted as Lesser and Greater Australia, while the continent retained the antique 'New Holland'.

Fourth, there is a North Pacific history and geography, reaching from East Asia northwards in an arc that takes in Kamchatka, the Bering Strait, the Aleutian islands, Alaska and the so-called Pacific Northwest in British Columbia. This is a coastal Pacific that extended to, and historically linked, Baja California, Alta California and the native societies in what formed the northern reach of New Spain. In this quarter of the Pacific, Chinese, Russian, Spanish, British and latterly American mariners battled for access to and influence over native traders of furs in particular. Multiple scientific expeditions were launched, in the manner of the earlier South Pacific journeys. Ryan Tucker Jones has re-oriented a familiar British and French historiography on natural history and scientific investigation to Russia and the North Pacific.[26] And David Igler's study *The Great Ocean* (2013) details how a North Pacific rim, as well as a cross-Pacific Canton–Hawai'i–America route flourished, partly from whaling and fishing, largely from trade in furs, and latterly transporting

---

[23] James Cook *The Journals of Captain James Cook on His Voyages of Discovery*, ed. J. C. Beaglehole and R. A. Skelton, 4 vols. (Cambridge, 1955), I, p. 279.

[24] Nicholas Thomas, *Islanders: The Pacific in the age of empire* (New Haven, CT, 2010).

[25] Alexander Ireland, *The geography and history of Oceania abridged, or, A concise account of Australasia, Malaysia, Polynesia, and Antarctica* (Hobart, 1863); Bronwen Douglas, 'Naming places: Voyagers, toponyms, and local presence in the fifth part of the World, 1500–1700', *Journal of Historical Geography*, 45 (2014): 12–24.

[26] Ryan Tucker Jones, *Empire of extinction: Russians and the North Pacific's strange beasts of the sea, 1741–1867* (Oxford, 2014).

The Pacific Ocean   71

goldseekers to and from California. His work has provided a much-needed integration of coastal North and South America into Pacific history.[27]

This work signals a fifth major geographical/historiographical orientation – the so-called Pacific rim, a construction often found in difficult scholarly and political relationship with the islands. The largest ocean on the planet also produces the longest coastline, and this geography has offered another, more recent way of comprehending the Pacific.[28] It is used often by scholars analysing US–East Asia geopolitical relations, including the Pacific War, and the increasingly linked economies of China, Hong Kong, Japan and the United States.[29] Another version includes coastal North America and South America into a 'pan-Pacific' history. This recognises that the geopolitical 'rim' was reinvented in the politico-cultural sphere. Any number of associations and non-government organisations were regionally organised on this geography, from the Pan Pacific Science Congresses (from 1920) to the Institute of Pacific Relations (from 1925) to the Pan Pacific Women's Association (from 1928).[30] Not incidentally, the first meetings and centre of organisational gravity for each of these pan-Pacific entities was Hawai'i. This had little to do with its Polynesian history, except in an antiquarian and later touristic sense, and much to do with its newer status as an apparent east–west crossroads, but one firmly under US sovereignty. The mythology of early twentieth-century Hawai'i as a model multi-ethnic community was safely propounded only because it was US territory.

Finally, historians have comprehended the Pacific on a vertical axis, that is, oceanographically and meteorologically, from the depth of the sea-bed to its tumultuous surface to the trade winds above. Humans and their material culture end up under the sea and maritime archaeology has become a key adjacent discipline for all oceanic histories. Sea mammals and fish in the Great Ocean have both sustained humans and become a valuable resource for extraction, and

---

[27] David Igler, *The Great Ocean: Pacific worlds from Captain Cook to the gold rush* (Oxford, 2013).

[28] Christopher L. Connery, 'Pacific rim discourse: The US global imaginary in the late cold war years', in Rob Wilson and Arif Dirlik, eds., *Asia/Pacific as space of cultural production* (Durham, NC, 1995), pp. 30–56.

[29] Bruce Cumings, *Dominion from sea to sea: Pacific ascendancy and American power* (New Haven, CT, 2009); Gary Y. Okihiro, 'Toward a Pacific civilization', *Japanese Journal of American Studies*, 18 (2007): 73–85.

[30] Tomoko Akami, *Internationalising the Pacific: The United States, Japan and the Institute of Pacific Relations, 1919–1945* (London, 2002); Fiona Paisley, *Glamour in the Pacific: Cultural internationalism and race politics in the women's pan-Pacific* (Honolulu, HI, 2009).

72   A. Bashford

historians have analysed aquatic life – tuna, sharks, corals, whales, sea lions, dugong, turtles – as economic history, ecological history and as the history of science.[31] Recently, signalling a broader interest in 'undersea' history, the Pacific has been historicised from an alternative 'below'.[32] The phenomenon of a single Pacific basin below the waves has often offered a geological unity that reassures historians trying to systematise a dizzying cultural and political diversity on and above the waves.[33] But this vast watery space has other divisions that impact on humans and non-humans alike, over time: the North Pacific current, the Pacific South Equatorial Current, the Peru cold-water current. The climatological and meteorological phenomenon of El Niño has become a manner of marking temporal, even historical, periods in the Pacific region.[34] The environmental determinism so common in 1930s historical geography may be returning, in a fashion, in a new climate-aware historiography.

Maritime, Imperial and Postcolonial Histories

Pacific history has engendered some of the world's most significant maritime history: studies of vessels, technologies, methods of navigation and maritime cultures.[35] Indigenous craft and navigation methods have fascinated maritime historians much as they did eighteenth-century European visitors.[36] The double-hulled canoe, techniques for dead reckoning, observations of westerly wind shifts in between prevailing trade winds and celestial navigation all continue as Pacific maritime knowledge, and are the subject of histories, documentaries and museum exhibits alike. And while there are some notable studies of steam technology in the

---

[31] Alistair Sponsel, 'From Cook to Cousteau: The many lives of coral reefs', in John Gillis and Franziska Torma, eds., *Fluid frontiers: Exploring oceans, islands, and coastal environments* (Cambridge, 2015), pp. 139–61; Iain McCalman, *The Reef: A passionate history* (Melbourne, 2013).

[32] Ryan Tucker Jones, 'Running into whales: The history of the North Pacific from below the waves', *American Historical Review*, 118 (2013): 349–77.

[33] Rainer F. Buschmann, 'The Pacific Ocean basin to 1850', in Jerry H. Bentley, ed., *The Oxford handbook of world history* (Oxford, 2011), pp. 565–80; Jerry H. Bentley, 'Sea and ocean basins as frameworks of historical analysis', *Geographical Review*, 89 (1999): 215–24.

[34] Richard H. Grove, 'The Great El Niño of 1789–93 and its global consequences: Reconstructing an extreme climate event in world environmental history', *Medieval History Journal*, 10 (2007): 75–98.

[35] A. D. Couper, *Sailors and traders: A maritime history of the Pacific peoples* (Honolulu, HI, 2009).

[36] Paul D'Arcy, *The people of the sea: Environment, identity and history in Oceania* (Honolulu, HI, 2006).

The Pacific Ocean   73

Pacific,[37] it is the 'age of sail' that steals attention in popular, museological and maritime archaeological investigations of the Pacific, the telling and retelling of the stories that the remote geography of the Pacific engendered: HMS *Bounty*'s mutiny; La Pérouse's South Sea expedition that simply vanished; New England whalers far from home in the Pacific, and Polynesian whalers far from home on Nantucket; beachcombers and European captives living well or ill with indigenous island and coastal communities. Both the Polynesian and European journeys have inspired re-enactment – also a form of history – as well as historical analysis of the genre of re-enactment itself, as a realist technology latterly turned affective.[38]

Pacific history has opened up a massive historiography on the comparative history of imperialism; of the Spanish, Portuguese, Dutch, French, British, German, American and Japanese intrusions into the islands and along the rim. How maritime empires became territorial empires – pastoral and plantation economies – over the eighteenth, nineteenth and twentieth centuries has yielded a rich historiography on law, treaties and land-taking from the coasts inwards. This insular and coastal geography of colonialism was quite different to the inland river and lake-oriented settlement in North America, for example. The Pacific is also a strange space of enduring, unfamiliar and remnant imperialism: Spain's failed venture to colonise the Solomon Islands;[39] France's last colonies (New Caledonia, the Marquesas);[40] New Zealand and Australia's imperial ambitions (Nauru, New Guinea, Samoa, Antarctica);[41] a self-evident, though constantly questioned, American Pacific empire (Hawai'i, Guam, Samoa, the Philippines); Russian designs on the North Pacific, its fish and furs; and bizarre international redistributions of sovereignty and experimental modes of rule after World War I (the German Pacific colonies turned Japanese, Australian and New Zealand mandates). A single island – Guam, for instance – distils the history and effects of successive Spanish, American and Japanese imperialism. Benedict Anderson

---

[37] Frances Steel, *Oceania under steam: Sea transport and the cultures of colonialism, c.1870–1914* (Manchester, 2011).

[38] Ben Finney, *Voyages of rediscovery* (Berkeley, CA, 1994); Iain McCalman and Paul Pickering, eds., *Historical reenactment: From realism to the affective turn* (Basingstoke, 2010).

[39] Martin Gibbs, 'The failed sixteenth century Spanish colonizing expeditions to the Solomon Islands, Southwest Pacific: The archaeologies of settlement process and indigenous agency', in Sanda Montén-Subías, María Cruz-Beccoral and Ruiz Martínez Apen, eds., *Archaeologies of early Spanish colonialism* (New York, 2016), pp. 253–80.

[40] Robert Aldrich, *France and the South Pacific since 1940* (London, 1993); Jean-Marc Regnault, ed., *François Mitterrand et les territoires français du Pacifique (1981–1988)* (Paris, 2003).

[41] Catharine Coleborne and Katie Pickles, eds., *New Zealand's empire* (Manchester, 2015).

74   A. Bashford

described a not dissimilar experience in the Philippines as 'historical vertigo'.[42]

'First contact' between indigenous people and Europeans is a particularly strong theme in Pacific history, from sixteenth-century Spanish–Chamorro relations through the very late contact between New Guinea highlanders and Australian goldseekers in 1930. The 'contact' theme in Pacific history has recently extended beyond close analysis of initial mis/understandings, exchange and violence on beaches and ships between visitors and locals, to an interest in communication between indigenous Pacific peoples themselves, some from faraway islands and coasts, whose language and culture was often, but not always, familiar. The cosmopolitanism of Pacific maritime sojourners has become an analytic counterweight to earlier and enduring celebrations of Europeans' global voyaging.[43]

Many, if not most Pacific histories written since the 1990s have been postcolonial revisions of eighteenth-century encounters. This has defined scholarship on Cook, for example, not least in a major debate between Marshall Sahlins and Gananath Obeyesekere about Cook's significance to Hawai'ians.[44] Other historians have tracked indigenous memory and oral histories about Cook, over two centuries.[45] The reinterpretation of conventional imperial histories to foreground and understand implications and viewpoints from an indigenous perspective extends to previous generations of historians as well, in part because the discipline of Pacific History was being institutionalised in the context of postwar decolonisation. The inaugural professor of the world's first department of Pacific History, at the Australian National University, was Cambridge-trained Jim Davidson. Appointed in 1950 he was an active participant in regional decolonisation, advising Samoan chiefs on independence, drafting constitutions for the Cook Islands, Nauru and New Guinea. His Cambridge PhD might have been the classic 'European penetration of the South Pacific, 1779–1842', but by 1967 his book *Samoa ma Samoa* detailed 'the emergence of the independent state of Western Samoa'.[46]

---

[42] Benedict Anderson, 'First Filipino', *London Review of Books*, 16 October 1997, 22.

[43] Thomas, *Islanders*; Nancy Shoemaker, *Native American whalemen and the world: Indigenous encounters and the contingency of race* (Durham, NC, 2015); Kate Fullagar, *The savage visit: New world peoples and popular imperial culture in Britain, 1710–1795* (Berkeley, CA, 2012).

[44] See Gananath Obeyesekere, *The apotheosis of Captain Cook: European mythmaking in the Pacific* (Princeton, NJ, 1992); Marshall Sahlins, *How 'Natives' think: About Captain Cook, for example* (Chicago, IL, 1995).

[45] Anne Salmond, *The trial of the cannibal dog: Captain Cook in the South Seas* (New Haven, CT, 2003); Maria Nugent, *Captain Cook was here* (Cambridge, 2009).

[46] J. W. Davidson, *Samoa ma Samoa: The emergence of the independent state of Western Samoa* (Melbourne, 1967).

The Pacific Ocean   75

Not colonisation but decolonisation was the important history to be told. Just as there is has been a 'contact' thematic in Pacific historiography, so there is particular indigenous history of decolonisation as Tracey Banivanua Mar argued,[47] and of political decolonisation that never happened, or is yet to unfold.[48]

Economy and Ecology

Economic historians have drawn China – in particular Guangzhao – into Pacific historiography, tracking the significance of 'Canton' trade, the word romanised and then internationalised from an original Portuguese transliteration of Guangdong. The Spanish seizure of Manila from Malay rajahs in 1571 established a 500-year history of Pacific-based intercontinental trade – comparable, that is, to the periodisation of the Atlantic world. Long the world's largest market, any number of ports, colonising expeditions, trade routes, island industries and shipping lines linked the oceanic region with Canton. Some economic historians argue that this Chinese–Spanish commerce became 'the prime impetus behind the birth of global trade'.[49] Certainly it created a template for Pacific-oriented wealth creation over the following centuries.[50] Marine commodities like bêche-de-mer from Fiji, pearlshells from the Torres Strait, furs from seals and otters in the north Pacific, all circuited through and gained their value because of, Cantonese markets.[51]

Another set of commodities was produced and extracted from insular and coastal land.[52] The sandalwood trade was especially significant over the nineteenth century connecting islands where it was grown and processed (Fiji, the New Hebrides, New Caledonia and Hawai'i) and Pacific

---

[47] Tracey Banivanua Mar, *Decolonisation and the Pacific: Indigenous globalisation and the ends of empire* (Cambridge, 2016); C. L. M. Penders, *The West New Guinea debacle: Dutch decolonisation and Indonesia, 1945–1962* (Honolulu, HI, 2002).

[48] Josette Kēhaulani Kauanui, *Hawaiian blood: Colonialism and the politics of sovereignty and Indigeneity* (Durham, NC, 2008); Noelani Goodyear-Ka'opua, Ikaika Hussey and Erin Kahunawaika'ala Wright, eds., *A nation rising: Hawaiian movements for life, land, and sovereignty* (Durham, NC, 2014).

[49] Dennis O. Flynn and Arturo Giráldez, 'Spanish profitability in the Pacific: The Philippines in the sixteenth and seventeenth centuries', in Dennis O. Flynn, Lionel Frost and A. J. H. Latham, eds., *Pacific centuries: Pacific and Pacific rim history since the sixteenth century* (London, 1999), p. 14.

[50] Kenneth L. Pomeranz, ed., *The Pacific in the age of early industrialization* (Farnham, 2009).

[51] Julia Martínez and Adrian Vickers, *The pearl frontier: Indonesian labor and indigenous encounters in Australia's northern trading network* (Honolulu, HI, 2015).

[52] Dorothy Shineberg, *They came for sandalwood: A study of the sandalwood trade in the southwest Pacific, 1830–1865* (Melbourne, 1967); Debra Ma, ed., *Textiles in the Pacific, 1500–1900* (Farnham, 2005).

76   A. Bashford

rim ports where it was traded, Sydney, Manila, Valparaiso and Canton, the major end market. Settler colonial societies created entirely new markets from the late eighteenth century. Salted pork, for example, was exported from New Zealand and Tahiti to feed the growing population of British and Irish in southeast Australia, from the late eighteenth century. The extraction and production as well as trade of these commodities involved increasingly complex negotiations between Europeans – both those who lived on the islands and intermittent traders – and locals. The authority of some monarchical dynasties, such as the Pomare in Tahiti and the Kamehameha in Hawai'i, was entrenched by the growing importance of such trade and through successful negotiations through much of the nineteenth century.[53] More recently mining – especially guano mining on islands along the Peruvian coast and phosphate mining on islands throughout Oceania – connected the Pacific to world economies. Great profits ensued, some as controversially extracted from islanders as effectively as the phosphate itself, as in the case of Nauru. In the end, Pacific Islanders may have negotiated more successfully within the economic context of eighteenth- and nineteenth-century maritime imperialism than twentieth-century globalisation.

Commercial exchange, extraction economies and invasion ecologies went hand-in-hand in the Pacific. There have been many costs. But one of the dividends has been a thriving tradition of Pacific ecological history. The Pacific is perhaps the major oceanic region in which ecological history, and environmental history more generally, has been thoroughly applied, from Alfred Crosby's focus on New Zealand in *Ecological Imperialism* onwards. The history of inter- and intra-species battles and exterminations, the concepts of resilience, invasion devastation or opportunistic flourishing, have each been thoroughly developed within Pacific-based history of science. In part this has been because the vastness of the ocean created island and coastal populations of non-human organisms if not entirely isolated, then certainly separated for many generations. In some instances, this isolation has been significant in evolutionary terms; the Wallace line, for example, marks the separation of Tasmania, Australia and New Guinea from Asia. And for humans, notwithstanding the historical and historiographical focus on connection across waters, distance and isolation have shaped history: contact with Europeans usually meant the devastating introduction of multiple unfamiliar microorganisms. These raised levels of infertility, morbidity and mortality, and introduced plant and animal species that changed seascapes and

---

[53] Brij V. Lal and Kate Fortune, *The Pacific islands* (Honolulu, HI, 2000), pp. 204–6.

The Pacific Ocean 77

landscapes in some instances very quickly. In the Pacific region, invasion ecology has long offered a rich conceptual, metaphorical as well as substantive mode through which to develop a demonstrably linked environmental and colonial history.[54]

Traffic: Slavery, Labour, Migration

Traffic in humans was always part of economic history and often part of maritime history. It has a long Pacific past. In both navy and merchant voyages, European mariners regularly captured adults and children from islands and coasts, but men and women characteristically held different value and had different experiences of captivity: as hostages on the one hand and, typically, as unwilling sexual labourers on the other. Sexual commerce was not an incidental but a problematically quotidian aspect of maritime, imperial and local cultures. Women were often enough objects of exchange between men, with little or no freedom of their own. As such the Pacific traffic in women must be seen as part of a maritime history of forced labour.[55]

While the forced movement of people for slave-based plantation economies defines Atlantic history, there is a less definitive but nonetheless significant history of coerced labour that unfolded in the Pacific. Historians have recently uncovered the extent to which an African diaspora extended from the Atlantic to the Pacific: any number of freed and escaped slaves from the Caribbean and North America ended up in Pacific ports, not infrequently re-entering a shadow network of forced labour via penal systems.[56] Other, more systematic if not official systems of slaving emerged in the Pacific world in nineteenth-century sequence to, and resulting from, the abolition of the slave trade in the Atlantic world. Many of the new South American republics banned slave labour in the early nineteenth century, for example, leaving a huge labour demand for the mid-nineteenth-century guano industry. China was one trans-Pacific source of contract labour. Easter Island was another, more coerced

[54] Alan Moorehead, *The fatal impact: The invasion of the South Pacific, 1767–1840* (New York, 1966); Alfred Crosby, *Ecological imperialism* (New York, 1986); Tom Griffiths and Libby Robin, eds., *Ecology and empire: Environmental history of settler societies* (Seattle, WA, 1997); J. R. McNeill, ed., *Environmental history in the Pacific world* (Aldershot, 2001); Iain McCalman and Jodie Frawley, eds., *Rethinking invasion ecologies from the environmental humanities* (London, 2014).

[55] Igler, *The Great Ocean*, ch. 3; Margaret Jolly, Serge Tcherkézoff and Darrell Tryon, eds., *Oceanic encounters: exchange, desire, violence* (Canberra, 2009).

[56] Cassandra Pybus, 'The world is all of one piece: The African diaspora and transportation to Australia', in Ruth Hamilton, ed., *Routes of passage: Rethinking the African diaspora* (East Lansing, MI, 2005), pp. 181–90.

78   A. Bashford

source. Around one thousand Rapanui and perhaps another thousand Micronesians were forced into mining labour in Peru. Unscrupulous captains of this trade were occasionally brought before French and British courts,[57] and trial records, as well as Rapanui oral histories taken in the 1970s, confirm the coercion of the traders still remembered as 'Peruvian slavers'. For Rapanui, this trade all but fatally compounded the pre-existing population decline from infectious diseases.[58]

For most polities in the Pacific, the legitimate – that is, governmental – response to abolition of slavery was authorisation of indentured or contracted labour systems, linking the Pacific and Indian Ocean worlds. Indian indenture to the Caribbean and across the Indian Ocean from the 1830s extended to Fiji in the 1870s. And from the 1860s opportunistic captains began moving Melanesian men and some women to sugar plantations in Queensland, a trade that British and colonial governments soon began to regulate.[59] Over these decades and into the twentieth century, hundreds of thousands of Japanese and Chinese were indentured to work in Hawai'i.[60]

Successive gold discoveries in California, the Australian colonies and then Otago in New Zealand created further demand for mobility, from which passenger lines derived great profit in the 1850s and 1860s, crossing from China and Hong Kong to San Francisco, via Hawai'i, and south-west to Sydney, Melbourne and Dunedin. In the last half of the nineteenth century, then, Pacific waters were constantly criss-crossed with vessels transporting contracted and free labourers, and migrants, to and fro. It became a busy ocean, increasingly so under steam. It also became a regulated ocean in this period, precisely because so much labour was indentured and observed in the shadow of the slave trade: captains and port-based agents were kept to minimum standards, at least on paper. All of this maritime movement of labourers also made Pacific coasts and ports key sites for a strident race-based nationalism. Coalescing around labour questions, the aspirational 'whiteness' of Pacific rim polities – Australia, New Zealand, Canada and the US – was defined by

[57] Grant McCall, 'European impact on Easter Island: Response, recruitment and the Polynesian experience in Peru', *Journal of Pacific History*, 11 (1976): 90–105. See also Hazel Petrie, *Outcasts of the gods? The struggle over slavery in Māori New Zealand* (Auckland, 2015).

[58] Finney, 'The other one-third of the globe', 289.

[59] Donald Denoon, 'Plantations and plantation workers', in Denoon, ed., *The Cambridge history of the Pacific Islanders*, pp. 226–32.

[60] Numbers for the South Pacific trade are set out in Lal and Fortune, *The Pacific Islands*, pp. 203–4, and C. Moore, J. Leckie and D. Munro, eds., *Labour in the South Pacific* (Townsville, Qld., 1990); Tracey Banivanua Mar, *Violence and colonial dialogue: The Australian-Pacific labor trade* (Honolulu, HI, 2007).

The Pacific Ocean

anti-Chinese, anti-Indian and anti-Japanese politics. A combination of proliferating maritime quarantine regulations and anti-Chinese labour/immigration laws made the Pacific the ocean in which border control shifted from intermittent emergency measures to quotidian and eventually normalised practice.[61] And this all played out in maritime sites and as maritime matters: customs, quarantine, inspections, deportations, refusals and provisional entries were increasingly the routine business of Pacific ports.

Overlaying this 'global colour line' by which so much of the Pacific was legally if not actually segregated, is a later twentieth-century diaspora. If Fiji is one site of an extended Indian diaspora, Australia, New Zealand and the United States are now home, or second home, to Fijian, Tongan, Samoan and Chamorro communities. Some of this out-migration has been voluntary, towards larger economies. Some has been unexpected and unwanted. There is a history of relocation and resettlement in the Pacific that is peculiarly oceanic, or more specifically, insular. Mining made some island homes literally unliveable: Ocean Island (Banaba), for example, where eighty years of phosphate mining (1900–79) stripped the island bare. Many Banabans relocated first to Fiji, and thence across the Pacific rim.[62] Other relocations are occurring now, or are imminent, as an effect of rising sea levels.[63]

Ways of Knowing

Pacific historiography is marked by a cross-cultural epistemology, different ways of knowing culture, nature and history.[64] Cosmologies clashed and converged. Christianity has been massively important in the Pacific context, the counter-reformation Spanish Catholic world extending to the Philippines, in early proselytising conflict with Islam, and eventually creating what remains one of the largest Catholic polities in the world.

---

[61] Adam McKeown, *Chinese migrant networks and cultural change: Peru, Chicago, Hawaii, 1900–1936* (Chicago, IL, 2001); McKeown, *Melancholy order: Asian migration and the globalization of borders* (New York, 2008); Marilyn Lake and Henry Reynolds, *Drawing the global color line: White men's countries and the question of racial equality* (Cambridge, 2008); Alison Bashford, 'Immigration restriction: Rethinking period and place from settler colonies to postcolonial nations', *Journal of Global History*, 9 (2014): 26–48.

[62] Katerina Martina Teaiwa, *Consuming Ocean Island: Stories of people and phosphate from Banaba* (Bloomington, IN, 2014).

[63] Jane McAdam, *Climate change, forced migration, and international law* (Oxford, 2012); McAdam, 'Lessons from planned relocation and resettlement in the past', *Forced Migration Review*, 49 (2015): 30–32.

[64] K. R. Howe, *Nature, culture, history: The 'knowing' of Oceania* (Honolulu, HI, 2000); Shino Konishi, Maria Nugent and Tiffany Shellam, eds., *Indigenous intermediaries: new perspectives on exploration archives* (Canberra, 2015).

80 A. Bashford

Christian denominations and nationalities folded into one another over successive eras – French and Catholic, British and Protestant, German and Lutheran.[65] In the process, ways of knowing, ways of believing and ways of speaking were shaped and resisted in relation to one another, as Vicente Rafael showed in *Contracting Colonialism*.[66] Religion was often politics. The London Missionary Society worked from an original Tahitian base, where the conversion of Pomare II in 1812 manifested as the earliest Christian kingdom in the Pacific and represented an alliance-politics of sorts that has been analysed as Polynesian imperialism.[67] Two centuries later, Christianity is the island Pacific's 'traditional' religion, making the region significant for the new study of global Christianities.[68]

Christian mission in the South Pacific coincided with, and often grafted onto, late Enlightenment scientific mission. Sometimes figured historiographically as a 'laboratory', the Pacific was rather more a 'field' for natural historians.[69] And given the remarkable biogeography that awaited them, it is little wonder that early natural historians, like the historians of science that later studied them, returned again and again to the Pacific. Bio-prospecting as much as navigation and charting was an explicit element of many, perhaps most, eighteenth- and nineteenth-century expeditions.[70] Islanders' knowledge was sought, sometimes demanded and sometimes exchanged; how to grow and process New Zealand 'flax', for example, momentarily an enticing prospect as a hemp substitute for sails and ropes. Commercial interests jockeyed with purer ambitions to gather good specimens, and millions of botanical, zoological and geological items returned to European and American collections, still displayed and stored in the Muséum national d'histoire naturelle and Jardin des Plantes in Paris, the Kew Botanical Gardens or the Museum für Naturkunder in Berlin. Because the Pacific was the Enlightenment's 'new world', modern ways of knowing the natural world – systems of

[65] Robert Aldrich, *The French presence in the South Pacific* (Basingstoke, 1990), ch. 2; John Gascoigne, 'Religion and empire in the South Seas in the first half of the nineteenth century', in Robert Aldrich and Kirsten McKenzie, eds., *The Routledge history of Western empires* (London, 2013), pp. 439–53.

[66] Vicente L. Rafael, *Contracting colonialism: Translation and Christian conversion in Tagalog society under early Spanish rule* (Durham, NC, 1993).

[67] Niel Gunson, 'Pomare II and Polynesian imperialism', *Journal of Pacific History*, 4 (1969): 65–82.

[68] Lal and Fortune, eds., *The Pacific Islands*, p. 200; Manfred Ernst, ed., *Globalization and the re-shaping of Christianity in the Pacific Islands* (Suva, 2007).

[69] Roy McLeod and Philip F. Rehbock, eds., *Darwin's laboratory: Evolutionary theory and natural history in the Pacific* (Honolulu, HI, 1994); Sujit Sivasundaram, *Nature's Godly empire: Science and evangelical mission in the Pacific, 1795–1850* (Cambridge, 2005).

[70] John Gascoigne, *Encountering the Pacific in the age of enlightenment* (Cambridge, 2014).

The Pacific Ocean 81

knowledge as well as units of knowledge – were built very much from these collections.[71]

In the same way, but with more serious implications, the Pacific has long been a site for the production of knowledge about human sameness and difference, and has drawn a great deal of scholarly interest in writing and revising histories of ethnography. Much was specifically 'seaborne ethnography', as Bronwen Douglas has argued.[72] A great deal of knowledge about human difference in Oceania – the invention of 'race' – rested on ideas about sex and gender.[73] And reproduction across 'race' has engaged historians of Pacific societies in large part because it engaged governments and lawmakers so strongly in past centuries.[74]

It is often claimed that the Pacific was a place in which Europeans thoroughly 'naturalised' and, later in the nineteenth century, 'biologised' indigenous people. Certainly a peculiar European view of the world invented 'savage' societies in the Pacific. Yet this was, at least originally, more a signifier of hunter-gathering economies, than a biological signifier of fixed race difference. Analysis of the 'biologising' of Pacific people can be overstated, and serves to misrepresent the cultural inquiry that governed most eighteenth-century accounts. These could be, and were, as dismissive, violent and hierarchical as the crudest post-Darwinian biological anthropology, and yet most European ways of knowing Pacific culture involved inquiry into politico-legal systems, cultures of birth and death, relations between men and women, linguistic variety, modes of thought about spiritual realms, kinship and history. The Pacific *has* been a site for the development of physical anthropology as well as comparative anatomy – even Te Rangi Hiroa proudly recounted his measurement of '424 heads of full-blooded Maoris'.[75] Yet such ways of knowing human difference belong to an historical period – and rather a shorter period than is usually claimed. Indeed, even as Te Rangi Hiroa wrote, other anthropologists and biologists were engaged in studies that were to undo the very idea of 'race', theoretically. Scientific investigations of mixed-race Pacific populations – almost despite their own ambitions and

---

[71] Alan Frost, 'The Pacific Ocean: The eighteenth-century's "new world"', *Studies on Voltaire and the Eighteenth Century*, 152–3 (1976): 803–9.

[72] Bronwen Douglas, 'Expeditions, encounters, and the praxis of seaborne ethnography: The French voyages of La Pérouse and Freycinet', in Martin Thomas, ed., *Expedition into empire: exploratory journeys and the making of the modern world* (New York, 2015), pp. 108–26.

[73] Shino Konishi, *The Aboriginal male in the Enlightenment world* (London, 2012).

[74] Damon Salesa, *Racial crossings: Race, intermarriage and the Victorian British empire* (Oxford, 2011).

[75] Te Rangi Hiroa, *Vikings of the sunrise*, p. 16.

82   A. Bashford

intentions – ended up challenging the viability of contemporary racial theories.[76]

Pacific Centuries

If, in scholarly terms, the Atlantic world is both a region and a period (c. 1500–1800), the Pacific world also has a temporal dimension. 'The Pacific century' was used in the late twentieth century as a forecasting signifier – the twenty-first century was going to be the Pacific century, in the light of rising Japanese and later Thai, Malaysian, Korean and Chinese economies. But by that century's end – 1999 – international relations scholars were already asking: 'whatever happened to the Pacific Century?'[77] To some extent the idea of a Pacific century became outmoded because it was linked so specifically to Japan. Yet it prompted economic historians to rethink the Pacific, and to nominate any number of previous 'Pacific centuries': not one, but at least five centuries, as Dennis O. Flynn, Lionel Frost and A. J. H. Latham indicated in their edited collection on the Pacific rim since the sixteenth century.[78]

In retrospect, however, the twentieth century might still best qualify as the Pacific century. If China dominated economically, and in the long view, Japan dominated Pacific history geopolitically in the twentieth century. That century began with a complete rearrangement of the region, as Japan asserted itself over Russia, and then allied itself with Britain and France in World War I, the Japanese Imperial Navy taking Germany's Micronesian colonies. And yet the end of the war signalled a marked shift in international relations across the Pacific, as Japanese governments pressed hard against the race-based immigration laws that so many Pacific rim countries continued to implement. Indeed the flurry of 'pan-Pacific' associations in the period was a precise response to Japanese dissatisfaction turned foreign policy. It is with good reason that the relatively new field of 'international relations' focused on the Pacific region. It was the Pacific War that globalised the second 'world' war, and historians are increasingly dating it not from 1939 to 1945, but from 1937 at the Japanese

---

[76] Warwick Anderson, 'Hybridity, race, and science: The voyage of the *Zaca*, 1934–1935', *Isis*, 103 (2012): 229–53.

[77] Rosemary Foot and Andrew Walter, 'Whatever happened to the Pacific Century?', *Review of International Studies*, 25 (1999): 245–69.

[78] Dennis O. Flynn, Lionel Frost and A. J. H. Latham, eds., *Pacific centuries: Pacific and Pacific rim history since the sixteenth century* (London, 1999). Two books emerged from a suite of 'Pacific centuries' conferences held in the 1990s, themselves responses to the declaration of an imminent 'Pacific century'; the other collection of essays is Sally M. Miller, A. J. H. Latham and Dennis O. Flynn, eds., *Studies in the economic history of the Pacific* (London, 1998).

The Pacific Ocean

invasion of China to September 1945, at the surrender of Japan, the strange seaborne ritual on USS *Missouri*.[79] It was a war fought through and in the Pacific. Islands were conquered (Guam), divided (Samoa) and bombed (Hawai'i). All of the ocean, land and people that had become part of the Japanese Empire, having been part of the Spanish, American, British and Australian empires, after the war had to decolonise again from their liberators and administrators.

The Cold War played out in the Pacific as well, not least with nuclear testing. The Marshall Islands was the so-called Pacific Proving Ground for early US testing, the apparent emptiness of the Pacific later inviting the French to experiment on Pacific atolls. The Pacific has also been a site of major anti-nuclear politics, both unofficial and, in the case of New Zealand, official. The mid-1980s Lange government declared New Zealand and its waters a 'nuclear free zone', banning nuclear-armed or nuclear-powered ships. The sinking of the Greenpeace protest vessel, the *Rainbow Warrior*, by French intelligence agents in 1985, entrenched a Pacific-based political stand-off.

The *Rainbow Warrior* sinking was an unlikely maritime affair in a jet-fuelled age. And yet, as with all oceans, containerisation has maintained – indeed increased – Pacific ocean traffic. The infrastructure of globalisation remains, in very large part maritime, as historians of global capitalism have shown. And the great volume of containerised cargo now transported across the ocean is the latest Pacific chapter for 'world-systems' theorists, always inclined to think historically.[80] It is this traffic, criss-crossing old Polynesian, galleon, whaling and naval routes, that daily connects the Pacific to world history as well as the world ocean.

Further Reading

There are now multiple general histories of the Pacific Ocean that treat the islands and rim, the North and the South together. Key single-authored books include Matt K. Matsuda, *Pacific worlds: A history of seas, peoples, and cultures* (Cambridge, 2012); Donald B. Freeman, *The Pacific* (London, 2010). David Armitage and Alison Bashford have edited *Pacific histories: Ocean, land, people* (Basingstoke, 2014). On the islands, a vast amount of information is gathered in Brij V. Lal and Kate Fortune, *The Pacific islands: An encyclopedia* (Honolulu, HI, 2000) and interpretations

---

[79] Christina Twomey and Ernest Koh, eds., *The Pacific war: Aftermaths, remembrance and culture* (London, 2015).

[80] Paul S. Ciccantell and Stephen G. Bunker, eds., *Space and transport in the world-system* (Westport, CT, 1998).

84   A. Bashford

in Paul D'Arcy, *The people of the sea: Environment, identity and history in Oceania* (Honolulu, HI, 2006) and Nicholas Thomas, *Islanders: The Pacific in the age of Empire* (New Haven, CT, 2010). Historiographically oriented studies include Doug Munro and Brij Lal, eds., *Texts and contexts: Reflections in Pacific Island historiography* (Honolulu, HI, 2005); Damon Salesa, 'The world from Oceania', in D. T. Northrop, ed., *A companion to world history* (Chichester, 2012), pp. 392–404; Margaret Jolly, 'Imagining Oceania: Indigenous and foreign representations of a Sea of Islands', *The Contemporary Pacific*, 19 (2007): 508–45. The linked geography of Oceania and history of racial classification is detailed in Bronwen Douglas, *Science, voyages, and encounters in Oceania, 1511–1850* (Basingstoke, 2014). For Pacific history that brings in the North and South American coastlines, see David Igler, *The Great Ocean: Pacific worlds from Captain Cook to the Gold Rush* (Oxford, 2013); Katrina Gulliver, 'Finding the Pacific world', *Journal of World History*, 22 (2011): 83–100, and for the history of a Spanish and Portuguese Pacific, see Rainer Buschmann, *Iberian visions of the Pacific Ocean, 1507–1899* (New York, 2014). On religion, and in particular Christianity in the Pacific, see the early work of Niel Gunson, *Messengers of grace: Evangelical missionaries in the South Seas 1979–1860* (Melbourne, 1978); Doug Munro and Andrew Thornley, *The covenant makers: Islander missionaries in the Pacific* (Suva, 1996); Hyaeweol Choi and Margaret Jolly, eds., *Divine domesticities: Christian paradoxes in Asia and the Pacific* (Canberra, 2014). For economic history of Māori trading and shipping, see Hazel Petrie, *Chiefs of industry: Māori tribal enterprise in early colonial New Zealand* (Auckland, 2006), and for broader economic histories, see Kenneth L. Pomeranz, ed., *The Pacific in the age of early industrialization* (Farnham, 2009). On the American Pacific, see Robert David Johnson, *Asia Pacific in the age of globalization* (Basingstoke, 2014). For natural history and the Pacific, see Ryan Tucker Jones, *Empire of extinction: Russians and the North Pacific's strange beasts of the sea, 1741–1867* (Oxford, 2014) and John Gascoigne, *Encountering the Pacific in the age of Enlightenment* (Cambridge, 2014). Artistic and literary cultural production has been examined, for example, in Khadija von Zinnenburg Carroll, *Art in the time of colony* (London, 2014) and Vanessa Smith, *Literary culture and the Pacific: Nineteenth-century textual encounters* (Cambridge, 2005).

3　The Atlantic Ocean

David Armitage[*]

There was a time before Atlantic history. Two hundred million years ago, in the early Jurassic, no waters formed either barriers or bridges among what are now the Americas, Europe and Africa. These landmasses comprised a single supercontinent of Pangea until tectonic shifts gradually pushed them apart. The movement continues to this day, as the Atlantic basin expands at about the same rate that the Pacific's contracts: roughly two centimetres a year. The Atlantic Ocean, at an average of about 4,000 kilometres wide and 4 kilometres deep, is not as broad or profound as the Pacific, the Earth's largest ocean by far, although its multi-continental shoreline is greater than that of the Pacific and Indian Oceans combined.[1] The Atlantic is now but a suburb of the world ocean. Despite the best efforts of international organisations to demarcate it precisely,[2] the Atlantic is inextricably part of world history, over geological time as well as on a human scale.

There was Atlantic history long before there were Atlantic historians. There were histories *around* the Atlantic, along its shores and within its coastal waters. There were histories *in* the Atlantic, on its islands and over its open seas. And there were histories *across* the Atlantic, beginning with the Norse voyages in the eleventh century and then becoming repeatable and regular in both directions from the early sixteenth century onwards, long after the Indian and Pacific Oceans had become so widely navigable.[3] For almost five centuries, these memories and experiences

---

[*] Special thanks to Phil Stern for his acute comments on this chapter.

[1] Jan Zalasiewicz and Mark Williams, *Ocean worlds: The story of seas on Earth and other planets* (Oxford, 2014), pp. 54, 56–57.

[2] International Hydrographic Bureau, *Limits of oceans and seas*, 3rd edn. (Monte Carlo, 1953), pp. 13, 18–19; Shin Kim, *Limits of Atlantic Ocean*, International Hydrographic Organization, Special publication, 23 (Seoul, 2003).

[3] Kirsten A. Seaver, *The frozen echo: Greenland and the exploration of North America, ca. A.D. 1000–1500* (Stanford, CA, 1996).

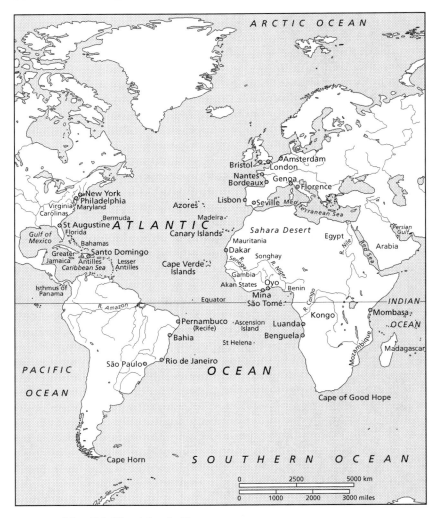

Map 3.1 The Atlantic Ocean

comprised the history of many Atlantics – north and south, eastern and western; Amerindian and African;[4] enslaved and free; Spanish and

---

[4] Paul Cohen, 'Was there an Amerindian Atlantic? Reflections on the limits of a historiographical concept', *History of European Ideas*, 34 (2008): 388–410; Thomas Benjamin, *The Atlantic World: Europeans, Africans, Indians and their shared history, 1400–1900* (Cambridge, 2009); John K. Thornton, *A cultural history of the Atlantic World, 1250–1820* (Cambridge, 2012); Jace Weaver, *The red Atlantic: American Indigenes and the making of the modern world, 1000–1927* (Chapel Hill, NC, 2015).

The Atlantic Ocean

Portuguese;[5] British, French, Dutch, creole and hybrid[6] – but not yet a single Atlantic history. More comprehensively Atlantic histories began to appear in the late nineteenth century; later, various species of political and geo-political Atlanticism flourished after the two world wars, but it would take until the latter part of the twentieth century for self-identified Atlantic historians to come onto the scene. Only in the early part of our own century did Atlantic history briefly emerge as a discrete field of study before oceanic history and global history engulfed it once more.[7]

In retrospect, Atlantic history appears to have peaked in the early 2000s. 'We are all Atlantic historians now', I provocatively declared in 2002, a notorious line usually quoted without its sceptical codicil: *'or so it would seem* from the explosion of interest in the Atlantic and the Atlantic world as subjects of study among historians of North and South America, the Caribbean, Africa and western Europe.'[8] Within less than a decade, almost thirty collective volumes on Atlantic history had appeared alongside countless articles, theses and monographs (and not just by historians).[9] In the words of one friendly critic at the time, Atlantic history was 'not merely trendy, but . . . clearly winning the day'.[10] It challenged the methodological nationalism that had informed professional history-writing since at least the late nineteenth century. It transcended national boundaries and largely ignored territorial frontiers. It stressed mobility and circulation and focused on exchange and hybridity, integration and communication. It treated the 'creation, destruction and re-creation of communities as a result of the movement, across and around the Atlantic

---

[5] John H. Elliott, *El Atlántico español y el Atlántico luso: divergencias y convergencias* (Las Palmas de Gran Canaria, 2014).

[6] Ira Berlin, *Many thousands gone: The first two centuries of slavery in North America* (Cambridge, MA, 1998), on 'Atlantic creoles'; Jorge Cañizares-Esguerra and Benjamin Breen, 'Hybrid Atlantics: Future directions for the history of the Atlantic world', *History Compass*, 11, 8 (August 2013): 597–609.

[7] Karen Ordahl Kupperman, *The Atlantic in world history* (Oxford, 2012); Christoph Strobel, *The global Atlantic 1400 to 1900* (Abingdon, 2015).

[8] David Armitage, 'Three concepts of Atlantic history' (2002), in David Armitage and Michael J. Braddick, eds., *The British Atlantic world, 1500–1800*, 2nd edn. (Basingstoke, 2009), p. 13 (my emphasis); for commentary, see Trevor Burnard, 'Only connect: The rise and rise (and fall?) of Atlantic history', *Historically Speaking*, 7 (2006): 19–21; Brian Ward, 'Caryl Phillips, David Armitage, and the place of the American South in Atlantic and other worlds', in Ward, Martyn Bone and William A. Link, eds., *The American South and the Atlantic world* (Gainesville, FL, 2013), pp. 8–44.

[9] Bernard Bailyn, 'The International Seminar on the History of the Atlantic World, 1500–1825: A report to the Mellon Foundation on the Seminar's work and accomplishments, 1995–2013' (Cambridge, MA, 2013), p. 12.

[10] Peter A. Coclanis, '*Drang Nach Osten*: Bernard Bailyn, the world-island, and the idea of Atlantic History', *Journal of World History*, 13 (2002): 170.

88   D. Armitage

basin, of people, commodities, cultural practices, and ideas'.[11] And it did so in a context defined by empires as well as states and within the perspective of developing political economy.[12] At its most ambitious, Atlantic history joined distinct regions and expanded conventional chronologies into narratives of large-scale change over three or four centuries. During these boom years, what was good for Atlantic history seemed to be good for oceanic history more generally, and even for transnational history *tout court*.

However, every boom risks a bust. Atlantic history's ascendancy was palpable but short-lived. The cause was less exhaustion than a certain repetition within the field along with increasing competition from without. Scholarly production of Atlantic histories hardly ceased but the field's adolescent energy waned and it was increasingly challenged as an historiographical inspiration. Its greatest booster and entrepreneur, Harvard historian Bernard Bailyn, noted in 2015 that Atlantic history had 'developed so swiftly that by 2010 some Atlantic historians had become Atlantic world weary and the basic idea was becoming passé'.[13] Supranational areas of study experienced their own growth spurts. New global histories, as well as other oceanic histories, began to overshadow and even to subsume Atlantic history. Atlantic world-weariness led to the sobering conclusions that the field had 'fallen on hard times', that it 'certainly ha[d] not lived up to the promises of its early supporters' and that 'this ocean was not necessarily more influential than local, regional or global factors in the everyday lives of many inhabitants of Africa, America and Europe'.[14] A new consensus was emerging. We were *not* all Atlantic historians now. We never had been. Probably, we never would be.[15]

At its zenith, Atlantic history sat mostly in splendid isolation. Its reigning vision was holistic but somewhat hermetic. It encompassed intercontinental and transoceanic connections but it was in denial about its eclectic ancestry and drew little sustenance from other oceanic histories. 'How had the idea of Atlantic history developed?', Bailyn asked in 2005.

---

[11] J. H. Elliott, 'Atlantic History: A circumnavigation', in Armitage and Braddick, eds., *The British Atlantic world, 1500–1800*, p. 259.

[12] Sophus Reinert and Pernille Røge, eds., *The political economy of Empire in the early modern world* (Basingstoke, 2013).

[13] Bernard Bailyn, 'Hot dreams of liberty', *New York Review of Books*, 62, 13 (13 August 2015), 50 (quoted).

[14] Patrick Griffin, 'A plea for a new Atlantic History', *William and Mary Quarterly*, 3rd ser., 68 (2011): 236; Richard J. Blakemore, 'The changing fortunes of Atlantic history', *English Historical Review*, 131 (2016): 867.

[15] Michelle Craig McDonald, 'There are still Atlanticists now: A subfield reborn', *Journal of the Early Republic*, 36 (2016): 701–13, offers a more upbeat view, based on recent publishing patterns in Anglophone journals.

The Atlantic Ocean   89

'Not in imitation of Fernand Braudel's concept of Mediterranean history', he replied, nor did he believe it was an extension of imperial history or the product of the history of encounters and exploration.[16] Now that Atlantic history is no longer even first among equals, it is clear that both the Mediterranean and the Indian Ocean challenge the Atlantic for chronological priority as maritime zones and as spaces of historical memory.[17] There is also a stronger case that the Pacific Ocean had been generating historical inspiration for decades before Atlantic history briefly asserted its predominance.[18] And it is more obvious than ever that the historiographies of other seas and oceans – the Red Sea and Black Sea; the Baltic and South China seas; the Southern Ocean and the Arctic Ocean – owe little debt to the historiography of the Atlantic.[19] Atlantic history is poised to become a consumer rather than a producer of models for other oceanic histories. Accordingly, this chapter attempts to show what those models have to offer Atlantic historians, in a post-Atlantic world of plurality and proliferation.

Atlantic History's Hundred Horizons

Before there was the Atlantic, or Atlantic history, there was a 'complex of seas', formed of many segmented and discontinuous Atlantics – even if they were not known by that name or placed in that frame.[20] There were no westward probes across the ocean until centuries after eastward-moving peoples had created pathways across the sea: to this extent, the history of the ocean's becoming '*the* Atlantic' must still start with Europe and with Europeans. Until the fifteenth century, most navigation was coastal, leading to cartographies both mental and formal that resembled road-maps more than navigational charts, much like early modern Japanese representations of a 'small eastern sea' rather than of an open Pacific

---

[16] Bernard Bailyn, *Atlantic History: Concept and contours* (Cambridge, MA, 2005), pp. 4–6.
[17] Molly Greene, 'The Mediterranean Sea'; Sujit Sivasundaram, 'The Indian Ocean', in this volume.
[18] Alison Bashford, 'The Pacific Ocean', in this volume.
[19] See the relevant chapters in this volume by Jonathan Miran, Stella Ghervas, Michael North, Eric Tagliacozzo, Alessandro Antonello and Sverker Sörlin.
[20] Fernand Braudel, *The Mediterranean and the Mediterranean world in the age of Philip II*, trans. Siân Reynolds, 2 vols. (London, 1972–73), I, p. 18; Barry Cunliffe, *On the ocean: The Mediterranean and the Atlantic from prehistory to AD 1500* (Oxford, 2017); Patricia Pearson, 'The world of the Atlantic before the "Atlantic world": Africa, Europe, and the Americas before 1850', in Toyin Falola and Kevin D. Roberts, eds., *The Atlantic World, 1450–2000* (Bloomington, IN, 2008), pp. 3–26; Benjamin Hudson, ed., *Studies in the Medieval Atlantic* (Basingstoke, 2012).

90   D. Armitage

Ocean.[21] The Norsemen who settled in what is now Newfoundland likely thought they were in Africa; Christopher Columbus probably went to his grave believing he had reached Asia. The waters they had crossed joined known parts of the world but did not display vast novel vistas; they would not appear on maps, or in European minds, until sixteenth-century Spanish navigational manuals and Dutch cartography began to reveal the full extent of what stood between Europe and Africa on one side and the Americas on the other. Yet even then, what oceanographers now think of as 'the' Atlantic long remained divided into sub-oceanic regions, particularly along a north–south axis bisected by the Equator. Oceanic currents, such as the Gulf Stream – first mapped by Benjamin Franklin in the late 1760s, though undoubtedly familiar long before in sailors' artisanal knowledge – created routes through the ocean that reinforced the distinctions.[22] At least until the early nineteenth century, denizens and historians of the ocean had to reckon with 'both Atlantics', as the pioneering hydrographer James Rennell termed them around 1830.[23] As late as the 1870s, the northern portion could still be called, in a reference work from the United States, 'the Atlantic proper', in contrast to the 'Ethiopic' sector, or South Atlantic.[24] 'The Atlantic is crossed daily by steamers', wrote the American oceanographer Matthew Fontaine Maury in 1861, 'the Pacific not once a year.'[25]

Until the late nineteenth century, then, there were at least two Atlantics. Above the Equator, lay the 'Mer du Nord', the 'North Sea' or, as Britons called it, with their eyes turned towards North America, the 'Western Ocean'. Beneath the Equator, there was a mostly separate oceanic system that emerged with voyaging back and forth between Africa and South America, particularly in the context of the trans-Atlantic slave trade: this was, variously, the 'Oceanus Ethiopicum', the 'Mare Aethiopicum',

[21] Marcia Yonemoto, 'Maps and metaphors of the "small Eastern Sea" in Tokugawa Japan', *Geographical Review*, 89 (1999): 169–87.

[22] Joyce E. Chaplin, 'The Atlantic Ocean and its contemporary meanings, 1492–1808', in Jack P. Greene and Philip D. Morgan, eds., *Atlantic history: A critical appraisal* (Oxford, 2009), pp. 36–39; Chaplin, 'Circulations: Benjamin Franklin's gulf stream', in James Delbourgo and Nicholas Dew, eds., *Science and empire in the Atlantic world* (Abingdon, 2007), pp. 73–96.

[23] James Rennell, *An Investigation of the currents of the Atlantic Ocean, and of those which prevail between the Indian Ocean and the Atlantic*, ed. Jane Rodd (London, 1832), p. 60; see ibid., pp. 69–70 on 'the two Atlantics'. Rennell's work appeared posthumously.

[24] George Ripley and Charles A. Dana, eds., *The American cyclopædia: A popular dictionary of general knowledge*, 16 vols. (New York, 1873), II, p. 69, quoted in Luiz Felipe de Alencastro, 'The Ethiopic Ocean – History and historiography, 1600–1975', *Portuguese Literary & Cultural Studies*, 27 (2015): 2.

[25] Matthew Fontaine Maury, *The physical geography of the sea and its meteorology* (1861), ed. John Leighly (Cambridge, MA, 1963), p. 37.

The Atlantic Ocean 91

'Oceano Australe', 'Oceano Meridionale' or 'Mare Magnum Australe'. The Afro-Latin Atlantic, with Brazil and Angola at its extremities, was the arena for the 'longest and most intense forced migration of the modern era', in which almost five million enslaved persons were transported westwards from Africa between 1556 and the end of the Brazilian slave-trade in 1850. As Luiz Felipe de Alencastro has persuasively argued, that mid-nineteenth-century moment marked a major watershed in Atlantic history by diminishing the significance of one maritime system – the South Atlantic Gyre in which currents and winds had determined routes of travel in the age of sail – at the point when steamships were liberating mariners and their vessels from the winds and allowed the northern and southern Atlantic systems to be more firmly sutured together.[26] It was not a coincidence that perhaps the greatest emancipated voice of the age, Frederick Douglass, proclaimed in 1852 that, 'Oceans no longer divide, but link nations together. From Boston to London is now a holiday excursion. Space is comparatively annihilated. Thoughts expressed on one side of the Atlantic, are distinctly heard on the other.'[27] Douglass was no doubt thinking of 'the Atlantic proper', but his words increasingly described the Atlantic basin as a whole, north and south as well as east and west.

The emergence of this integrated Atlantic – post-emancipation, post-colonial, if not quite (or perhaps ever) post-imperial – made possible the imagination of larger Atlantic histories in the sense of historical accounts that took the Atlantic basin as their bailiwick. Indeed, a narrative arising from this moment and constructed around the rise and fall of the slave-trade and the histories of slavery and emancipation, may be the most promising point of origin for Atlantic history itself. W. E. B. Du Bois's *The suppression of the African slave-trade to the United States of America, 1638–1870* (1896) is emblematic of this post-emancipation historiography, a history of the black Atlantic a century before the sociologist Paul Gilroy made the term fashionable while using Du Bois's own concept of 'double consciousness' as a lens.[28] Du Bois's was a study on an intercontinental scale over a *longue durée* of almost 250 years. Without his

---

[26] Alencastro, 'The Ethiopic Ocean', 1, 6; see also Kenneth Maxwell, 'The Atlantic in the eighteenth century: A southern perspective on the need to return to the "big picture"', *Transactions of the Royal Historical Society*, n.s. 3 (1993): 209–36.

[27] Frederick Douglass, 'What to the slave is the fourth of July?: An address delivered in Rochester, New York, on 5 July 1852', in *The Frederick Douglass papers, series one: Speeches, debates, and interviews*, ed. John W. Blassingame, 5 vols. (New Haven, CT, 1979–92), II, p. 387.

[28] W. E. B. Du Bois, *The suppression of the African slave-trade to the United States of America, 1638–1870* (New York, 1896); Paul Gilroy, *The Black Atlantic: Modernity and double consciousness* (Cambridge, MA, 1993).

92   D. Armitage

work, studies such as C. L. R. James's *The Black Jacobins* (1938) or Eric Williams's *Capitalism and slavery* (1944) would have been inconceivable. Nor might we have had the single greatest macroscope for viewing the Atlantic as a dynamic, destructive, circulatory system – the online Trans-Atlantic Slave Trade Database detailing nearly 36,000 voyages carrying as many as 12.5 million people across the ocean.[29] There was a black Atlantic history almost before there was any other Atlantic history, and it placed bondage and forced displacement of subaltern populations at the heart of the Atlantic story.

As if to answer this black Atlantic vision, a distinctly white and racially charged Atlantic also emerged briefly in the early twentieth century. This was the geo-political vision of an Atlantic world imagined by the German political geographer Karl Haushofer in the 1920s. Haushofer is perhaps better known now for his vision of Pacific history – another early and anomalous precursor to a burgeoning field of oceanic history – but the two emerged in tandem in the pages of his journal, the *Zeitschrift für Geopolitik*.[30] There, the Atlantic world (*Atlantische Welt*) comprised the continents of the Americas, the oceans around them and only the sub-Saharan parts of Africa. Haushofer clearly separated this from another sphere of influence with its own independent history and destiny, the 'Old World' (*Alte Welt*) of Europe, North Africa and the Arabian peninsula. This *Atlantische Welt* connected the Americas to Africa but not to Europe, and hence a racialised and creolised hemisphere with oceanic projections.[31] This was an Atlantic world outside of any Atlantic history that had been, or ever would be, imagined again.

The next wave of Atlantic histories came during what, from an Atlantic perspective, was the inter-war period.[32] In the closing stages of the First World War, the American journalist Walter Lippmann began to write of an 'Atlantic community', which was initially North Atlantic in scope but which he later extended to include various Latin American countries. His idea went underground during an era of American isolationism but resurfaced later as the backstory for the institutionalised Atlantic

---

[29] www.slavevoyages.org/ (accessed 31 March 2017); David Eltis and David Richardson, *Atlas of the Transatlantic slave trade* (New Haven, CT, 2010).

[30] On Haushofer's Pacific vision, see Alison Bashford, 'Karl Haushofer's *Geopolitics of the Pacific Ocean*', in Kate Fullagar, ed., *The Atlantic world in the antipodes: Effects and transformations since the eighteenth century* (Newcastle upon Tyne, 2012), pp. 120–43.

[31] See the world map from *Zeitschrift für Geopolitik*, 1, 4 (1924), reproduced in William O'Reilly, 'Genealogies of Atlantic history', *Atlantic Studies*, 1 (2004): 79.

[32] For more on these genealogies of Atlantic history, see Sylvia Marzagalli, 'Sur les origines de l' "Atlantic history": paradigme interprétatif de l'histoire des espaces atlantiques à l'époque moderne', *Dix-huitiéme Siècle*, 33 (2001): 17–31; O'Reilly, 'Genealogies of Atlantic history'.

The Atlantic Ocean

community erected after the next great war. Lippmann emerged afresh as a promoter of Atlanticism as a species of internationalism in the era of US-led building of international institutions, from the Atlantic Charter (1941) and the United Nations to UNESCO to NATO, that is often held to be the seedbed for Atlantic history as an integrated field of focus.[33] It is from this moment that we get the initial conception of 'Atlantic world' as a geopolitical expression of an Atlantic community and as a historical entity in the writings of diplomats and legal internationalists but not yet among historians.[34] It was in the early 1970s that the idea of an 'Atlantic world' first broke free of these origins to migrate into broader historiography. It only became a widespread term of art in the new century, when its usage ballooned in historical work after 2000: six scholarly articles in the English used the term in their titles in the 1990s but over fifty did so in the 2000s, and there has been a similar pattern of invocations since 2010.[35]

The post-Second World War genealogy of Atlantic history underpinned a narrative with a durable chronology and implied geography. European westward expansion into oceanic space led to waves of emigration premissed on the dispossession of Indigenous peoples and the destruction or transmutation of their communities in order to facilitate settler colonialism, initially under the supervision of European metropoles. The increasingly insatiable slave trade pumped expendable labour into a system of early capitalist production, leading to escalating inequality and racial domination. Those hierarchies did not collapse when perceived political oppression and the creole response to it sparked a series of 'Atlantic revolutions' that led to political independence, the formation of new nation-states (which were retrofitted with their own national histories) and, with a delay of decades and sometimes as a result of civil war, the emancipation of the enslaved. This was the teleological narrative that informed Atlantic history at the height of its fortunes in the early twenty-first century. It settled into a timeline between the late fifteenth century and the first third of the nineteenth century but inevitably missed the watershed of 1850 and the later Brazilian abolition of 1888 and only

---

[33] Bailyn, *Atlantic History*, pp. 6–30, is the classic account of this genealogy of Atlantic history.

[34] See, for example, Arnold Ræstad, *Europe and the Atlantic world*, ed. Winthrop W. Case (Princeton, NJ, 1941); Ræstad, *Europe and the Atlantic world* (Oslo, 1958); Claude Delmas, *Le monde Atlantique* (Paris, 1958); Robert Strausz-Hupé, James E. Dougherty and William R. Kintner, *Building the Atlantic world* (New York, 1960).

[35] The first use of 'Atlantic world' in the title of a historical monograph in English seems to be K. G. Davies, *The North Atlantic world in the seventeenth century* (Minneapolis, MN, 1974). JSTOR articles with the words 'Atlantic World' in the title appeared at the following rate: 1970s (1); 1980s (2); 1990s (6); 2000s (52); 2010–16 (32).

94   D. Armitage

belatedly incorporated the Haitian Revolution as a pivotal event. It was, by accident or design, but still without acknowledgment, an Atlantic history whose chronology revealed its geography as still centred on that 'proper' Atlantic above the Equator.

This was a history of the North Atlantic as the Mediterranean of modernity, strung between European expansion and early industrialisation and informed by a liberal story of oppression relieved by revolution and emancipation, both personal and political. In the hands of the French historian Jacques Godechot and his American collaborator, R. R. Palmer, this political narrative produced a history of modern Western civilisation with the Atlantic at its heart. However, the Atlantic itself was more a hole than a centre. Their germinal paper, 'Le problème de l'Atlantique', presented in Rome in 1955, depicted an Atlantic world without an ocean: like Palmer's great solo work, *The age of the democratic revolution* (1959–64), their piece can hardly be said to contribute to Atlantic history as an oceanic history, though Godechot himself had written the first maritime history of the Atlantic in French in 1947.[36] (The first English-language histories of the Atlantic, published in 1957 by two mariner-writers, the American Leonard Outhwaite and the Australian Alan Villiers, were popular works firmly focused on the North Atlantic.)[37] It would take students of the early modern Hispanic Atlantic inspired by Fernand Braudel in the 1950s, such as Vitorino Magalhães Godinho, Huguette Chaunu and Pierre Chaunu and Frédéric Mauro, to apply Mediterranean models to the Atlantic and its regions, even if Braudel himself found their work 'arbitrary' for failing to achieve his holistic ambitions.[38] As a result, these avatars of Atlantic history were rarely invoked later as originators of the field, in favour of dry-footed historians like Palmer who had little interest in the history of the Atlantic Ocean *per se*.

[36] Jacques Godechot, *Histoire de l'Atlantique* (Paris, 1947); R. R. Palmer and Jacques Godechot, 'Le problème de l'Atlantique du XVIIIᵉ au XXᵉ siécle', in *Relazioni del X Congresso Internazionale di Scienze Storiche (Rome, 4–11 Settembre 1955)*, 6 vols. (Florence, 1955), V, pp. 175–239; Palmer, *The age of the democratic revolution: A political history of Europe and America, 1760–1800*, introd. David Armitage (Princeton, NJ, 2014).

[37] Leonard Outhwaite, *The Atlantic: A history of an ocean* (New York, 1957); Alan Villiers, *Wild ocean: The story of the North Atlantic and the men who sailed It* (New York, 1957). (Villiers also wrote an early work of Indian Ocean history: *The Indian Ocean* (London, 1952); Sivasundaram, 'The Indian Ocean', pp. 37–38 above.) Their descendant is Simon Winchester, *Atlantic: A vast ocean of a million stories* (London, 2010).

[38] Vitorino de Magalhães Godinho, 'Problèmes d'économie atlantique: Le Portugal, flottes du sucre et flottes de l'or, 1670–1770', *Annales ESC*, 5 (1950): 184–97; Huguette Chaunu and Pierre Chaunu, *Séville et l'Atlantique, 1504–1650*, 8 vols. (Paris, 1955–59); Frédéric Mauro, *Le Portugal et l'Atlantique au XVIIe siècle, 1570–1670: étude économique* (Paris, 1960); Alencastro, 'The Ethiopic Ocean', 35–37.

The Atlantic Ocean

Until the explosion of self-consciously Atlantic history in the late 1990s and early 2000s, scholarship flowed largely in the channels cut after the Second World War. These intellectual conduits directed Atlantic history into imperial and national histories, within a chronology from encounter to emancipation between the late fifteenth and early nineteenth centuries. The major exceptions were those African historians like Philip Curtin who followed Du Bois and his successors in studying the long-term dynamics of the slave trade: their work necessarily affirmed the established periodisation of Atlantic history, but it penetrated deeper into the South Atlantic context and into Africa, it integrated the Caribbean more firmly within Atlantic history and it focused on a slave-system driven by national entities, in Portugal and Britain especially, but decidedly supranational and intercontinental in scope.[39]

The challenge for Atlantic history in the late twentieth century was threefold: first, to integrate the various streams of Atlantic history – political, economic and cultural; black and white Atlantics; national and transnational histories; second, to press against conventional chronological and geographical boundaries; and third, to define the identity of the field without cutting it off from other areas of historical inquiry. The rapid maturation and equally speedy dissolution of Atlantic history in the early 2000s only partly rose to those challenges. To be sure, as the proliferation of seminars and conferences, monographs and articles demonstrated, Atlantic history offered an expansively integrative approach at just the moment when historians were becoming increasingly sceptical that a national frame was adequate to capture the processes, both local and global, in which they were interested. The major syntheses that emerged in the wake of this expansion of monographic work, in the form of textbooks and surveys as Atlantic history became a widespread teaching field, consolidated this integrative tendency, especially by combining the black, white and 'red' (or Indigenous) Atlantics into multi-ethnic narratives.[40] They were less successful in breaching the apparently impenetrable barrier of the mid-nineteenth century: the moment when both Atlantics were finally joined into a single communications system continued to mark the outer limit of Atlantic history, at least chronologically. Historians of early globalisation centred on the late nineteenth-century Atlantic economy, students of the US Civil War era and scholars of migration who note the movement of sixty-five million Europeans across the ocean between 1830 and 1930, have made the case

---

[39] See, for example, Philip Curtin, *The Atlantic slave trade: A census* (Madison, WI, 1969).
[40] See especially Benjamin, *The Atlantic world*, and Thornton, *A cultural history of the Atlantic world, 1250–1820*, as well as the guide to 'Further Reading' for this chapter.

96   D. Armitage

for a 'long Atlantic'.[41] However, what Emma Rothschild calls 'provincialism in time' has proved more resilient than provincialism in space, and this longer Atlantic has yet to become established historiographically.[42]

The third challenge, of defining Atlantic history, remained productively unresolved even at the zenith of Atlantic history's success. To establish its identity, some historians, like Bailyn, engaged in genealogy, to discover their ancestors and to display their pedigree, even if at some cost in constraining originality while affirming continuity. In response, others (including myself) turned to morphology, to display the family resemblances among related strains of Atlantic history.[43] These joint efforts may have briefly shaped the course of the field, just before its identity was once more subsumed into broader currents of historical inquiry. Sometimes, the best way to go forward is to look backwards; in the remainder of this chapter, I will suggest three new routes for Atlantic history, in light of recent oceanic history more broadly, and building on my earlier effort to dissect the field.

Three (More) Concepts of Atlantic History

Fifteen years ago, I proposed three concepts of Atlantic history to anatomise existing approaches and to point up prospective pathways for the field: these were *circum*-Atlantic history, *trans*-Atlantic history and *cis*-Atlantic history.[44] By circum-Atlantic history, I meant 'the history of the Atlantic as a particular zone of exchange and interchange, circulation and transmission': in short, Atlantic history as transnational history.[45] Trans-Atlantic history is 'the history of the Atlantic world told through comparisons' between empires, nations, states and similar communities

---

[41]   Kevin H. O'Rourke and Jeffrey G. Williamson, *Globalization and history: The evolution of a nineteenth-century Atlantic economy* (Cambridge, MA, 1999); Douglas R. Egerton, 'Rethinking Atlantic historiography in a postcolonial era. The Civil War in a global perspective', *Journal of the Civil War Era*, 1 (2011): 79–95; Robert E. Bonner, 'The salt water Civil War: Thalassological approaches, ocean-centered opportunities', *Journal of the Civil War Era*, 6 (2016): 243–67; Donna Gabaccia, 'A long Atlantic in a wider world', *Atlantic Studies*, 1 (2004): 10–12.

[42]   Emma Rothschild, 'Late Atlantic history', in Canny and Morgan, eds., *The Oxford handbook of the Atlantic world, 1450–1850*, p. 647; for exceptions, see Daniel T. Rodgers, *Atlantic crossings: Social politics in a progressive age* (Cambridge, MA, 1998), and the essays in the fourth part of Falola and Roberts, eds., *The Atlantic world, 1450–2000*, pp. 275–358 ('Globalization and its discontents'), on the twentieth-century Atlantic world.

[43]   Bernard Bailyn, 'The idea of Atlantic history', *Itinerario*, 22 (1996): 19–44, revised and expanded in Bailyn, *Atlantic history*, pp. 1–56; O'Reilly, 'Genealogies of Atlantic history'; Armitage, 'Three concepts of Atlantic history'.

[44]   Armitage, 'Three concepts of Atlantic history', 17–29.

[45]   Joseph Roach, *Cities of the dead: Circum-Atlantic performance* (Cambridge, MA, 1996), was the source of the term.

The Atlantic Ocean   97

or formations, such as cities or plantations – that is, Atlantic history as international, interregional or, as we might now say, inter-polity history.[46] And cis-Atlantic history comprises 'the history of any particular place – a nation, a state, a region, even a specific institution – in relation to the wider Atlantic world', or Atlantic history conceived as local history and even as microhistory.[47]

This typology was not exhaustive and I intended the three categories to be mutually reinforcing: circum-Atlantic history made trans-Atlantic history possible and both depended on cis-Atlantic histories; these emerged in turn from circum- and trans-Atlantic connections and circulations. At the time, and for many years after, they adequately captured the bulk of work conducted as the history of an Atlantic world that was largely defined against inter-oceanic and global connections, conceived of as a holistic, multi-continental system and viewed as the sum of experiences above the waves and on the territories adjoining and within the Atlantic Ocean. By now, they no longer seem as comprehensive as they once did, not least because they were derived mostly inductively, from existing practices within Atlantic history itself.

The evolution of oceanic history in the last decade suggests a pressing need to extend my original trichotomy to take account of more recent developments, within and beyond Atlantic history, and to imagine new prospects for Atlantic history itself. With these goals in mind, let me offer three *more* concepts of Atlantic history in addition to my original triad:

1. *Infra*-Atlantic history – the subregional history of the Atlantic world.
2. *Sub*-Atlantic history – the submarine history of the Atlantic world.
3. *Extra*-Atlantic history – the supraregional history of the Atlantic world.

My aim in the latter part of this chapter is to describe each approach, with examples drawn from Atlantic history and its historiographical neighbours, to account for their significance and to suggest how each

---

[46] I take the term 'inter-polity' from the work of Lauren Benton and Adam Clulow: for example, Benton and Clulow, 'Legal encounters and the origins of global law', in Jerry H. Bentley, Sanjay Subrahmanyam and Merry E. Wiesner-Hanks, eds., *The Cambridge world history*, VI, 2: *The construction of a global world, 1400–1800 CE: Patterns of change* (Cambridge, 2015), pp. 80–100.

[47] Lara Putnam, 'To study the fragments/whole: Microhistory and the Atlantic world', *Journal of Social History*, 39 (2006): 615–30. For self-consciously cis-Atlantic histories, see, for example, Stephen K. Roberts, 'Cromwellian towns in the Severn basin: A contribution to cis-Atlantic history?', in Patrick Little, ed., *The Cromwellian Protectorate* (Woodbridge, 2007), pp. 165–87; Daniel Walden, 'America's first coastal community: A cis- and circumatlantic reading of John Smith's *The Generall Historie of Virginia*', *Atlantic Studies*, 7 (2010): 329–47; Steven A. Sarson, *The tobacco-plantation South in the early American Atlantic world* (Basingstoke, 2013).

98   D. Armitage

can draw Atlantic history into closer and more productive dialogue with other oceanic histories. These three new concepts supplement but do not supplant my earlier trichotomy. Taken together, they can offer novel ways to re-energise the field of Atlantic history and to increase its integration with other areas of historical analysis.

Infra-Atlantic History

Infra-Atlantic history is the inverse of circum-Atlantic history as 'the history of the ocean as an arena distinct from any of the particular, narrower, oceanic zones that comprise it'.[48] In contrast to that integrative approach, it focuses instead on those more specific and bounded regions that flow into or abut upon the larger ocean but which have their own integrity as islands and archipelagos, littorals and beaches, straits, gulfs and seas in their own right. It is the history of the peoples who inhabited these sub-regions, who lived by the sea or pursued maritime lives in coastal and insular waters. This is not the Atlantic as a congeries of cis-Atlantic histories, because there is no assumption that those places should be connected to a larger circuit of communication. Nor is it the Atlantic as a 'world' or a 'system' but instead as a series of distinct spaces and the competing visions that emerged from them. To paraphrase a distinction Greg Dening made for Pacific history, it is history *in* the Atlantic rather than history *of* the Atlantic.[49]

Infra-Atlantic history draws inspiration from adjacent oceanic histories that have also attempted to break down wider oceans into their component parts. As Jonathan Miran notes in his essay on the Red Sea in this volume, 'most maritime spaces are innately fractured, fragmented and unstable arenas'; with this, he affirms the argument of Peregrine Horden and Nicholas Purcell that the Mediterranean should be spared from Braudelian synthesis by decomposition into many microecologies or Sugata Bose's similar claims in favour of the dizzyingly various 'hundred horizons' visible in the Indian Ocean arena.[50] It has been suggested that the future of global history in an age of resurgent nationalism, populism and anti-globalism lies in narrating disintegration as well as

---

[48] Armitage, 'Three concepts of Atlantic history', 18.

[49] Greg Dening, 'History "in" the Pacific', *The Contemporary Pacific*, 1 (1989): 134–39; compare Blakemore, 'The changing fortunes of Atlantic history': 862, on the attendant 'risk of losing the impulse to search for connections across boundaries or on an Atlantic scale' that might come with history 'in' rather than 'of' the Atlantic.

[50] Miran, 'The Red Sea', in this volume, p. 171; Peregrine Horden and Nicholas Purcell, *The corrupting sea: A study of Mediterranean history* (Oxford, 2000); Sugata Bose, *A hundred horizons: The Indian Ocean in the age of global empire* (Cambridge, MA, 2006).

The Atlantic Ocean   99

integration.[51] On this view, a segmented Atlantic has as much to reveal as a coordinated one. This is because it is more likely to reflect particular experiences than to fall into the traps of Eurocentrism – the assumption that the Atlantic was a European preserve or invention – or whiggism, the premise that Atlantic integration was inevitable, even irreversible.

Infra-Atlantic history can be discovered first throughout the islands of the Atlantic. That search takes us back to one possible root of the term 'Atlantic' itself. Around 355 BCE, Plato in the *Timaeus* imagined the island empire of Atlantis, in the western ocean beyond the Mediterranean 'frog-pond', which warred with Athens before disappearing in a cataclysmic flood. The first European voyages into the Atlantic lent his myth fresh plausibility – or, at least, utility in accounting for earlier links with the Americas – though it later became a western analogue to the Indian Ocean's Lemuria, a sunken superpower around which identities later swirled.[52] The first recorded westward explorer of the Atlantic was Plato's near-contemporary, the island-hopping Pytheas of Massalia (Marseille), who made it to Britain, Orkney and Shetland and possibly even Iceland in the fourth century BCE.[53] Long thereafter, the Atlantic would be a realm of imaginary islands – the Fortunate Isles, St Brendan's Isle, the Island of the Seven Cities and Ultima Thule, among others – before Europeans learned that it was indeed a sea fringed with many insular formations, from Orkney and Shetland in the north to the Canaries and the Azores in mid-Atlantic and the Greater and Lesser Antilles in the Caribbean.[54] All had their own infra-Atlantic histories before trans-Atlantic contact and their inhabitants would continue to live such histories even when they became more deeply implicated in an emergent Atlantic world.

The Atlantic gradually came into focus as a sea *with* islands, but was it also a sea *of* islands? Pacific studies prompt the question.[55] In that oceanic history, the paradigm of a sea of islands expresses Indigenous

---

[51] Jeremy Adelman, 'What is global history now?', *Aeon Magazine* (2 March 2017): https://aeon.co/essays/is-global-history-still-possible-or-has-it-had-its-moment (accessed 31 March 2017).

[52] *Plato's Atlantis story: Text, translation and commentary*, ed. Christopher Gill (Liverpool, 2017); Pierre Vidal-Naquet, *The Atlantis story: A short history of Plato's myth*, trans. Janet Lloyd (Exeter, 2007), pp. 56–62; Sumathi Ramaswamy, *The lost land of lemuria: Fabulous geographies, catastrophic histories* (Berkeley, CA, 2004).

[53] Barry Cunliffe, *The extraordinary voyage of Pytheas the Greek* (London, 2001).

[54] John R. Gillis, *Islands of the mind: How the human imagination created the Atlantic world* (Basingstoke, 2004); compare Andrew Jennings, Silke Reeploeg and Angela Watt, eds., *Northern Atlantic islands and the sea: Seascapes and dreamscapes* (Newcastle upon Tyne, 2017).

[55] Paul D'Arcy, 'The Atlantic and Pacific worlds', in Coffman, Leonard and O'Reilly, eds., *The Atlantic world*, pp. 207–26; Damon Salesa, 'Opposite footers', in Fullagar, ed., *The Atlantic world in the antipodes*, pp. 283–300.

100   D. Armitage

consciousness of attachment and importance; it reframes as plenitude what outsiders put down as the absence or insignificance of territories in the 'Earth's empty quarter'.[56] There were no Indigenous Atlantic equivalents to the immense colonising voyages of the Polynesian navigators, which made islands into stepping-stones across vast oceanic expanses. The 'Atlantic Mediterranean', populated by islands from the Canaries to the Azores and joined together by Atlantic winds, could hardly compare with these, though the Caribbean islands and the adjacent coastal regions of southern North America and northern South America have a claim to be a 'trans-oceanic Mediterranean' or even an 'Atlantic Oceania', albeit on a far smaller scale than anything within the Pacific.[57] Territories such as Ascension Island, Tristan da Cunha and St Helena remained remote from each other and from the five continents until well into the twentieth century, and for much of the eighteenth century, St Helena had functioned as a gateway to the Indian Ocean world while the Falkland Islands 'open[ed] ... facilities of passing into the Pacifick Ocean'.[58] These were islands *in* the Atlantic, but not quite *of* it.

Mediating *between* the Atlantic, its islands and the lands that surround it are its coasts and beaches. All maritime activity begins from these regions where land and sea meet but their potential within Atlantic history has only just begun to be explored.[59] Within the historiography of the Pacific, the beach holds a special place as a metaphor for the meeting of cultures and a space where mutual understandings and misunderstandings were performed and identities continually reshaped.[60] The beach has not functioned as illuminatingly in Atlantic historiography,

[56] Epeli Hau'ofa, 'Our sea of islands' (1993), in Hau'ofa, *We are the ocean: Selected works* (Honolulu, HI, 2008), pp. 27–40; R. G. Ward, 'Earth's empty quarter? Pacific islands in a Pacific world', *The Geographical Journal*, 155 (1989): 235–46.

[57] Felipe Fernández-Armesto, *Before Columbus: Exploration and colonisation from the Mediterranean to the Atlantic, 1229–1492* (Basingstoke, 1987), p. 152; David Abulafia, 'Mediterraneans', in W. V. Harris, ed., *Rethinking the Meditereanean* (Oxford, 2005), pp. 82–85; John R. Gillis, 'Islands in the making of an Atlantic Oceania, 1500–1800', in Jerry H. Bentley, Renate Bridenthal and Kären Wigen, eds., *Seascapes: Maritime histories, littoral cultures, and transoceanic exchanges* (Honolulu, HI, 2007), pp. 21–37. On the Caribbean, compare Joshua Jelly-Schapiro, *Island people: The Caribbean and the world* (New York, 2016), pt. II, 'The Lesser Antilles: Sea of islands'.

[58] John McAleer, 'Looking East: St Helena, the South Atlantic and Britain's Indian Ocean world', *Atlantic Studies*, 13 (2016): 78–98; George Anson, *A voyage around the world, in the years MDCCXL, I, II, III, IV*, ed. Richard Walter (London, 1748), p. 92, cit. ibid., 79, on the Falklands. On the importance of islands more generally, the classic work remains Richard H. Grove, *Green imperialism: Colonial expansion, tropical island Edens, and the orgins of environmentalism, 1600–1860* (Cambridge, 1995).

[59] For more general inspiration, see Alison Bashford, 'Terraqueous histories', *The Historical Journal*, 60 (2017): 253–73.

[60] Greg Dening, *Beach crossings: Voyaging across times, cultures and self* (Carlton, Vic., 2004).

The Atlantic Ocean
101

perhaps because of a later European association with the seaside as a location for leisure and pleasure, aesthetics and athletics.[61] Infra-Atlantic history might restore significance to such spaces by doing what Henry David Thoreau punningly called '*littorally* . . . walking down to the shore, and throwing your line into the Atlantic', to look for more local and bounded objects of study where the 'ocean is but a larger lake'.[62] Here were points of interaction between the human and the natural (especially protein-rich resources such as fish) and between land and sea – oceanic histories in miniature, in effect.

The histories of frontiers and borderlands have been largely terrestrial and located within the interiors of continents but there is great potential for examination of the 'saltwater frontier' where incomers and indigenes, especially, met from the early fifteenth century in Africa and from the early sixteenth century onwards in the Americas, both Caribbean and continental. Exchange and interchange, followed often by conflict and dispossession, took place first in these liminal spaces, as native habitations were transformed into bridgeheads for settlers to protect themselves by sea or project their power over land, for example along the eastern seaboard of seventeenth-century North America.[63] 'The American coasts can be said to have been Europe's initial New World frontier', and that idea can be extended around the edges of the Atlantic world, especially along its western shores.[64]

Infra-Atlantic history extends well beyond the moment of early interactions. After the initial period of encounter and occupation, European powers attempted to integrate new territories and subjects into their networks of sovereignty and authority. Imperial entanglement was always incomplete because a patchwork of corridors and enclaves rendered empires uneven in their penetration and, like any network, made up as much of holes as linkages. Within the Atlantic world, coasts, rivers, estuaries and islands were sites for the elaboration of empire, both on the fringes of continents and in archipelagos like the West Indies where empires competed for control cheek by jowl with one another in contested 'interpolity microregions' well into the nineteenth century.[65] When

[61] Alain Corbin, *The lure of the sea: The discovery of the seaside in the western world, 1750–1840*, trans. Jocelyn Phelps (Cambridge, 1994).
[62] Henry D. Thoreau, *Cape Cod* (1865), ed. Joseph J. Moldenhauer (Princeton, NJ, 1988), pp. 92, 98.
[63] Andrew Lipman, *The saltwater frontier: Indians and the contest for the American coast* (New Haven, CT, 2015).
[64] John R. Gillis, *The human shore: Seacoasts in history* (Chicago, IL, 2012), p. 91.
[65] Lauren Benton, *A search for sovereignty: Law and geography in European empire, 1400–1900* (Cambridge, 2010); Jeppe Mulich, 'Microregionalism and intercolonial relations: The case of the Danish West Indies, 1730–1830', *Journal of Global History*, 8 (2013): 72–94;

102   D. Armitage

examined at this granular level of micro-regions, infra-Atlantic history shows that two features of Atlantic history usually assumed to have an elective affinity, connectivity and integration, were only contingently related: to be enmeshed within Atlantic networks was not necessarily to be part of an ever more entangled Atlantic world. Yet infra-Atlantic history, may still appear superficial, in the literal sense of the term. Like most species of Atlantic history, it starts on the surface of land and ocean and builds upwards and outwards from there. To go deeper, we need to consider 'sub-Atlantic' history.

Sub-Atlantic History

Sub-Atlantic history is history from below – not in the traditional, social-historical, meaning of that phrase as the history of those beneath the elites, but rather as history that took place 'below the water line' or 'below the waves'.[66] The term 'sub-Atlantic' seems to have emerged at that pivotal moment in the middle of the nineteenth century when the two Atlantics were increasingly united by the advent of steam navigation and when the telegraph joined both sides of the Atlantic for the first time: for example, the *Oxford English Dictionary*'s earliest instances of 'subatlantic' come from 1854 and 1875, respectively: 'subatlantic telegraphy' and the 'sub-atlantic cable enterprise'.[67] More recently, the word has been invoked, with reference to Caribbean thinkers such as Édouard Glissant and the late Derek Walcott, to cover the realm of 'the sub-Atlantic as a repository of historical memory'.[68] Sub-Atlantic history can cover all these senses and more, to denote the world beneath the waves of the Atlantic, its currents, sea-floor and waters, as well as the denizens of marine ecosystems, human interactions with the natural world of the Atlantic, and the history that took place *within* the ocean itself.[69]

Benton and Mulich, 'The space between empires: Coastal and insular microregions in the early nineteenth-century world', in Paul Stock, ed., *The uses of space in early modern history* (Basingstoke, 2015), p. 152.

[66] Marcus Rediker, 'History from below the water line: Sharks and the Atlantic slave trade', *Atlantic Studies*, 5 (2008): 285–97; Ryan Tucker Jones, 'Running into whales: The history of the North Pacific from below the waves', *American Historical Review*, 118 (2013): 349–77.

[67] *OED*, s.v., 'sub-Atlantic'.

[68] James Delbourgo, 'Divers things: Collecting the world under water', *History of Science*, 49 (2011): 162; see ibid., 167, on 'a sub-Atlantic unity made by the deaths of Africans' in the poetry of Derek Walcott.

[69] More generally, see John Gillis and Franziska Torma, eds., *Fluid frontiers: New currents in marine environmental history* (Cambridge, 2015).

The Atlantic Ocean 103

Sub-Atlantic history remedies the striking absence of 'one area of inquiry ... from Atlantic history: the ocean itself', considered as 'a single oceanic unit, a huge bioregion differentiated by human activities at different rates in specific subregions'.[70] It can be an adjunct to infra-Atlantic history, as the examination of a particular segment of the ocean and its interactions with animals, land and humans, an approach exemplified in Jeffrey Bolster's richly illuminating history of the fishing banks of the Northwestern Atlantic.[71] Oceans may appear to be timeless, the profound and unchanging stage for what, in Braudelian terms, might appears to be the spume of events on the crest of its waves. By contrast, sub-Atlantic history reveals the history of the sea as a variable and shifting entity transformed by human activity (for example, through overfishing or by polluting) as well as by more overarching processes like climate change. Sub-Atlantic history accordingly brings Atlantic history more fully into alignment with environmental history as a whole.[72]

Sub-Atlantic history should also encompass the histories of activities beneath the ocean. The Atlantic does not have the same large migratory populations of aquatic animals on the scale of the Pacific, with its whales, fish and pinnipeds, for example; human migration and settlement in pursuit of those creatures has not shaped Atlantic history to the same degree as it has the human history of the Pacific.[73] However, humans have long hunted whales up into the high Arctic reaches of the Atlantic and demands for protein from dried fish determined sailing and settlement patterns in the North Atlantic and colonial linkages between New England and the Caribbean (for provisioning the enslaved population) in the eighteenth century.[74] Access to the products of mammals and fish thereby shaped forms of Atlantic integration for centuries, as did the winds and currents of the basin until the advent of steam. Much Atlantic history has taken for granted the ocean and its inhabitants that

---

[70] Jeffrey Bolster, 'Putting the ocean in Atlantic history: Maritime communities and marine ecology in the Northwest Atlantic, 1500–1800', *American Historical Review*, 113 (2008): 21, 24.

[71] Jeffrey Bolster, *The mortal sea: Fishing the Atlantic in the age of sail* (Cambridge, MA, 2012).

[72] For an important overview, see J. R. McNeill, 'The ecological Atlantic', in Canny and Morgan, eds., *The Oxford handbook of the Atlantic world, 1450–1850*, pp. 289–304.

[73] Jones, 'Running into whales'.

[74] See, for instance, David J. Starkey, 'Fish and fisheries in the Atlantic world', in Cofffman, Leonard and O'Reilly, eds., *The Atlantic world*, pp. 55–75; Peter E. Pope, *Fish into wine: The Newfoundland plantation in the seventeenth century* (Chapel Hill, NC, 2004); Christopher P. Magra, *The fisherman's cause: Atlantic commerce and maritime dimensions of the American Revolution* (Cambridge, 2009).

104   D. Armitage

drove these developments. Future Atlantic historians will want to look *at* the ocean, as well as across it, to discern its true historical dimensions.

Consciousness of the ocean *qua* ocean also forms part of sub-Atlantic history. Because most white inhabitants of the Atlantic world until the early nineteenth century shared a post-Roman prejudice against swimming, 'it is most certain that the *Indians*, and the Negroes excel[led] all others in [the] Arts of Swimming and Diving'. For this reason, Africans, African Americans and Native Americans were on the leading edge of submarine knowledge-gathering in the Atlantic, for example working to recover specimens for Sir Hans Sloane in Jamaica, diving for pearls or salvaging materials from wrecks.[75] They were also more likely to fall victim to ferocious fauna like sharks: 'the shark and the slave trade had gone together from the beginning'.[76] More generally, while the geography of the Atlantic was reasonably well known by the late sixteenth century, its oceanography and hydrography only began to explored in the late eighteenth century. Before then, although fishermen and sailors possessed vernacular understandings of the winds and waters of the Atlantic and its animal populations, exploration of the ocean was confined to coastal waters. The first deep-sea sounding of the Atlantic took place from HMS *Racehorse* in the Norwegian Sea in 1773 but major scientific work on the deep ocean did not take off until the late nineteenth century, with the *Challenger* expedition of 1872–76.[77] The invention of sonar allowed much deeper investigation and led, in the 1950s, to the great achievement of Marie Tharp and Bruce Heezen in mapping the mid-Atlantic ridge – a breakthrough not just for sub-Atlantic history but also for the emergent theory of plate tectonics.[78] More than half a century later, the Atlantic, like much of the rest of the world's deep oceans, still remains largely uncharted territory – an inner space awaiting scientific exploration, but also ripe for historical investigation as well.

[75] Delbourgo, 'Divers things'; Kevin Dawson, 'Enslaved swimmers and divers in the Atlantic world', *Journal of American History*, 92 (2006): 1327–55; Melchisédec Thévénot, *The art of swimming: Illustrated by proper figures with advice for bathing* (London, 1699), sig. [A11]^r, quoted, ibid., 1333.

[76] Rediker, 'History from below the water line', 286.

[77] Richard Ellis, *Deep Atlantic: Life, death, and exploration in the abyss* (New York, 1996); Helen Rozwadowski, *Fathoming the ocean: The discovery and exploration of the deep sea* (Cambridge, MA, 2005); R. M. Corfield, *The silent landscape: The scientific voyage of HMS Challenger* (Washington, DC, 2005); Michael S. Reidy, *Tides of history: Ocean science and her majesty's navy* (Chicago, IL, 2008); Reidy and Rozwadowski, 'The spaces in between: Science, ocean, empire', *Isis*, 105 (2014): 338–51.

[78] Bruce C. Heezen, Marie Tharp and Maurice Ewing, *The floors of the oceans*: I, *The North Atlantic*, The Geological Society of America, Special paper, 65 (1959); Hali Felt, *Soundings: The story of the remarkable woman who mapped the ocean floor* (New York, 2012).

The Atlantic Ocean 105

The world beneath the waves of the Atlantic may be the least developed form of Atlantic history for the moment. However, it is likely to burgeon as oceanic history becomes more deeply shaped by environmental history. The non-human history of the Atlantic – the historical study not only of its other creatures, but of its waters and winds and how they have in turn interacted with human activity – is only likely to expand, as we can already see from recent work on Caribbean hurricanes, for instance.[79] Meanwhile, the world beneath the waves – shipwrecks, drowning, the imagining of the depths – is already attracting literary attention.[80] The submarine realm may be the final frontier for Atlantic history but advances in history from below the waves in other oceanic historiographies suggest its time will soon come, especially as it combines with emerging work on the exploitation, management and governance of the oceans in other fields.[81] When it does, it will be one more means to join Atlantic history with adjacent oceanic histories. To see the promise of that conjunctive turn, we now turn finally to my third and last additional concept, *extra*-Atlantic history.

Extra-Atlantic History

Extra-Atlantic history is the history of the Atlantic told through its linkages with other oceans and seas.[82] On its eastern side, it opens into the Mediterranean through the Straits of Gibraltar; on the western shore, only the isthmus of Panama, less than 80 kilometres at its narrowest, separated it from – or linked it to – the Pacific before the digging of the Panama Canal. Like the Pacific, the Atlantic is part of the Great Ocean Conveyor Belt and its climate is subject to the variations of the El Niño/ Southern Oscillation.[83] At its southern extremes, the Atlantic joins the Pacific, the Indian Ocean and the Southern Ocean; and thanks to climate change and the retreat of the ice, the widening North-West Passage will soon link the Atlantic with the Pacific through the Arctic Ocean again. As sub-Atlantic history reveals, and as this volume repeatedly proves, the

[79] Greg Bankoff, 'Aeolian empires: The influence of winds and currents on European maritime expansion in the age of sail', *Environment and History*, 23 (2017): 163–96; Matthew Mulcahy, *Hurricanes and society in the British Greater Caribbean, 1624–1783* (Baltimore, MD, 2009); Stuart B. Schwartz, *Sea of storms: A history of hurricanes in the Greater Caribbean from Columbus to Katrina* (Princeton, NJ, 2015).

[80] For example, Steve Mentz, *At the bottom of Shakespeare's ocean* (London, 2009); Mentz, *Shipwreck modernity: Ecologies of globalization, 1550–1719* (Minneapolis, MN, 2015).

[81] John Hannigan, *The geopolitics of deep oceans* (Cambridge, 2016).

[82] Peter Coclanis has called this 'Conjuncto-Atlantic' history: Coclanis, 'Atlantic world or Atlantic/world?', *William and Mary Quarterly*, 3rd ser., 63 (2006): 739.

[83] Zalasiewicz and Williams, *Ocean worlds*, p. 89.

106   D. Armitage

oceanographic connections among the oceans ensure that any attempt to separate them will be artificial and constraining. There is a myth of oceans as well as a myth of continents.[84] The means to break such myths is by acknowledging those continuities. Oceans connect.[85] Atlantic history links to many other oceanic histories. If taken in isolation, its own history might simply appear to be arbitrarily infra-oceanic. And if the Atlantic is too large to capture some historical processes, it is certainly too small to encompass those that operated on interoceanic, transregional and global scales.

From the fifteenth century onwards, historical actors would never have mistaken the Atlantic for a discrete oceanic realm. For Columbus, what would later be known as the Atlantic was a gateway to Asia, an alternative to a Mediterranean and trans-continental route increasingly blocked by the Ottoman Empire. His successors in the sixteenth, seventeenth and eighteenth centuries who sought a North-West Passage likewise assumed the Atlantic was not bounded and land-locked. Throughout the early modern world, globe-trotting cosmopolitans – sailors, soldiers, merchants, clerics, pilgrims and the like – moved between oceanic worlds, Mediterranean, Atlantic and Indian Ocean.[86] Slave-traders and planters who carried forms of staple production and of enforced labour from the Mediterranean and the Atlantic islands across the ocean assumed – like promoters of import substitution for goods like wine, olives and silk from Richard Hakluyt to John Locke and beyond – that climate connected the Atlantic Americas with the lands around the Mediterranean in southern Europe and North Africa. With the large-scale extraction of silver from mines in Mexico and Peru, the first empire on which the sun never set – the Spanish Monarchy – became the vehicle for the first circuit of early modern globalisation with the Manila galleons as its conveyor-belt from 1571 to 1815.[87] When the Philippines were administered from the viceroyalty of New Spain, it was clear even by the late sixteenth century that the Hispanic Atlantic world extended far across the Pacific. Indeed, in

---

[84] Martin W. Lewis and Kären E. Wigen, *The myth of continents: A critique of metageography* (Berkeley, CA, 1997); Philip E. Steinberg, *The social construction of the ocean* (Cambridge, 2001).

[85] Kären E. Wigen and Jessica Harland-Jacobs, eds., '*Special issue: Oceans connect*', *Geographical Review*, 89, 2 (April 1999); Rila Mukherjee, ed., *Oceans connect: Reflections on water worlds across time and space* (Delhi, 2013).

[86] Alison Games, 'Beyond the Atlantic: English globetrotters and transoceanic connections', *William and Mary Quarterly*, 3rd ser., 63 (2006): 675–92; Games, *The web of Empire: English cosmopolitans in an age of expansion, 1560–1660* (Oxford, 2008); Emma Rothschild, *The inner life of empires: An eighteenth-century history* (Princeton, NJ, 2011).

[87] Dennis O. Flynn and Arturo Giráldez, 'Born with a "silver spoon": The origin of world trade in 1571', *Journal of World History*, 6 (1995): 201–21.

The Atlantic Ocean

the eyes of European powers well into the eighteenth century, the North American continent remained a geopolitical bridge between the Atlantic and Pacific worlds.[88]

The political economy of empires and transnational trading companies likewise shaped the linkages between the Atlantic and other oceanic regions. The English East India Company could not have functioned in the Indian Ocean without its Atlantic outpost on St Helena; its Scottish successor and competitor, the short-lived Company of Scotland Trading to Africa and the Indies of the late seventeenth century, proposed a bi-hemispheric vision of global trade centred on the Isthmus of Darién (hence its popular name, the Darien Company).[89] Until the opening of the Suez Canal, the Cape of Good Hope was the pivot between the Atlantic world and the Indian Ocean, a 'tavern of the seas' where empires joined and oceans connected: up until 1869, the two oceanic worlds could not be distinguished.[90] Commodities such as rice, indigo and breadfruit were transplanted from the Indian Ocean and Pacific Ocean into the Atlantic as staples for settlers and the enslaved and products for intercontinental commerce; the tea dumped into Boston harbour on the eve of the American Revolution came from China to North America in East India Company ships. Later demands for labour especially after emancipation, drew Chinese and Indian workers into the region, joining Atlantic migration to global circuits of mobility and transportation in the nineteenth and early twentieth centuries.[91] It was only in the twentieth century that the Atlantic was perceived to be a 'world', entire of itself, and distinct from global history more generously conceived. Now is the

---

[88] Paul W. Mapp, *The elusive west and the contest for Empire, 1713–1763* (Chapel Hill, NC, 2011).

[89] Philip J. Stern, 'British Asia and British Atlantic: Comparisons and connections', *William and Mary Quarterly*, 3rd ser., 63 (2006): 693–712; Stern, 'Politics and ideology in the early East India Company-State: The case of St. Helena, 1673–1696', *Journal of Imperial and Commonwealth History*, 35 (2007): 1–23; Douglas Watt, *The price of Scotland: Darien, union and the wealth of nations* (Edinburgh, 2006).

[90] Kerry Ward, '"Tavern of the seas"? The Cape of Good Hope as an oceanic crossroads during the seventeenth and eighteenth centuries', in Jerry H. Bentley, Renate Bridenthal and Kären E. Wigen, eds., *Seascapes: Maritime histories, littoral cultures, and transoceanic exchanges* (Honolulu, HI, 2007), pp. 137–52; Gerald Groenewald, 'Southern Africa and the Atlantic world', in Coffman, Leonard and O'Reilly, eds., *The Atlantic world*, pp. 100–16.

[91] Madhavi Kale, *Fragments of empire: Capital, slavery, and Indian indentured labor migration in the British Caribbean* (Philadelphia, PA, 1998); Adam McKeown, 'Global migration, 1846–1940', *Journal of World History*, 15 (2004): 155–89; Donna R. Gabaccia and Dirk Hoerder, eds., *Connecting seas and connected ocean rims: Indian, Atlantic, and Pacific Oceans and China Seas migrations from the 1830s to the 1930s* (Leiden, 2011); Reed Ueda, *Crosscurrents: Atlantic and Pacific migration in the making of a global America* (New York, 2016).

108   D. Armitage

time to reconnect it to that broader history, to bring Atlantic history out of almost one hundred years of solitude.

★ ★ ★ ★ ★

All three of these newer Atlantic histories, infra-Atlantic, sub-Atlantic and extra-Atlantic, expand and deepen Atlantic history, both in time – beyond its default boundaries within early modern history – and in space: beneath its surface, across its waters and into the broader reaches of the world ocean as a whole. By drawing methods and inspirations from other oceanic histories, they may help to bring Atlantic historiography into a more productive and enduring dialogue with oceanic history *tout court*. They might also provide remedies for some of the Atlantic world-weariness that has beset the field in recent years. If Atlantic history does have a future, it will be as a subset of world history viewed through the lenses of oceanic history.[92] We are all global oceanic historians now – even the avowed Atlanticists among us.

Further Reading

Among existing oceanic histories, Atlantic history is particularly well supplied with handbooks, companions and survey volumes. To experience the evolution and consolidation of the field in recent years, one could read sequentially Jack P. Greene and Philip D. Morgan, eds., *Atlantic history: A critical appraisal* (Oxford, 2009); Nicholas Canny and Philip Morgan, eds., *The Oxford handbook of the Atlantic world, 1450–1800* (Oxford, 2011); Joseph C. Miller, Vincent Brown, Jorge Cañizares-Esguerra, Laurent Dubois and Karen Ordahl Kupperman, eds., *The Princeton companion to Atlantic history* (Princeton, NJ, 2015); and D'Maris Coffman, Adrian Leonard and William O'Reilly, eds., *The Atlantic world* (Abingdon, 2015).

Important edited collections from the earlier boom in Atlantic history include David Armitage and Michael J. Braddick, eds., *The British Atlantic world, 1500–1800* (Basingstoke, 2002; 2nd edn, 2009); Horst Pietschmann, ed., *Atlantic history: History of the Atlantic system, 1580–1830* (Göttingen, 2002); Wim Klooster and Alfred Padula, eds., *The Atlantic world: Essays on slavery, migration, and imagination* (Upper Saddle

---

[92] As argued by various historians in recent years: for example, Coclanis, '*Drang Nach Osten*'; Coclanis, 'Atlantic world or Atlantic/world?'; Lauren Benton, 'The British Atlantic in global context', in Armitage and Braddick, eds., *The British Atlantic world, 1500–1800*, 2nd edn, pp. 271–89; Canny, 'Atlantic history and global history'; Cécile Vidal, 'Pour une histoire globale du monde atlantique ou des histoires connectées dans et au-delà du monde atlantique?', *Annales HSS*, 67 (2012): 391–413.

The Atlantic Ocean 109

River, NJ, 2005); Jorge Cañizares-Esguerra and Erik R. Seeman, eds., *The Atlantic in global history, 1500–2000* (Upper Saddle River, NJ, 2007); James Delbourgo and Nicholas Dew, eds., *Science and empire in the Atlantic world* (New York, 2008); Toyin Falola and Kevin D. Roberts, eds., *The Atlantic world, 1450–2000* (Bloomington, IN, 2008); and Bernard Bailyn and Patricia L. Denault, eds., *Soundings in Atlantic history: Latent structures and intellectual currents, 1500–1830* (Cambridge, MA, 2009).

In 2002, I noted that Atlantic history had not yet suffered 'death by a thousand textbooks'; the texts that soon appeared greatly helped to move the field forward, among them Douglas R. Egerton, Alison Games, Jane G. Landers, Kris Lane and Donald R. Wright, *The Atlantic world: A history, 1400–1888* (Wheeling, IL, 2007); Thomas Benjamin, *The Atlantic world: Europeans, Africans, Indians and their shared history, 1400–1900* (Cambridge, 2009); Karen Ordahl Kupperman, *The Atlantic in world history* (Oxford, 2012); John K. Thornton, *A cultural history of the Atlantic world, 1250–1820* (Cambridge, 2012); Catherine Armstrong and Laura M. Chmielewski, *The Atlantic experience: Peoples, places, ideas* (Basingstoke, 2013); and Anna Suranyi, *The Atlantic connection: A history of the Atlantic world, 1450–1900* (Abingdon, 2015).

Atlantic history is also now well supplied with economical overviews of the field and its fortunes. See especially Bernard Bailyn, *Atlantic history: Concept and contours* (Cambridge, MA, 2005); John G. Reid, 'How wide is the Atlantic Ocean? Not wide enough!', *Acadiensis*, 34 (2005): 81–87; Trevor Burnard, 'Only connect: The rise and rise (and fall?) of Atlantic history', *Historically Speaking*, 7 (2006): 19–21; Alison Games, 'Atlantic history: Definitions, challenges, and opportunities', *American Historical Review*, 111 (2006): 741–57; Jorge Cañizares-Esguerra and Benjamin Breen, 'Hybrid Atlantics: Future directions for the history of the Atlantic world', *History Compass*, 11, 8 (August 2013): 597–609; Richard J. Blakemore, 'The changing fortunes of Atlantic history', *English Historical Review*, 131 (2016): 851–68; and Michelle Craig McDonald, 'There are still Atlanticists now: A subfield reborn', *Journal of the Early Republic*, 36 (2016): 701–13.

The expanding possibilities for articulating Atlantic history with other histories, oceanic and global, can be tracked in David Eltis, 'Atlantic history in global perspective', *Itinerario*, 23 (1999): 141–61; Donna Gabaccia, 'A long Atlantic in a wider world', *Atlantic Studies*, 1 (2004): 1–27; Philip J. Stern, 'British Asia and British Atlantic: Comparisons and connections', *William and Mary Quarterly*, 3rd ser., 63 (2006): 693–712; Paul W. Mapp, 'Atlantic history from imperial, continental, and Pacific perspectives', *William and Mary Quarterly*, 3rd ser., 63 (2006): 713–24; Peter A. Coclanis, 'Atlantic

110   D. Armitage

world or Atlantic/world?', *William and Mary Quarterly*, 3rd ser., 63 (2006): 725–42; Lauren Benton, 'The British Atlantic in global context', in Armitage and Braddick, eds., *The British Atlantic world, 1500–1800* (2nd edn.), pp. 271–89; Nicholas Canny, 'Atlantic history and global history' and Peter A. Coclanis, 'Beyond Atlantic history', in Greene and Morgan, eds., *Atlantic history*, pp. 317–36, 337–56; Emma Rothschild, 'Late Atlantic history', in Canny and Morgan, eds., *The Oxford handbook of the Atlantic world, 1450–1850*, pp. 634–48; Douglas R. Egerton, 'Rethinking Atlantic historiography in a postcolonial era: The Civil War in a global perspective', *Journal of the Civil War Era*, 1 (2011): 79–95; Kate Fullagar, ed., *The Atlantic world in the Antipodes: Effects and transformations since the eighteenth century* (Newcastle upon Tyne, 2012); Cécile Vidal, 'Pour une histoire globale du monde atlantique ou des histoires connectées dans et au-delà du monde atlantique?', *Annales HSS*, 67 (2012): 391–413; Paul D'Arcy, 'The Atlantic and Pacific worlds', in Coffman, Leonard and O'Reilly, eds., *The Atlantic world*, pp. 207–26; Christoph Strobel, *The global Atlantic 1400 to 1900* (Abingdon, 2015); and John McAleer, 'Looking east: St Helena, the South Atlantic and Britain's Indian Ocean world', *Atlantic Studies*, 13 (2016): 78–98.

Part II

Seas

4 The South China Sea

Eric Tagliacozzo

The South China Sea has been one of the busiest waterways in global history; its pedigree is ancient, even as its modern geopolitical importance remains undisputed. Few oceanic spaces have generated as much conflict as a region *per se* than this particular body of water. Yet the history of connection, both via trade and via political contacts, between China and the various polities of Southeast Asia has been more steady and influential than any more recent history of geostrategic unease. Ancient tribute missions travelled across the placid waters of the South China Sea for some two thousand years, and there was a constant stream of vessels putting the worlds of East and Southeast Asia in conversation with one another, through the transmission of ideas, materiel and people. Most of this traffic moved with the natural rhythms of weather – the seasonal monsoons pushing boats north and south, each at their proscribed time of year – until steam travel began in earnest in the mid-nineteenth century. A number of scholars have described the dynamics of this system in holistic terms, giving us an idea of the mechanics of oceanic connection over several thousand kilometres of open water.[1] The present chapter aims to look at these patterns over the *longue durée*, and queries what kind of place the South China Sea was for most of its history, before the contemporary era made it a byword for international conflict.

The first part of this chapter looks at the earliest and medieval connections across this vast body of water, as medieval China, in particular (especially in the T'ang and Sung periods) became aware of the tropical polities of Southeast Asia, and started to produce records about their relative size and location at the far bottom of the South China Sea. This

---

[1] For comprehensive statements on some of these processes, see Andre Gunder Frank, *ReOrient: Global economy in the Asian age* (Berkeley, CA, 1998); Takeshi Hamashita, *China, East Asia, and the global economy: Regional and historical perspectives* (New York, 2008); and Kenneth Hall, *A history of early Southeast Asia* (Lanham, MD, 2011). These three books approach these ideas from global, East Asian and Southeast Asian viewpoints; taken together, they give us a good window on how to think about the South China Sea as a totality.

113

Map 4.1 The South China Sea

contact eventually became routinised into 'tribute-trade', a particular pattern of interaction that China forged with most of its neighbours, whether these were territorial or oceanic in nature. The second part then queries the changing dynamics of what (in a Western context) we might call the early modern South China Sea, as a larger retinue of actors started to pass through this space, and shape its destiny through their presence. Arabs, Persians, Japanese and other sea-faring peoples all contributed to this history, but it was the arrival of Europeans in a number of national guises – Portuguese, Spanish, Dutch, French and English – that would have the most impact, although this was not felt immediately, but

The South China Sea 115

rather after the initial 'contact period'. The penultimate part describes the new template that developed as a result of this quickening of contact, as more and more people scattered around the South China Sea were brought into its widening economic embrace, particularly through the trade in environmental products. The ecology of the South China Sea changed as a result of this trade, but so did political configurations. Finally, the last part looks at the new arrangements that came about as a result of political conquest and incorporation, as the lands surrounding the South China Sea began to be claimed by various actors, and spheres of influence were carved into what formerly had been a freewheeling, liquid space.

Early and Medieval Templates: The South China Sea as a Region

The dynamics of trade and contact in the South China Sea stretch far back into Antiquity. Han Chinese chronicles first mentioned an episodic trade with the *Nanyang* (Southern Ocean) countries in 140 BCE, with the *Han Shu Ti Li Chih* laying out these early contacts as being undertaken in both Chinese and foreign ships. By the Six Dynasties Period (219–580 CE) and the T'ang (618–906 CE), however, most of this traffic seems to have been from the Middle East: coastal inhabitants from Arabia and Persia who specialised in carrying low-bulk, high-value goods (such as resins and spices) from the Indian Ocean, through the conduit of Southeast Asia and the South China Sea, and up the China coasts. However, Chinese continued to travel along the maritime nexus, regardless of who owned the boats. The monk Fa Hsien (337–422 CE) was one such sojourner, outlining Buddhist communities in India and south Sumatra; he is also perhaps the first recorded Chinese to land in Borneo.[2]

Moving in the other direction, north across the South China Sea, the larger world in which Fa Hsien found himself also started sending trade missions to China at this time, with a Javanese embassy arriving for the first time in 430 CE. and the Chinese list of known area potentates expanding to six, one century later.[3] The rise of Srivijaya in the seventh century concretised these contacts into a regulated trade, with monsoon-climate forest products being pushed north in exchange

[2] Paul Wheatley, *The golden Khersonese* (Kuala Lumpur, 1961), pp. 37–41, 108. This judgment was based on Wheatley's transcription of the toponym *Ye-po-ti*, which he ascribed as Borneo.
[3] See O. W. Wolters, *Early Indonesian commerce: A Study of the origins of Srivijaya* (Ithaca, NY, 1974), p. 151.

116   E. Tagliacozzo

for items like ceramics, gongs and ceremonial flags from China.[4] The travelling Chinese scholar I-ching, who composed his 'A record of the Buddhist religion as practised in India and the Malay Archipelago 671 to 695 CE' at the very end of this century, while still in-situ in Southeast Asia, augmented China's knowledge of the region even more.[5] It was in these earliest centuries that the first proto-ethnological sketches on the traditions and customs of Southeast Asians appear in Chinese sources, showing a concerted Sinic curiosity about the strange worlds to the south.[6]

Yet it was only really in the Sung Dynasty (960–1279 CE) that Chinese maritime trade with Southeast Asia substantially grew to become an important national industry. This renaissance was due to several inter-related factors. First, commerce was institutionalised during these years by the erection of mercantile and shipping offices in a number of important ports along the east and southeastern seaboard, with Hang-zhou, Ming-zhou, Guang-zhou and Chuan-zhou serving as the major sites of activity. This allowed traders to be brought under official protection and jurisdiction, as well as under the careful tax-collecting eyes of the central government. Second, court officials were also sent abroad to renew old mercantile contacts and encourage new ones, fully outfitted with gifts befitting the generosity of emperors who expected substantial South Seas ecological tribute in return. Third, the Sung Court also started ambitious ship-building projects in the southern provinces of Fujian and Guangdong, so that ocean-going junks would be fully outfitted with the most up-to-date technologies for piloting, depth-sounding and direction-finding. The growth of this new industry enabled contact across the South China Sea to a degree that was previously unseen. And finally, kiln-building was also stimulated in these same southern coastal provinces, to provide China with an export industry to pay for the rising volume of biota that was being funnelled north from places like Southeast Asia. The revival of Taoism during the Sung (with its concomitant needs

---

[4] Grace Wong, *Chinese celadons and other related wares in Southeast Asia* (Singapore, 1977), pp. 81–91.

[5] Robert Nicholl, 'A study in the origins of Brunei', *Brunei Museum Journal*, 7, 2 (1990): 26.

[6] See, for example, early writings on the customs of the people of *P'oni* (Brunei): notices exist describing a people who were skilled at throwing chiselled knives with edges like a saw; punished murderers and thieves with amputation of the hand; sacrificed to ancestors on nights with no moon; floated ceramic bowls downriver in religious rites; and wove cloth from local plants called '*kupa*' and '*tieh*'. John Chin, *The Sarawak Chinese* (Kuala Lumpur, 1981), p. 2, has shown how all of these early descriptions were in some way or another true of the peoples of the area: the first and second of the Muslim population of Brunei, the third of the Kadayans, the fourth of the Melanaus (for water-spirit propitiation) and the fifth of many Malay and Dayak villages along the Brunei coasts.

The South China Sea   117

for ritual paraphernalia like scented wood, ivory and mother of pearl) was one reason for this gradual influx of commodities.[7] Wang Gungwu has identified another factor as the growth of a new leisure class, looking to enjoy the refinements of elite living such as rare birds, aphrodisiacs and gemstones.[8] Nanyang ecological products were also becoming more and more integrated into the Chinese pharmacopoeia, with area products like bezoar, rhino horns, tortoiseshell and camphor being used as antipyretics, analgesics, diuretics and tonics respectively.[9] The Superintendent of Trade in Ch'uan-zhou, Chau Ju Kua, wrote in his *Chu Fan Chi* (1225 CE) that many of these commodities (such as sandalwood and *gaharu* wood) were sent directly from the Nanyang.[10] Commerce grew so fast that at the start of the dynasty that one-fiftieth of Chinese income derived from these exchanges; by the late Sung, however, the taxes on South Seas commodities alone constituted a tenth of all funds in the hands of the Imperial administration.[11]

Merchants from China sailing across the South China Sea to Southeast Asia hoping to barter for these commodities stimulated a maritime 'Golden Age' for overseas Chinese trade. The killing of much of the Muslim population of Canton in 878 toward the end of the T'ang had already discouraged long-distance Arab shipping in the area, but technological innovations in junk construction simultaneously catapulted Chinese vessels into the forefront of the ocean-going trade. By the middle of the Sung junks could carry up to 600 tons of cargo and 300 merchants and crew in voyages down to Southeast Asia: this in ships over 100 feet long, with beams and depths running thirty feet at the widest points.[12] As these journeys became more and more frequent, captains

---

[7] Aurora Roxas-Lim, *The evidence of ceramics as an aid in understanding the pattern of trade in the Philippines and Southeast Asia* (Bangkok, 1987).

[8] Wang Gungwu, *The Nanhai trade: Early Chinese trade in the South China Sea* (Singapore, 2003), p. 57.

[9] Daniel Reid, *Chinese herbal medicine* (Hong Kong, 1987), pp. 96–97, 118, 184.

[10] Robert Nicholl, 'An age of vicissitude in Brunei 1225–1425', *Brunei Museum Journal*, 7, 1 (1990): 8.

[11] Roxas-Lim, *The evidence of ceramics*, p. 28.

[12] K. K. Kwan and Jean Martin, 'Canton, Pulao Tioman, and Southeast Asian maritime trade', in [Southeast Asian Ceramic Society, West Malaysia chapter], *A ceramic legacy of Asia's maritime trade: Song Dynasty Guangdong wares and other 11th to 19th century trade ceramics found on Tioman Island, Malaysia* (Kuala Lumpur, 1985), p. 52. For other good accounts of the nautical dimension to the Nanyang trade, see Pierre Yves Manguin, 'The Southeast Asian ship: An historical approach', *Journal of Southeast Asian Studies*, 2 (1980): 266–76; Pierre Yves Manguin, 'Relationship and cross-influence between Southeast Asian and Chinese ship-building tradition', *IAHA Conference*, Manila, 21–25 November 1983; Pierre Yves Manguin, 'Sailing instructions for Southeast Asian seas, 15–17 centuries', *SPAFA Workshop*, Cisarua, West Java, 1984; also J. V. G. Mills, 'Chinese navigators in Insulinde around A.D. 1500', *Archipel*, 18 (1979): 69–83; and Ma Huan, *Ying-yai Shenglan: The overall survey of the ocean's shores*, trans. Feng Ch'eng-Chün (Cambridge, 1970).

118   E. Tagliacozzo

acquired specialised knowledge: the distances between various cities, the ebb and flow of local tides, storm and typhoon frequencies, and the location of dangerous shoals and reefs. There were at least two main routes along the *Jiao-Guang* ('Eastern Sea Route') that could take a trading junk to Southeast Asia, in search of the products of the region.[13] Both left the Middle Kingdom with the northeastern monsoon in winter, with the first moving south along the coasts of the Southeast Asian mainland and returning up through Borneo, the Philippines and eventually Taiwan.[14] Another alternative, which Mills unearthed from the *Wu-pei-chih* charts, followed a direct route across the South China Sea in the opposite direction, stopping at Luzon, Mindoro, the Visayas and Sulu before snaking down to the northern parts of Borneo.[15] In either case, junks seemed to rely less on charts than on *portolans* or rutters (sailing directions), with specimens published during the fourteenth and fifteenth centuries (such as the 1304 *Nan hai Chih* and Ma Huan's *Ying-yai Sheng lan*) providing very detailed references.[16]

Archaeological work completed along (for example) the Borneo coasts in the last half-century has drawn a picture for us of how these earliest contacts with China helped organise societies up and down the coasts of the South China Sea. A significant portion of the evidence is metallurgical; along with Brunei, the Sarawak Delta seems to have been one of the initial regions involved in the international commercial web, based on especially T'ang and Sung Dynasty artefacts unearthed in the region. Decades ago, Tom Harrisson and the Sarawak museum excavators he led found pottery, crucibles and graveyards and Chinese cash-string coins in the Sungei Ja'ong and Bongkisam sites, as well as small gold figurines compatible with schools of Tantric Buddhism.[17] Extant ceramics, especially, placed the inter-connected delta sites within a dateable time sequence, starting in the early eighth century and then disappearing away from the trade orbit around the time of the fall of the Mongol Dynasty in China (1368 CE). Based on this evidence (or a lack of it after this

---

[13] Grace Wong, 'An account of the maritime trade routes between Southeast Asia and China', in *Studies on Ceramics* (Jakarta, 1978), p. 201.

[14] See Victor Purcell, *The Chinese in Southeast Asia* (London, 1965), p. 18.

[15] J. V. G. Mills, 'Malaya and the *Wu-pei-chih* charts', *Journal of the Malay Branch of the Royal Asiatic Society* 15 (1973): 19; see also Roderich Ptak, 'Notes on the word "Shanhu" and Chinese coral imports from maritime Asia, 1250–1600', *Archipel*, 39 (1990): 65–80.

[16] J. V. G. Mills, 'Arab and Chinese navigators in Malaysian waters', *Journal of the Malay Branch of the Royal Asiatic Society*, 47 (1974): 42–51; also Carrie Brown, 'The Eastern Ocean in the *Yung-lo Ta Tien*', *Brunei Museum Journal*, 4 (1978): 46–58.

[17] See Tom Harrisson, 'Recent archaeological discoveries in East Malaysia and Brunei', *Journal of the Malay Branch of the Royal Asiatic Society*, 40 (1967): 141.

The South China Sea 119

date), scholars hypothesised the existence of a 'Ming Gap' for Southeast Asia's involvement with the China Trade, across the South China Sea. They pointed to extensive amounts of Ming and Ch'ing wares that were coming to light along the coasts, around the old capital (Kota Batu) at the same time.[18] But further investigations since these digs in the 1960s have somewhat diluted the 'Ming Gap' thesis, as post-Sung export wares have been unearthed in the Delta, although still in smaller numbers than previous years.[19] The supposition about the rhythms of Sino/Southeast Asian coastal settlement still largely stands in principle, however: the earliest sites in coastal Borneo, for example, were located in Brunei as well as in the Delta, with a later shift in importance to Sarawak, before a final recapturing of dominance by Brunei at the start of the Ming Dynasty.

Situated right on the main trade routes of the South China Sea, Brunei and its environs seem to have held a symbolic importance to the Chinese from an early date. *P'oni* (the Chinese transcription of the city/region) is mentioned in court chronicles in 517 CE (possibly the earliest definitive Chinese record of Borneo, as Fa Hsien's exact itinerary is still unclear). Subsequent notices in 522, 616, 630 and 690 CE show us the growth of Chinese contacts with this polity – whatever their exact nature may have been – over the centuries.[20] By 977 CE two Muslim envoys appeared in the Chinese court as ambassadors of the 'King of Brunei', which led to the first *direct* contact between the kingdoms as chronicled by the Sung.[21] This Muslim angle to Sino/Southeast Asian interactions continued up until the rise of the Mongols in the later thirteenth century, with likely the oldest Chinese inscription in all Southeast Asia unearthed in a Chinese merchant's tomb outside of Brunei city ('Here lies *P'u*' ([apparently 'Abu', an Islamicised Chinese from Chuan-zhou in Fujian]). The date on the grave stele was 1264 CE.[22]

---

[18] Tom Harrisson, 'A fine wine pot (For Brunei)', *Sarawak Museum Journal*, 9, n.s., 13–14 (Jan.–Dec. 1959): 132; and Harrisson, 'The Borneo finds', *Asian Perspectives*, 5 (1961): 253.

[19] See for example Lucas Chin, 'Trade pottery discovered in Sarawak from 1948 to 1976', *Sarawak Museum Journal*, 46 (1977): 25; and John Guy, *Oriental trade ceramics in South-East Asia, ninth to sixteenth centuries* (Singapore, 1986), p. 35. A Fujian export shard with the inscription 'Muhammad is the Prophet' in Arabic has also recently been found here; destined for Muslim markets further west, it is extremely rare. See Pengiran Karim Pengiran Osman, 'Notes on a blue-and-white sherd (with Arabic inscription) found at Kota Batu archaeological site', *Brunei Museum Journal*, 7 (1991): 10–21.

[20] John Chin, *The Sarawak Chinese* (Kuala Lumpur, 1981), p. 2. Yet see the questioning of the temporal continuity of P'oni in J. W. Christie, 'On Po-ni: The Santubong sites of Sarawak', *Sarawak Museum Journal*, 35 (1984–85): 80.

[21] Grace Wong, 'An account of the maritime trade routes between Southeast Asia and China', in *Studies on Ceramics* (Jakarta, 1978), p. 56.

[22] Wolfgange Franke and Ch'en T'ien-fan, 'A Chinese tomb inscription of A.D. 1264 recently discovered in Brunei', *Brunei Museum Journal*, 3 (1973): 91–96.

120   E. Tagliacozzo

The founding Ming Emperor commissioned a special piece to be written about the nature of tribute and trade relations with Southeast Asia, this separate from the regular notices printed in the *Ming-shih*. By this time parts of the South China Sea were already becoming important as ecological-collecting depots, and therefore had grown important to the Chinese court.[23] Fei Hsian, who journeyed on the Admiral Zheng He's ships to Southeast Asia, described good relations in his *Hsing Cha Sheng Lan*, while the early fifteenth century chronicler Wang Ta-yuan (in his *Tao i chih lio*) also was impressed with the wealth of trade, singling out tortoiseshell, gold dust and aromatic wood exports.[24] A last evidence of this high regard stands in a grave complex just skirting of Nanjing, where the chief of a Southeast Asian delegation was interred in 1408 CE, after contracting an illness in such an unaccustomed northern climate. The Chinese Emperor closed the court for three days, assigning some of the ambassador's relatives to remain and to perform the yearly ritual sacrifices.[25] When further embassies arrived in the early 1400s, heralding the union of area potentates in the east and south of the South China Sea, the region was already vital to the Chinese court. The extended Sulu basin was known to the Chinese as one of the most vital regions in the Nanyang, a market-theatre for all sorts of products native to this arena.[26]

Changing Patterns: The Early Modern South China Sea

A new stimulus began slowly to change South China Sea trading and political contacts in the sixteenth century, one that signalled a shift in earlier commercial relationships and the beginning of new systems befitting a complicated, emerging world. European ships began to touch down in both China and Southeast Asia, first only a few Portuguese *carracks* and *caravels*, but later the traders, explorers and representatives of a range

---

[23] See Carrie Brown, 'An early account of Brunei by Sung Lien', *Brunei Museum Journal*, 2 (1972): 219.

[24] Sin Fong Han, 'A study of the occupational patterns and social interaction of overseas Chinese in Sabah, Malaysia' (PhD diss., University of Michigan, 1971), p. 37; W. W. Rockhill, 'Notes on the relations and trade of China with the Eastern Archipelago and the coasts of the Indian Ocean during the Fourteenth Century', *T'oung Pao*, 16 (1915): 266.

[25] Robert Nicholl, 'The tomb of Maharaja Karna of Brunei at Nanking', *Brunei Museum Journal*, 5 (1984): 35.

[26] Wang Gungwu, 'China and Southeast Asia: 1402–24', in Jerome Ch'en and Nicholas Tarling, eds., *Studies in the social history of China and Southeast Asia* (Cambridge, 1970), pp. 375–402. See also Omar Matussin and Dato P. M. Sharaffuddin, 'Distributions of Chinese and Siamese ceramics in Brunei', *Brunei Museum Journal*, 4 (1978): 59–60.

The South China Sea 121

of maritime polities (England, Spain and Holland), one after another.[27] Coercive policies were eventually put forward by all of these countries, as each attempted to nudge commerce to benefit their own distant exchequers. A Ming dynasty memorial from 1530 CE recounted the evolving state of affairs as being dangerous; already dark clouds were seen to be on the horizon.[28] The anxious tone of the memorial was certainly justified, as numerous Southeast Asian polities that had earlier shipped tribute to China now dealt with the more aggressive trade impetuses of various European powers. This was certainly a gradual shift. But the general violence and predation that spread along the maritime pathways of the South China Sea eventually changed the nature of the sea routes. In the case of Southeast Asia, and the polities that had traditionally participated in this trade, these changes were to be significant over the longer term and encompassed the ways in which many regional peoples led their everyday lives.

It has already been shown that Southeast Asia was known to the medieval Chinese through a series of essays and court records, which tabulated the region's growth in the international maritime orbit of the Sung and Yuan era. Inscribed in the form of records of tribute, these notices don't tell us much about the character of regional cities, and even less about urbanisation in the South China Sea as a result of the trade with China.[29] Via Chau Ju Kua, the aforementioned superintendent of trade in Chuan-zhou, we certainly do know that the walls of some Southeast Asian ports were built of timber, and that the populations could be relatively large. These things imply the presence of local logging, not just for urban wall construction but also for building of houses.[30] For this to have happened on a scale for Chinese chroniclers to notice, and to specifically comment on these issues, the scope of these urbanising activities must have been sizable, with concomitant effects such as deforestation. Still other Chinese sources stated that area kings wore Chinese silks on formal occasions, and that there had been miscegenation going on with Chinese traders for quite a long time.[31] All of these descriptions give us

---

[27] See John E. Wills, Jr., ed., *China and maritime Europe, 1500–1800: Trade, settlement, diplomacy and missions* (Cambridge, 2011).

[28] Victor Purcell, *The Chinese in Southeast Asia* (London, 1965), p. 22.

[29] For four theoretical discussions on the nature and dimensions of Southeast Asian port cities at the dawn of European contact, see Richard O'Connor, 'A theory of Indigenous Southeast Asian urbanism', Research Notes and Discussions Paper, Singapore, Institute of Southeast Asian Studies, 1983, and Peter Reeves, Frank Broeze, and Anthony Reid, all in Frank Broeze, ed., *Brides of the sea: Port cities of Asia from the 16th–20th centuries* (Kensington, NSW, 1989).

[30] Frederick Hirth and W. W. Rockhill, transl., *Chau Ju Kua: His work on the Chinese and Arab trade in the 12th and 13th Centuries* (Taipei, 1967 reprint of 1911 original), p. 63.

[31] Robert Nicholl, 'A study in the origins of Brunei', *Brunei Museum Journal*, 7 (1989): 7, and Nan Sin Feng, *The Chinese in Sabah, East Malaysia* (Taipei, 1975), p. 29.

122   E. Tagliacozzo

useful clues to longer-term processes that were happening in the region, and which seem to be have been deemed important enough to put into documents by Chinese observers from afar.

However, it was only with the arrival of Western observers in the early 1600s that more solid descriptions were left on how the trade of the South China Sea spurred the gradual urbanisation of cities in the region. The Venetian chronicler Antonio Pigafetta, who visited Southeast Asia in the early 1520s after Magellan's death in the Philippines, left an eye-witness account of growing ports, complete with the trappings of trans-regional trade. Pigafetta's ship was sometimes met by indigenous vessels whose sides were decorated with gold, which then led them past brick walls (implying the existence of kilns) into palaces defended by cannon.[32] Cushions and carpets were laid down for their comfort, while silk trappings and Chinese banners were common, as well as locally mined gold and precious stones. Palace windows revealed phalanxes of guardsmen, all equipped with 'cutlasses and shields', and elephants came marching into audience halls, casting Chinese ceramics as presents.[33] Currency from China was sometimes used as regional tender too, with the measures and weights of the Middle Kingdom sometimes regulating transactions in the markets of area ports.[34]

A half-century later, with the Spanish now embedded in several parts of the South China Sea, an anonymous Spanish account gives us further information – strategic here – on the dynamics of urban sultanates.[35] Because of widening trade radials, some cities were now casting their own cannon-shot of heavy cast iron, in fact importing the raw materials from offshore islands where the ores occurred plentifully, and naturally. Harpoons, pikes and lances were also being forged, allowing local metallurgical industries to keep active, while gunpowder was imported from Chinese merchants, usually via Siam. Spanish ships would attack, occupy and ultimately surrender a number of South China Sea ports all in the next few years, but what is vital for our purposes is to acknowledge the accumulation in local cities of cutting-edge technology and material wealth, all through regional contacts in the trade with China. Metallurgy, mining and the acquisition of precious metals were all happening on an increasingly large scale, as

---

[32] See the exegesis provided in Peter Bellwood and Matussin bin Omar, 'Trade patterns and political development in Brunei and adjacent areas AD 700–1500', *Brunei Museum Journal*, 4 (1980): 5–180.

[33] See John Carroll, 'Aganduru Moriz' account of the Magellan expedition at Brunei (1521)', *Brunei Museum Journal*, 6 (1985): 54.

[34] John Chin, *The Sarawak Chinese* (Kuala Lumpur, 1981), p. 7.

[35] See J. S. Carroll, 'Franscisco de Sande's invasion of Brunei 1578: An anonymous Spanish account', *Brunei Museum Journal*, 6 (1986): 47–71.

The South China Sea   123

Southeast Asian ports used their local environment both for construction, and for defensive purposes.

Sinic visitors and subjects were a vital part of the population balance of South China Sea ports, all to the south of China. In late sixteenth- and early seventeenth-century chronicles, they appear as pilots, captains, pepper merchants and ambassadors, as well as debtors and slaves on the run.[36] And by the late eighteenth century, a large commerce with 'sister emporia' to the north like Macao was developing, with scores of ships plying between the two regions to conduct the lucrative trade in Southeast Asia's natural products.[37] William Millburn, an English East India Company scribe, noted a few decades later (in 1813) that commerce with China was still vital, though the same English writer chronicled that although Spanish dollars were now the main currency of some area ports, Chinese copper cash was still accepted.[38] The age-old imports of trade continued to come down from the coasts of China (iron bars, glassware, gongs and coarse cutlery), all paying for the biota that Southeast Asian cities collected in her ports. In fact, as shipping, warehousing, packing and storage centres, numerous South China Sea entrepôts had sprouted up along many of the region's rivers, all at least partly in response to Chinese trade.[39] Unusual (and possibly even unnecessary) before the trade with China became ubiquitous, these complexes would eventually develop into multi-functional, complex exchange-centres geared towards the amalgamation of South China Sea products.

Into Modernity: New Political, Ecological and Economic Systems

The Chinese clearly looked south at the South China Sea and saw ungoverned, maritime space. The idea that travelling beyond the pale of civilisation led to dangerous realms was commonplace; geographies beyond

---

[36] See Don Juan de Arce's letter of 21 March 1579, in Blair, ed., *The Philippine islands*, IV, p. 195; Admiral Olivier van Noort's commentary of 26 December 1600 in Pieter de Hondt, ed., *Historische beschryving der reizen of nieuwe en volkoome verzameling van de aller waardigste en zeldsaamste zee en landtogten*, 21 vols. (The Hague, 1747–67), XVII, p. 33; the same admiral's description over the course of the new year, 1601, in *Nederlandsche reizen: tot bevordering van den koophandel na de meest afgelegene gewesten des aardkloots*, 14 vols. (Amsterdam, 1784), II, p. 240; and the letter of Sultan Hassan of Brunei to Spanish Governor Tello, 27 July 1599, in Blair, ed., *The Philippine islands*, XI, p. 120.

[37] Pierre Yves Manguin, 'Brunei trade with Macao at the turn of the 19th Century', *Brunei Museum Journal*, 6 (1987): 17.

[38] See William Millburn, *Oriental commerce: Containing a geographical description of the principal places in the East Indies, China, and Japan, with their produce, manufactures, and trade*, 2 vols. (London, 1813).

[39] For two excellent regional overviews, see Anthony Reid, *Southeast Asia in the age of commerce*, 2 vols. (New Haven, CT, 1988–93); Victor Lieberman, *Strange parallels: Southeast Asia in global context, 800–1830*, 2 vols. (Cambridge, 2003–9).

124   E. Tagliacozzo

the orbit of Chinese administration were often described as being wild, and completely untamed. In his moving exegesis on T'ang exotics, *The vermilion bird* (1967), Edward Schafer showed how the T'ang described Vietnam, for example, as a place of screaming monkeys and miasmic mists – covered by impenetrable and unhealthy jungle.[40] This notion of exile is one that comes up again and again in Chinese descriptions of the southern frontier, from descriptions of parts of Yunnan in the southwest (bordering Siam and Burma) to other borders during the Ch'ing (1644–1911 CE). Even spaces as comparatively 'familiar' as maritime Taiwan were deemed to be frontiers, sites where Ming rebels like Koxinga, the Spanish, the Dutch and assorted other 'bandits' and 'pirates' (some of them Japanese, such as the famous *wako* of the sixteenth century) held sway. Chinese pioneering families who visited Taiwan often began as adventurers, but eventually became elites over generations in their adopted homes, still out on the polity's distant extremities.[41] A number of these patterns and their political and cultural legacies along China's South China Sea borders are crucial even now, both vis-à-vis Taiwan on China's southeastern coasts, as well as in other places.[42]

The South China Sea may have been deemed beyond the pale of what the Chinese considered 'civilisation', but there was clearly bounty there to be exploited. This ecological history of this particular sea, which brought it into a complex union with an increasingly globalised modernity, is still being pieced together by historians.[43] One of the most important classes of goods were sea-products. Regional sea peoples such as the Bajau, for example (scattered throughout much of Southeast Asia), had traditionally devoted most of their labour in food collection for their own needs, gathering crustaceans, fish and turtle eggs from the sea. Yet as the importance of trade with China grew in the South China Sea over the eighteenth century, they often began to be pressed into unwilling

[40] Edward Schafer, *The vermilion bird: T'ang images of the south* (Berkeley, CA, 1967).
[41] Burton Watson, trans., *The Columbia book of Chinese poetry: From early times to the thirteenth century* (New York: 1984).
[42] C. Patterson Giersch, *Asian borderlands: the transformation of Qing China's frontier* (Cambridge, MA, 2006); Joanna Waley-Cohen, *Exile in Mid-Qing China: Banishment to Xinjiang, 1758–1820* (New Haven, CT, 1991); Peter Perdue, *China marches west: the Qing conquest of central Eurasia* (Cambridge, 2005); Shih-Shan Henry Tsai, *Maritime Taiwan: Historical encounters with the east and the west* (Armonk, NY, 2009), ch. 2; Johanna Menzel Meskill, *A Chinese pioneer family: the lins of Wu-feng, Taiwan, 1729–1895* (Princeton, NJ, 1979).
[43] The most important history here is James Francis Warren's *The Sulu zone, 1768–1898: The dynamics of external trade, slavery, and ethnicity in the transformation of a Southeast Asian maritime state* (Singapore, 1981), but Heather Sutherland's work, most of it in article form, has also been very important; for example, Sutherland, 'Trepang and Wangkang: The China trade of eighteenth century Makassar, 1720s–1840s', *Bijdragen tot de Taal-, Land- en Volkenkunde*, 156 (2000): 451–72.

The South China Sea

service by more martial peoples. The Taosug of the southern Philippines (and other groups) used them to provide different sorts of marine resources: mother-of-pearl, tortoise shells, rattan and *trepang*, all of which the Chinese valued highly. Tortoise- and turtle-shell of several species – leatherback (*Dermochelys coriacea*), green (*Chelonia mydas*) and hawksbill (*Eretmochelys imbricata*) – had been traded up to China from Southeast Asia's waters for centuries already. By the time of Dalrymple's and Forrest's visits in the late eighteenth century (two prominent European travellers/observers), coastal peoples had made these commodities a vital mainstay of the trade.[44]

Mother-of-pearl exports were also very profitable by the beginning of the nineteenth century,[45] the finest specimens being extracted from the same coral beds – often thirty miles wide and ringing whole islets – from where pearls were collected.[46] Rattan, too, was gathered for bulk-shipment to South China, with early commentators noting that Southeast Asian bays were overgrown with the plants, the supply of which would grow back even if hundreds of tons were extracted annually for export.[47] The pliable fibres of the plant were very cheap, as a single piece of cotton trade-cloth could fetch hundreds of strands of rattan in the late nineteenth century.[48] The Bajau even became skilled manufacturers of salt, some of which was procured by the solar evaporation of brine, other portions coming from the bleaching of *nipa* palm ashes. What was not utilised locally, was traded inland for other China export products.[49]

---

[44] See Jennifer Elkin, 'Observations of marine animals in the coastal waters of Western Brunei Darussalam', *Brunei Museum Journal*, 7 (1992): 74–80; Roderich Ptak, 'China and the trade in tortoise-shell' in Roderich Ptak, ed., *China's seaborne trade with South and Southeast Asia* (Abingdon, 1999); 'Doctor de Sande's report on the visit of the Portuguese to Brunei, August 1578', in Emma Blair, ed., *The Philippine islands*, 55 vols. (Cleveland, OH, 1903–9), IV, p. 221; Alexander Dalrymple, *A plan for extending the commerce of this kingdom, and of the East-India-company* (London, 1769), pp. 76–82; Thomas Forrest, *A voyage to New Guinea, and the Moluccas, from Balambangan: Including an account of Magindano, Sooloo, and other islands; and illustrated with thirty copperplates* (London, 1779), p. 405.

[45] Milburn, *Oriental commerce*, II, p. 513.

[46] Alexander Dalrymple, 'An account of some nautical curiosities at Sooloo', in Dalrymple, *An historical collection of several voyages and discoveries in the South Pacific Ocean*, 2 vols. (London, 1770), I, pp. 1–14.

[47] Alexander Dalrymple, *Oriental repertory*, 2 vols. (London, 1793–1808), II, p. 534; and Forrest, *A voyage to New Guinea*, p. 88.

[48] Spenser St John, *Life in the forests of the Far East*, 2 vols. (London, 1862), I, p. 403.

[49] David E. Sopher, *The sea nomads: A study based on the literature of the maritime boat people of Southeast Asia* (Singapore, 1965), p. 138; for a good overview on salt as a commodity in this trade, see Bernard Sellato, 'Salt in Borneo', in Pierre le Roux and Jaques Ivanoff, eds., *Le sel de la vie en Asia du Sud-Est* (Bangkok, 1993), pp. 263–84. Coral was also exported to China from the Bornean coastal strand; see Ptak, 'Notes on the word "Shanhu" and Chinese coral imports from maritime Asia'.

126   E. Tagliacozzo

In these ways local Bajau economies across a decent-sized swathe of the South China Sea was re-fashioned along entirely new lines, all in the interests of the money to be made from the rising marine goods commerce to the Middle Kingdom.[50]

Still another important product exported out of Southeast Asia and up across the South China Sea to Canton was pearls. Garnered from the mollusc *Melegrina margarita*, the placuna was pounded into powder for use in Chinese pharmacopeias, while larger and finer specimens were traded, and eventually soldered into jewellery.[51] Writings about the quality and value of Southeast Asian pearls extend all the way back in European records to Tomé Pires' time, when the Portuguese itinerant sailor described pearls being traded as 'beads' to Chinese sellers in 1515.[52] Only a few years later, Southeast Asian pearls were disparaged as being of inferior quality, though Pigafetta said that they were still pricey enough to use as ransom-items to obtain the freedom of political hostages.[53] These exports of Southeast Asian waters largely kept their reputation over the next several hundred years, however, with Chinese texts like the *Huang Ching Zhi Gong Tu* ('Illustrations of the tributaries of the Ch'ing Empire') outlining them as among the most vital products of the region.[54] The Chinese court understood that these items were vital to the littoral communities on Southeast Asia's coasts; Western observers also understood this, and eventually figured out ways to get their own share of this lucrative trade.[55]

However, no single product illustrates the mechanics of marine goods-extraction across the South China Sea – and the politics that attended this extraction – better than *trepang* (edible sea-cucumber), which found a useful habitat for itself in the placid waters off much of insular Southeast Asia. The region's sea peoples never took to eating these animals, even in times of significant hardship, yet by the nineteenth century Taosug *datus* (princes) had organised through regional slaving expeditions an

---

[50] See Clifford Sather's fine book, *The Bajau Laut: Adaptation, history, and fate in a maritime fishing society of South-Eastern Sabah* (Kuala Lumpur, 1997).

[51] Warren, *The Sulu zone*, p. 80.

[52] Tomé Pires, *The Suma Oriental of Tomé Pires, an account of the East, from the Red Sea to Japan, written in Malacca and India in 1512–1515, and The book of Francisco Rodrigues, rutter of a voyage in the Red Sea, nautical rules, almanack and maps, written and drawn in the East before 1515*, trans. Armando Cortesão (London, 1944), p. 123.

[53] Ronald Bishop Smith, *George Alvares, the first Portuguese to sail to China* (Lisbon, 1972), p. 12; Antonio Pigafetta, 'The first voyage round the world', and 'De Moluccis Insulis', in Blair, ed., *The Philippine islands*, XXXIII, p. 211; I, p. 328.

[54] Geoffrey Wade, 'Borneo-related illustrations in a Chinese work', *Brunei Museum Journal*, 6 (1987): 1–3.

[55] Wade, 'Borneo-related illustrations', p. 3; Fray Casimiro Diaz in Blair, ed., *The Philippine islands*, XLII, p. 185; Dalrymple, *A plan for extending*, pp. 76–82.

The South China Sea 127

estimated 20,000 sea-peoples per year for their collection, often in fleets of scores of boats.[56] More than five-dozen species of these *holothurians* were local to Southeast Asian waters, and these were graded into qualities of first, second and third class, depending on size, colour and the difficulty of procurement.[57] China preferred the whitish-grey trepang, which were normally found on coral bottoms and at considerable depths. Dark-grey or black varieties were less valued but were eaten nonetheless. Southeast Asians often went to much trouble to get these animals, with Aboriginal Australians still remembering the sea-cucumber voyages of Makassar *prahus* to the coasts,[58] and Bajau mythology eulogising '*trepang* heroes' who outwitted sharks and giant stingrays.[59] The Taosug even built a series of freshwater wells on isolated islands as an encouragement for 'Free Bajaus' to search for holothurians offshore.[60] New technologies were also brought to the coasts of various parts of Southeast Asia to better facilitate the gathering process, altering further local modes of livelihood.[61] Warren has estimated that by the 1830s almost 70,000 people – most of them slaves and other appropriated 'sea-peoples' – were involved in marine products procurement, most of them under the auspices of the Sultan of Sulu.[62] Almost all of the ocean produce they collected was eventually heading north to the coasts of Ch'ing China, across the placid waters of the South China Sea.

This confluence between the ecological and the political is important because it shows how mastery of the sea became equated with entrance into the wealth of the modern world system, which was expanding exponentially at this time, as Kenneth Pomeranz and others have shown.[63]

---

[56] Warren, *The Sulu zone*, p. 70.

[57] Kolff described the sorting, preparation, and drying process of *trepang* in Borneo waters in the 1830s and 40s; see D. H. Kolff, *Voyages of the Dutch brig of war Dourga*, trans. George Windsor Earl (London, 1840), pp. 172–75; see also Frederick Wernstedt and J. E. Spencer, *The Philippine island world: A physical, cultural, and regional geography* (Berkeley, CA, 1967), p. 595.

[58] See Leonard Andaya, 'The Bugis Makassar diasporas', *Journal of the Malay Branch of the Royal Asiatic Society*, 68 (1995): 119–38; also see the complex ethno-historical study of Gene Ammarell, *Bugis navigation* (New Haven, CT, 1999).

[59] Dalrymple, 'An account of some nautical curiosities at Sooloo', in Dalrymple, *Historical collection of several voyages and discoveries in the South Pacific Ocean*, I, p. 12.

[60] Forrest, *A voyage to New Guinea*, pp. 372–74; and Dalrymple, *Oriental repertory*, II, p. 530.

[61] Sopher, *The sea nomads*, pp. 246–47.

[62] Warren, *The Sulu zone*, p. 73; for cargo manifests heading north to Macao around this time which include *trepang*, see Pierre Yves Manguin, 'Brunei trade with Macao at the turn of the 19th century', *Brunei Museum Journal*, 6 (1987): 18. For a new overview of these patterns, see Jennifer Gaynor, *Intertidal history in island Southeast Asia: Submerged genealogy and the legacy of coastal capture* (Ithaca, NY, 2016).

[63] Kenneth Pomeranz, *The great divergence: China, Europe, and the making of the modern world economy* (Princeton, NJ, 2001).

128   E. Tagliacozzo

The littoral strand of southern China – Guangdong and Fujian provinces in particular – were becoming the site of an enormously complex exchange, with China being pried open to global commerce by an increasingly voracious Western world. The 'Canton system', as the broad outlines of the process of trade were called, functioned for decades, but became more and more unequal in nature until the Opium Wars of 1839 to 1842 permanently shifted the balance toward exploitation. Over the rest of the nineteenth century and into the twentieth, South China was gradually turned into an economic cash-cow for Western trade interests, who flooded the market with opium to pay for the very great variety of goods that were in demand back in Europe and the Americas.[64] The Spanish conquest of the southern Philippines in the last third of the nineteenth century put an end to the Sulu Sultanate as the main conveyor belt for some of this intra-Asian commerce.[65] In coastal Vietnam, too, a period of great instability ensued in the early nineteenth century, as the Tay-Son rebellion (1771–1802) displaced old elites, and the maritime sea-scape between that country and China was thrown into chaos for two decades. The resulting Nguyen Dynasty which took over the Vietnamese court in 1802 was Confucian, and largely anti-trade, but was eventually humbled later in the century by the French, who landed in the Mekong delta region in 1859, and in a series of steps between 1862 and the late 1880s proceeded to take over the entire country. The South China Sea coasts of Cambodia followed as a protectorate around that same time.[66]

Further to the south, in the bottom extremities of the South China Sea, the dynamics of incorporation were eventually similar. The British began with a few small bases, including the tiny island of Balambangan in 1763, and gradually carved out more of a trading presence in the region, especially with the acquisition of Singapore in 1819. The so-called 'Straits Settlements' proved not to be enough to slake the thirst for influence in this arena, however, with the pull of the China market too strong, and Southeast Asia too tempting to provide an entrance to it from the comparative safety of the lower South China Sea. Portions of the Malay Peninsula and Borneo followed in terms of British incorporation,

---

[64] See Paul van Dyke, *The Canton trade: Life and enterprise on the China coast, 1700–1845* (Hong Kong, 2007); and van Dyke, *Merchants of Canton and Macao: Success and failure in eighteenth century Chinese trade* (Hong Kong, 2016).

[65] Laura Lee Junker, *Raiding, trading, and feasting: The political economy of Philippine chiefdoms* (Honolulu, HI, 1999); also Oona Paredes, *A mountain of difference: The Lumad in early colonial Mindanao* (Ithaca, NY, 2013).

[66] Li Tana, *Nguyen Cochinchina: Southern Vietnam in the seventeenth and eighteenth centuries* (Ithaca, NY, 1998); Nola Cooke, Li Tana and James Anderson, *The Tongking gulf through history* (Philadelphia, PA, 2011); Dian Murray, *Pirates of the south China coast, 1790–1810* (Palo Alto, CA, 1987).

The South China Sea 129

sometimes indirectly and at other times more directly, with the Pangkor Engagement signalling a real 'forward policy' in 1874.[67] Only a year earlier the Dutch made their own intentions clear at the very bottom of the South China Sea, as centuries-old settlements were eventually expanded from 1873 onward with the start of the Aceh War to include most of the rest of what we now term to be 'Indonesia'.[68] These processes were political and were accomplished through treaties, but they were also very much technological feats, marrying the new technologies of hydrography, surveillance and military hardware with epidemiological sciences, all in the service of the state.[69] The sea was eventually marked off and cordoned; empires which had existed mostly in name as putative 'spheres of influence' now resembled polities closer to the reality of the name. By the twentieth century it is no exaggeration to say that the South China Sea – for so long in its history the epitome of an open *mare liberum* – was now more of a closed sea. Trade and travel still crossed its seas, but lines on the map had politically cordoned off its shores.[70] This is the world of the South China Sea that we have inherited today, and which now makes up part of a nation-state-driven world.[71]

It is, in fact, the South China Sea of the twentieth into the twenty-first centuries that shows us how fragile this history of movement, trade and political accommodation has become. This broad maritime space is still criss-crossed by shipping as it always has been; indeed, the raw tonnage of transport is higher now than it ever has been in historical time. Yet there are worrying signs that an epoch of *mare clausum* – closed seas – could be approaching. China has claimed most of the islands of the South China Sea – including the Spratly and Paracel chains – and has begun fortifying them, building atolls into islets and islets into actual bases. The neighbouring countries of the region, including Japan, Taiwan and the nations of ASEAN, have reacted by putting forth their own claims.[72] American

---

[67] J. M. Gullick, *Malay society in the late nineteenth century: The beginnings of change* (Oxford, 1987).

[68] Robert Cribb, *The Late colonial state in Indonesia: Political and economic foundations of the Netherlands East Indies, 1880–1942* (Leiden: 1994).

[69] Eric Tagliacozzo, *Secret trades, porous borders: Smuggling and states along a Southeast Asian frontier, 1865–1915* (New Haven, CT, 2005).

[70] Eric Tagliacozzo and Wen-Chin Chang, eds., *Chinese circulations: capital, commodities and networks in Southeast Asia* (Durham, NC, 2011); Eric Tagliacozzo, Helen Siu and Peter Perdue, eds., *Asia inside out*, vol. I: *Changing times* (Cambridge, MA, 2015); Eric Tagliacozzo, Helen Siu and Peter Perdue, eds., *Asia inside out*, vol. II: *Connected places* (Cambridge, MA, 2015).

[71] Anthony Reid, ed., *The last stand of Asian autonomies: Responses to modernity in the diverse states of Southeast Asia and Korea, 1750–1900* (London, 1997).

[72] Probably the most important scholar thinking over the strategic implications of the contemporary South China Sea has been Michael Leifer; see a useful compendium of his

sea-power has tried to guarantee rights of international navigation and adjudication by international courts of disputes but it is anyone's guess if there is the willpower present to deny actual encroachments on territory. The Hague makes occasional pronouncements on the issue but is remote. As further resources are discovered in the region (including offshore oil and natural gas), and as jockeying continues over balance-of-power issues astride the sea-routes, the world will be watching to see if the status quo is kept. Abandoning centuries of free access and free travel – the historical legacy of human interaction in this arena – seems not to be in the interest of practically any of the interested parties.[73]

Conclusion

The South China Sea has a history that is at once local and trans-local; it has been the great space of separation between Asian polities for thousands of years, but also the main connective tissue to knit this space into a single web of contact and interaction. It is this inherent paradox that makes this particular sea interesting. Though we can indeed see something of 'East' and 'Southeast Asian' worlds developing over the *longue durée* for much of this period the politics and economics of these regions were linked, and were in fact continually maintained through the seasonal passage of vessels heading north and south. Some of these ships were engaged in diplomacy, keeping the centuries-old pattern of vassalage and semi-vassalage to China amongst the polities of the Nanyang intact, and regulated over time. But even more of the vessels had commercial motives, trading in a wide variety of goods that both the northern and southern rims of the South China Sea wanted, each from one other. High-status and often high-technology goods (for the time) travelled south, for the most part, and ecological produce, both of the seas and of the forests of Southeast Asia, one of the world's most bio-diverse regions, travelled north. Each side received something it desired, whether luxury goods (in the case of China) that helped to power the rise of a new and increasingly vigorous commercial class, or status-items (in the case of the Nanyang), showing investiture and recognition by the Middle Kingdom, the great medieval hegemon to the north.

work provided in Chin Kin Wah and Leo Suryadinata, eds., *Michael Leifer: Selected works on Southeast Asia* (Singapore, 2005).

[73] See Alice Ba, 'ASEAN's stakes: The South China Sea's challenge to autonomy and agency', *Asia Policy*, 21 (2016): 47–53; Alex Calvo, 'China, the Philippines, Vietnam and international arbitration in the South China Sea', *The Asia-Pacific Journal*, 13, 43, 2 (26 October 2015): http://apjjf.org/-Alex-Calvo/4391 (accessed 31 March 2017).

The South China Sea   131

By the early modern age, some of these patterns began to change in the encircling waters of the South China Sea. A quickening of commerce, brought about by the entrance of a variety of new actors to the scene (some of them Asian, some of them not), pushed the rate of travel and contact to new heights. Ethnic actors from both previously marginalised parts of the South China Sea region and beyond it came in greater numbers; they brought more wealth with them too. And for the first time, they began to stay in the region in larger numbers than just a trickle of men trading in ports. This re-aligned some of the commercial and political relations of Southeast Asia, empowering some (such as the Sulu Sultanate) and enslaving others (such as many of the region's 'sea peoples'), in new bonds of hierarchical integration. Where the China market had been the engine for much of this sea's trade in the past, the world market started to take on more importance into the later eighteenth and early nineteenth centuries. By that time, some of the Europeans who had trickled into the region took on a more menacing aspect, as they planted flags in the ground and claimed some coasts abutting this most central of seas. We have seen the beginnings of that process here, and those seeds brought out a bitter fruit in the form of colonialism and empire, different versions of which stretched from parts of the South China coasts all the way down to the land- and sea-scapes of Southeast Asia. We still, in fact, live with the legacy of those times even now, as we run our fingers over the colours of the map that make up the various margins of the modern South China Sea.

Further Reading

There are a number of studies that treat the history of the South China Sea through interesting windows. Andre Gunder Frank's *ReOrient: Global economy in the Asian age* (Berkeley, CA, 1998) gives a nice global take on this regional place; Takeshi Hamashita's *China, East Asia, and the global economy: Regional and historical perspectives* (New York, 2008) then does so via an East Asian angle, while Kenneth Hall's *A history of early Southeast Asia* (Lanham, MD, 2011) complements this from the Southeast Asian side of things. For the early period, the great classic from China's vantage is arguably Edward Schafer's *The vermilion bird: T'ang images of the south* (Berkeley, CA, 1967), while the annotated translation of Frederick Hirth and W. W. Rockhill, entitled *Chau Ju Kua: His work on the Chinese and Arab trade in the 12th and 13th Centuries* (Taipei, 1967, reprint of the 1911 original) tells us what the South China Sea polities looked like from the locus of China's thirteenth-century coasts. To get onto the water

132   E. Tagliacozzo

itself, see Wang Gungwu's classic *The Nanhai trade: Early Chinese trade in the South China Sea* (Singapore, reprint 2003), and O. W. Wolters's seminal *Early Indonesian commerce: A study of the origins of Srivijaya* (Ithaca, NY, 1974), which provides the Southeast Asian point of view. For medieval times, Roderich Ptak, ed., *China's seaborne trade with South and Southeast Asia* (Abingdon, 1999) is very good in sketching out the broad parameters; an eminent authority on the ships themselves is Pierre Yves Manguin; see his 'The Southeast Asian ship: An historical approach', *Journal of Southeast Asian Studies*, 2 (1980): 266–76; and Pierre Yves Manguin, 'Relationship and cross-influence between Southeast Asian and Chinese ship-building tradition', IAHA Conference, Manila, 21–25 November 1983. The great, well-known debate about the nature and outlines of Early Modern Southeast Asia and the South China Sea as a region can be found in Anthony Reid, *Southeast Asia in the age of commerce*, 2 vols. (New Haven, CT, 1988 and 1993), and Victor Lieberman, *Strange parallels: Southeast Asia in global context, 800–1830*, 2 vols. (Cambridge, 2003–9). Looking south from China to complement these works is John Wills, *China and maritime Europe, 1500–1800: Trade, settlement, diplomacy and missions* (New York, 2010); looking more broadly across the entire seascape of Asia at this time is Frank Broeze, ed., *Brides of the sea: Port cities of Asia from the 16–20th centuries* (Kensington, NSW, 1989). A 'frontier approach' is adopted in C. Patterson Giersch, *Asian borderlands: The transformation of Qing China's frontier* (Cambridge, MA, 2006); for the Taiwanese angle on things, see both Shih-Shan Henry Tsai, *Maritime Taiwan: Historical encounters with the East and the West* (Armonk, NY, 2009); and also Johanna Menzel Meskill, *A Chinese pioneer family: The Lins of Wu-feng, Taiwan, 1729–1895* (Princeton, NJ, 1979). Exciting scholarship has been done on the trade systems of the South China coasts in Paul van Dyke, *The Canton trade: Life and enterprise on the China coast, 1700–1845* (Hong Kong, 2007), and also in his *Merchants of Canton and Macao: Success and failure in eighteenth century Chinese trade* (Hong Kong, 2016). From Southeast Asia, the Philippine world is very well covered in both James Francis Warren's *The Sulu zone, 1768–1898: The dynamics of external trade, slavery, and ethnicity in the transformation of a Southeast Asian maritime state* (Singapore, 1981), and in Laura Lee Junker's *Raiding, trading, and feasting: The political economy of Philippine chiefdoms* (Honolulu, HI, 1999). Vietnam and Cambodia's mainland coasts are well-described in Li Tana, *Nguyen Cochinchina: Southern Vietnam in the seventeenth and eighteenth centuries* (Ithaca, NY, 1998); Nola Cooke, Li Tana and James Anderson, *The Tongking Gulf through history* (Philadelphia, PA, 2011); and in Dian Murray's excellent *Pirates of the South China Coast, 1790–1810* (Palo Alto, CA, 1987). Still standing alone in its broad insights is Kenneth

The South China Sea 133

Pomeranz's *The great divergence: China, Europe, and the making of the modern world economy* (Princeton, NJ, 2001). A feel for the connections forged by the commodities themselves can be found in Eric Tagliacozzo and Wen-Chin Chang, eds., *Chinese circulations: Capital, commodities and networks in Southeast Asia* (Durham, NC, 2011). Eric Tagliacozzo also describes the arrival of coercion into the 'linking seas' in *Secret trades, porous borders: Smuggling and states along a Southeast Asian frontier, 1865–1915* (New Haven, CT, 2005). Finally, the end of old systems is laid out very well in Anthony Reid, ed., *The last stand of Asian autonomies: Responses to modernity in the diverse states of Southeast Asia and Korea, 1750–1900* (London, 1997).

5   The Mediterranean Sea

Molly Greene

The Mediterranean Sea looms large in the Western world, and thus also in Western historiography. It is the *Ur*-sea. This is true for several reasons. First, it is the birthplace of Greco-Roman, and thus European, civilisation.[1] Second, the successful navigation of the sea stretches very far back in human history, to thousands of years before the beginning of the Christian era, and the written and archaeological record is abundant. This distinguishes the study of the Mediterranean from the fields of Pacific and Atlantic history. Finally, from the early medieval period Europeans formed an idea of themselves and of Europe in opposition to Islam, and it is the Mediterranean which purportedly served as the watery frontier, 'the historic dividing line separating two groups conceived of as opposites'.[2] Nevertheless, the Mediterranean is a frontier that has been routinely crossed by both sides and, at times, the Europeans have found it expedient to advocate for Mediterranean unity, rather than enmity. The current refugee crisis, in which (mostly) Muslim refugees have been crossing from the southern and eastern shores to the northern shores of the inland sea, with many thousands dying in the attempt, is but the latest iteration of a very ancient Mediterranean dynamic: it is a frontier but one that is routinely crossed.

The division of the sea into its Muslim and Christian halves has been an essential framework for writing about the history of the Mediterranean. The early twentieth-century Pirenne thesis, although by now the subject of sustained critique, remains one of the best known paradigms in medieval history; it argued that it was the arrival of the Muslim armies in the Mediterranean in the seventh century that destroyed the unity of the

---

[1] However, not everyone is in agreement about where to locate the origins of Europe. See Michael Z. Wise, 'Idea of a unified cultural heritage divides Europe', *The New York Times*, 29 January 2000. The organisers of a project to build a Museum of Europe argued that the starting point should be Charlemagne and the ninth-century Holy Roman Empire. The Greek government was quick to object.

[2] Linda Darling, 'The Mediterranean as a borderland', *Review of Middle East Studies*, 46 (2012): 55.

134

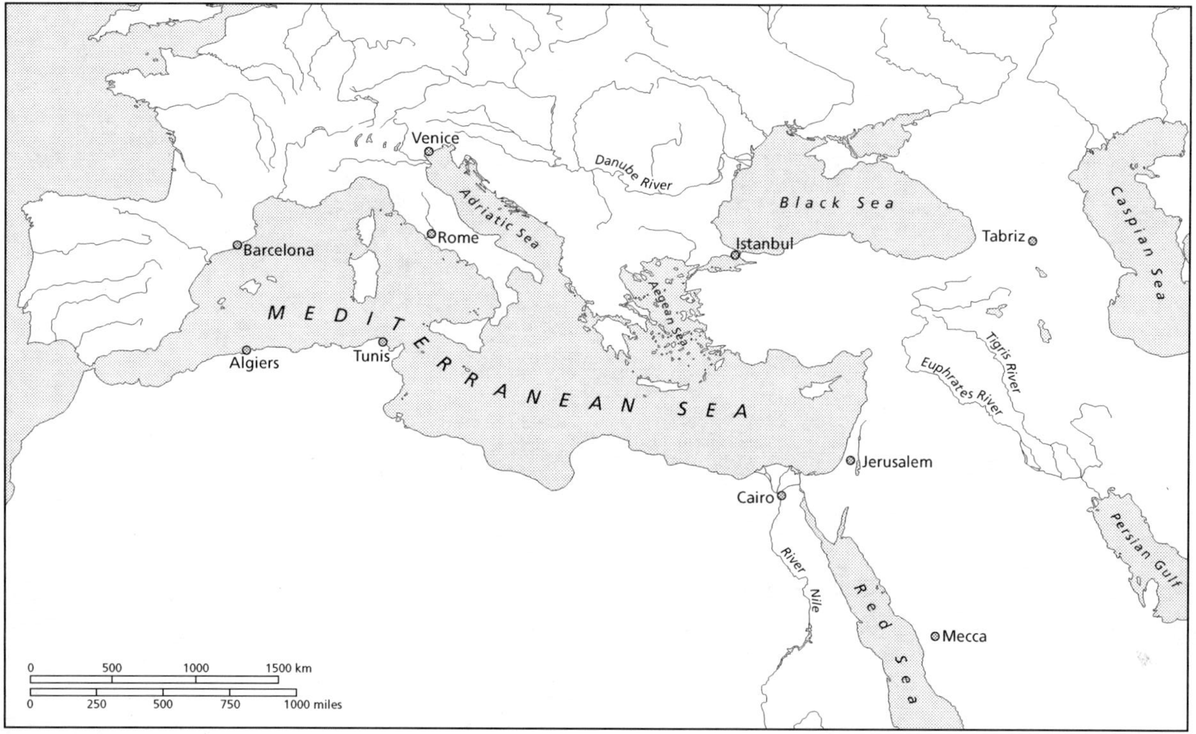

Map 5.1 The Mediterranean Sea

136   M. Greene

Roman world. A more recent trend in writing about the Mediterranean seeks to downplay, if not entirely ignore, religious divides in favour of an environmental approach that emphasises the essential unity of the region. This was the thesis of Fernand Braudel's magnum opus *La Méditerranée et le Monde Méditerranéen à l'époque de Philippe II*, published in 1949. Between the northern and southern limits of the cultivation of the olive tree, Braudel argued, the repetitions and cycles of environmental time structured human experience in more consequential ways than the supposed ruptures and breaks brought on by the rise and fall of empires and the eruptions of religious conflict. The afterlife of Braudel's book (the English translation of which appeared only in the early 1970s) was rather peculiar. Although widely hailed as a major accomplishment of the *Annales* school of historical writing, it did not inspire a new field of Mediterranean studies and sat for a long time in splendid isolation.[3]

Since the 1990s this has changed. There has been both a general uptick in scholarly interest in the Mediterranean, alongside a more focused return to Braudel, with the goal of grappling with his legacy. Work in the latter vein has attempted to tackle two major criticisms of *La Méditerranée*, namely the charge of environmental determinism and the relative unimportance of human actors in Braudel's narrative.[4] Peregrine Horden and Nicholas Purcell's massive *The corrupting sea: a study of Mediterranean history*, published in 2000, is a landmark in the field and a self-proclaimed response to Braudel. Against Braudel's emphasis on a unified Mediterranean environment, they posit instead extreme fragmentation, the Mediterranean as a possibly endless series of microecologies.[5] But they share the Braudelian vision of a world connected by the sea itself, perhaps even more than Braudel, since the distinctive ecologies of the Mediterranean make autarky an impossibility. It is interesting that, although Horden and Purcell are deeply interested in the Mediterranean environment, in their view it is not the environment that drives change

---

[3] See Peregrine Horden, 'Introduction', in Peregrine Horden and Sharon Kinoshita, eds., *A companion to Mediterranean history* (Chichester, 2014) for a discussion of the reasons behind this.

[4] The two are, of course, related. These concerns are in line with the new dialectical approach in environmental history, which considers not only how the environment shapes human society but how humans shape their environment. Cultural and environmental history are moving closer together, with historians asking how humans thought about, harnessed and used the natural world around them. See Alan Mikhail, 'Introduction: Middle East environmental history: The fallow between two fields', in Alan Mikhail, ed., *Water on sand: Environmental histories of the Middle East and North Africa* (Oxford, 2013).

[5] They make this argument through four case-studies: the Beqaa Valley, south Ertruria, the Aegean island of Melos and Cyrenacia in North Africa. Peregrine Horden and Nicholas Purcell, *The corrupting sea: A study of Mediterranean history* (Oxford, 2000).

The Mediterranean Sea 137

but rather the decisions made by local actors to diversify agriculture in order to mitigate risk. In the words of one reviewer: 'All social and economic history, the authors argue, should be placed squarely in the context of relations of production, rather than in transitory technological or environmental changes.'[6] To foreground relations of production is, of course, to foreground social relations and power.[7] By so doing, the authors are well within the mainstream of environmental history today, which rejects environmental determinism.

Other post-Braudelian works on the Mediterranean continue the emphasis on human agency, sometimes pushing it even further. The editors of *Mediterranean diasporas: Politics and ideas in the long nineteenth century* write that, instead of the more usual focus on trade and economic history, 'the originality of this volume lies in the fact that it sees the Mediterranean, first and foremost, as a place of intellectual communication'.[8] Peter Miller, editor of *The sea: Thalassography and historiography*, took the unusual approach of excavating the history of Braudel the administrator, rather than Braudel the scholar. Looking at Braudel's tenure at the VIe section of École des Hautes Études, it turns out that the projects he encouraged and the people he admired all had a very human-centred approach to history: 'This Braudel was not the one for whom human life was mere "froth on the waves".'[9] All of the chapters in the Miller volume insist on the intersection of cultural and economic history, a closing of the divide between materialist and cognitive accounts of the past.

In writing about the environmental history of the Mediterranean, historians like Horden and Purcell are able to draw on a long tradition of scholarship on the classical and medieval world to help them make their claims. For example, they would not have been able to take on, and to refute, arguments about the nature of Greek and Roman agriculture – its supposedly primitive nature, for example, according to Moses Finley – were it not for the fact that these topics have figured so prominently in the Western historical tradition. Here we see how the treatment of the Mediterranean as an environmental and ecological unit is connected to

---

[6] James and Elizabeth Fentress, 'Review article: The hole in the doughnut', *Past and Present*, 173 (2001): 208.

[7] 'Complexity and sophistication are to be found in abundance in Mediterranean social relations rather than in Mediterranean productive techniques.' Fentress, 'Review article', 208.

[8] Maurizio Isabella and Konstantina Zanou, eds., *Mediterranean diasporas: Politics and ideas in the long nineteenth century* (London, 2015), p. 3.

[9] Peter N. Miller, 'Introduction: The sea is the land's edge also', in Peter N. Miller, ed., *The sea: Thalassography and historiography* (Ann Arbor, MI, 2013), p. 8.

138   M. Greene

the much older tradition of historical writing about the Mediterranean, discussed in the opening to this chapter, which finds its origins in the significance that Mediterranean Antiquity holds for European history.

Against the Mediterranean

In sharp contrast to these well-established scholarly traditions, other academic fields resist the idea of the Mediterranean as a legitimate category of historical research. Anthropologists and historians of the Muslim world have been particularly prominent in these critiques. This brings us to a consideration of Muslims who live along its southern, eastern and northeastern shores, whose relationship to the inland sea is quite different. An essential part of the rejection of 'the Mediterranean' or 'Mediterranean studies' is the very term itself, 'Mediterranean', and what it implies about the place of Muslims in it. Mediterranean is a Roman/Latin word, of Greek origin. Until the nineteenth century it was never used by the Muslims of North Africa and the Levant.[10] In addition, the Europeans expanded their usage of the term into the concept of the 'Mediterranean region', in that same century, at the exact moment when Britain and France were establishing their regional dominance. Braudel's connected and unified Mediterranean was very much a sea that was stitched together by Europeans and it is certain that the intensification of the European presence across the Mediterranean was experienced as something considerably worse than 'connection' by Muslims from Algeria to Istanbul.[11] In the most lethal use of 'Mediterranean'-type thinking French colonial officials fervently promoted Algeria's classical past as a way of turning their new conquest into a part of France. This connection between the word and European imperialism or, at the very least, Eurocentrism is an anxiety that the field of Mediterranean history shares with Atlantic and Pacific history. Historians of the Atlantic, for instance, worry that they still tend to view Atlantic history (whatever that may mean) from the perspective of Europe and to divide up the Atlantic, and even a compact area such as the Caribbean, along imperial lines. This is an unfortunate irony, given that one of the original motivations

---

[10] Susan Alcock notes that even today there are no Arabic journals devoted to the Mediterranean. Susan E. Alcock, 'Alphabet soup in the Mediterranean basin: The emergence of the Mediterranean serial', in W. V. Harris, ed., *Rethinking the Mediterranean* (Oxford, 2005), pp. 314–36.

[11] See Peregrine Horden and Nicholas Purcell, 'The Mediterranean and the new thalassology', *American Historical Review*, 111 (2006): 722–40, for a discussion of the intertwining of the Mediterranean and European imperialism.

The Mediterranean Sea

for the study of bodies of water was 'to escape the restrictions of the nation-state'.[12]

For the Arabic writers of the medieval period the sea was a barrier, not a bridge; it separated two adversarial shores.[13] Nor did they call it the Mediterranean. The Arabic translation of the word – *al-Mutawassit* – started to be used only in the nineteenth century; it appears in none of the medieval maps and makes only a rare appearance in the chronicles or geographical texts.[14] Instead, what the Europeans saw as one sea was viewed as many by the Arabs: the 'Rūmi/Byzantine Sea, the Shāmi/Syrian sea, the Akhdar/Green Sea and the Mālih/Salty Sea. This did not signal a cultural predisposition against maritime endeavours, since the Indian Ocean and the Red Sea were viewed as part of the Islamic world.[15] Rather, it stemmed from the fact that their Christian adversaries came from across the Mediterranean Sea and, from the tenth century onwards, were increasingly successful in their campaigns to retake territory they had lost and to conquer other areas anew. These campaigns culminated, in the medieval period, in the Crusades. Even when, over the course of several centuries, Muslim armies managed to drive the Europeans out of Egypt and the Levant, their attitude towards the coastline remained cautious. When the Mamluks retook Damietta from the French in 1251, they destroyed the city's fortifications: '[they]demolished all the ramparts, razing them to the ground in order to prevent the Christians from ever making use of the city, they took all the Stones and carried them to the River Nile'.[16]

The tradition of multiple names for this body of water continued into the early modern period, as did the view that the sea was a source of danger, not connection. This is unsurprising considering the reality of European piracy and, in the case of North Africa, actual naval attacks. Speaking of a late sixteenth-century Moroccan traveller, Matar observes that: 'Common to him and other Muslims was the image of a terrifying sea, not because Arabs or Muslims had a religiously engrained or

---

[12] Alison Games, 'Atlantic History: Definitions, challenges and histories', *American Historical Review*, 111 (2006): 744. The Games and the Horden and Purcell articles are part of an *AHR* Forum entitled 'Oceans of History' in the June 2006 issue.

[13] Here I am drawing heavily on the unpublished paper of Nabil Matar, 'The Mediterranean through Arab eyes: 1598–1798'. I thank him for sharing his work with me and for allowing me to reference it for this chapter. In the article Matar notes that major works of Mediterranean history continue to be written with no use of Arabic or Ottoman sources.

[14] The word is clearly an adoption of the Western term, since both carry the idea of 'in the middle'.

[15] Matar, 'The Mediterranean', 5, 6.

[16] Megan Cassidy-Welch, '"O Damietta": War, memory and crusade in thirteenth-century Egypt', *Journal of Medieval History*, 40 (2014): 346–47.

140   M. Greene

an instinctive hostility to the sea but because they feared attacks from European fleets.'[17] In this period North Africans moved inland as a response to British and French bombardments of the shoreline, a pattern that we see in the Greek islands as well, where coastal villages were abandoned in favour of settlement in the interior of the islands.[18] In the latter case the attacks were more likely to come from an assortment of Catholic corsairs and pirates.

Andrew Hess, another scholar of North Africa, does not concern himself with the Muslim view of the Mediterranean *per se*. Nevertheless, he stands in firm opposition to the idea of a coherent Mediterranean world, spanning the northern and southern shores, at least in the early modern period. His book *The forgotten frontier: A history of the sixteenth-century Ibero-African frontier*, was pioneering in its day and remains an essential text on the western Mediterranean.[19] Hess argues that three events in 1492, 'three shocks to the old order', shattered what had previously been a dense network of contact and movement between Muslim North Africa and Andalusia.[20] These were Columbus's journey to the New World, the expulsion of the Jews from Spain and the defeat of the last Muslim kingdom, Granada, on the Iberian peninsula. In the wake of these events, both sides (even the victorious Christian side) decided to call a halt to their battles with each other in favour of directing their attentions elsewhere. In his words: 'contrasting Mediterranean civilizations separated themselves at the Strait of Gibraltar, ending their history of integration in a little-known exchange of ambassadors and border populations'.[21] As a result, 'the wide belt of cultural pluralism of the late fifteenth century, the zone including both Hispano-Muslims and the Christian-Muslim military border in North Africa, shrank to a thin line'.[22] What remained in the western Mediterranean was a watery frontier that separated Spain

[17] Matar, 'The Mediterranean', 8. Matar also points out, however, how remarkably quickly North African elites absorbed the European view that the Arabs were not a seafaring people. In 1699 the ruler of Morocco wrote to James II that he, Mulay Ismail, belonged to 'a people who knew nothing of the sea', despite the fact that just fifty years prior North Africans had sailed as far north as Iceland and Ireland. Matar, 'The Mediterranean', 11.

[18] Matar, 'The Mediterranean', 10. See Molly Greene, *Catholic pirates and Greek merchants: A maritime history of the Mediterranean* (Princeton, NJ, 2010) for the history of Catholic piracy in the Mediterranean.

[19] Andrew Hess, *The forgotten frontier: A history of the sixteenth century Ibero-African frontier* (Chicago, IL, 1978). What the Hess book does share with Braudel, however, is that it did not open up a new field of study. That may be changing, as discussed below.

[20] Hess, *The forgotten frontier*, p. 7.

[21] Hess, *The forgotten frontier*, p. 7. Hess makes the interesting point, for global historians, that this separation took place even as breakthroughs in maritime technology were creating a closer-knit world economy.

[22] Hess, *The forgotten frontier*, p. 10.

The Mediterranean Sea 141

from North Africa. Two mutually antagonistic foes glared at each other over this divide, with only violent entrepreneurs such as the so called Barbary corsairs willing to sail out into these now hostile waters.

The Ottoman Mediterranean

Having considered the response of scholars of the Muslim world, let us look at the related, but distinct field of Ottoman history.[23] Ottomanists have grappled with the question of the Mediterranean mostly from the perspectives of Ottoman mercantile activity and state policy towards naval matters, with the understanding, of course, that both easily shade into questions of cultural difference. For example, when it comes to maritime history, naval prowess on the high seas has long been viewed as an essential mark of state vigour and success, while a global trading presence has been taken as a mark of cultural openness and sophistication. Although such views are no longer stated so frequently or openly, there is a long tradition of such thought in academic circles and this tradition certainly affects writing on the Ottomans and the Mediterranean: (supposed) Ottoman weakness on and disinterest in the sea is seen as an indictment of Ottoman civilisation itself. As recently as 1999 Predrag Matvejević, in a book that won four European literary prizes, wrote 'the Turks came from the depths of Asia' and 'have no feeling for the sea. They have always been more warriors than sailors.'[24] It is this kind of stereotyping to which Cemal Kafadar responded in his article 'A death in Venice (1575): Anatolian Muslim merchants trading in the Serenissima', published just a few years before Matvejevi's book.[25] By telling the story of a Muslim merchant in Christian Venice, Kafadar was doing far more than documenting an individual life; he was taking on the interwoven cultural narratives of (supposedly unique) Muslim fear of the sea, xenophobia and lack of business acumen.

It is clear, then, that Ottoman historians and historians of the medieval Muslim world have had to grapple with similar culturally inflected narratives about Muslims and the sea. But there are significant differences between the two fields that reflect the dissimilar geopolitical realities of

---

[23] The Ottomans called the sea the Ak Deniz, or white sea. This name comes from the Central Asian system of associating directions with colours. Matar, 'The Mediterranean', 12.

[24] Predrag Matvejević, *Mediterranean: A cultural landscape*, trans. Michael Henry Heim (Berkeley, CA, 1999), p. 77. His remarks on the Romans, unsurprisingly, are far more nuanced: 'The ancient Romans were not a seafaring nation, though they were able to keep their waters safe and supply them with ports' (p. 77).

[25] Cemal Kafadar, 'A death in Venice (1575): Anatolian Muslim merchants trading in the Serenissima', *Journal of Turkish Studies*, 10 (1986): 191–217.

142   M. Greene

the two worlds. Viewed from the widest possible angle, the merchants, scholars and diplomats of medieval Islam travelled along mostly land routes that began in Spain in the west, ran through the Maghreb to Egypt, then across the Red Sea to Arabia and, beyond that, the Indian Ocean.[26] The Mediterranean, particularly the northern shores, was tangential to their itineraries.

The Ottomans, on the other hand, united the northern and southern shores of the eastern Mediterranean for the first time in almost a millennium when they conquered Egypt in 1517. The Mediterranean was at the very centre of their empire and, as the strongest Muslim power in the early modern world, they effectively pulled the weight of the Muslim world further west than it had been since the Umayyads in the seventh century. Reflecting this reality, Ottoman historians have quite energetically contested the assertion that Europeans took hold of the Mediterranean as early as the Crusades and never let go. The eastern Mediterranean was not, in fact, a European lake during the Ottoman period. The Europeans were present, of course (particularly the French), but the vital routes linking Alexandria to Istanbul and Volos to Thessaloniki and the islands to Izmir and so on, were crowded with a wide variety of Ottoman vessels.[27]

More recently, Ottoman historians have moved from an investigation of merchants to rethinking the relationship between the state and the Mediterranean. This rethinking has focused on the period after the Ottoman defeat at Lepanto because it is then, the argument goes, that the Ottomans turned their back on the sea. Wisely putting to one side the narrow equation of maritime history with naval history, such work has demonstrated an active engagement with the sea, not in the sense of naval affairs, but in terms of effective legal and diplomatic responses to the turbulent conditions of the seventeenth and eighteenth centuries, when piracy and then the Seven Years' War created havoc in the sultan's waters.[28]

---

[26] This is the world described so memorably in Amitav Ghosh, *In an antique land* (London, 1992).

[27] See Eyal Ginio, 'When coffee brought about wealth and prestige: The impact of Egyptian trade on salonica', *Oriente Moderno*, n.s. 25 (2006): 93–107 for the important ties between Egypt and Thessaloniki; Alan Mikhail, *Nature and empire in Ottoman Egypt: An environmental history* (Cambridge, 2011), for the traffic in wood between southern Anatolia and Egypt; and Molly Greene, *A shared world: Muslims and Christians in the early modern Mediterranean* (Princeton, NJ, 2000), for shipping in Ottoman Crete.

[28] See in particular Michael Talbot, *British–Ottoman relations, 1661–1807: Commerce and diplomatic practice in eighteenth-century Istanbul* (Woodbridge, 2017), and Joshua M. White, *Piracy and law in the Ottoman Mediterranean* (Palo Alto, CA, 2017).

The Mediterranean Sea 143

To the vexed question of how, if at all, to define the Ottoman Mediterranean, Joshua White has given a very clear answer: the Ottoman Mediterranean was defined not by the action of its navies or the faith of its inhabitants but by the fact that it was a unified legal space. What he means by this is the fact that, in the post-Lepanto world when the scourge of piracy spread across the Mediterranean (similar to what was happening in the Atlantic and Indian Oceans), foreigners and Ottoman subjects alike turned repeatedly to the Ottoman legal bureaucracy for assistance in confronting the problems created by piracy. This bureaucracy, in turn, responded in ways that were both creative and effective. Here we shall consider only the role played by the Ottoman Şeyhülislam (also known as the mufti), the Empire's chief jurisconsult, in these cases.[29]

As early as 1611 Venetian authorities began soliciting *fetvas* from the mufti to strengthen their case against the North Africans who were wreaking havoc on their shipping. In 1624 a particularly brazen series of attacks carried out by the North Africans, with the cooperation of local officials, in the Adriatic and Ionian Seas – among other things over 700 Venetian subjects were carried off into slavery – produced outrage in both Istanbul and Venice.[30] In the meetings that followed and the delegations that moved across the Mediterranean – first the Ottomans to Tunis and then the Tunisians to Istanbul – the mufti's intercession was sought by all sides. By their actions, White argues, it seems that the officials in Istanbul (and the Venetians) knew that it was not enough to say that the Tunisians' actions contravened the treaties (*ahdnames*) negotiated between Venice and the sultan's representatives, based as they were on secular law. Inevitably, the religious question came up. Were the North Africans pirates or were they *gazis*, fighting the Islamic Holy War?

It took the mufti to tell the Tunisians, in the *fetvas* that he wrote, that their activities were not a *halal gaza*, a religiously permissible raid, and that they were contravening not just the sultan's law, but God's law as well.[31] Although the resolution of this particular case is not apparent, unfortunately, in the historical record, the fact that both the Tunisians and the Venetians approached the mufti directly to write a *fetva* that would be favourable to their side, as well as the fact that the Venetians kept copies of the *fetvas* that were issued over the course of the seventeenth century, shows that the Şeyhülislam was considered an important person

---

[29] See Joshua M. White, 'Fetva diplomacy: The Ottoman Şeyhülislam as trans-imperial intermediary', *Journal of Early Modern History*, 19 (2015): 199–221. The Ottoman response, however, was not confined to the role of the Şeyhülislam.

[30] White, 'Fetva diplomacy', 211–12.

[31] White, 'Fetva diplomacy', 213.

144   M. Greene

in resolving these types of problems. Given longstanding assumptions about the absence of the Ottomans from maritime and naval history, it is revealing that in his 1724 publication *A General History of the Pyrates*, Captain Charles Johnson, in explaining the governance of Atlantic pirate ships, wrote 'The Quarter-Master's opinion is like the Mufti's among the Turks; the Captain can undertake nothing which the Quarter-Master does not approve.'[32]

The Ottomans have not typically figured at all in the story of the Seven Years' War (1754–63). To the extent that there has been an Ottoman perspective on the war at all, it has come from Greek historians who have underlined the boost given to Greek shipping during the war due to the neutrality of Greek ships.[33] Now it is clear that the Ottomans moved decisively to limit the damage to themselves and their merchants from British/French hostility in their waters.[34] Through a series of decrees the sultan extended his sovereignty out to sea, going beyond the consensus held in both Europe and the empire at the time that a state's sovereignty only extended as far as the reach of a cannon ball shot from port. Their reason for so doing was to establish an expansive zone in the Aegean where the British and the French were not allowed to attack each other's shipping. Besides the general disruption, the Ottomans were particularly concerned since much of Ottoman internal seaborne trade was carried on French ships.

Because of the existing configuration prior to the war, the new policy tended to be punitive towards the British and protective of the French. This was because the French had a more established presence in the eastern Mediterranean than did the British. The new Ottoman policy meant that Ottoman petitioners, both Christian and Muslim, who had suffered attacks while onboard French ships, were able to get restitution in Istanbul. British diplomats in the capital complained long and loudly about the rules but they complied; during this period, Ottoman merchants were paid tens of thousands of gurush (an Ottoman silver coin) in compensation by the British authorities.

These interventions on the part of Ottoman historians are important, not just for the relationship between the Ottomans and the Mediterranean, but also for the narrative of Mediterranean history itself. In his recent article 'The medieval Mediterranean' (2014), Dominique

---

[32] Quoted in White, 'Fetva diplomacy', 200.

[33] See Stelios A. Papadopoulos, ed., *The Greek merchant marine (1453–1850)* (Athens, 1972).

[34] See Michael Talbot, 'Ottoman seas and British privateers: Defining maritime territoriality in the eighteenth century Levant', in P. W. Firges, Tobias P. Graf, Christian Roth and Giilay Tulasoglu, eds., *Well-connected domains: Towards an entangled Ottoman history* (Leiden, 2014), pp. 54–70.

The Mediterranean Sea 145

Valérian argues that, in a divided sea, it was in the medieval period that rules were developed for regulating relationships across the religious frontier: 'From this plurality of normative systems arose the difficult problem of regulating relationships in the Mediterranean (both in times of peace and times of war); the Middle Ages is the period when these rules were invented and progressively accepted and shared, most persisting into modern times.'[35] This interpretation places the Ottoman Empire in a passive role; it simply inherited an international framework that was already in place. New research demonstrates instead that the Ottomans must be given a far more active role in the development of international law in the Mediterranean.[36]

The Mediterranean and Global History

Resistance to the Mediterranean as a legitimate category of research has also come from broad intellectual trends both in history and in anthropology. Area studies – which operated under the assumption 'that knowledge was culturally and historically specific' – came under attack from the 1990s due to several major shocks to the world system; the rise of China, the fall of the Berlin Wall and the financialisation of the global economy. In a recent article on the rise of global history Jeremy Adelman writes: 'As ideological differences dissolved and the marketplace reintegrated the remaining parts of the world into a new assemblage, what fundamental differences were there to justify the existence of idiographic, particularist, context-dependent knowledge?'[37] It seemed that the universal laws of the market were soon going to be in operation everywhere, with a similar result.

At the same time that area studies were being put on the defensive, anthropologists, too, began to cast a critical eye on their own discipline. As early as 1984 Michael Herzfeld, one of the leading anthropologists of

---

[35] Dominique Valérian, 'The medieval Mediterranean', in Horden and Kinoshita, eds., *A companion to Mediterranean history*, p. 86.

[36] See also the articles of Will Smiley. His focus is on the longstanding Ottoman–Russian relationship but he shows how emerging treaty law between the two adversaries also found its way into the Mediterranean where, after 1770, the Russians became major players. Will Smiley, 'The burdens of subjecthood: The Ottoman state, Russian fugitives and interimperial law', *International Journal of Middle East Studies*, 46 (2014): 73–93; Smiley, '"After being so long Prisoners, they will not return to Slavery in Russia": An Aegean network of violence between empires and identities', *Journal of Ottoman Studies*, 44 (2014): 221–34.

[37] Jeremy Adelman, 'The forked roads to global history: A new world history', forthcoming in Masashi Haneda, ed., *Gulobaru hisutori-no kanosei* [The Potential of Global History] (Tokyo, 2017).

146   M. Greene

the Mediterranean (even as, over many decades, he has very deliberately wrestled with the Mediterranean as a legitimate intellectual category), castigated anthropologists for their development of the analytical category of the 'culture area'. Such a concept, he wrote, encouraged stereotyping – the very opposite of what the field desired. Instead they should be engaged in 'intensely localized' ethnography and then synthesising these studies into 'a globally effective portrait of humankind'.[38] We see here, too, an emphasis on the global which Adelman described, although the methodology remains rooted in the local.

Recently, the pendulum has begun to swing back in the other direction, although that 'other' is not identical to what was left behind in the 1990s. Local context matters, but the larger framework is a history of global integration rather than an understanding of a particular place. Some global historians, for example, are warning against the dangers of imposing a false uniformity across the entire globe – Thomas Friedman's flat world – arguing that we must be more sensitive to 'the varieties of histories of integration'.[39] In their 2006 article in the *American Historical Review*, Horden and Purcell made the case, yet again, for the importance of the Mediterranean and defended it against charges of imperialism, exclusivism, and cultural and environmental determinism. They were careful, however, to connect the Mediterranean to the concerns of global history. The study of the inland sea, they argue, 'throws up questions and models that may help the global historian to understand how the new constituent regions of world history have actually interacted' and 'it is in the study of long-distance interaction even more than in comparison that the greatest advantage of the new regional history lies'.[40]

The new global history, however, can lead in a different direction. In his article on the history of the field, Adelman makes a point that, while seemingly obvious, has not received sufficient attention: global disintegrations are as much a part of the historical narrative as the better known triumphs of integration.[41] Given recent developments – Brexit must now stand alongside the fall of the Berlin Wall in 1989 – it seems likely that an interest in historical processes of disintegration will grow.

Here the Mediterranean has much to offer because historians have proclaimed its demise as a unified area at least three times. The earliest, and still the most famous breakup, came in the seventh century, and was

---

[38] Michael Herzfeld, 'The horns of the Mediterraneanist dilemma', *American Ethnologist*, 11 (1984): 439.

[39] Adelman, 'The forked roads to global history'.

[40] Horden and Purcell, 'The Mediterranean and the new thalassology', 732, 740.

[41] Adelman, 'The forked roads to global history'.

The Mediterranean Sea 147

made famous by the Pirenne thesis. In sharp contrast Hess's *Forgotten frontier*, which argues that a hostile frontier divided the formerly integrated western Mediterranean, is little known outside of the specialised fields of early modern North African and Spanish history.[42] This obscurity is not due to any deficiencies in Hess's scholarship. Rather it is the direct result of the marginalisation of the Mediterranean in the early modern world as the European journeys of exploration diminished the importance of the Mediterranean in the world economy.[43]

Critics of the Pirenne thesis have convincingly shown that, by the time the Arabs showed up in the Levant and in North Africa, there was little of the Roman Mare Nostrum left; trade between the eastern and western half of the Mediterranean had been dwindling for a long time prior to the seventh century. Responses to Hess have been slow in coming but they raise similar questions about the relationship between military conquest and trade patterns. In this case, however, the argument is that trade not only did not dry up in the wake of 1492 (or 1581, when an Ottoman/Habsburg truce signalled the end of military engagement in the Mediterranean between the two great powers), but that Spanish commerce with the Maghrib actually grew in the early modern period.[44] On both sides of the supposedly impenetrable and violent frontier, various actors used the ransoming of captives as a vital source of funds and as a way to justify trade, formally prohibited, with the enemy. The Spanish Crown placed North Africa under a system of 'permanent exception' to the prohibition, and if a Christian merchant sought a licence to trade with the Maghrib, 'all he had to do was declare that he would use his profits to ransom Christians rather than invest them in goods to be redistributed back in Spain'.[45] On the North African side we see the Pasha of Algiers taking steps to ensure the safe arrival of the Mercedarians (one of the Spanish religious orders of redemption) in Algiers, instructing the viceroy of Majorca to warn them about the presence of English corsairs in the area. He took this step even though at this time (1604) Algiers was formally an English ally, and the Mercedarians were the agents of an

[42] The Spanish Empire, of course, is a major scholarly field but most of the attention goes to Spain's possessions in the so-called New World, rather than to its Mediterranean commitments.

[43] For the difficulties of writing Mediterranean history after 1492, see Molly Greene, 'Beyond the northern invasions: The Mediterranean in the seventeenth century', *Past and Present*, 174 (2002): 40–72.

[44] Daniel Hershenzon, 'The political economy of ransom in the early modern Mediterranean', *Past and Present*, 231 (2016): 72. Hershenzon's notes also provide an excellent bibliography of the new writing on the western Mediterranean in the early modern period.

[45] Hershenzon, 'The political economy of ransom', 72.

148   M. Greene

enemy state. The Pasha, of course, had his eye on the generous ransoming budget the Mercedarians were bringing with them.[46]

This new work on the western Mediterranean suggests that the early modern period was not so different from what had come before. For many centuries Muslims and Christians had learned how to share the common space, across the religious divide. Diplomacy and shared practices, both of which were on full display in the North African–Spanish relationship, were the essential building blocks of this post-Roman unity.[47]

This brings us to the third iteration of the demise of the Mediterranean. As many scholars have noted, the Mediterranean seems to dissolve with the advent of modernity which, in the case of the inland sea, is conventionally seen to arrive with Napoleon's armies. In Naor Ben-Yehoyada words, 'where the one ends the other starts'.[48] Through a combination of economic globalisation and nation-state consolidation, the argument goes, the Mediterranean disintegrated over the course of the nineteenth and the twentieth centuries. Whether or not one agrees, the possibility that global integration in some areas was accompanied by disintegration elsewhere is certainly a question worth exploring. One highly distinctive fact about the Mediterranean in the modern age does stand out. Across the globe the rise of European hegemony has been perceived as a series of encounters (in the case of the Americas) or re-encounters (in China, for example). In the Mediterranean, modernity unfolded within 'a discourse of *historical separation*'.[49] The countries of northwestern Europe, the place where modernity was seen to reside, forgot or buried their long history of engagement in the Mediterranean and turned the latter into an historical Other. Over the course of the eighteenth century, for example, French Enlightenment thinkers turned North Africa into a wild and unknown land, despite the fact that the city-states of southern Europe had been signing treaties with North African polities since the medieval period.[50] This process of Othering takes us back to Hess and earlier pronouncements on the death of the Mediterranean. The idea that the Mediterranean cannot be modern is projected backwards as historians look for the moment of its demise: 'histories of the Mediterranean [that]

---

[46] Hershenzon, 'The political economy of ransom', 75.
[47] Valérian, 'The medieval Mediterranean', 86.
[48] Yehoyada, 'Mediterranean modernity?', 107. In my discussion I am drawing heavily on Yehoyada's article; more than any other scholar he has grappled with the problem of writing about the Mediterranean in the modern era.
[49] Yehoyada, 'Mediterranean modernity?', 109. The emphasis is in the original.
[50] See Ann Thomson, *Barbary and Enlightenment: European attitudes towards the Maghreb in the eighteenth century* (Leiden, 1987). The two shores were assigned different places however. North Africa and the Levant were passive, they could only 'react' to history. Southern Europe was 'out of history'. Yehoyada, 'Mediterranean modernity?', 110.

The Mediterranean Sea 149

date the sea's death to earlier periods – as early as the turn of the sixteenth century or as late as the beginning of the nineteenth – not because they agree on the conditions for the sea's end, but rather because all accounts construct their respective Mediterraneans in opposition to the present'.[51]

A more self-conscious approach is called for. The Mediterranean is an awkward piece in the puzzle that makes up the globe; perhaps we can learn something from this awkwardness. Why does the Mediterranean seem to vanish with the advent of modernity? When alternative candidates are proposed as the bearers of modernity, in an attempt to question the northwestern European monopoly on the birth of the modern, they are always drawn from 'other early-modern imperial and economic cores far from the circum-Mediterranean lands'.[52] But why? And how should we understand the distinctive discourse of historical separation? Taking on these questions would be beneficial for both Mediterranean and for global history.

On Cosmopolitanism

In all three moments of disintegration, the breakdown in commercial relations is at the same time a moment of cultural separation.[53] But these are the exceptional moments in Mediterranean history. The inland sea is better known, perhaps even renowned, for a vibrant commercial life which has never been stymied by ethnic, linguistic and religious boundaries. This multi-ethnic, multi-religious and multi-linguistic commercial tradition is at the heart of the Mediterranean's famous 'cosmopolitanism', a word that is used by popular and academic historians of the region alike.

The scholarly discussion on Mediterranean cosmopolitanism is multifaceted and wide-ranging but at its heart is the historical experience of the multi-ethnic and multi-religious port cities of the central and eastern Mediterranean. Which cities, exactly, and how far back the concept extends – does it predate the nineteenth century? – is an essential part of the debate. A powerful dose of nostalgia is wrapped up with the notion of cosmopolitanism; the port-cities, it is imagined, were places of 'urbaneness, refinement, and inter-cultural co-existence and conviviality'.[54]

---

[51] Yehoyada, 'Mediterranean modernity?', 117.

[52] Yehoyada, 'Mediterranean modernity?', 108.

[53] 'To state it baldly, I believe that the separation of the Mediterranean world into different, well-defined cultural spheres is the main theme of its sixteenth-century history': Hess, *The forgotten frontier*, p. 3.

[54] Yehoyada, 'Mediterranean modernity?', 116.

150   M. Greene

In part as a reaction to this romantic strain, scholars have pushed back hard and worked to look at cosmopolitanism more critically. Merchants, diplomats, travellers, pirates and intermediaries of all sorts have always been the quintessential cosmopolitan figures of the Mediterranean world, precisely because they are boundary-crossers. One of the most important new interpretive frameworks to emerge in recent years is the argument that intermediaries not only crossed boundaries, they were instrumental in their creation and their maintenance. This also means that cosmopolitan figures did not dissolve boundaries but, in fact, were dependent upon them for their survival.[55] It was Natalie Rothman's 2012 book *Brokering empire: Trans-imperial subjects between Venice and Istanbul* that first made this argument and subsequent work on boundary crossers has proved to be equally fruitful.[56]

As Venetian supremacy broke down, the Venetians had to accept the participation of Ottoman subjects in the trade between the *Serenissima* and the eastern Mediterranean. Different terms for the variety of Ottomans who showed up in Venice began to make their appearance in the documents produced by the state bureaucracy. Rothman traces the history of the word 'Levantini' in Venetian commercial discourse. Originally applied by the state to a specific group of merchants – the diasporic Sephardi Jews coming from the Ottoman Empire – it came to encompass all Ottoman merchants trading in Venice. As part of its linguistic travels, it went from a focus on diasporic commercial activity to a term that referred to a specific group of people, of presumed provenance and particular character traits, the 'Levantini' who were the 'Natives or Inhabitants of the Levant, the Eastern People'.[57] Crucially, this unfolded with the enthusiastic participation of those merchants and fortune-seekers from the eastern Mediterranean who at times were keen to present themselves as 'Levantini' to the authorities, while at other times they rejected the term for themselves but insisted that it should be applied to others. Whichever position they took, their role 'underscores the important mediation performed by those claiming to be "in-between" in the

---

[55] Another critique of the cosmopolitanism literature goes off in another direction, by pointing out that the port-cities – usually represented as happy fugitives from state authority – were in fact dependent upon state projects of modernisation for their success. For a good example of this, see Khaled Fahmy, 'For Cavafy, with love and squalor: Some critical notes on the history and historiography of modern Alexandria', in Anthony Hirst and Michael Silk, eds., *Alexandria: Real and imagined* (Aldershot, 2004), pp. 263–80.

[56] See for example, Hussein Fancy, *The mercenary Mediterranean: Sovereignty, religion and violence in the medieval Crown of Aragon* (Chicago, IL, 2016), a study of the Muslim mercenaries who served the Crown of Aragon. Fancy shows how warfare both bound and separated the medieval Mediterranean.

[57] Rothman, *Brokering empire*, p. 213.

The Mediterranean Sea

process of articulating categories of difference and developing metropolitan practices of boundary-marking and boundary crossing'.[58] Venice in the sixteenth and seventeenth centuries became a cosmopolitan city; that is, it attracted foreign merchants of widely varying religious, linguistic and ethnic backgrounds. They certainly co-existed but their co-existence was marked less by conviviality and refinement, as the nostalgia industry would have it, but rather by an incessant process of boundary making and remaking.

Francesca Trivellato makes similar points about the famously cosmopolitan city of Livorno in the early modern period.[59] Sephardi Jews were encouraged to settle in the city and were offered extraordinary privileges as inducement. As a result, the Jewish community in Livorno emerged as the second largest Sephardic settlement, after Amsterdam, in Europe.[60] Nevertheless, this relentlessly commercial society was fully conscious of differences between Jews and non-Jews and boundaries were carefully policed, both by state authorities and by community leaders. In fact, Trivellato argues, it was the clarity of such boundaries that allowed economic cooperation to flourish.[61] The famously protean character of Mediterranean boundary crossers, she warns, should not be exaggerated. Everyone, including the Medici, understood that the Sephardi habit of using Christian pseudonyms when trading with merchants in Iberia was 'a conventionally accepted fiction used to bypass legal restrictions'.[62] It did not mean that Sephardi merchants were uncertain in their religious identity.

One of the debates around Mediterranean cosmopolitanism concerns the relationship between early modern cosmopolitanism (the two cases discussed here) and the (mostly Ottoman) cities of the nineteenth century. The scholars working on these two periods tend to write from different traditions and are rarely in conversation with each other. Bringing them together would be an exciting and worthwhile project to explore as we think about the future of Mediterranean history. Such a collaboration would also have the great benefit of bridging one of the most intractable

---

[58] Rothman, *Brokering empire*, p. 213.

[59] Francesco Trivellato, *The familiarity of strangers: The Sephardic diaspora, Livorno, and cross-cultural trade in the early modern period* (New Haven, CT, 2009). Livorno was a creation of the Medici and they heavily promoted its image as a diverse city. In 1676 they issued a new golden coin, upon which they carved the image of the city and the motto 'Diversis gentibus una' (many diverse people, one city): Trivellato, *The familiarity of strangers*, p. 96.

[60] Trivellato, *The familiarity of strangers*, p. 5.

[61] Trivellato, *The familiarity of strangers*, p. 96.

[62] Trivellato, *The familiarity of strangers*, p. 19.

152   M. Greene

divides in the field, namely the chasm between the early modern and the modern Mediterranean.

The Mediterranean Graveyard

It is impossible to ignore the twenty-first-century tragedy that has been unfolding in the Mediterranean. The numbers of refugees and migrants crossing the Mediterranean are simply extraordinary. To take only one eight-month period, by the end of August 2015 some 300,000 people had attempted the crossing to Europe from either Turkey or North Africa and 2,500 perished in the course of the journey.[63] Yehoyada has pointed out that – in keeping with the conventional separation between the historical study of the Mediterranean and the Mediterranean of the twenty-first century – there has been little attempt to consider these vast human waves in the context of earlier periods in the history of the inland sea.[64]

The fact of so many desperate people drowning just a few hundred miles from European territory (it is only 290 miles from the west coast of Libya to the Italian island of Lampedusa) certainly underlines the argument that Braudel's unified Mediterranean was attractive and compelling only when the Europeans dominated it.[65] When it is migration from the southern shores to the northern ones, the response is radically different. Fortress Europe, however, is not a new phenomenon. The city of Marseille, for example, grew to be one of the most important ports in the eighteenth-century Mediterranean even as it rigorously excluded anyone who was not a subject of the French king. The difference is that in earlier periods the Muslims of the southern and eastern shores were connected to vast hinterlands and to points further east – such as India – which meant that the Mediterranean was not as important. Now, with the desperate conditions that have engulfed much of Africa and the Middle East, crossing the Mediterranean looms as an avenue of escape. Braudel was certainly correct to point out that the Mediterranean has always been affected by events and trends that unfold far from its shores.

We have seen that successive waves of connection and separation between the Christian and Muslim halves of the Mediterranean have structured much of the writing about the sea. It is also the case that dramatic pronouncements of separation and divergence – whether it be

---

[63] www.unhcr.org/en-us/news/latest/2015/8/55e06a5b6/crossings-mediterranean-sea-exceed-300000-including-200000-greece.html (accessed 12 July 2016).
[64] Yehoyada, 'Mediterranean modernity?', 107.
[65] And of course the crossing from Turkey to Greece is only a few miles. The island of Lesvos is clearly visible from the Turkish coastline.

The Mediterranean Sea

the Pirenne thesis, Hess's frontier in the western Mediterranean and the dagger of nationalism which supposedly finished a connected maritime world – have consistently been qualified and modified, such that the current weight of scholarly opinion falls on the side of connection. It turns out that even in the tremendously hostile western Mediterranean after 1492 Spanish merchants coming to North Africa were more than willing to do business even with the Muslim and the Jewish communities they had recently forced out of Iberia (and the reverse was true as well).[66] Willingness to do business, however, does not mean that cosmopolitan societies were either desired or achieved.

This history of connection even within a larger context of hostility raises questions about how to think about current events in the Mediterranean. On the one hand the unprecedented deaths at sea, combined with anti-immigrant sentiment in Europe would suggest that now, more than ever perhaps, the Mediterranean is a frontier. But, using past historiography as a guide, we should be alert to the possibility that the current crisis echoes, in part, the long history of exchange – licit and illicit – across the inland sea and that now, as then, such projects always require partners on both shores.

Further Reading

Peregrine Horden and Nicholas Purcell's weighty study, *The corrupting sea: A study of Mediterranean history* (Oxford, 2000), has become the indisputable reference point for the ongoing debates on Mediterranean unity, history in the *longue durée* and environmental/ecological approaches to the sea's history. Another influential *histoire totale*, with a specific focus on the declining importance of the Mediterranean in the early modern period, is Faruk Tabak's *The waning of the Mediterranean 1550–1870: A geohistorical approach* (Baltimore, MD, 2008). Several good general histories of the Mediterranean have been published in recent years: Peregrine Horden and Sharon Kinoshita have edited *A companion to Mediterranean history* (Chichester, 2014) and David Abulafia edited *The Mediterranean in history* (New York, 2003). The chronological and thematic sweep of both volumes is admirably broad and helpful but, as with most general studies of the Mediterranean, coverage of the European shores is stronger than that of the Muslim Mediterranean.

See Cyprian Broodbank's *The making of the Middle Sea: A history of the Mediterranean from the beginning to the emergence of the classical world*

---

[66] Hershenzon, 'The political economy of ransom'.

(New York, 2013) for the first emergence of the Mediterranean. O. R. Constable's *Housing the stranger in the Mediterranean world: Lodging, trade and travel in Late Antiquity and the Middle Ages* (Cambridge, 2003) covers the transition from the ancient to the medieval world through the perspective of institutions of hospitality. Medieval Iberia continues to attract the attention of historians. For Mediterranean historians, Hussein Fancy's *Sovereignty, religion and violence in the medieval Crown of Aragon* (Chicago, IL, 2016) is especially attractive because of its close attention to events on the southern shores, in today's North Africa, and their important consequences for the history of Iberia. Fancy's work also engages with the literature on boundary crossers that is an essential theme in E. Natalie Rothman's *Brokering empire: Trans-imperial subjects between Venice and Istanbul* (Ithaca, NY, 2012). Eric Dursteler's *Renegade women: Gender, identity and boundaries in the early modern Mediterranean* (Baltimore, MD, 2011) focuses on women who crossed between Islam and Christianity. For the medieval period in the east, see Angeliki Laiou's *Economic history of Byzantium from the seventh through the fifteenth centuries* (Washington, DC, 2002) which provides, among other things, a Byzantinist perspective on Latin domination of the Mediterranean in the late medieval and early modern period. On the Islamic Mediterranean in the medieval period, see Hassan Khalilieh's *Admiralty and maritime laws in the Mediterranean Sea (ca. 800–1050): The Kitab Akriyat al-Sufun vis-à-vis the Nomos Rhodion Nautikos* (Leiden, 2006). Molly Greene's *Catholic pirates and Greek merchants: A maritime history of the Mediterranean* (Princeton, NJ, 2010) also looks westward from the east, this time during the Ottoman centuries. Greene's is also one of the few studies of Christian, as opposed to Muslim, piracy. Alberto Tenenti's *Piracy and the decline of Venice, 1580–1615* (Berkeley, CA, 1967) remains a classic, as does Godfrey Fisher's *Barbary legend: War, trade and piracy in North Africa, 1415–1830* (Oxford, 1957). J. H. Pryor's *Geography, technology and war: Studies in the maritime history of the Mediterranean, 649–1571* (Cambridge, 1988) and John Guilmartin's *Gunpowder and galleys: Changing technology and Mediterranean warfare at sea in the 16th century* (London, 2003) are essential reading for maritime warfare in the pre-modern Mediterranean. For studies of the port cities of the Mediterranean, see Lois Dubin *Port Jews of Habsburg Trieste: Absolutist politics and Enlightenment culture* (Stanford, CA, 1999), Daniel Goffman, *Izmir and the Levantine world, 1550–1650* (Seattle, WA, 1990) and Edhem Eldem, Bruce Masters and Daniel Goffman, *The Ottoman city between East and West: Aleppo, Izmir and Istanbul* (Cambridge, 1999.) See *Cities of the Mediterranean: From the Ottomans to the present day*

The Mediterranean Sea

(London, 2010), ed. Biray Kolluoğlu and Meltem Toksöz, for a study that connects the Mediterranean and the concerns of global history. Nabil Matar's studies have opened the previously unknown connections between Morocco and England in the early modern period. See his *Britain and the Islamic world, 1558–1713* (Oxford, 2011). Ann Thompson's *Barbary and Enlightenment: European attitudes towards the Maghreb in the eighteenth century* (Leiden, 1987) effectively conveys French engagement with the Mediterranean, while Thomas Gallant's *Experiencing dominion: Culture, identity and power in the British Mediterranean* (Notre Dame, IN, 2002) is a study of the expansion of British power in the region in the nineteenth century. We still lack a synthetic study of the Napoleonic era in the Mediterranean but Daniel Panzac's *Barbary Corsairs: The end of a legend, 1800–1820* (Leiden, 2005) explores what the Napoleonic wars meant for the maritime world of North Africa. Maurizio Isabella and Konstantina Zanou, eds., *Mediterranean diasporas: Politics and ideas in the long nineteenth century* (London, 2015) considers the dramatic events of the nineteenth century from a Mediterranean, rather than a European, viewpoint, including the Muslim world. Julia Clancy-Smith's *Mediterraneans: North Africa and Europe in an age of migration 1800–1900* (Berkeley, CA, 2010) makes for particularly interesting reading, considering the situation in the Mediterranean today.

6   The Red Sea

Jonathan Miran

The Red Sea has long been perceived as a place, a concept and a mythical arena. The idea of the Red Sea has inhabited the minds of Jews, Christians and Muslims who, for many centuries, have conjured up evocative images of the miraculous biblical account of the parting of the Red Sea and its crossing. Arguably, these are among the most visually arresting scenes in monotheist scriptures. From the historian's perspective, the Red Sea seems to present a fundamental paradox: though, since prehistoric times, it has been one of the busiest and most important sea lanes on the globe, a singular maritime space and among the first seas to be mentioned in recorded history, it has long been perceived a transitional space and a sea without a history of its own.

Oceans and seas have always captured the human imagination. Seas have reputations, and the dry, blazingly hot and generally inhospitable environment of the Red Sea basin's littorals has usually unwittingly cast it in a negative light. In his 2010 bestselling epic on the Atlantic, Simon Winchester wrote about those inland seas which seem 'strangely still, starved of any readily apparent vitality'. Together with the Coral Sea and Sea of Japan which 'are somehow stripped of any true kind of oceanic liveliness', the Red Sea, Winchester continues, 'bathed in its ocher fog of desert sand, seems perpetually half dead'.[1] Just like deserts that can be imagined as seas, the Red Sea is an example of an aquatic space that historians and other writers have, on the whole, tended to represent as a sort of desert (in a negative sense) – an empty space, an ahistorical place, and an area of deprivation to be promptly traversed on the way to the more propitious areas located beyond it.

Those accounts that have treated the Red Sea as a historical subject mostly view it from a macro-historical perspective as a transitional space, a maritime corridor in the long-distance trade between the Mediterranean and the Indian Ocean and as a border separating Africa from Arabia. The

---

[1] Simon Winchester, *Atlantic: Great sea battles, heroic discoveries, titanic storms, and a vast ocean of a million stories* (New York, 2010), p. 21.

156

The Red Sea

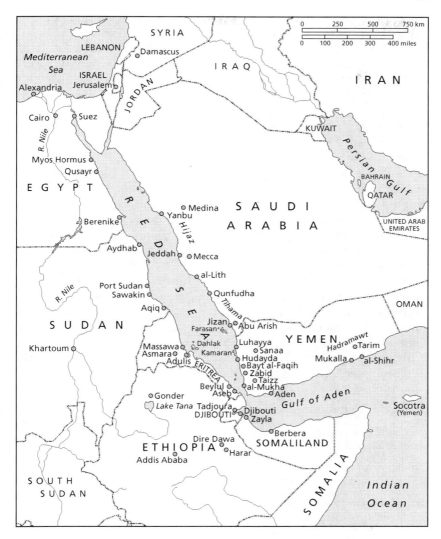

Map 6.1 The Red Sea

history of the Red Sea, in this view, has been exclusively defined by its functional relationship to the Mediterranean and the Indian Ocean – an indispensable hyphen between the two, at times serving as an interface, or a bridge, at others as a barrier. Emblematic of this *non-lieu* representation is the oft-cited phrase referring to the Red Sea as 'an extreme

158   J. Miran

example of a sea on the way to somewhere else'.[2] Such attitudes are also mirrored in accounts of Mediterranean and Indian Ocean history, which mention the Red Sea only in passing, if at all. In his famous study of the Mediterranean, Fernand Braudel said very little about the Red Sea, which he basically saw as located within the continuum of warm deserts extending from western Africa to Arabia and Iran (a so-called 'Greater Sahara'), and described in his chapter on the boundaries of the 'Greater Mediterranean'.[3] Negative perceptions or mere disregard for a historical Red Sea *per se* die hard. For example, the omission of an entry on the Red Sea in the four-volume *Oxford encyclopedia of maritime history* published as late as 2007 is perplexing.[4]

Why has the Red Sea as a historical *space* and *place* not attracted enough scholarly attention? One reason is the way that knowledge has been produced about this area. Rooted in the meta-geographical division of the world into continents and sub-continental regions, the African/Middle Eastern Studies divide has thwarted a more integrative approach to this region and has unwittingly masked the Red Sea as an in-between space, separating Africa from the Middle East.[5] In turn, this has obscured the animated historical connections, circulations and exchanges across the Red Sea area. Different area studies research centres, funding programs, journals and conferences did little to promote alternative conceptions of space. The division of fields of enquiry on the basis of this logic goes even further to separate the northern African Red Sea shores – mainly Egypt, but sometimes the Sudan (attached to Middle Eastern studies)

[2] William Facey, 'The Red Sea: The wind regime and location of ports', in Paul Lunde and Alexandra Porter, eds., *Trade and travel in the Red Sea: Proceedings of Red Sea project I held in the British Museum, October 2002* (Oxford, 2004), p. 7.

[3] Fernand Braudel, *The Mediterranean and the Mediterranean world in the age of Philip II*, 2 vols., trans. Siân Phillips (London, 1972). Though one can note that already in the early nineteenth century, the French naturalist Jean Baptiste Bory de Saint-Vincent (1778–1846) theorised about the Mediterranean as a concept, and identified the Red Sea (*la Méditerranée Erythréenne*) as one of nine such 'Mediterraneans' in the world. See Jean Baptiste Bory de Saint-Vincent, 'Mer', in *Dictionnaire classique d'histoire naturelle*, 17 vols. (Paris, 1822–31), X, p. 381.

[4] John B. Hattendorf, ed., *The Oxford encyclopedia of maritime history*, 4 vols. (Oxford, 2007). Two other recent and quite surprising examples that neglect to even mention the Red Sea as a potentially worthwhile subject for historians are David Abulafia's essay on the role of different 'Mediterraneans' (or sub-Mediterraneans) in world history and Markus Vink's survey of Indian Ocean studies and the 'New Thalassology': Abulafia, 'Mediterraneans', in William V. Harris, ed., *Rethinking the Mediterranean* (Oxford, 2005), pp. 64–93; Markus P. Vink, 'Indian Ocean studies and the "new thalassology"', *Journal of Global History*, 2 (2007): 41–62.

[5] A self-consciously provocative Afro-centric dissension from this logic is expressed in Ali A. Mazrui, 'Towards abolishing the Red Sea and re-Africanizing the Arabian peninsula', in Jeffrey C. Stone, ed., *Africa and the sea: Colloquium at the University of Aberdeen (March 1984)* (Aberdeen, 1985), pp. 98–103.

The Red Sea 159

from the Horn of Africa (attached to African studies). In sum, the Red Sea falls through different conceptual grids and areas of expertise: Egypt is usually studied as part of the Arab world and the Middle East, the Sudan somewhere in between the Middle East and Africa, and Ethiopia is sometimes isolated within its own rich, yet rather insular, tradition of Ethiopian studies rooted in Oriental philology and Semitics.

A similar argument about the fragmentation of knowledge production, diffusion and accessibility could be made about the division of the Red Sea littorals among nine modern nation-states, if we are to include the Gulf of Aqaba and the Gulf of Aden (which we should): Israel, Jordan, Saudi Arabia, Yemen, Egypt, Sudan, Eritrea, Djibouti and the self-declared Republic of Somaliland, a list of nation-states that includes some of the poorest and richest countries in the world and a region that is today associated with poverty, conflict and overall instability. Most of these nation-states have their political and economic centres in their interiors and – conveniently oblivious to a more dynamic transregional view of the past – have developed national histories that perceive the Red Sea littorals as peripheral and marginal. The politicisation of nation-state-centred narratives about history and culture have also obscured the cultural hybridity and cosmopolitanism that has characterised Red Sea port towns and littorals throughout history.

Geography and Naming

Located at the interface between Mediterranean Europe, Africa and Asia, the Red Sea is the saltiest and one of the hottest seas in the world and among its most distinctive maritime spaces. The world's northernmost tropical sea, it is a narrow strip of water about 2,000 kilometres long extending from Suez in the north to the Strait of Bab al-Mandab in the south; its average width is about 280 kilometres and it covers an area of approximately 438,000 square kilometres, which is roughly equivalent to the size of Iraq or Sweden. Until the opening of the Suez Canal in 1869 that connected the Red Sea with the Mediterranean, the basin's only natural opening was at Bab al-Mandab, a strait about thirty kilometres wide. The climate of its arid littorals is less than pleasant, with torrid mean annual temperatures in the southern coastal areas of the basin. The northern part of the basin is practically rainless, while rainfall in the southern area is light and irregular. All along its coasts are shallow coral reefs and shoals, which make sailing particularly treacherous and require expert navigational skills. Some of its shores are bordered by steep mountains which make its coasts difficult to access from both land and sea, explaining in part the thin inhabitation of its littorals and the absence of large

160   J. Miran

port cities with sizeable populations. No permanent rivers or streams flow into the Red Sea, further contributing to its high levels of salinity. That, coupled with high degrees of humidity, has not favoured the preservation of its urban coastal centres. For example, towns such as Mokha in Yemen, Sawakin in Sudan or Zayla in Somaliland, all of which were relatively important port towns as late as the eighteenth and nineteenth centuries, are nowadays partly in ruins and barely inhabited.[6]

If, however, one is to consider the basin's landed surroundings as forming part of the broader Red Sea area, then these arduous and challenging geographic conditions should not mask the more propitious and soundly populated lands behind these barren coasts: the rich Nile Valley, the fertile Ethio-Eritrean and Yemeni highland plateaux, and the Hijazi range of mountains with its oases. Historically, polities in these hinterlands were not always sea-oriented, though they often established trading communities in outposts on the Red Sea coasts and their economic exigencies and political undertakings were at times played out in the broader Red Sea regional arena.

For the sea-centred historian concerned with patterns of maritime mobility, the location of port towns and entrepôts and spatial integration, the Red Sea's single most critical feature is unquestionably its wind regime. It is characterised by northerly and northwesterly winds in the northern part of the basin throughout the year, and variable seasonal southerly winds (in winter) and northerly winds (in summer) in the southern part of the basin.[7] Winds in the Gulf of Aden are governed by the monsoon system: southwest from June to September and northeast from October to May. Inauspiciously impacting water currents, these wind systems made navigation in the Red Sea infamously onerous. In some cases, long-distance merchants went as far as preferring to move goods between the Indian Ocean and the Mediterranean via the terrestrial trade routes in western Arabia rather than risking the hazards of Red Sea navigation. In other cases, trade goods were moved by sea by local and regional cabotage networks that were relatively slow. All in all, the Red Sea wind regime was critical in shaping shipping patterns, the circulation of goods, trading spheres and the location of port towns. In more than one way it divided the Red Sea into two spheres of navigation with far-reaching historical implications. This held true, at least until the

---

[6] Ruth Lapidoth, *The Red Sea and the Gulf of Aden* (The Hague, 1982), pp. 1–12, and Alasdair J. Edwards and Stephen M. Head, eds., *Red Sea* (Oxford/New York, 1987), esp. ch. 1 by Stephen M. Head (pp. 1–21).

[7] Facey, 'The Red Sea'. See also G. R. Tibbetts, 'Arab navigation in the Red Sea', *Geographical Journal*, 127 (1961): 322–34.

The Red Sea   161

nineteenth-century introduction of steamship navigation (1830s) and opening of the Suez Canal (1869).

The multiple appellations given to the Red Sea are in some cases suggestive of the historical layering of political dominance or hegemonic aspirations, geographic constructions and naming practices, as well as culturally rooted imaginings (both external and local). In the Hebrew Bible it is called *Yam Suf* (Heb.), or 'Sea of Reeds'. In Antiquity, the Greek *Erythrà thálassa* referred to a far broader aquatic space than the Red Sea, and included the entire Indian Ocean from Egypt to China. In the early Christian era some appellations referred to the 'Persian Gulf' (*Persikòs kólpos/sinus Persicus*) and to the 'Arabian Gulf' (*Arábios kólpos/ sinus Arabicus*) to designate the Red Sea proper. Interestingly, from the ninth century onwards, Arab cartographers such as al-Khwarizmi, Ibn Hawqal or Yaqut al-Hamawi, named different parts of the Red Sea following their contiguous terrestrial areas, giving *Bahr al-Kulzum*, or 'Sea of Clysma' (ancient Suez), *Bahr al-Hijaz*, 'Sea of Hijaz', *Bahr Mekka*, 'Sea of Mecca', *Bahr al-Yaman*, 'Sea of Yemen', *Bahr Habesh*, 'Sea of Abyssinia/Ethiopia' and so on. Yaqut included the Gulf of Aden (*Khalij Barbara*) in the Red Sea. In Arabic we also have *al-Halij al-'Arabi*, 'The Arabian Gulf', *Khalij Ayla*, 'Gulf of Ayla' (or the Gulf of Aqaba), and in Turkish, *Shab denizi*, the 'Coral Sea'. But our current usage is traced back to the ancient *Erythrà thálassa*, and to the Romans, who translated that to *Mare Rubrum*. From these came *al-Bahr al-Ahmar* in Arabic, *Bahrä Ertəra* in Ethiopic (Ge'ez) and *Qäyyəh Bahri* in Tigrinya. It was only in the fourteenth and fifteenth centuries that European cartographers applied and fixed the appellation *Mare Rubrum* ('Red Sea') to refer to the maritime space that we now identify by that name (sometimes represented on European medieval maps in vermilion).[8]

Historiographic Perspectives, Old and New

Though attitudes to the Red Sea as a historical space have been generally characterised by scholarly apathy, there have been exceptions to this trend, mostly in France. A case in point is the work of Albert Kammerer (1871–1951), a career diplomat and a non-professional geographer and historian who developed a life-long passion for the Red Sea region (and

---

[8] C. H. Becker and C.F. Beckingham, 'Baḥr al-Ḳulzum', in *Encyclopaedia of Islam*, 2nd edn.: http://dx.doi.org/10.1163/1573-3912_islam_SIM_1062 (accessed 31 March 2017); Alexis Wick, *The Red Sea: In search of lost space* (Oakland, CA, 2016), pp. 83–86; Emmanuelle Vagnon and Éric Vallet, eds., *La fabrique de l'océan Indien. Cartes d'Orient et d'Occident (Antiquité–XVIe siècle)* (Paris, 2017), pp. 111–31.

162   J. Miran

the 'Orient', more broadly) after being posted in Egypt in 1922. In 1925 Kammerer published an article titled 'La mer Rouge à travers les âges' ('The Red Sea through the ages') in which he recognised the sea basin as a geographical and historical entity and called for the writing of its history. Adopting a thematically driven *longue durée* approach, he surveyed this history from ancient Egypt and the aromatics trade, to the history of different ports in the Greco-Roman period, to Arab navigation in the medieval period, down to the role of the Red Sea in intra-European politics since the eighteenth century.[9] One wonders whether Kammerer was influenced or inspired by Lucien Febvre (1878–1956), whose classic primer of historical geography appeared only three years beforehand.[10] Albert Kammerer went on to publish his monumental multi-volume eclectic work on the history of the Red Sea region, *La Mer Rouge, l'Abyssinie, l'Arabie . . .* (1929–52).[11] In the preface to the first volume of this *tour de force*, Kammerer recognised what he perceived to be the oft-overlooked fundamental historical cohesiveness of the Red Sea:

It is the history of a geographic region that is more homogeneous than is commonly thought, where a purely Semitic civilization developed. It comprises not only Arabia and the Red Sea itself, in other words the history of navigation and the commercial links between the Indies ('*les Indes*') and the Mediterranean, but it includes also the part of Africa that has a coast on the Red Sea (minus Egypt); in other words, Ancient Ethiopia, the medieval lands of Prester John, or Abyssinia of modern times.[12]

An equally interesting effort to write the Red Sea into the historical narrative is the 'introduction' to that same volume written by the French statesman and historian Gabriel Hanotaux (1853–1944), and titled somewhat bombastically 'The secret of the Red Sea: the Erythraean origins of Western thought'.[13] Hanotaux opened his essay by stressing the critical geopolitical role of the Red Sea as a major trade route in the

---

[9] Albert Kammerer, 'La mer Rouge à travers les âges', *La Revue de Paris*, 32, 2 (March–April 1925): 109–41.

[10] Lucien Febvre, *La Terre et l'évolution humaine: introduction géographique à l'histoire* (Paris, 1922). Translated into English as Lucien Febvre in collaboration with Lionel Bataillon, *A geographical introduction to history*, trans. E. G. Mountford and J. H. Paxton (London, 1925).

[11] Albert Kammerer, *La Mer Rouge, l'Abyssinie et l'Arabie depuis l'Antiquité*, 4 vols. (Cairo, 1929–35), and Kammerer, *La Mer Rouge, l'Abyssinie et l'Arabie aux XVIe et XVIIe siècles*, 3 vols. (Cairo, 1947–52).

[12] Kammerer, *La Mer Rouge, l'Abyssinie et l'Arabie depuis l'Antiquité*, I, pp. xxvii–xxxiii (my translation).

[13] Gabriel Hanotaux, 'Introduction: Le secret de la mer Rouge. Les origines Érythréennes de la pensée occidentale', in Kammerer, *La Mer Rouge, l'Abyssinie et l'Arabie depuis l'Antiquité*, I, pp. iii–xxv.

The Red Sea   163

world. Placing the Red Sea firmly in global history – but interestingly
positioning it also vis-à-vis the Mediterranean and its history – Hanotaux
went as far as claiming that in at least three different historical moments
the fate of this sea determined the fate of 'Civilisation' itself: the first
was when Alexander the Great took Tyre and then went on to establish
Alexandria (331 BCE); the second moment was when the Portuguese
appeared at the Bab el-Mandeb and challenged the privilege enjoyed by
the trading cities of the Mediterranean (sixteenth century), and the third
case was when, following the opening of the Suez Canal (1869), 'Lesseps
breathed back to the Mediterranean the life which had abandoned it
and gave back to it this Oriental commerce that Christopher Columbus
missed when he landed in America'.[14] After highlighting the Red Sea's
role as 'one of the points of departure of Civilization', Hanotaux established its geographic and ethnic unity. The people who inhabit that space,
he wrote, 'constitute an ethnic corridor between East and West'. These
are the Semitic people, whose history, he thought, was tied to the history
of the Red Sea in its broadest sense (he included the Jordan Valley, the
Dead Sea, up to Damascus) and whose history is rooted in the histories
of Judaism, Christianity and Islam. Referring to the peoples of the Red
Sea region as *'nos Erythréens'* (our Erythraeans, to be understood as 'Red
Sea people'), who were 'splendidly isolated' from other people living in
more fluvial and agricultural settings, Hanotaux claimed their ethno-cul-
tural homogeneity.

Though studies relating to various topics in and around the Red Sea
were undertaken in the second half of the twentieth century, only rarely
did they adopt a sea-centred approach inclined to look at the region as a
coherent historical and geographical unit, or that focused on phenomena
on both shores of the basin. One exception is Roger Joint-Daguenet's
Histoire de la mer Rouge, a rather flawed semi-scholarly two-volume survey of the political history of the Red Sea region over the past 3,500 years
published in 1995 and 2000.[15] Far more important is the work of historian Michel Tuchscherer who, since the early 1990s, has published studies on trade, currency flows, the coffee economy, Red Sea islands and the
multifarious relationships between the African and Arabian coasts of the
Red Sea between the sixteenth and nineteenth centuries.[16]

---

[14] Hanotaux, 'Introduction', pp. viii–ix.
[15] Roger Joint-Daguenet, *Histoire de la Mer Rouge. De Moïse à Bonaparte* (Paris, 1995);
Joint-Daguenet, *Histoire de la Mer Rouge. De Lesseps à nos Jours* (Paris, 2000).
[16] Representative works include Michel Tuchscherer, 'Le commerce en mer Rouge aux
alentours de 1700: flux, espaces et temps', in Rika Gyselen, ed., *Circulation des monnaies,
des marchandises et des biens*, vol. V (Bures-sur-Yvette, 1993), pp. 159–78; Tuchscherer,
'Trade and port cities in the Red Sea-Gulf of Aden region in the sixteenth and seventeenth centuries', in Leila Tarazi Fawaz and C. A. Bayly, eds., *Modernity and culture: From*

164   J. Miran

Current historiographical trends associated with the shift toward maritime conceptions of space, or the so-called oceanic turn (also, the 'New Thalassology'), are reviving interest in the Red Sea as a historic space and a distinct region that deserves to be studied.[17] The appearance of a spate of Red Sea-related monographs and special journal issues, as well as the organisation of panels, workshops and conferences in recent years, reflect the growing realisation on the part of the new ocean-centred historians that small(er) maritime arenas are excellent sites for testing aquatic-centred approaches. The last fifteen years have witnessed a noteworthy renewal and propelling of Red Sea studies.[18] Archaeologists and historians such as Timothy Power and myself recognise that the space between the Indian Ocean and the Mediterranean should be historicised as an integrated maritime space whose historical trajectories and orientations were not limited to the sole role of bridging the Mediterranean Sea and the Indian Ocean.[19] Such efforts to recast the history of the region with the Red Sea as an organising framework for historical and social scientific analysis allow us to think more usefully about the Red Sea as a region *sui generis*.

New thinking about the Red Sea recognises more fully and unequivocally that the particularly narrow bodies of water in the Red Sea and Gulf of Aden constitute an arena of multilayered, interconnected and overlapping circuits and networks characterised by brisk flows of people, goods and ideas. In other words, and transcending traditional characterisations

---

the Mediterranean to the Indian Ocean (New York, 2002), pp. 28–45; Tuchscherer, 'Coffee in the Red Sea area from the sixteenth to the nineteenth century', in William Gervase Clarence-Smith and Steven Topik, eds., *The global coffee economy in Africa, Asia, and Latin America, 1500–1989* (Cambridge, 2003), pp. 50–66; Tuchscherer, 'Les échanges commerciaux entre les rives africaine et arabe de l'espace mer Rouge golfe d'Aden au seizième et dix-septième siècles', in Lunde and Porter, eds., *Trade and travel in the Red Sea*, pp. 157–63; Tuchscherer, 'Îles et insularité en mer Rouge à l'époque ottomane (XVIe–début XIXe siècle)', in N. Vatin and G. Veinstein, eds., *Insularités ottomanes* (Paris, 2004), pp. 203–19.

[17] To my knowledge, it was only in 2014 that Michael Pearson, a leading historian of the Indian Ocean, has included the Red Sea in a list of potentially promising maritime spaces to be studied in a general historiographic essay on oceanic history. Michael Pearson, 'Oceanic history', in Prasenjit Duara, Viren Murthy and Andrew Sartori, eds., *A companion to global historical thought* (Chichester, 2014), p. 338.

[18] In this context one should mention the United Kingdom-based 'Red Sea Project' and the six international conferences that it has convened between 2002 and 2013. (See precise references to the conference proceedings in the Further Reading section below.)

[19] Jonathan Miran, ed., 'Special issue: Space, mobility and translocal connections across the Red Sea Area since 1500', *Northeast African Studies*, 12 (2012): ix–307 and Miran, 'Mapping space and mobility in the Red Sea region, c. 1500–1950', *History Compass*, 12, 2 (February 2014): 197–216. An application of such orientation for the first centuries of the Islamic era is Timothy Power, *The Red Sea from Byzantium to the Caliphate, AD 500–1000* (New York, 2012).

The Red Sea

of this area, new studies, for example by John Meloy on Mamluk Jiddah and the Hijaz, and Eric Vallet's work on the Yemeni Rasulid state, increasingly take into account the interactions of both coasts of the Red Sea as well as the multiple dimensions of regional and transregional trading ambits between Egypt and India. This approach helps to bring into sharper focus the host of inter- and intra-regional and transmarine political, commercial and religious circuits and networks that produced spaces with varying degrees of cohesiveness and integration.[20] Other work, for example, by Steven Sidebotham on Roman Berenike, Roxani Eleni Margariti on medieval Aden, Li Guo on thirteenth-century Qusayr, Nancy Um on Mokha in the seventeenth and eighteenth centuries, Philippe Pétriat on the Hadrami merchants in nineteenth- and twentieth-century Jiddah and my own work on Massawa in the same period, explores, among other themes, the ways in which transcoastal and transregional connections and interactions – including the broader Indian Ocean and the Mediterranean regions – shaped Red Sea port towns, their social and cultural environments, characteristics and cosmopolitan urban societies.[21] Much like the Arabian/Persian Gulf, such work increasingly inserts the Red Sea into conversations on the broader picture of Indian Ocean history.[22]

The place and role of the Red Sea region in global history is also gradually gaining greater recognition and attention. As much as it has long served as an important route from Europe and the Mediterranean to Indian Ocean Asia, cross-Red Sea social and cultural contact, circulation and exchanges spurred the development of vibrant civilisations emerging in northeast Africa and south Arabia in the first millennium

---

[20] John L. Meloy, *Imperial power and maritime trade: Mecca and Cairo in the later Middle Ages* (Chicago, IL, 2010); Eric Vallet, *L'Arabie marchande. Etat et commerce sous les sultans rasulides du Yémen (626–858 / 1229–1454)* (Paris, 2011).

[21] Steven E. Sidebotham, *Berenike and the ancient maritime spice route* (Berkeley, CA, 2011); Roxani Eleni Margariti, *Aden and the Indian Ocean trade: 150 Years in the life of a medieval Arabian port* (Chapel Hill, NC, 2007); Li Guo, *Commerce, culture and community in a Red Sea port in the thirteenth century: Arabic documents from Quseir* (Leiden, 2004); Nancy Um, *The merchant houses of Mocha: Trade and architecture in an Indian Ocean port* (Seattle, WA, 2009); Philippe Pétriat, *Le négoce des lieux saints. Négociants hadramis de Djedda, 1850–1950* (Paris, 2016); Jonathan Miran, *Red Sea citizens: Cosmopolitan society and cultural change in Massawa* (Bloomington, IN, 2009). One could add to the list two articles on the port of Sawakin: Jay Spaulding, 'Suakin: A port city of the early modern Sudan', in Kenneth R. Hall, ed., *Secondary cities and urban networking in the Indian Ocean realm, c. 1400–1800* (Lanham, MD, 2008), pp. 39–53; Andrew C. S. Peacock, 'Suakin: a northeast African port in the Ottoman Empire', *Northeast African Studies*, 12 (2012): 29–50.

[22] An example is Edward A. Alpers, *The Indian Ocean in world history* (New York, 2014). New sea-centred perspectives on the history of the Arabian/Persian Gulf are brought together in Lawrence G. Potter, ed., *The Persian Gulf in history* (New York, 2009) and Potter, ed., *The Persian Gulf in modern times: People, ports, and history* (New York, 2014).

166   J. Miran

of the Common Era. The Red Sea area has also been the site of global-scale imperial struggles between world powers, at least since Antiquity.[23] Furthermore, the region has been the source of prized commodities such as frankincense and myrrh, coffee, mother-of-pearl and pearls, which have been used in religious ritual and as traditional medicine, or have shaped fashion trends and modes of sociability in different parts of the world. The birth of Islam and the most spectacular of annual global pilgrimage flows (the *hajj*) are also centred on this region. For example, in his transregional/translocal history of Southeast Asians and the *hajj*, Eric Tagliacozzo firmly locates the Red Sea in its regional context noting that 'few places in the world can boast as complex a history as the Red Sea and its coasts in the early modern era', or that the Red Sea was 'one of the most important spaces on the planet' around the turn of the twentieth century.[24] The connection between mobility on a global scale and the Red Sea region is also at the centre of Valeska Huber's work on the Suez Canal as a lynchpin of different forms of mobility.[25] These are but a few examples that underscore the importance of the Red Sea in world history.

Discovering the Red Sea

Few seas have been the subject of descriptions for as long a time as the Red Sea.[26] Naturally, periods characterised by international commercial expansion and imperial vying spawned the production of new knowledge about the Red Sea from the particular vantage points of outsiders to the region (focused on long-distance transit trade and strategic importance). Adding to the reasons accounting for a Red Sea blind spot, I tend to agree with Timothy Power who speculated that the focus on the transit trade in what came to be such paramount historical sources as the mid-first-century CE anonymous Greco-Roman merchant guide the *Periplus of the Erythraean Sea (Periplus Maris Erythraei)* and the Jewish merchant letters preserved in the Cairo Geniza has deeply influenced scholarly perceptions of the Red Sea.[27] The challenge today is to construct an alternative

---

[23] See G. W. Bowersock, *The Throne of Adulis: Red Sea wars on the eve of Islam* (Oxford, 2013).

[24] Eric Tagliacozzo, *The longest journey: Southeast Asians and the pilgrimage to Mecca* (New York, 2013), pp. 5, 56.

[25] Valeska Huber, *Channelling mobilities: Migration and globalisation in the Suez Canal region and beyond, 1869–1914* (Cambridge, 2013).

[26] See George F. Hourani, *Arab seafaring in the Indian Ocean in ancient and early medieval times* (Princeton, NJ, 1951, rev. ed. 1995), pp. 17–36; Power, *The Red Sea*, pp. 6–10; Mark Horton, 'The human settlement of the Red Sea', in A. J. Edwards and S. M. Head, eds., *Red Sea*, pp. 347–51.

[27] Power, *The Red Sea*, p. 14.

The Red Sea   167

framing of Red Sea history – one that dynamically interweaves the local, regional and the supraregional, or the global – by using some of those same historical descriptions. This section explores some such sources and, in the process, also serves to provide a temporal framework of Red Sea history in the broadest of brushstrokes.

Though navigation in the Red Sea was already recorded during the Bronze Age Pharaonic state – most famously Queen Hatshepsut's expedition to the Land of Punt around 1400 BCE (Dynasty XVIII) – it was under the Ptolemaic dynasty (332 BCE–30 BCE) that enduring Red Sea maritime communications were significantly expanded and consolidated. The Ptolemaic rulers of Egypt invested state resources in the Red Sea, established a number of ports on the sea's western shores (e.g. Berenike), and laid the foundations for the famous 'India trade'.[28] This began the process of further integrating the Red Sea region into what would later become a more or less coherent regional space. Early accounts of the Red Sea date to the second century BCE; Agatharchides of Cnidus's *On the Erythraean Sea* (c. 110 BCE) provides the earliest meaningful account of the Red Sea, as well as of the geography and ethnography of its African and Arabian coasts.[29] Other accounts date from the beginning of the Christian era. Strabo's (64 BCE–21 CE) *Geography* and Pliny the Elder's (23 CE–79 CE) *Natural History* both include valuable information about the Roman trade with India, but also about the Red Sea region, its inhabitants and its natural history.

The production of knowledge about the Red Sea in this period reached its peak with the mid-first-century CE anonymous Greco-Roman merchant guide the *Periplus of the Erythraean Sea* (*Periplus Maris Erythraei*).[30] The composition of a merchant handbook by an experienced mariner describing in detail the area between the Mediterranean and India may well have reflected the apex of the India trade in the Roman era. The *Periplus* provided detailed information about sailing conditions, winds, reefs, harbours, entrepôts, markets, trade goods, traders, trading practices and ethnographic descriptions of the coastal inhabitants of the Red Sea and the western Indian Ocean (to which the appellation *Maris Erythraei* referred). All in all, intensified political, commercial, social and cultural exchanges in the Red Sea during the

[28] See Sidebotham, *Berenike and the ancient maritime spice route*.
[29] Agatharchides of Cnidus, *On the Erythraean Sea*, trans. and ed. by Stanley M. Burstein (London, 1989).
[30] *Periplus Maris Erythraei: Text with introduction, translation and commentary*, ed. Lionel Casson (Princeton, NJ, 1989).

168   J. Miran

two centuries before and after the start of the Common Era integrated and consolidated 'the Red Sea as a discrete unit of human geography', in Power's words.[31]

The rise of Islam in western Arabia and its gradual spread north and south, through land and sea, induced a new phase of knowledge production on the Red Sea. Arab geographers and travellers such as Al-Masudi (tenth century), Ibn Jubayr (twelfth/thirteenth centuries), Ibn al-Mujawir (thirteenth century) and Ibn Battuta (fourteenth century), provided descriptions that usually highlighted the fickle winds and the hazards of sailing in Red Sea waters. The production of nautical information culminated with Ahmad ibn Majid's exhaustive mariner's pilot *Kitab al-fawa'id fi usul al-bahr wa'l-qawa'id* ('The book of profitable things concerning the first principles and rules of navigation'), written around 1490 CE.[32] Ibn Majid devoted a chapter of his nautical compilation to the Red Sea (*Qulzum al-'Arab*) providing detailed information on sailing routes, winds, currents, shoals, reefs, islands and harbour entrances among other subjects. Revealingly, his descriptions did not extend north beyond Jiddah; the northern half of the Red Sea was ignored. A qualitatively different set of sources from the medieval Islamic period that has recently been utilised in enlightening studies are letters, especially those written by Jewish traders and preserved in the Cairo Geniza. Roxani Eleni Margariti utilised such documents to carefully reconstruct the history of Aden and its commercial and shipping connections between Egypt and India.[33] Li Guo read fragments of papers shedding light on the operation and activities of Abu Mufarrij and his family's shipping business in Qusayr al-Qadim (Egypt) during the late Ayyubid and early Mamluk eras (thirteenth century).[34] Eric Vallet, for his part, draws on an impressive array of archives compiled for the Yemeni Rasulid sultans between the thirteenth and fifteenth centuries, to reconstruct the history of Aden as well as multiple dimensions of regional and transregional trading ambits in the Red Sea, Gulf of Aden and western Indian Ocean region.[35]

The sixteenth century represented a momentous turning point in Red Sea history. The Ottoman conquest of Mamluk Egypt (1516–17) and the

---

[31] Power, *The Red Sea*, pp. 9–10. For a useful summary of findings resulting from excavations in the ancient ports of Adulis, Berenike and Myos Hormos, see Eivind Heldaas Seland, 'Archaeology of trade in the Western Indian Ocean, 300 BC–AD 700', *Journal of Archaeological Research*, 22 (2014): 380–83.

[32] G. R. Tibbetts, *Arab navigation in the Indian Ocean before the Portuguese* (London, 1971); Tibbetts, 'Arab navigation in the Red Sea', *The Geographical Journal*, 127 (1961): 322–34.

[33] Margariti, *Aden and the Indian Ocean trade*.

[34] Guo, *Commerce, culture and community in a Red Sea port in the thirteenth century*.

[35] Vallet, *L'Arabie marchande*.

The Red Sea 169

advances of Portuguese ambitions in the western Indian Ocean brought these two powers to compete over ascendancy in the area and inscribed the Red Sea into the arena of global imperial politics. The most pertinent of several Portuguese Red Sea 'explorers' was Dom João de Castro (1500–48) whose expedition from the island of Socotra to Suez in 1541 may be considered the first European scientific exploration of the Red Sea. The result was an exhaustive survey of the African coastlines. Full of geographical, nautical and historical information, making learned references to Greco-Roman writers about the region, De Castro's *Roteiro do Mar Roxo* represents an important source for the study of the Red Sea at this time and served as an invaluable source of information for later Europeans. It is telling that the pioneer twentieth-century historian of the Red Sea, Albert Kammerer, edited, introduced and annotated De Castro's rutter.[36]

The European Enlightenment in the eighteenth century marked a new era for the production of 'scientific' geographic knowledge about areas outside Europe.[37] The Red Sea was one of the first areas to be explored and studied, mostly by way of an interest in the history of Egypt, but also in ancient history and the ancient world more broadly. The middle of the eighteenth century inaugurated the beginning of a long-standing French fascination with the Red Sea. The geographer and cartographer Jean-Baptiste Bourguignon d'Anville (1697–1782) produced the first – to my knowledge – rigorous scientific attempt to describe the topography of the Red Sea in his *Mémoires sur l'Egypte ancienne et moderne, suivis d'une Description du Golfe Arabique ou de la Mer Rouge* (Paris, 1766). In the sixty pages devoted to the Red Sea, d'Anville described his efforts to draw up a map of the Red Sea as an integrated space (*Golfe Arabique ou Mer Rouge*, 1765), making exhaustive references to Greek, Roman, Arab, Ottoman, Portuguese, French and English sources and unpublished manuscript maps.[38]

---

[36] Albert Kammerer, *Le routier de Dom Joam de Castro. L'exploration de la mer Rouge par les Portugais en 1541* (Paris, 1936). See also Timothy J. Coates, 'D. João de Castro's 1541 Red Sea voyage in the greater context of sixteenth-century Portuguese-Ottoman Red Sea rivalry', in Caesar E. Farah, ed., *Decision making and change in the Ottoman Empire* (Kirksville, MO, 1993), pp. 263–85.

[37] See Anne Marie Claire Godlewska, *Geography unbound: French geographic science from Cassini to Humboldt* (Chicago, IL and London, 1999).

[38] Cartographic representations of the Red Sea were not new to the eighteenth century. In the sixteenth and seventeenth centuries Iberian and Dutch atlases included cartographic representations that framed the Red Sea as a cohesive spatial unit. Two superb publications that reproduce historic cartographic representations of the Arabian Peninsula and the Indian Ocean, offer much to the Red Sea historian. Khaled al Ankary, *La Péninsule Arabique dans les cartes européennes anciennes. Fin XVe–début XIXe siècle* (Paris, 2001); Vagnon and Vallet, eds., *La Fabrique de l'océan Indien*.

170   J. Miran

Not unlike the early sixteenth century, the turn of the nineteenth century positioned the Red Sea at the centre of global imperial rivalry, this time between the French and the British. Napoleon's invasion of Egypt (1798–1801) was in part motivated by the objective of hindering British communications with India via the Red Sea. The British, for their part, were looking for new ways to speed up access to India. Technological developments proved crucial in the next few decades and the gradual introduction of steam navigation propelled a series of hydrographic and nautical charting surveys culminating with the publication in 1841 of Robert Moresby's *Sailing directions for the Red Sea*.[39] These dynamics climaxed in the opening of the Suez Canal in 1869, which, arguably, constituted the single most transformative event in the history of the Red Sea.[40] All in all, the introduction of regular steamship navigation, the opening of the canal, and the imposition of regimes of mobility by European colonial empires, established the basin's role as a major global waterway and cemented its pivotal strategic position in the world.

As suggested in the context of Albert Kammerer's scholarly enterprise, the 1920s and 1930s present particular interest for the Red Sea historian. In France, journalistic, literary and scholarly fascination with the Red Sea produced a boom of publications that captured the popular imagination. Investigative journalists (*Grands reporters*) such as Albert Londres and Joseph Kessel travelled to the region and produced intrepid first-hand accounts that denounced abiding slave trafficking, rampant piracy, smuggling and the harsh labouring conditions of Red Sea pearlers.[41] Such politically progressive undertakings were blended with (or fuelled) by an *esprit d'aventure* that seized the popular imagination at times removed from such high-minded political inspiration. No one epitomised this trend better than the eccentric adventurer, maverick and prolific writer Henry de Monfreid, who published *Les Secrets de la mer Rouge* in 1931 (translated into English in 1934 and released as a feature film in 1937). *Les Secrets* quickly became a classic of the travel-adventure writing genre and Monfreid continued to release many more books recounting

[39] Sarah Searight, 'The charting of the Red Sea', *History Today*, 53 (2003): 40–6. For French efforts in this field, see Georges, R. Malécot, 'Quelques aspects de la vie maritime en mer Rouge dans la première moitié du XIXe siècle', *L'Afrique et l'Asie Modernes*, 164 (1990): 22–43.

[40] Huber, *Channelling mobilities*, and Colette Dubois, 'The Red Sea ports during the revolution in transportation, 1800–1914', in Fawaz and Bayly, eds., *Modernity and culture from the Mediterranean to the Indian Ocean*, pp. 58–74.

[41] Joseph Kessel, *Marchés d'esclaves* (Paris, 1930) and *Fortune carrée* (Paris, 1932), Albert Londres, *Les pêcheurs de perle* (Paris, 1931).

The Red Sea 171

his Red Sea adventures, real and imagined, to popular acclaim. Some of Monfreid's books are still in print in French.

Imagining the Red Sea: Boundaries, Mobility and Spatial Integration

How should we think about the Red Sea and write its history/histories? The insight that most maritime spaces are innately fractured, fragmented and unstable arenas is certainly valid even for a maritime space as relatively small and circumscribed as the Red Sea.[42] This goes to the heart of the challenge of writing oceanic and sea histories. Given that sea-centred scholarship on Red Sea history is still in its infancy, one can offer more questions than answers. If we are to apply David Armitage's three-fold schema of *circum*-Atlantic, *trans*-Atlantic and *cis*-Atlantic history to the Red Sea, most studies to date correspond to the *cis*-Red Sea concept (which can be the history of a port town or a region within a Red Sea context). In this and other essays, I try to make the case for employing a *circum*-Red Sea approach (the transregional history of circulation and exchanges in the Red Sea World) to a space characterised by geographical and historical unity.[43]

A first conceptual problem encountered by the Red Sea historian is that of boundaries: what and where is the Red Sea region, area or world? What are its contours? Unstable notions of space and borders inevitably raise the question of connections between the Red Sea and the Mediterranean on the one hand, and the Indian Ocean, on the other. A closely connected question is whether to include the Gulf of Aden and the important port of Aden within the confines of Red Sea history, or even a Red Sea world. The crucial factor here is the peculiar wind regimes that limited mobility and shaped spaces of activity in the Red Sea area. In some periods, the Gulf of Aden was far more integrated with the southern half of the Red Sea than the southern and northern halves were connected to each other. This practically made the southern half of the Red Sea an appendage of the Indian Ocean. This point would support the thesis that until the introduction of steamship navigation in the mid-nineteenth century, the Red Sea was not an entirely integrated space since its different wind regimes effectively divided it into two. One

---

[42] Karen Wigen, 'Introduction, *AHR* Forum: Oceans of History', *American Historical Review*, 111 (2006): 717–21.

[43] David Armitage, 'Three concepts of Atlantic history', in David Armitage and Michael J. Braddick, eds., *The British Atlantic world 1500–1800*, 2nd edn. (Basingstoke, 2009), pp. 18–20.

172   J. Miran

could hence advance the argument that this made the Red Sea a barrier between the Mediterranean and the Indian Ocean, rather than a bridge. But this view is construed from the sole perspective of international long-distance trade. We know well that navigational challenges perhaps slowed down, but did not cut communications on all levels of mobility in the Red Sea basin (different sea vessels, cabotage networks, the interconnectedness of seaborne and overland transportation arrangements).

A set of conceptual dilemmas wrestled with by historians of maritime spaces is whether they should limit themselves to writing about those people who crossed the sea and lived on its coastlines and in its port cities and islands, or should they include the lands bordering the sea (and if yes, how far inland?). A case for extending the boundaries of the Red Sea world inland can be made when evoking – once again – alternative overland transportation undertakings that grew out of the adversities of Red Sea navigation. The moving of goods overland – for example, from Aden to the North, along the Arabian littoral – was a way to compensate for difficult sailing conditions in the northern half of the basin. Merchants and shippers adapted and adjusted to the limitations posed by natural conditions by the dynamic *complementarity* of sea and land. This serves to make the case for a dynamic regional approach that does not limit Red Sea history to water and coast.

There is no question that the role of states and empires (both local and external) in integrating parts of the Red Sea could be critical. Economic, commercial, taxation, administrative policies, security practices and the policing of waters could promote spatial, but also political, economic and social integration. In turn, the sea itself could play a role in promoting state formation and developing hegemonic ambitions in the Red Sea region. Intimately related is the role of states in establishing regimes of navigation and the policing of waters – and the ways by which local actors made efforts to circumvent them (e.g. smuggling, contraband and piracy). The question of spatial integration also raises the issue of economic interdependence among Red Sea (coastal – hinterland and intercoastal) populations. What was the nature of economic interdependence between different parts of the Red Sea region and to what extent has economic interdependence created coherent economic, social and, perhaps, cultural spaces in parts of the basin?

In light of such issues, can we indeed imagine the Red Sea as a coherent region, and what specific political, commercial or technological factors could promote greater or lesser integration? Are parts of it more integrated than others and are there periods in which integration is more apparent? One example of an avenue for thinking about cultural integration is the question of architectural continuity, or what has been

The Red Sea   173

coined by Derek H. Matthews in the early 1950s the 'Red Sea style'.[44] Matthews proposed that the built form around the rim of the Red Sea was characterised by a shared, coherent and unified architectural style. Confirming Matthews's notion of Red Sea architectural unity, art historian Nancy Um went further to argue that 'the Red Sea style represents a tangible case of sustained cross-cultural contact across a linked maritime region and thus moves beyond the conventional modern limits of continent and nation'.[45]

Space and Scale between the Local, Regional and Global

The principal challenge for future historians of the Red Sea is to construct a schema that captures multiple scales – from the local to the regional and the global – and that explores the dynamic interrelationships between them. One can think of this as interweaving microhistory, regional history and global history.[46] In this last section I propose a method for thinking about space, mobility and circulation in the Red Sea area that engages the problem of scale. In part inspired by the work of historians such as Michel Tuchscherer, a useful way to construct the foundation for a multi-scale conceptual framework is to examine three macro-level economic and commercial ambits. This helps to better explore the set of interconnected moving parts that could determine evolving configurations of space and boundaries, changing patterns of mobility, commodity flows, inter- and intra-regional exchanges, the rise and decline of particular trade networks and the fluctuating location and hierarchies of Red Sea port towns, among other subjects.

The first long-distance/international transit trade system linked the Indian Ocean with the Mediterranean. This is the macro-level setup that has shaped conventional characterisations of the Red Sea as a conduit. We encounter here commodities extracted or produced *outside* the Red Sea area, such as spices (the famed 'spice trade'), textiles, muslin cloth, silk, pottery, glassware, ironware and teak. On this level the Red Sea served as a transit space connecting producers and consumers located beyond its littorals and immediate inlands. This system involved entrepôt ports,

---

[44] Derek H. Matthews, 'The Red Sea style', *Kush*, 1 (1953): 60–87.

[45] Nancy Um, 'Reflections on the Red Sea style: Beyond the surface of coastal architecture', *Northeast African Studies*, 12 (2012): 243–72 (244).

[46] Among the work that has inspired my thinking on the subject is Francesca Trivellato, 'Is there a future for Italian microhistory in the age of global history?', *California Italian Studies*, 2 (2011): http://escholarship.org/uc/item/0z94n9hq (accessed 31 March 2017); Bernhard Struck, Kate Ferris and Jacques Revel, 'Introduction: Space and scale in transnational history', *The International History Review*, 33 (2011): 573–84.

174   J. Miran

sophisticated international financial arrangements and long-distance mercantile networks whose origins were removed from the Red Sea littorals proper. The role, operation and impact of different trading networks in the Red Sea area – for example, Cairene, Alexandrian, Maghribi, Turkish, Gujarati, Hadrami but also Syrian, Greek and Armenian – is central for delineating not only commercial orbits but also social and cultural spaces between the Indian Ocean and the Mediterranean, Africa and Arabia.[47] More work could be done to reconstruct the rise, decline and the social and cultural impact of different trading networks on the formation and transformation of Red Sea urban communities. For example, the histories of South Asian merchants and migrants who either circulated between India and the Red Sea or settled in different Red Sea localities for temporary periods or for good deserve further attention. What were the exact provenance and modes of organisation of South Asian brokerage and financing and how did it connect with systems of production, labour and distribution?[48] These dynamics could then be compared to those characterising other South Asian networks, notably in the Arabian/Persian Gulf and in the southwestern Indian Ocean.[49] In periods such as the early modern era, the factors accounting for the establishment, operation and decline of particular networks raise compelling questions as to the spatial boundaries of the Red Sea area. Rooted, among other factors, in the singular wind regime, in some ways this division rendered the northern part of the basin – dominated by Egyptian merchants – an extension of the Mediterranean trading world, and the southern – dominated by South Asian merchants – an appendage of the western Indian Ocean trading system.[50]

Transit trade was only one sphere of economic activity in the area. A second inter-regional intermediate commercial arrangement married

---

[47] See, for example, Nelly Hanna, *Making big money in 1600: The life and times of Isma'il Abu Taqiyya, Egyptian merchant* (Syracuse, NY, 1998); Michel Tuchscherer, 'Activités des Turcs dans le commerce de la mer Rouge au XVIIIe siècle', in Daniel Panzac, ed., *Les villes dans l'empire ottoman* (Paris, 1991), pp. 321–64; Pétriat, *Le négoce des lieux saints*.

[48] On South Asians in the Red Sea area, see chapters in Ashin Das Gupta, *Merchants of maritime India, 1500–1800* (Aldershot, 1994); Richard Pankhurst, 'The "Banyan" or Indian presence at Massawa, the Dahlak Islands and the Horn of Africa', *Journal of Ethiopian Studies*, 12 (1974): 185–212; Paul Bonnenfant, 'La marque de l'Inde à Zabîd', *Chroniques Yéménites*, 8 (2000): http://cy.revues.org/7 (accessed 31 March 2017).

[49] For these areas, see for example James Onley, 'Indian communities in the Persian Gulf, c. 1500–1947', in Potter, *The Persian Gulf in modern times*, pp. 231–66; Pedro Machado, *Ocean of trade: South Asian merchants, Africa and the Indian Ocean, c. 1750–1850* (Cambridge, 2014).

[50] See André Raymond, 'A divided sea: The Cairo coffee trade in the Red Sea area during the seventeenth and eighteenth Centuries', in Fawaz and Bayly, eds., *Modernity and Culture from the Mediterranean to the Indian Ocean*, pp. 46–57.

The Red Sea 175

a regional system of production and consumption with a cross-regional commercial setup in which different commodities produced *in* parts of the Red Sea area, their hinterlands and aquatic zones, were exported to Egypt and the Mediterranean and further to Europe on the one hand, and to the Gulf, South and Southeast Asia and East Africa on the other. Similarly, commodities from the Mediterranean and the Indian Ocean were imported *into* the Red Sea region for consumption in the Ethiopian region, the Nile Valley, Yemen and the Hijaz as well as in the Red Sea ports. Goods extracted or produced in the Red Sea area and exported include the aromatics trade – especially frankincense and myrrh – animal skins, gold, gems, ivory, ebony, pearls, mother-of-pearl and tortoise-shells, but also slaves, and later, most famously, coffee. Importations for consumption in the Red Sea area included rice and grain (from India and Iraq), textiles (from India and Egypt), as well as a variety of metals and manufactured goods shipped via Egypt into the Red Sea. Merchants handled complex arrangements between the Red Sea-based agents of distant businesses and those traders who were more 'local' to the Red Sea area: Egyptians, Hijazis, Yemenis, Hadramis and Somalis who usually lived in port towns and coordinated the linking of land-bound with seaborne transportation networks. Shipping arrangements included the regional operations of distribution and supply between the more important ports and smaller towns and fishing villages, mostly run by coast-based Red Sea traders and shippers.

Studying the trajectories of particular commodities or merchants from a 'global micro-historical' perspective may be a particularly useful way to illuminate multiple connections that animated local, regional and global actors and networks. Tracing the circuits of labour, financing, commercialisation and consumption of commodities such as coffee, pearls and mother-of-pearl allows us to bring into sharper focus multiple unexplored connections between local, regional and global historical processes. Though dwarfed by the Persian Gulf, the Red Sea pearling industry – to take one example – serves a case in point. The production, trade and consumption of pearls and mother-of-pearl from the Dahlak and Farasan archipelagos involved distinct infrastructures of financing, labour and commercialisation that brought together an assortment of Red Sea and western Indian Ocean actors. In the case of Dahlaki pearling banks, divers who were either northeast African slaves or freed slaves and Arabs from the Arabian Red Sea coastlands provided the labour; Gulf, Hijazi, Yemeni or Dahlaki (Eritrean) boat owners handled fishing crews and provided for transportation, whereas Indian and Arab merchants financed pearl-fishing enterprises and purchased the luxurious marine products that found their way to Bombay and to consumers in

176   J. Miran

the capitals of Europe, to the button-producing factories of northern Italy, Austria-Hungary and, perhaps, to the religious souvenir carving industry which flourished in Bethlehem in Palestine.[51]

The third system was inter-coastal and intra-regional. In some ways it overlapped with the intermediate regional system, and was characterised chiefly, but not exclusively, by the economic dependence of the Arabian side of the Red Sea on the African part which faced it. The largely barren lands of the Hijaz and other regions of Arabia were supplied with foodstuffs produced in the Egyptian and Sudanese Nile Valley, or in the Ethiopian highlands and in Somalia. For example, the Hijaz with its holy cities depended heavily on grain produced in the Nile Valley, which tied it to the political economy of food production and consumption in the Red Sea. An interesting related aspect that marries environmental, economic and religious dynamics was the establishment of special pious endowments (*waqfs*) in Egypt whose role it was to supply the Hijaz with grain. Accordingly, some of the most fertile lands in the Nile Valley were especially allotted for the production of wheat for the inhabitants of western Arabia.[52] The dynamics of grain production, commercialisation and consumption in the Red Sea area reveal at times a fine balancing act between ecological constraints, climatic conditions, commercial dynamics and political circumstances.[53] Much like the intermediate economic-commercial sphere, the inter-coastal system was operated by local and regional traders; many were based in the various Red Sea ports and smaller harbour villages, and involved a networks of boats and cabotage arrangements.

All in all, and although they sometimes overlapped and were complementary and interdependent, these three spheres, propelled chiefly by economic and commercial forces, animated a dense web of multiple differentiated trade arrangements, shipping networks, currency, credit and debt systems and labour networks. They thus produced variegated spaces

[51] Miran, *Red Sea citizens*, pp. 99–110. I am currently at work on an essay on a prominent Red Sea pearl merchant with the working title 'Secrets of the Red Sea: The legendary 'Alī al-Nahārī and the early twentieth-century global pearling boom.'

[52] Michel Tuchscherer, 'Approvisionnement des villes saintes d'Arabie en blé d'Egypte d'après des documents ottomans des années 1670', *Anatolia Moderna*, 5 (1994): 79–99 and Colin Heywood, 'A Red Sea shipping register of the 1670s for the supply of foodstuffs from Egyptian *Wakf* sources to Mecca and Medina (Turkish documents from the archive of 'Abdurrahman 'Abdi' Pasha of Buda, I)', *Anatolia Moderna*, 6 (1996): 111–74. For more on Egyptian–Hijazi economic relations in the Ottoman period, see Suraiya Faroqhi, *Pilgrims and sultans: the Hajj under the Ottomans, 1517–1683* (London, 1994) and André Raymond, *Artisans et commerçants au Caire au XVIIIe siècle*, 2 vols. (Damascus, 1973–74).

[53] See, for example, Steven Serels, 'Famines of war: The Red Sea grain market and famine in Eastern Sudan, 1889–1891', *Northeast African Studies*, 12 (2012): 73–94.

The Red Sea 177

between the Mediterranean and the Indian Ocean. One propitious way to examine how the three systems were interwoven is to examine the relationship between seasonal rhythms, production cycles (for example, wheat in Egypt, coffee in Yemen, cotton in India), and transportation patterns (affected by the wind regime but also by the Muslim pilgrimage) and their impact on the circulation of commodities and people.

Of many potentially promising subjects, one set of themes that is already attracting scholarly attention and that deserves to be at the forefront of future scholarly efforts involves the impact of extensive inter- and intra-regional migration and exchanges in the basin and beyond it on the social and cultural makeup of Red Sea urban communities and littoral societies. Red Sea port towns mediated connectivities between inland producing areas and forelands and between overseas commerce and inland consumers. Migratory flows in and out of towns were shaped by the spatial positioning and re-positioning of labour and trading flows and networks that resulted from the cyclical ebb and flow of commercial abatement and boom periods. It was not rare that large segments of the inhabitants of a given town were migrants from both forelands and inlands. Indeed, in many cases, 'outsiders', or 'strangers' (for example, Hadramis, Gujaratis) were the most prominent and powerful inhabitants of Red Sea ports (for example, Jiddah, Massawa, Aden). In other words, some Red Sea port towns were where actors involved in all or some of the orbits that I have described above met – at times settling together and forming new hybrid and cosmopolitan communities and spaces. Can we discern singular 'Red Sea cosmopolitanisms' in port towns? And if yes, what were their specific features, orientations and were they comparable to one another and to those in the broader Indian Ocean world?

Yet migration into Red Sea towns and littorals did not only involve powerful merchants and entrepreneurs. One subject that has not been studied thoroughly enough is the social and cultural integration of those many northeast Africans who either migrated or were moved in slavery to the Arabian coasts and who remained in its towns.[54] Africans clearly played a role in shaping the societies and cultures into which they were gradually absorbed. In some places such as the Yemeni Tihama region, extensive inter-coastal exchanges produced Arabian-African

---

[54] In an article published twenty years ago and yet to be taken up on, Edward Alpers showed how a close and thorough reading in European accounts and descriptions of Arabian port towns (for example, Jeddah, al-Qunfudha, Jizan, al-Luhayya, Hudaydah, Mukalla, and Aden) may illuminate such cultural traces. Edward A. Alpers, 'The African diaspora in the northwestern Indian Ocean: Reconsideration of an old problem, new directions for research', *Comparative Studies of South Asia, Africa and the Middle East*, 17 (1997): 62–81.

178   J. Miran

hybrid border spaces that were perceived as socially and culturally distinct by inland communities. For example, Africans introduced to the Tihama musical instruments, styles and rhythms, which developed into what musicologists have referred to as 'Red Sea music'.[55] All in all, both high- and low-status migrants – traders, entrepreneurs, agents, labourers, slaves and freed slaves – who settled more durably in urban settings negotiated their social, religious, political, cultural roles and positions in the townscapes of their respective locales. Future work on such subjects may help us identify new forms and features of cultural unity or cohesiveness in the Red Sea region or in parts thereof.

★ ★ ★ ★ ★

A critical subject that begs further study is the question of Red Sea identity. For millennia the Red Sea has been an area characterised by hybridity, where people from the inlands and others coming from abroad met, sometimes mixed, creating idiosyncratic urban or coastal cultures. In the twentieth century, the modern nation-state has all too often obfuscated and attempted to erase past complex local and regional identities. New scholarship should take on the task to recover complex senses of identity expressed by or ascribed to the peoples of the Red Sea. It would be important to ask whether the inhabitants of the Red Sea littorals and its islands have shared in the past or still share some type of consciousness or *mentalité* – in the sense evoked by *Annales* historians – that is particularly associated with the coast or the sea. Did Red Sea port town and other coastal dwellers, as well as islanders, develop any sense of consciousness or identity as 'Red Sea people' or did they identify with more local/regional littoral or offshore sea spaces (mirroring the more localised naming of the Red Sea described above)? The question of identities and cultural and symbolic representations connected to the Red Sea and expressed by or about the inhabitants of the Red Sea littorals is only beginning to receive attention.

A propitious way to further explore notions of identity in the Red Sea area is to analyse 'local' historical accounts of the region or of particular Red Sea port cities, produced by professional and non-professional historians and writers in Egypt, the Sudan, Saudi Arabia, Eritrea, Djibouti, Somaliland and Yemen.[56] This should however not be limited to local histories.

---

[55] Anderson Bakewell, 'Music', in Francine Stone, ed., *Studies on the Tihāmah. The report of the Tihāmah expedition 1982 and related papers* (Harlow, 1985), p. 105; Leila Ingrams, 'African connections in Yemeni music', *Musiké*, 2 (2006): 65–76.

[56] See for example the following urban histories of the port cities of Hudayda, Massawa, Sawakin and Jiddah: Aḥmad 'Uthmān Muṭayyir, *Al-Durra al-farīda fī tārīkh madīnat al-Ḥudayda* (al-Ḥudayda, 1984); Ibrāhīm al-Mukhtār, *Al-Jāmi' li-akhbār jazīrat Bādī* (Unpublished manuscript, Asmara, 1958); Muḥammad Ṣāliḥ Ḍirār, *Tārīkh Sawākin*

The Red Sea   179

Studying the different cultural expressions (poetry, prose, songs, folk tales) of littoral societies such as Tihami Yemenis, the Afar in Eritrea and Djibouti, the Arabian Rashayda pastoralists of the eastern Sudan and Eritrea, or indeed island communities such as those inhabiting the Farasan and Dahlak archipelagos, may illuminate our understanding of the ways that Red Sea coastal dwellers constructed identities that related to their maritime environment.[57]

One revealing anecdotic example of a derogatory appellation used by inlanders to refer to Red Sea coastal and urban cosmopolitan communities, and employed on both sides of the Red Sea, is *tarsh al-bahr* ('spew/ vomit of the sea'). Originally used by Arabs to refer to non-Arab pilgrims arriving to the Hijaz and Mecca, the expression is now sometimes employed by the inhabitants of the inland Najd region of Saudi Arabia to pejoratively designate the cosmopolitan inhabitants of the Hijaz and the port of Jiddah.[58] Similarly, on the other side of the Red Sea, in the context of mid-twentieth-century Eritrean nationalism, some Tigre-speaking inlanders referred to those urban cosmopolitan Arabs in the port of Massawa as the *tarsh al-bahr*, or those whom the sea has spat out onto the Eritrean shores, and who were 'foreign' to Eritrea, and therefore less legitimate in making claims in nationalist politics.[59] This example could suggest how an external designation may have promoted both a sense of identity as coastal dwellers and a shared identity with other littoral people in the broader Red Sea basin.

Further Reading

There is still no single volume scholarly history of the Red Sea. For a comprehensive treatment of its physical and natural features, see Alasdair J. Edwards and Stephen M. Head, eds., *Red Sea* (Key Environments Series) (Oxford and New York, 1987). The published proceedings of six 'Red Sea Project' conferences offer new findings on an array of

---

wa-al-Bahr al-Ahmar (Khartoum, 1981); 'Abd al-Qudūs al-Anṣārī, *Tārīkh madīnat Jiddah* (Jiddah, 1963); Aḥmad b. Muḥammad al-Ḥadrāwī, *Al-Jawāhir al-mu'adda fī faḍā'il Jiddah* (Cairo, 1909).

[57] For example, Dionisius A. Agius, 'The Rashayda: Ethnic identity and Dhow activity in Suakin on the Red Sea coast', *Northeast African Studies*, 12 (2012): 169–216; Agius, John P. Cooper, Lucy Semaan, Chiara Zazzaro and Robert Carter, 'Remembering the sea: Personal and communal recollections of maritime life in Jizan and the Farasan Islands, Saudi Arabia', *Journal of Maritime Archaeology*, 11 (2016): 127–77; Agius, *The life of the Red Sea dhow: A cultural history of Islamic seaborne exploration* (London, 2018).

[58] Madawi al-Rasheed, *A most masculine state: Gender, politics and religion in Saudi Arabia* (New York, 2013), pp. 187–88.

[59] Miran, *Red Sea citizens*, pp. 23, 289, n. 55.

180   J. Miran

pertinent themes: Paul Lunde and Alexandra Porter, eds., *Trade and travel in the Red Sea region* (Oxford, 2004); Janet C. M. Starkey, ed., *People of the Red Sea* (Oxford, 2005); Janet C. M. Starkey, Paul Starkey and T. J. Wilkinson, eds., *Natural resources and cultural connections of the Red Sea* (Oxford, 2007); Lucy Blue, John Cooper, Ross Thomas and Julian Whitewright, eds., *Connected hinterlands* (Oxford, 2009); Dionisius A. Agius, John P. Cooper, Athena Trakadas and Chiara Zazzaro, eds., *Navigated spaces, connected places* (Oxford, 2012); and Dionisius A. Agius, Emad Khalil, Eleanor Scerri and Alun Williams, eds., *Human interaction with the environment in the Red Sea: Selected papers of Red Sea Project VI* (Leiden, 2017). An effort to promote the study of the Red Sea region as an integrated space is Jonathan Miran, 'Space and mobility in the Red Sea region, 1500–1950', *History Compass*, 12, 2 (February 2014): 197–216; see also Jonathan Miran, ed., 'Special issue: Space, mobility and translocal connections across the Red Sea Area since 1500', *Northeast African Studies*, 12 (2012): ix–307. For Roman Berenike and its local, regional and global connections, see Steven E. Sidebotham, *Berenike and the ancient maritime spice route* (Berkeley, CA, 2011). On Christians, Jews and inter-imperial contestations in the southern Red Sea region in Late Antiquity, see G. W. Bowersock, *The Throne of Adulis: Red Sea wars on the eve of Islam* (Oxford, 2013). For an integrated approach to the Red Sea in the early Islamic centuries, see Timothy Power, *The Red Sea from Byzantium to the Caliphate AD 500–1000* (New York, 2012). The history of Aden and its commercial connections between the eleventh and thirteenth centuries is detailed in Roxani Eleni Margariti, *Aden and the Indian Ocean trade: 150 years in the life of a medieval Arabian port* (Chapel Hill, NC, 2007). On the operation of a family shipping business in late Ayyubid and early Mamluk Qusayr, see Li Guo, *Commerce, culture and community in a Red Sea port in the thirteenth century: Arabic documents form Quseir* (Leiden, 2004). For a massive study of Rasulid Yemen, the Red Sea and the western Indian Ocean, see Eric Vallet, *L'Arabie marchande. Etat et commerce sous les sultans rasulides du Yémen (626–858 / 1229–1454)* (Paris, 2011). The relationship between the Sharifate of Mecca and Mamluk Egypt is the subject of John L. Meloy, *Imperial power and maritime trade: Mecca and Cairo in the later Middle Ages* (Chicago, IL, 2010). On the Ottoman empire and the Red Sea, see Salih Özbaran, 'Ottoman expansion in the Red Sea', in S. Faroqhi and K. Fleet, eds., *The Cambridge history of Turkey, Vol. 2. The Ottoman Empire as a world power 1453–1603* (Cambridge, 2013), pp. 173–201 and Alexis Wick, *The Red Sea: In search of lost space* (Oakland, CA, 2016). For the commercial history of the early modern Red Sea, see

The Red Sea 181

Michel Tuchscherer, 'Trade and port cities in the Red Sea-Gulf of Aden region in the sixteenth and seventeenth centuries', in L. T. Fawaz and C. A. Bayly, eds., *Modernity and culture from the Mediterranean to the Indian Ocean* (New York, 2002), pp. 28–45; Michel Tuchscherer, 'Le commerce en mer Rouge aux alentours de 1700: flux, espaces et temps', in R. Gyselen, ed., *Circulation des monnaies, des marchandises et des biens*, Vol. V (Bures-sur-Yvette, 1993), pp. 159–78. On the history of coffee, see Michel Tuchscherer, 'Coffee in the Red Sea area from the sixteenth to the nineteenth century', in W. G. Clarence-Smith and S. Topik, eds., *The global coffee economy in Africa, Asia, and Latin America, 1500–1989* (Cambridge, 2003), pp. 50–66. On the urban history of the port of Mocha and its wider connections, see Nancy Um, *The merchant houses of Mocha: Trade and architecture in an Indian Ocean port* (Seattle, WA, 2009) and C. G. Brouwer, *Al-Mukha: Profile of a Yemeni seaport as sketched by servants of the Dutch East India Company (VOC), 1614–1640* (Amsterdam, 1997) and its two sequels on the seventeenth-century commerce of this port published in 2006 and 2010. The nineteenth-century transport revolution and its impact on the Red Sea is the subject of Colette Dubois, 'The Red Sea ports during the revolution in transportation, 1800–1914', in Fawaz and Bayly, eds., *Modernity and culture from the Mediterranean to the Indian Ocean*, pp. 58–74. The opening of the Suez Canal and its implications is analysed in Valeska Huber, *Channelling mobilities: Migration and globalisation in the Suez Canal region and beyond, 1869–1914* (Cambridge, 2013). A social history of the port of Massawa in the second half of the nineteenth century is Jonathan Miran, *Red Sea citizens: Cosmopolitan society and cultural change in Massawa* (Bloomington, IN, 2009). On Hadrami merchants and entrepreneurs in the Red Sea region, see Janet Ewald and William Gervase Clarence-Smith, 'The economic role of the Hadhrami diaspora in the Red Sea and Gulf of Aden, 1820s to 1930s', in U. Freitag and W. G. Clarence-Smith, eds., *Hadhrami traders, scholars, and statesmen in the Indian Ocean, 1750s-1960s* (Leiden, 1997), pp. 281–96 and Philippe Pétriat, *Le négoce des lieux saints. Négociants hadramis de Djedda, 1850–1950* (Paris, 2016).

7 The Sea of Japan/Korea's East Sea

Alexis Dudden

A decades-long naming dispute at the International Hydrographic Organisation centres on the body of water that straddles 40 degrees north latitude and rests between 130 and 140 degrees east longitude.[1] Oceanographers refer to this sea as one of the northern Pacific Ocean's 'marginal seas', and depending where you stand along its spiky coastline, its deep blue hues are variously known as the Sea of Japan, Korea's East Sea or simply the East Sea. This essay does not advocate one name in preference over another, while ideas for new names regularly appear. During the first decade of this century, for example, a Japanese woman thoughtfully suggested, 'The Blue Sea', while a former president of South Korea proposed the 'Sea of Friendship' or the 'Sea of Understanding'.[2] Agreement on a new name is remote, however, leaving international news broadcasters such as CNN to explain regional military tensions taking place in 'waters off the Korean Peninsula'.[3]

For millennia, a steady stream of human traffic has crossed over this sea's northern and southern openings, largely from the Asian continent moving eastwards to what is now called Japan. Thus, the name East Sea originated as a directional term (literally, 東海), with the first known

---

[1] The third edition of the International Hydrographic Organisation's technical publication, *Limits of oceans and seas* (Monte Carlo, 1953), remains the standard, yet is widely agreed to be out of date. (A fourth edition appeared in 2002 with few updates.) Deprived of its sovereignty during Japanese occupation in the first half of the twentieth century, Korea could not participate in the initial name-giving moment in 1928. Upon gaining entry to the United Nations in 1991, South and North Korea became eligible to participate in the naming process, dating the public element of this international dispute from this moment. See Kyodo News, 'Sea of Japan name dispute rolls on', *Japan Times*, 3 May 2012, p. 3.

[2] Letter to the editor, *Asahi Shimbun*, 20 August 2002; on the sidelines of the November 2006 APEC meeting in Hanoi, South Korean President Roh Moo-hyun suggested several alternative names to Japan's Prime Minister Abe Shinzo; see *Asahi Shimbun*, 8 January 2007.

[3] For example, Ryan Browne and Steve Almasy, 'North Korea's missile test fails, U.S. Military Says', *CNN*, 29 April 2017: http://edition.cnn.com/2017/04/28/world/north-korea-missile-launch/ (accessed 30 April 2017).

The Sea of Japan/Korea's East Sea 183

Map 7.1 The Sea of Japan/Korea's East Sea

written record of it carved into an early fifth-century stele commemorating the life of King Gwanggaeto the Great, the nineteenth monarch of Goguryeo, northernmost of Korea's ancient dynasties.[4] The first known reference to the East Sea as such outside of East Asia appears to have been in the thirteenth-century travelogue of Giovanni de Pian del Carpini, a contemporary and follower of Francis of Assisi who wrote one

---

[4] In Korean and English see studies by Soh Jeong-Cheol and Park Young-Min, beginning with their most current, *East Sea or Sea of Japan: History and truths* (Seoul, 2015), p. 321, which features an excellent reproduction of the Gwanggaeto stele and accompanying explication.

184 A. Dudden

of the earliest European accounts of areas under Mongol control and contact.[5]

Although modern technologies have replaced earlier days of sail, intense north winds make this sea notoriously difficult to cross. Most ancient navigators headed along its coastlines to the few straits that offered a better chance of safe passage: the Korea or Tsushima Straits, the Kanmon Straits, the Tsugaru Straits, the Soya or La Pérouse Strait, and the Strait of Tartary. Very little river water discharges into this sea – barely 1 per cent of its volume – and today places called Russia, North Korea, South Korea and Japan contain its 978,000 square surface kilometers. Russia claims almost half of this sea's total 7,600-kilometer coastline even though Russian explorers were the last to show up in the region. Their seventeenth-century designation for the sea – the Japan Sea – named the area to which they were heading and appears to have relied on or was coterminous with Matteo Ricci's 1602 map of the world, that – for the first time historians are aware of – designated this body of water in Chinese characters as '日本海' (Japan Sea).[6] Notably, the 'Japan' piece (日本) as understood in European translation derives from Marco Polo's famous thirteenth-century phonetic transliteration of China's name for the country: 'Ciapangu' (as it appeared verbatim on Martin Behaim's astonishing 1492 globe). The word ultimately Europeanised as Giappone in Italian, Japon in French and Yaponskey in Russian, as it would thus appear to name the sea on seventeenth-century Russian maps: Японское море (*Yaponskey More*). There seems to be no evidence that any Japanese used the name Sea of Japan in print before the late eighteenth-century until the painter and illustrator Shiba Kokan printed it on his 1792 map of the world (the famous 'Chikyu Zenzu': 地球全図).[7]

In 1928, when the International Hydrographic Organisation agreed to Japan's request for the sole name, 'Sea of Japan', Korea could not

[5] Referenced in Soh and Park, *East Sea or Sea of Japan*, pp. 130–31; see also friar Giovanni DiPlano Carpini, *The story of the Mongols: Whom we call the Tartars*, trans. Erik Hildinger (Wellesley, MA, 2014).

[6] The University of Minnesota Libraries have published an online interactive version of the Matteo Ricci map that has a zoom feature clearly illustrating this. See University of Minnesota Libraries, *Matteo Ricci, Li Zhizhao, and Zhang Wentao: Map of the World 1602* online at: www.lib.umn.edu/bell/riccimap (accessed 31 March 2017).

[7] Shiba Kokan's 1792 map labels the ocean '日本内海' (Japan's Inland Sea), which is interesting because today what Japanese refer to as their Inland Sea is off the southern coast of the country while at the same time this map depicts the Pacific Ocean as '日本東海' (Japan's East Sea). Waseda University in Tokyo archives this map in its collections and has a useful online link that enables zeroing in on the labels for these seas: http://archive.wul.waseda.ac.jp/kosho/ru11/ru11_00809/ru11_00809_0001/ru11_00809_0001.html (accessed 31 March 2017).

The Sea of Japan/Korea's East Sea

object because it was under Japanese occupation. That said, the collection of early modern European maps that current international arbitration tribunals favour seem equally divided between references to the Sea of Japan and East Sea/Korea's East Sea. Thus, Korean geographer Ryu Yeon-Taek explains that the Korean government today prefers a dual naming scheme for this sea until all parties involved – including Russia and indigenous groups – settle on an alternative new name.[8] The most famous of the early modern European maps is French count of La Pérouse, Jean-François de Galaup's 1797 map of his explorations of the northern Pacific – known widely as the 'La Pérouse Map' – which shared the 'Sea of Japan' terminology with Matteo Ricci's 1602 map of the world and that of numerous Russian explorers as well. At the same time, different European mapmakers chose otherwise: British Royal Geographer, James Wyld, printed 'Sea of Korea' on his 1823 map, Dutch engraver, Peter Schenk the Younger, used 'Mare Orientale' (East Sea) on his 1708 map, and Dutch publisher Pieter van der Aa chose 'Mer de Corée' (Korean Sea) for his 1706 publication (the European term for Korea deriving from awareness of Korea's Goryeo Dynasty [918–1392]).[9] Of note, for his part, the renowned French cartographer Gilles Robert Vaugondy's splendidly colourful 1750 map, 'Empire du Japon', used two names: 'Mer du Corée' and 'Mer du Japon'.[10]

[8] In a working level paper, Ryu Yeon-Taek succinctly spells out the government's plan: 'The naming of the body of water separating the Korean peninsula and the Japanese Archipelago is a matter for negotiations between neighboring states. However, taking into account the unresolved naming differences between the Republic of Korea and Japan for the same sea area, the Republic of Korea proposes a plausible alternative to enable the publication of the 4th edition of IHO Publication S-23. The option is to publish names and spatial details of the sea area in question incorporating dual naming principles according the IHO Technical Resolution . . . Basically based on the important recommendation of the IHO Technical Resolution A 4.2.6, the Republic of Korea proposes that the body of water separating the Korean peninsula and the Japanese Archipelago should have dual names, namely, "East Sea/Sea of Japan".' See Ryu Yeon-Taek, 'The International Hydrographic Organisation and the *East Sea/Sea of Japan* issue', in Korea Hydrographic and Oceanographic Administration, ed., *Sea names, heritage, perception, and international relations* (Seoul, 2015), p. 200.

[9] Today, North Korea refers to the ocean as '조선동해' in Korean (the Joseon Sea) which at once relies on the name in play on many Korean maps during the Joseon Dynasty (1392–1910), '朝鮮東海' (the Joseon Sea); it is also the word for Korea that the government of North Korea uses for itself to distinguish itself in Korean from South Korea. Although some readers may be sceptical, *Wikipedia*'s 'Sea of Japan naming dispute' entry page arguably has the best compilation of the numerous maps in question: https://en.wikipedia.org/wiki/Sea_of_Japan_naming_dispute (accessed 31 March 2017).

[10] The private map collector, David Rumsey, maintains an astonishing online archive of historical maps and cartographic material. His link to the Vaugondy 'Empire du Japon' map is here: www.davidrumsey.com/luna/servlet/detail/RUMSEY~8~1~3984~500001:L-Empire-du-Japon,-divise-en-sept-p (accessed 31 March 2017).

186   A. Dudden

Any Neolithic-era name that may have been in play among the indigenous Nivkh, Orok and Ainu people – whose few descendants still live along the thin stretches of water where mainland Russia breaks off towards Sakhalin Island – failed to make the grade of modern maps, although they treasure their ancestors' boots and clothes made of salmon-skin hides. Fishing formed the basis of these communities' existence, and at least for the Ainu, a god of the sea that storytellers call Repun appears in drawings either as a whale or as a male figure with a harpoon. Legend relates tales of Repun's beneficence in fish catches when the hunt on land was meagre, yet none of the storytelling groups seems to have had a specific name for the ocean that Repun makes bountiful, nor, however, did they have writing.[11]

Names Change or Stay the Same

During the first half of the twentieth century, Japan transformed much of Northeast Asia into the Empire of Great Japan (大日本帝国), renaming places and people according to the imperial architects' worldview.[12] In 1928 when the Japanese government gained international recognition for the name, 'Sea of Japan', a very different history was in motion for this sea. Japanese officials in Tokyo were preparing to expand their nation's hoped for rule over the world's 'eight directions under one roof' (八紘一宇) from an envisioned new capital in northeastern China that they would call Shinkyo in Japanese (literally, 'New Capital'). However, when the empire collapsed in 1945 this city returned to the name it had before: Changchun. Although the Japanese empire disintegrated before Shinkyo would replace Tokyo, during the 1930s the imperial government and its related emigration companies sent millions of Japanese into the empire's reaches on a migration course over the now officially named Sea of Japan that reversed the paths that were historically followed over this water – now moving from east to west. At the same time, the Japanese government and these companies also transferred similar numbers of colonial subjects to the homeland (as the core Japanese islands came to be called) following the more traditional flow from west to east.

Noticeably, much of the twentieth-century movement took place on an ocean network that had not been so active for over a thousand years. From 698 to 926 a realm known in Korean as Balhae (Bokkaikoku in

---

[11] Michael Ashkenazi, *Handbook of Japanese mythology* (New York, 2008); also David L. Howell, *Geographies of identity in nineteenth-century Japan* (Berkeley, CA, 2005).
[12] See Todd Henry, *Assimilating Seoul: Japanese rule and the politics of public space in colonial Korea, 1910–1945* (Berkeley, CA, 2014).

The Sea of Japan/Korea's East Sea   187

Japanese) encompassed much of today's North Korea and the Russian Federation's Maritime Province before the Mongols conquered it. From ports along its extensive coastline, such as today's Kim'chaek in North Korea, delegations regularly crossed the sea to Japanese ports on the country's north central coast from which they would carry their trade and envoys south overland by river, canal and portage routes to Kyoto, which was then capital. All of this greatly enhanced the ongoing development of ancient Japan with people, poetry and painting, too.[13]

Japanese historians such as Amino Yoshihiko demonstrate that the Chinese characters for Japan (日本) gained traction in the mid-seventh and early eighth centuries when Korean and Chinese emissaries and monks travelling on Balhae's routes as well as essential ones developed much earlier by competing kingdoms in southern Korea crossed through this sea's southern straits surrounding Tsushima Island (where some of their tombs remain today). Collectively, they brought texts from the Tang capital at Chang'an (now Xi'an) that referenced Japan with these Chinese characters. As Amino explains, 'It is also important that we recognize that this influence came to Japan via the sea, which functioned as both a transportation route and an obstacle to intercourse.'[14] The name 'Japan' (日本), Amino further explains, literally translates as the 'source of the sun . . . reflect[ing] a strong consciousness of the Tang empire on the Chinese mainland . . . [And, moreover, unusually] the name 日本 signifies a natural phenomenon or orientation and . . . is neither the name of the place of origin of the dynastic founders nor that of a dynasty or tribe.'[15] At the time that Japan's early chieftains settled on this name 日本 to help centralise their rule, the ill-fated Baekje Kingdom in southern Korea (18 BCE–660 CE) was nearing the end of its abundant overseas transfer of goods and people through the sea's southern passage to the Wa realm, as the southern Japan region was commonly known beforehand (and may also have included southern Korea). Together with yet another southern Korean realm called Gaya, renowned for ironwork and metallurgy, Korean intercourse laid the foundations for the archive of Japan: writing, systems of law and literature, urban planning, Buddhism,

---

[13] See Amino Yoshihiko, *Chusei Saiko: Retto no chiiki to shakai* [Rethinking the medieval: Region and society of the archipelago] (Tokyo, 1986); also William Johnston, 'From feudal fishing villages to an archipelago's peoples: The historiographical journey of Amino Yoshihiko', Edwin O. Reischauer Institute of Japanese Studies, *Occasional Papers in Japanese Studies*, 2005-1 (2005). See also Alan Christy's excellent translation of one of Amino's seminal works: Amino Yoshihiko, *Rethinking Japanese history*, trans. Alan Christy (Ann Arbor, MI, 2012).

[14] Amino, *Rethinking Japanese history*, p. 264.

[15] Amino Yoshihiko, 'Deconstructing "Japan"', trans. Gavan McCormack, *East Asian History*, 3 (1992): 123.

188   A. Dudden

pottery, weapon design and production, and, likely, even the proto-members of the Japanese imperial family as well as tens of thousands of other people moving from west to east.[16]

Although southwestern Korea's Baekje's rulers once had extensive relations with overseas counterparts, they failed to forge alliances with regional chiefs in what was becoming Japan, which might have helped them to withstand local rivalries as well as Chinese encroachment. Conversely, the Balhae Kingdom's rulers in what is now North Korea viewed interaction with ancient Japan's early leaders as elemental to their own security in order to withstand Tang advances as well as local competition. Part of this worldview entailed at least fifty diplomatic exchanges over the sea between Korea and Japan during the latter ninth and early tenth centuries. Also at the time, there is indication of a Balhae–Japan naval alliance in the making in part to attempt to conquer the eighth century's magnificent Silla Dynasty in southeastern Korea. That never materialised, however, and although speculative, this failure would surely have pleased the legendary late seventh-century Silla King Munmu. At the kingdom's height, Munmu ordered his 682 entombment in an offshore rocky grave, still visible from Korea's southeastern coast near the ancient capital of Gyeongju (which counted over one million inhabitants at the time he died). With his sarcophagus in the sea, Munmu vowed that his spirit would become a dragon to protect his people from advances by water, especially from what Koreans and Chinese have referred to for nearly two thousand years as 'wako' (倭寇), a derogatory term that conveys barbarity and translates as 'Japanese pirates' – literally 'dwarf pirates' (thus, Japanese distaste for the term). Like 'East Sea', this term is first recorded in writing on the 414 Gwangaetto stele, exclaiming the great northern king's defeat of a marauding 倭寇 raid in 404. Peak pirate activity arose over a thousand years later during the fifteenth and sixteenth centuries, however, which Japanese historian Murai Shosuke explains as a moment when Japan itself had entirely devolved from centralised rule into an era of internally warring clans.[17] At the time, there were several pirate raids near the area of King Munmu's tomb, yet it appears that the pirates preferred to head to the Chinese coast, turning south in the Korea Straits into the East China Sea to places such as Ningbo and Xiamen.

---

[16] William Wayne Ferris, 'Ancient Japan's Korea connection', *Korean Studies*, 20 (1996): 1–22.
[17] Murai, Shōsuke, *Chūsei wajinden* (Tokyo, 1993) [村井章介(中世倭人伝)]; see also Hiroshi Mitani, 'A protonation-state and its "unforgettable other"', in Helen Hardacre, ed., *New directions in the study of Meiji Japan* (Leiden, 1997), pp. 293–310; and Ōta Kōki, *Wakō: Nihon Afure Katsudōshi* (Tokyo, 2004) [太田弘毅『倭寇: 日本あふれ活動史』].

The Sea of Japan/Korea's East Sea   189

Connective Threads

Noticeably, the ninth- and tenth-century diplomatic ocean network between the northern area of Korea and Japan evaporated as quickly as the more recent twentieth-century reverse immigration routes from Japan to the continent. Today, contemporary Korean memories of violence that originate with Japan's modern occupation of the country (1910–45) stand at odds with Japanese memories of the cataclysmic and total collapse of the nation's empire and destruction of the homeland (1945). Such collective memory often combusts into nationalistic flames, which occlude history on both sides of the current naming dispute that surrounds this sea. Thoughtful voices push back, however, and urge understanding the ocean as a 'connective zone'.[18] For example, Japanese historian Furayama Tadao has argued that the entire region – including Russia and indigenous areas – is best contextualised as 'another world, another culture' in order to break it free from nationalistically determined definitions.[19]

It can be jarring to move back and forth between the countries surrounding this sea and to jump through different chronological time periods at once, yet, in the case of this sea, it is historically productive. Put differently, exploring this sea's richness via spots along its coastlines and islands – rather than one nation at a time or time period after time period – helps create a sense of this oceanic history as a connective place for the region and beyond as well as its future possibilities.

To begin, this body of water's vital and unusually warm current is its most crucial thread. Over the course of the past fifteen to twenty million years that the Japanese main islands have been back-arc spreading from the Asian mainland and tectonically creating the physical space for this body of water to come into being, this famous ocean current – also known as the Japan Current – has brought fish larvae, plankton and other food to the myriad creatures inhabiting this sea.[20] In short, as

---

[18] Furumaya Tadao, '*Nihonkai "Mitsu no Kako"*' [The three pasts of the Sea of Japan], in Shinoda Akira, ed., *Tsunagaru Nihonkai* [The connecting Sea of Japan] (Tokyo, 2007), p. 59.

[19] Two Japanese language publications that underscore the broad possibilities for such an approach include Matsumoto Kenichi, *Kaigansen no Rekeishi* [A history of the coastline] (Tokyo, 2009) and Ariyoshi Sawako, *Nihon no shimajima: Mukashi to ima* [Japan's islands: Then and now] (Tokyo, 2012); in English, see Joseph P. Stoltman, 'Aspiring for a harmonious global society: The role of geography education', keynote address at the International Conference on Geographic Naming and Geographic Education, Northeast Asia History Foundation, Seoul, 2014.

[20] The best general treatment in English of the Kuroshio is Joyce E. Jones and Ian S. F. Jones, 'The Western Boundary Current in the Pacific: The development of our

190   A. Dudden

the nineteenth-century English geographer and hydrographer Alexander George Findlay described, the Kuroshio is 'a remarkable stream'.[21] At 46 degrees north latitude, Japan's life-giving Kuroshio Current even makes for pleasant swimming during summer months at the sea's northernmost reaches on the beaches of the lush, tiny island of Moneron, off the southern tip of Russia's Sakhalin Island. Moneron is the only landmass in the Straits of Tartary, and its astonishing diversity makes it the Russian Federation's first national marine park. The island's name originates with the French navigator Jean François de La Pérouse's 1787 visit to the region who named it after his expedition's chief engineer, Paul Merault Monneron (although the island is spelled without two 'n's').[22] The French name stands today even though the great Japanese cartographer, Mamiya Rinzo, and his colleagues visited and mapped it during their great 1808–9 expedition north through Sakhalin and eastern Siberia.[23] Japanese called the island Kaibaito until 1945, reworking the Ainu name Todomoshiri into Chinese characters – literally 'place of sea lions' in both Japanese and Ainu. In August 1945, the Soviets reverted to the French name when they subsumed control of it together with all of Sakhalin. Moneron's human population comes and goes with the transient Ainu and vanished Japanese having given way to equally nomadic Russians, today arriving as eco-tourists to frolic with the island's resident sea lions that sunbathe on basalt boulders or browse among the jewellery stores of sea stars and anemones underneath the waves.[24]

Hydrographer Arthur Findlay published numerous texts during the second half of the nineteenth century, but his *North Pacific directory* became the American and European ship captain's essential guide, ultimately becoming a helpful template for Japanese and Korean hydrographers who continue to engage this science and make significant

---

oceanographic knowledge', in Keith R. Benson and Philip F. Rehbock, *Oceanographic history: The Pacific and beyond* (Seattle, WA, 2002), pp. 86–95, esp. pp. 89–90.

[21] Alexander George Findlay, *North Pacific directory: A directory for the navigation of the North Pacific Ocean with its descriptions of its coasts, islands, etc., from Panama to Behring Strait and Japan, its winds, currents, and passages* (London, 1870), p. 597.

[22] See John Dunmore, *Where fate beckons: The life of Jean-Francois de la Pé* (Fairbanks, AK, 2008). (The name of Moneron Island is spelled slightly differently from the navigator, Monneron.)

[23] Brett L. Walker, 'Mamiya Rinzo and the Japanese exploration of Sakhalin Island: Cartography and empire', *Journal of Historical Geography*, 33 (2007): 283–313.

[24] The Japanese name for the island (Kaibaito) was an intentionally Japanised Chinese character reading of the indigenous Ainu name, Todomoshiri, which literally means 'Sea lions live here'; the best English-language treatment of Ainu people and their world stems from an exhibition at the Smithsonian's Arctic Studies Center in 2000. Co-curated by William Fitzhugh and Chisato Dubreuil, the catalogue they co-edited is splendid: *Ainu: Spirit of a northern people* (Seattle, WA, 2001).

The Sea of Japan/Korea's East Sea   191

refinements to Findlay's initial observations of this sea.[25] Importantly, Findlay captured a moment that marked this ocean's global trajectory, making his work historically significant beyond its precise measurements of currents and ocean depths. In the book's second edition (1870), he observed, 'The period which has elapsed [since 1850] has held a more important influence on the social and commercial progress of the world than any recorded in history, and in no part has this change been more evident than in the countries around the North Pacific Ocean.'[26] The text added a key detail that guided this shift that was only at that time being appreciated beyond the region: 'The Japanese Current . . . is an immense stream . . . and is exactly analogous to the Gulf Stream in the North Atlantic.'[27]

Forking in two at the tip of the Ryukyu Islands in the East China Sea, one trajectory heads north around Tsushima Island, splitting in two again into the Tsushima Current and the East Korea Warm Current, which together bring southern saline-charged nutrients across the sea to the Tsugaru Strait, between Hokkaido and Japan's primary island, Honshu. There, they recombine and break free into the Pacific to rejoin the current's southern branch in the North Pacific gyre. Within that great whorl – the largest ecosystem on earth – the Kuroshio conveys its warmth to the southern islands of Alaska and the coastline of British Columbia before heading back again across the Pacific. Unfortunately, today this means that the current contributes to one of the planet's greatest challenges: the Great Pacific Garbage Patch, a man-made collection of insoluble plastic and chemical particulate gunk, most conservatively estimated to be the size of France, although likely larger than the United States.

The Kuroshio's warm northerly branch makes Vladivostok Russia's only ice-free Pacific port and home to the Russian Pacific fleet. Distressingly, throughout the Cold War Russia took enormous licence with its control over these waters and dumped astonishing amounts of radioactive waste up through the 1990s, including two nuclear reactors off the coast of North Korea in 1978.[28] Today, North Korea maintains several

---

[25] For example, Uda Morihiro, *The results of simultaneous oceanographical investigation in the Japan Sea and its adjacent waters in May and June, 1932* (Tokyo, 1934); Lee Ki-Suk and Kim Woong Seo, *Ocean atlas of Korea, the East Sea* (Incheon, 2011).

[26] Findlay, *North Pacific directory*, p. i.

[27] Findlay, *North Pacific directory*, p. 597.

[28] The Russian report, known as the Yablokov Report, covers all of the northern Pacific and makes clear in total that between 1950 and 1990, the former Soviet Union dumped twice the amount of toxic waste as previously imagined: 2.5 million curies. See William J. Broad, 'Russians describe extensive dumping of nuclear waste', *The New York Times*, 27 April 1993, Science section.

192   A. Dudden

nuclear facilities along this ocean's coastline, while South Korea operates three. For its part, Japan operates the world's largest nuclear plant, the Kashiwazaki-Kariwa facility, south of Niigata, an area of Japan known in earlier times as Echigo, this coast's central port and critical to the country's early modern economy for rice, fish, timber and salt, among many other goods. Merchants along this coastline perfected a near shore trade route known as the 'Kitamaebune' (literally the 'northern bound ships'), which operated annually from the mid-seventeenth century through the advent of Western schooners in the region. Although the sails on these ships remained too weak in the face of this sea's ferocious northerly winds to accomplish more than one trip per year, the 'Kitamaebune' trade was integral to the calculus of the world's first commodity exchange at Osaka (in 1800 Osaka rivalled Paris in manifold ways, especially in terms of market economy).[29] Ships departed from Osaka's ports on Japan's southern face into the Inland Sea and headed west through the Kanmon Straits dividing Honshu and Kyushu, and from there cruised along Japan's northern coastline to what is today southern Hokkaido. This greatly added to the process of bringing the 'barbarian lands' (蝦夷) into Japanese consciousness, which in 1869 were renamed Hokkaido and colonised as the first piece of Japan's modern empire. Throughout such discordant human histories, the 360 currently known fish species in this sea do their best to thrive, with herring and sardines the most lucrative commodities, and giant octopus and squid holding the greatest mystery.[30]

This sea's expanse and terrible storms have long provided a natural security barrier for Japan – or, in the historian Amino Yoshihiko's words, 'an obstacle to intercourse' – challenging potential invaders such as the Mongols, who tried twice in 1274 and 1281 to cross its waters' narrowest reaches in the south, only to get trapped and repelled by typhoons – the original 'divine winds' (*kamikaze*).[31] Ironically, however, the very richness of life within this sea ultimately reeled in the outside world during the eighteenth and nineteenth centuries, making it the object of intense focus among Europeans and Americans, who finally 'opened' the region to global trade. The reason was straightforward and had nothing to do

---

[29] See James L. McClain and Osamu Wakita, eds., *Osaka: The merchants' capital of early modern Japan* (Ithaca, NY, 1999).

[30] A good primer through the lens of climate change and the effect of the Anthropocene is Kyung-Il Chang, Chang-Ik Zhang, Chul Park, Dong-Jin Kang, Se-Jong Ju, Sang-Hoon Lee and Mark Wimbush, eds., *Oceanography of the East Sea (Japan Sea)* (Cham, 2016); also Ian Jared Miller, Julia Adeney Thomas and Brett Walker, eds., *Japan at nature's edge: The environmental context of a global power* (Honolulu, HI, 2013).

[31] See Thomas D. Conlan's translation with historical interpretation, *In need of a little divine intervention: Takezaki Suenaga's scroll of the Mongol invasions of Japan* (Ithaca, NY, 2010).

The Sea of Japan/Korea's East Sea

with imperialising apologetics of civilisation and enlightenment so prevalent elsewhere in the world at the time. Counterbalancing the warm current in this sea is a cold water stream that heads straight down from the Arctic, providing optimal breeding conditions for the then most prized creatures of all: whales.

Whaling was not at all a foreign import to this sea. For millennia, open-boat, near-shore whaling practices were standard.[32] Eight thousand-year-old petroglyphs depicting whales and whale-hunting scenes were discovered in 1971 along an ancient riverbed in Bangudae, near South Korea's port city of Ulsan and the centre of its whaling industry until Korea joined the international moratorium on whaling in 1986. At Bangudae, along a stream bed are several sites of these astonishing rock carvings – the world's oldest known – which were drawn at a time when the people living there trapped whales in nets after the huge creatures ventured inland in long disappeared brackish rivers and marshes (these, in turn, are just upstream from some of the planet's most perfectly preserved 100 million year-old herbivorous dinosaur footprints, left in the mud millions of years before the nearby sea existed, let alone before anything resembling a human arrived). The drawings visible today identify distinct species of whale including the northern right, the humpback, the right whale, the grey whale and the sperm whale.[33] Seals, sea turtles and an ancient salmon are depicted, too.

Likewise, on the opposite side of this sea along Japan's northern coasts and islands, 15,000-year-old burial mounds confirm the consumption of whale meat, and Ainu legends recount whale-hunting and worship alike. To the outrage of many today, the government of Japan eschews global bans on whaling, and although Japan's butcher ships do not hunt in this sea, the Japan Whaling Association, a private organisation established in 1988, explains the nation's right to kill cetaceans in the Southern Ocean by summoning this northern sea's thousand-year-old harpooning techniques as justification for the current slaughter.[34]

All this notwithstanding, the industrial whaling practices that European and American whalers introduced here in the nineteenth century would

---

[32] The onshore techniques mirrored what Native American Nantucket Indians taught Quaker colonists in New England who became the founding names in the United States' whale oil business. See Nancy Shoemaker, *Native American whalemen and the world: The contingency of race* (Chapel Hill, NC, 2015).

[33] In English, see Sarah M. Nelson, *The archaeology of Korea* (Cambridge, 1993); Kim Won-yong, *Art and archaeology of ancient Korea* (Seoul, 1986); also Brian Fagan, 'Discovering a lost world', *Current World Archaeology* (24 January 2014): www.world-archaeology.com/travel/cwa-travels-to-the-petroglyphs-of-bangudae.htm (accessed 31 March 2017).

[34] See Hiroyuki Watanabe, *Japan's whaling: The politics of culture in historical perspective* (Melbourne, 2009).

194   A. Dudden

change whaling techniques forever for Japanese and Koreans – as well as make it impossible for Japanese and Korean leaders to keep their borders closed. In the mid-nineteenth century, ungainly whaling barks from the world's predominant ports in places such as New Bedford, Massachusetts, cruised this sea during the summer's 'hunting' season, able to boil strips of blubber on board during a voyage. The process called 'trying out' was such that a single ship could contain hundreds and often thousands of barrels of oil ready to sell when it entered port. This did away with countless middlemen and built new exchange markets in places such as Lahina, Maui and Port Lloyd on what is now Chichijima of the Ogasawara Islands, and allowed whaling ships to return north multiple times to their kill in this sea and others in the North Pacific before returning home. All of this captured social geographer David Harvey's understanding of the 'elimination of spatial barriers and the struggle to "annihilate space by time" essential to capital accumulation'.[35] Using the example of the bark *Charles W. Morgan*, which was built and outfitted in New Bedford in 1841 for roughly $50,000 (a sum that amortised during the first of its eighty voyages), owners and investors were especially pleased when the price of whale oil peaked in 1856 at $1.77 per gallon. (A barrel held roughly 32 gallons.)[36] They still lived comfortably when it was less than half of that in 1888, the year the National Geographic Society was established, and the *Morgan* spent the hunting season in this sea cruising along both the Japanese and Korean coasts.

Deeply entwined, therefore, in the international rhetorical fanfare of 'opening' Japan to the world in the mid-nineteenth century – Korea would follow a decade later – were the ways in which the first-comer United States government acted on behalf of the whaling industry in its endeavours. Ships' logbooks to the regions of the northern Pacific including this sea were collectively known on many nineteenth-century American maps as the 'Japan Grounds' for the whales and prized pinnipeds such as the spotted seals and sea lions hunted there and reveal the precarious nature of an entire area on the verge of forced engagement with Americans and Europeans and their commercial treaties of the industrial world.[37] In 1851, Mercator Cooper, the only American whaling captain at the time known as a private individual to have made it

---

[35] David Harvey, 'Between space and time: Reflections on the geographical imagination', *Annals of the Association of American Geographers*, 80, 3 (1990): 425.

[36] The Mystic Seaport Museum of America and the Sea in Mystic, CT and the New Bedford Whaling Museum in New Bedford, MA both have exceptionally rich digital collections.

[37] See Noell Wilson, *The birth of a Pacific nation: Hokkaido and U.S. whalers in nineteenth century Japan* (book manuscript in progress).

The Sea of Japan/Korea's East Sea   195

safely in and out of Tokyo Bay (on Japan's Pacific coast) spelled this out in a letter to American government representatives:

I think their ports should be opened for the convenience of whalers as we have so many ships cruising along their coast none of which in case of wreck gain any assistance from them and from their distance from other ports they would perish before they could obtain help. As they are it would be more than useless for any ship to enter their ports.[38]

As part of a global moment, whaling ships grew in intensity in the Sea of Japan/East Sea, where they increasingly encountered and rescued stranded Japanese fishermen from far-flung rocks. Ironically, the Japanese government's determination to regulate everything on land – in this instance boat length – helped speed along its own collapse.[39] In rigidly attempting to force Japanese to remain within a tightly drawn perimeter around the country, the Tokugawa shogun's command for ever-smaller boats created the unforeseen by-product of more castaways as smaller boats were more easily tossed about in storms. The castaways, in turn, encountered foreign whalers, which increased foreigners' knowledge about 'locked Japan' (in Herman Melville's famous words). Graveyards along Japan's coasts remember many 'lost at sea', not necessarily drowned but stranded.[40]

Meanwhile, captivity narratives were wildly popular in American literature, with plots revolving mainly around the feared red man – American

---

[38] Mercator Cooper papers, Letter dated 9 February 1851, MSS 85 Subgroup 2, Series A, Folder 1. (Archival collection of New Bedford Whaling Museum, New Bedford, Massachusetts.)

[39] It was not that Japanese did not know how to build larger ships. Just prior to the Tokugawa shogun's 1636 implementation of laws limiting vessel size, Japanese traders coursed the East and South China Seas along the Chinese coast, Vietnam, Indonesia, Malaysia and the Philippines on ships known as the 'Red Seal' fleet for the colour of the shogunal mark that gave them permission to do so. 200 sailors rode aboard each of these ships that rivalled the great European galleons of the day (the Tokugawa government allowed about 350 of these ships during the first decades of its rule). In 1613 on the other side of the country in the northeastern Sendai domain, with the shogun's permission lord Date Masamune funded 800 shipwrights, 700 blacksmiths and approximately 3,000 carpenters in Ishinomaki harbor to build a Spanish-style galleon known both as the *Date Maru* and the *San Juan Bautista*. It was 500 tons (about 180 feet long), with three masts and sixteen cannons, and it made two full Pacific crossings to Mexico under Hasekura Tsunenaga's command. All of this happened, however, just as shogunal authorities were beginning to cordon off Japan's ports, ordering everyone fixed in place and proscribing Spaniards and Christianity altogether while severely curtailing travel abroad for Japanese. The shogun sold most of the Red Seal ships to Chinese traders, and in 1618 disposed of the *San Juan Bautista* to Spaniards in the Philippines; a replica of it made in 1993 survived the awful 11 March 2011 earthquake and tsunami which laid waste to the harbour and town where the original was built.

[40] Matsumoto, *Kaigansen no Rekeishi*.

196   A. Dudden

Indians – abducting white boys and girls.[41] There does not, however, seem to be a fictional account of a white man being taken hostage in Japan, making Ranald MacDonald's official testimony detailing his real life 1848–49 capture along Japan's northwestern coast and his subsequent imprisonment all the more sensational then as well as historically significant today.[42] In 1848, MacDonald, a half-Chinook, half-Scot self-promoting adventurer (by his own account) used the money he earned working the 'Japan Grounds' on a ship called the *Plymouth* to purchase a small boat and keep it on deck with the express intent of having the captain lower him overboard along the northwest coast of Japan. MacDonald knew about the shogun's strict laws forbidding foreigners' access (although he does not seem to have known that the exclusion decree was rescinded in 1848); he claimed, nonetheless, that his 'principal motive in this was . . . the mere gratification of adventure'.[43] He made clear that he wanted the adventure that he got, yet once his story came to the attention of American journalists and officials who desired certain ends, its details were too useful to be spun into anything less than a hostage crisis involving an innocent American trapped by heathen on the anti-Christian island of Japan (in their collective telling, that is).

Beginning with the fallout from MacDonald's testimony together with that of several other American sailors who had been taken prisoner in northern Japan after their ship *Lagoda* wrecked, newspaper columnists urged the US Congress to take action against Japan whose leaders in the act of capturing MacDonald and the others 'forfeit all claim to respect as a civilized people, and may justly be regarded as hostile to the human race'.[44] Ultimately, such views prevailed in the appropriations debates that would fund Commodore Matthew Perry's enormously expensive and highly militarised expeditions to Japan between 1852 and 1854 to open ports to trade. Doing so, Congress at once assuaged whalers'

[41] Paul Gilmore, *The genuine article: Race, mass culture, and American literary manhood* (Durham, NC, 2001).

[42] For the fullest account, see Frederick Schodt, *Native American in the land of the shogun: Ranald MacDonald and the opening of Japan* (Berkeley, CA, 2003); also Imanishi Yuko, *Ranald MacDonald* (Tokyo, 2013).

[43] Schodt, *Native American in the land of the shogun*, pp. 191–93.

[44] Schodt, *Native American in the land of the shogun*, p. 303. All of this becomes even more important in light of Japanese officials' response to Matthew Perry's requests for information about shipwrecked sailors during his visit. Included in the first volume of Perry's journals of the expedition is an account given to the Americans concerning the well-being of twenty-three American sailors missing between 1847 and 1850, with assurances – which Perry accepted in full – that they had long been repatriated through Dutch auspices (1847, seven Americans; 1847, thirteen Americans; 1849, three Americans): see Matthew Calbraith Perry, *Narrative of the expedition of an American squadron to the China Seas and Japan: Performed in the years 1852, 1853 and 1854*, 3 vols. (Washington, DC, 1856–57), I, p. 471.

The Sea of Japan/Korea's East Sea

interests while also aligning with strategic planners who wanted to 'get' Japan before the British did to secure an American foothold in Asia.

International law at the time concurred with public discussion. In appointing Perry, United States' Acting Secretary to the Navy, C. M. Conrad, emphasised:

> When vessels are wrecked ... on their shores, their crews are subjected to the most cruel treatment ... [and with] great barbarity.[45]

American commercial interests, he explained, were thus the cause of civilisation's progress:

> Every nation has undoubtedly the right to determine for itself the extent to which it will hold intercourse with other nations. This same law of nations, however, which protects a nation in the exercise of this right imposes upon her certain duties which she cannot justly disregard . . . none is more imperative than that which requires her to succor and relieve those persons who are cast by the perils of the ocean upon her shores.[46]

In sum, the United States government argued that because Japanese leaders flouted international laws (of which they were unaware), the use of force if necessary was justified.

Meanwhile, to achieve its aim this power politics view of the sea would outright ignore this ocean's connective possibilities such as friendly encounter. On 11 April 1850, the whaling ship *Hannibal* from New London, Connecticut, sailed along Japan's northwestern coast, several hundred miles south of where MacDonald had gone ashore. The ship's logbook describes the scene:

> Light breeze. Land in sight and about 20 Jappanese Junks – Stood in for land and at 2 ½ PM when about 3 miles distant lowered 3 boats and pulled for the shore – taking guns and fishing gear. Saw along the shore great numbers of seal on the rocks – on landing found a party of Jappanese capturing seals for their oil and hides. Second mate gave a sailor's knife and a short piece of towline for a fine looking calf. We got neither fish nor game – but returned aboard. Got up in chains and anchors ready to go.[47]

The *Hannibal*'s log-keeper, Nathaniel Saxton Morgan, was 17 and from Hartford, Connecticut. The next day – roughly three years before

---

[45] Conrad to Kennedy, 5 November 1852, in Matthew Calbraith Perry, *Correspondence relative to the naval expedition to Japan* (n.p., 1855), p. 4.

[46] Ibid., p. 5.

[47] 'Whaling voyage of the ship Hannibal. Capt Sluman Grey on a three years cruise bound to the North Pacific and Arctic Oceans' (Nathaniel Saxton Morgan, age 16 log-keeper). Logbook of the *Hannibal* (Log 862): Mystic Seaport Archival Collection, Mystic, CT. The second mate was Fitch Way, twenty-six years old from Montville, CT.

Matthew Perry's 'shock and awe' entrance into Tokyo harbour – Morgan described what he could see of Honshu and Hokkaido:

The island of Nippon on one side and the mainland of Japan on the other. The land appears in a high state of cultivation and covered with luxuriant verdure. In passing through the straits we saw several apparently large towns and cities and immense herds of cattle – the Capt ordered the boats to be got ready to go on shore and shoot bullock but the wind freshening we stood our course which I think all for the best. We had a fine view of both sides of the straits – the island of Nippon and the Mainland – the wind some of the time being ahead we had to tack from shore to shore – This land is surely a paradise – lovely in the extreme.[48]

Experiences like Morgan's and a number of other Americans and Europeans contradicted the United States' politically desired ends, which at that moment rested on making the Japanese government fully submit to American terms for trade. All of this makes this sea's possibilities even more important today when thinking about contemporary pressures to 'open' North Korea, whose eastern coastline and people are integral to this connective world.

Ironically, too, the history of modern whaling connects to an additional contemporary security problem in this sea. Japan's Oki Islands and Korea's Ulleugndo are among the sea's remarkably few island groups – the largest of which also include Russia's Sakhalin and Japan's Sado. Both Oki and Ulleungdo have rich fishing traditions that include whaling, and today they boast cultures centred on squid and cuttlefish – with the squid-shaped public telephone booth near Oki Island's main ferry port perhaps globally unique. Geologically distinct, Oki and Ulleungdo have ancient histories of kingly visits and/or exiles as early as the sixth and seventh centuries and also medieval era 'wako' (倭寇) pirate raids. Both are covered by similarly tall, thick grasses that in the sea's wild wind make it appear at times as if green waves are carrying the ocean itself up the islands' respectively steep inclines. Of note, however, one of Northeast Asia's key flashpoints centres on several spiky spits of land that stand between Ulleungdo and the Oki Islands, and which hold one of the most surreal security distinctions in the contemporary world: the United States military is potentially obligated under separate agreements with South Korea and Japan to defend this territory for each side even though both sides claim the islands as 'integral' to their nations. The sharply pointed volcanic outcrop that Koreans know as Dokdo and Japanese call Takeshima is the focus of this bipolar state of affairs. The United States government tries hard to hide its complicit involvement in creating this

---

[48] Logbook of the *Hannibal*, 12 April 1850, Mystic Seaport Archival Collection.

The Sea of Japan/Korea's East Sea 199

mess among allies by publishing maps that label the islands with their nineteenth-century European name, the Liancourt Rocks, after a French whaling ship that nearly wrecked on them in 1849.[49]

Tragedy in a Connective Sea

In another key, tragedy offers a complementary approach to understanding connection in any body of water, which also works around nationalist impulses. Put another way, the hard fact of what the poet T. S. Eliot evoked as 'death by water' impels grasping the foreboding totality of any sea as well as its connective possibilities.

In Russian terms, the sea it shares with Japan and Korea remains in many ways less part of the nation's past than of its future – as does much of Russia's far east, which commands most of this ocean's shoreline, urging forward the significant expansion of its naval bases in the region today. With only a few intrepid Russian explorers reaching this region in the late seventeenth and eighteenth centuries – and chiefly taking an interest in this sea as a means to head onwards to the fabled 'Isles of Gold' as Europeans then described Japan – for Russians the first substantial introduction to this ocean's far reaches came in the very late nineteenth century in Anton Chekhov's *The island: A journey to Sakhalin*.[50] Chekhov's chronicle results from a government assignment to compile a convict census of the penal colony that was Sakhalin Island between 1868 and 1905. It was the last jail built in the notorious Romanov corrective system where over 30,000 political and criminal offenders endured or succumbed to the worst conditions in the empire. The distance to Sakhalin from Moscow (where most of the prisoners originated) is 'nearly one-quarter of the earth's circumference', and, having survived this trek, upon arrival the innkeeper greeted Chekhov by flatly asking why he had come to 'this godforsaken hole'.[51] Chekhov's prose detailed not only the prisoners' death-in-life conditions, but also makes a composite sketch of the nearly 10,000 'former convicts who were required to remain in exile and had been granted settler status, of family members who had accompanied the prisoners from

---

[49] Ariyoshi, *Nihon no shimajima*, pp. 298–341; also see Alexis Dudden, 'Korea-Japan's rocky standoff: Something more?', in Jeff Kingston, ed., *Asian nationalisms reconsidered* (London, 2015), pp. 103–15.

[50] Anton Chekhov, *The island: A journey to Sakhalin*, trans. Luba Terpak and Michael Terpak (New York, 1967); see also Vlas Doroshevich, *Sakhalin: Russia's penal colony in the Far East*, trans. Andrew A. Gentes (London, 2011); James McConkey, *To a distant island* (Philadelphia, PA, 2000).

[51] Quoted in McConkey, *To a distant island*, p. 146.

200   A. Dudden

need or love or both, and of the children born either on the island or on the lengthy trip to it'.[52]

In 1905, the southern half of Sakhalin Island became a war spoil for Japan as a result of its nation's defeat of Russia – the final moments of victory for Japan in a decisive naval battle at the opposite end of this sea in the Tsushima Straits. By 1945, nearly 400,000 Japanese would colonise their portion of this large island, with emigration companies' promotional films playing in Japanese movie theatres featuring the ice-breaker voyages that would convey settlers as well as the unimaginably deep snows that this ocean's winters bring.

These snows conceptually connect back much further in time to engage the sum total of countless images and histories within Japan that continue to colour for Japanese an enduring perception of this entire region, its coastline, and sea beyond as 'the backside of Japan' (literally, *Ura Nihon* as it all remains commonly called in Japanese addition to the more proper geographic names). Some of the most revealing among these histories revolve around the port city of Niigata (earlier Echigo), located where the Amurian plate and the Okhotsk plate converge and appear to make Japan itself twist sideways north. Importantly, the bleak-ness that this area engenders within Japanese society intersects with cen-turies' long practice of using this sea itself as a place for banishment and exile. During Japan's classical and early medieval eras, when court officials decided that certain emperors, priests and poets were guilty of heretical thought, they expelled them from the splendour of the capitals at Kyoto and Kamakura on the country's southern face and put them out to sea at Maze, among other departure ports, close to Niigata.

Regardless that this sea did not have a name in Japanese until about 200 years ago – or maybe because of it – the frequent absence of even a horizon line instilled dread as inky dark skies become one with even darker waters. Among others, Emperor Juntoku endured twenty winters off of Niigata's coast on Sado Island in its coffin-like fog and thunder snows before his death in 1241, while the dramatist Zeami Motokiyo, Japan's most famous Noh author, was exiled to Sado for the year in 1434 on charges that are still unclear. During the early modern era, police in Edo (today's Tokyo) regularly sent prisoners and poor people to work to their deaths in the gold mine on Sado. In the 1930s and 1940s the mine continued to operate, exchanging the labour source from disen-franchised Japanese to enslaved colonial Koreans and Allied prisoners of war. Testimony given during British inquiry into Japanese war crimes

---

[52] McConkey, *To a distant island*, pp. 6, xi.

The Sea of Japan/Korea's East Sea 201

revealed the intentional murder on Sado Island in August 1945 by mine blast of 387 Allied prisoners.[53] Japan's other spots of remote exile in this sea included the Oki Islands. The sum total of these histories colour for Japanese in the country's powerful spots at Kyoto and eventually Tokyo an enduring view of all of it – including the sea – as hinterland Japan.

Moreover, the utter destruction of Japan's modern empire enshrouded this region in the image of defeat, not least because at the empire's height in the 1930s it was filled with such promise for its planners. Niigata became the main exit point for several million Japanese soldiers and settlers heading to secure their nation's 'Manifest Destiny' in northern Korea and northeastern China, on a historically reversed migration pattern of people moving from Japan to the continent. On 1 September 1931, the Japanese Railway Company opened the new Joetsu trunk line from Tokyo to Niigata, which conveyed Japanese emigrants to ocean liners such as the *Gassan*, which alone took tens of thousands of Japanese to ports such as Wonsan and Najin on the northeastern Korean coast from which point they would head inland to seek their fortunes on the continent.[54] The total devastation of the Japanese empire in 1945 meant that roughly six million settlers out of a Japanese population of 72 million – the preponderance having relocated to north China – worked their way back to Japan as best they could, although 'home' and 'return' for many people were strange concepts having been born and raised abroad, never having set foot in Japan proper.[55] In addition, in August 1945, the Soviet Union took captive as many as 700,000 Japanese soldiers and civilians – many of them included the settlers to the southern half of Sakhalin – imprisoning them in Siberian gulags where a horrifically high death rate prevailed (up to 60,000 fatalities).[56] Russia held hundreds of thousands of these

---

[53] The contested story about the possible murder of British POWs on Sado Island stems from a 1948 war criminal investigation, which American General Douglas MacArthur ordered destroyed. See Gregory Hadley and James Oglethorpe, 'MacKay's betrayal: Solving the mystery of the "Sado Island prisoner-of-war massacre"', *Journal of Military History*, 71 (2007): 1–24; BBC, *WW2 People's War: An Archive of World War Two Memories – Written by the public, gathered by the BBC*, 15 October 2014: www.bbc.co.uk/history/ ww2peopleswar/user/89/u246489.shtml (accessed 31 March 2017).

[54] See Kazuko Kuramoto, *Manchurian legacy: Memoirs of a Japanese colonist* (East Lansing, MI, 2004); Louise Young, *Japan's total empire: Manchuria and the culture of wartime imperialism* (Berkeley, CA, 1999).

[55] Lori Watt, *When empire comes home: Repatriation and reintegration into postwar Japan* (Cambridge, MA, 2010).

[56] Andrew Barshay, *The gods left first: The captivity and repatriation of Japanese POWs in Northeast Asia, 1945–1956* (Cambridge, MA, 2010); also Paul Murayama, *Escape from Manchuria: The rescue of 1.7 million Japanese civilians trapped in Soviet-occupied Manchuria following the end of World War II* (Mustang, OK, 2016).

202   A. Dudden

people in labour camps as late as 1956, with a few not returning to Japan until the 1990s. The majority of survivors arrived home over the sea to Niigata.

In the immediate wake of the Allied forces' 1945 destruction of Japan, the Korean War erupted (1950–53). Amid what was predominantly a series of land and air campaigns, the United Nations led a naval blockade that was the longest in modern history at the North Korean port of Wonsan from February 1951 to July 1953. Shortly before it began, however, on 23 December 1950 the SS *Meredith Victory* set sail from there to Geoje Island near Busan on Korea's far southern coast, about 500 miles away. Today that ship is known informally as the 'Ship of Miracles' partly because of the Christmas season with which its action coincided and partly because of what it accomplished: the greatest humanitarian rescue operation from land by ship. Captain Leonard LaRue ordered his crew to unload all weapons and extraneous supplies from the *Meredith* and refit the 10,000-ton cargo ship designed for sixty crewmembers and twelve passengers to accept as many refugees as possible. With little food or water, nearly 14,000 people stood one against another for three wintry days at sea, disembarking along the country's southern coast on 26 December 1950.

Following the 1953 armistice between the United States and North Korea, yet before Japan resumed formal relations with either North or South Korea, in 1959 an unusual ferryboat service was launched that regularly departed the Japanese port of Niigata for the North Korean port of Wonsan. A Soviet-flagged passenger ship, the *Kurilion,* first set sail from Japan in December 1959, evolving during the next two decades into the North Korean-built *Mangyonbong.* The ship continued to course back and forth with its passengers atop water that was dominated underneath its surface by US and Russian submarines playing precarious games of cat and mouse with one another. The ferryboat itself drew little reaction in Japan although the Niigata-based 'Japanese North Korean Return Assistance Association' tried hard to give it a place of pride, regularly touring the city's schoolchildren and ladies' associations aboard the ship, holding festive and well-documented parties for those leaving Japan (recording the restaurant, the menu, who attended, whether they wore traditional Korean dress or Western fashions), and marking the ship's commemorative moments (10,000th passenger, 50,000th, fifteenth year) with banners and posters hung throughout the city's downtown area. In short, no one in Niigata appeared to feel that there was anything to hide or fear about any of it.

The passengers who rode this ferry included groups of children of Korean ethnicity in Japan on required school field trips to the 'Fatherland',

The Sea of Japan/Korea's East Sea   203

as well as people visiting relatives and tourists.[57] Additionally, a group of people only decades later understood to be part of a much more confusing scheme rode this ship too. In the mid-1950s, Japanese and North Korean leaders and the International Committee of the Red Cross organised and legitimated the planned removal of Koreans in Japan to North Korea as part of the 'Great Patriation of the Fatherland'.[58] Between 1959 and 1984, roughly 93,000 people crossed this sea this way, yet they were never allowed to leave North Korea (as they had been promised they would). Only recently have the inner workings of this history come to light, raising problematic questions of 'who knew what when?' and 'did ethnic cleansing really take place in postwar Japan?' Most pressingly now as North Korean refugees to Japan and elsewhere recount stories of their lives: 'Can anything be done to help those still alive and wanting to get out?'[59]

An equally complicated Cold War history of this sea worked in the other direction, and only confirmed in 2002: North Korea's state-sponsored abduction of Japanese citizens in the 1970s and 1980s.[60] In what seems like a pitch for a really bad movie, the horrific reality involved North Korean scuba-diving frog agents emerging from the sea and kidnapping Japanese citizens as they went about their daily lives along the coast: two were in their car on a date at the beach, for example, while another, Yokota Megumi, was thirteen years old in 1977 and walking home from badminton practice at her Niigata middle school when she was snatched. In 2002, following headline-grabbing revelations, five returned to Japan by plane; their children and spouses followed two years later, with the most awkward case involving an abducted Japanese woman, who after her kidnapping was forcibly married to Charles Robert Jenkins, an American who had deserted his army post along the demilitarised zone in South Korea in 1965 to protest the war in Vietnam by defecting north. The couple had two children while living in Pyongyang, and following an extremely elaborate diplomatic dance to exempt Jenkins from immediate extradition upon arrival in Japan (as the US–Japan Alliance would require), they live now in seclusion on Sado Island.

---

[57] See Sonia Ryang, *North Koreans in Japan: Language, ideology, and identity* (Boulder, CO, 1997).

[58] See Tessa Morris-Suzuki, *Exodus to North Korea: Shadows from Japan's Cold War* (Lanham, MD, 2007).

[59] Kyoko Matsumoto, 'Japanese abductee possibly hospitalized in Pyongyang', *The Japan Times*, 16 October 2016: www.japantimes.co.jp/news/2016/10/16/national/japanese-abductee-possibly-hospitalized-pyongyang/ (accessed 31 March 2017).

[60] See Robert S. Boynton, *The invitation only zone: The true story of North Korea's abduction project* (New York, 2015).

204   A. Dudden

The nightmare abduction plan aimed to train spies perfectly fluent in 'native' Japanese; the 93,000 repatriates trapped there – with most now dead – having long been deemed of dubious patriotism as far as their allegiance to North Korea was concerned, thus untrustworthy regardless of language fluency (and this includes the several thousand Japanese women who accompanied Korean husbands 'home' to a North Korea most had never seen before).[61] The practical details of this plan were launched in the late 1940s, shortly after the official creation of separate South and North Korean regimes when North Korean intelligence agents routinely kidnapped South Korean fisherman all along the Korean peninsula's east coast to gain information as well as to increase their population. Unsurprisingly, Koreans were sympathetic to the plight of abducted Japanese yet collectively bewildered by the levels of outrage over a few Japanese compared with the thousands of their own similarly lost to this sea.

There is no tangible evidence that the *Mangyongbong* ferry and the abducted Japanese are of a piece, yet when the abductee story broke in Japan in 2002, the surrounding maelstrom swept the ferry and its history into its midst. Overnight, the ship itself became one with kidnapping Japanese, its separate and sad history moot. In this context, the sea itself continues to resonate hard all around. What, then, of the few boats of North Korean refugees who appear on it now? Known as 'ghost ships' in Japan where in addition to the Russian coastline the small craft wash ashore with skeletons or decomposing corpses – the numbers increasing during winter months when the winds shift – eighty appeared along various spots of Japan's northern coastline in 2013, sixty-five in 2014, and forty or so in 2015. Thus, in such light it is noticeable that the intense international discussion about what might happen to North Korea's 22 million people should the country collapse contains little productive conversation about a potential exodus over the sea.

Equally important to consider, the name of the sea did not matter to the 269 people of sixteen nationalities who died on 1 September 1983 when Korean Airlines (KAL) Flight 007 crashed into the waters off of Moneron Island. En route from New York to Seoul, the plane was 300 miles off of its charted course and deep in Russian air space at the height of the Cold War. With no response from KAL pilot Captain Chun

---

[61] Anna Fifield, 'Japanese women who have escaped from North Korea find little sympathy at home in Japan', *Washington Post*, 15 September 2014: www.washingtonpost.com/world/japanese-women-who-have-escaped-from-north-korea-find-little-sympathy-at-home/2014/09/14/4a843e15-a3d1-40cd-bfb2-d2f886b67dfa_story.html?utm_term=.44847b07d14a (accessed 31 March 2017).

The Sea of Japan/Korea's East Sea

Byung-in to verbal or hand communication or warning shots, the pilot of a Soviet Su-interceptor, Major Gennadi Osipovich, shot at the hydraulics systems near the passenger plane's tail, causing it to spiral out of the sky for several horrible minutes and disintegrate on impact.[62] Nearly ten years later in 1992, following the collapse of the Soviet Union Russian President Boris Yeltsin transferred flight transcripts and other materials to victims' families, who, thus, would learn that their loved ones had died aware of their impending deaths, which only compounded grief relating to the fact that very few human remains and only tiny bits of debris were ever found.[63] With the information, Hans Ephraimson-Abt, father of twenty-two-year-old Alice who died, told reporters, 'We have been struggling to know what happened for years to our loved ones. Now we face the agonizing recognition that their death was neither painless nor instant.'[64]

Setting aside a never-ending cycle of speculation, the reality of this sea at this moment in human history was primed for controversy. Recovery teams faced a web of man-made impediments in the form of Cold War lines drawn on top of the water that could not be crossed. Which side would conduct search and recovery operations? Where? United States' alliance structures with South Korea and Japan versus Russia determined that the South Korean owners of the airplane designated American and Japanese rescue teams. For its part, the Soviet Union included Moneron and Sakhalin Islands off whose shores Russian military divers searched for the plane, which they presumed they would find. It had entirely disintegrated, however, leaving only mangled pieces the size of a car door at best. During the weeks to come, civilians on the two islands hunted for scant shards of the jet and its passengers as they washed ashore.

Meanwhile, although twelve-mile national territorial limits in the sea were standard at the time throughout the world, Japan had three-mile limits in this sea's northern and southern straits so that American ships could carry nuclear weapons with greater breathing room. Only in 2009 did Japanese officials confirm the long-suspected detail about Japan's

---

[62] Similar to other cataclysmic tragedies at sea such as the 1994 sinking of the ferryboat *Estonia* in the North Sea and the 2014 crash of Malaysia Airlines Flight 370 in the Southern Indian Ocean, alternative explanations abound for what happened to KAL Flight 007. For lucid explication, see William Langewiesche, *The outlaw sea: A world of freedom, chaos, and crime* (New York, 2005), pp. 101–26.

[63] Seymour Hersh, '*The target is destroyed*': *What really happened to Flight 007 and what America knew about it* (New York, 1986).

[64] Hans Ephraimson-Abt, quoted in Celestine Bohlen, 'Tape displays the anguish on the jet the Soviets downed', *The New York Times*, 16 October 1992, p. A6; Ephraimson-Abt is chairman of American Association for Families of K.A.L. 007.

206   A. Dudden

unusually constrained control over its own sea.[65] The American over-lord sleight of hand transgressed international territorial norms in the sea and undercut Japan's legally enshrined 'non-nuclear' status – a post-1945 proscription on possessing nuclear weapons on land and sea – and only added more barriers to the aftermath of the KAL disaster in the waters northwest of Japan's northernmost island of Hokkaido. Today, on Hokkaido's northern tip at Cape Soya is a plea for peace embod-ied in monument to the plane's victims, a soaring concrete structure in the shape of an enormous *origami* crane, like the little paper ones at Hiroshima and Nagasaki.

In Closing

The city of Niigata's lone skyscraper houses an organisation called the Economic Research Institute for Northeast Asia (ERINA).[66] This is Niigata's flashiest venue, and fitting, therefore, that the consulates of the People's Republic of China, the Russian Federation and the Republic of Korea have their offices on floors just above and below ERINA's. The challenge for ERINA's ideas about the sea it overlooks – how best to invest Japanese capital in Russian oil exploration in Yakutsk, among others, or how best to transport landlocked Mongolian rare earth minerals to mar-ket – is not a matter of high-level political connections. Instead, it revolves around the degree of autonomy that municipalities all along the shores of this body of water can exercise as well as how much voice local and regional governments and municipalities can achieve. Moreover, ERINA consciously addresses the limitations that the outdated architecture of a defeated Japan and enduring Cold War mindset impose on this sea.

The former governor of Niigata prefecture, Hirayama Ikuo, a respected economist at the Bank of Japan and now university president, explained some of these hurdles: 'When ERINA wants to make a policy pro-posal, it has to go through five different desks at the Foreign Ministry (in Tokyo): Russia, China, South Korea, North Korea, and the United States. You can imagine what happens.'[67] Looked at differently, ERINA's backers want to exploit resources and rely on the open possibility of

---

[65] Japan Coast Guard, 'For the safety navigation in Japanese coastal waters' (Tokyo, 2009): www.kaiho.mlit.go.jp/syoukai/soshiki/toudai/navigation-safety/en/pdf/english.pdf (accessed 31 March 2017).

[66] Established in 1993, ERINA hosts meetings and sponsors publications regarding the potential linkages and development of this sea area. See: www.erina.or.jp (accessed 31 March 2017).

[67] Hirayama Ikuo in interview with author, 13 November 2009; see also, Hirayama, *Watashi wa Konna Shiji ni naritakatta* (Tokyo, 2009), p. 169.

The Sea of Japan/Korea's East Sea 207

the sea as a transport network. They view this body of water's connective tissue as primary for its surrounding lands ideally in which regional inhabitants would have greater control over policy direction and profit allocation. Regardless of the ultimate decision over this sea's name – or maybe as part of it – all who share its coastlines will want to determine a name for it that has connective meaning to it and to all of its life forms in order to hold the region together rather than further dividing it.

Further Reading

There are plentiful excellent studies of the Pacific Ocean broadly conceived, beginning with David Armitage and Alison Bashford, eds., *Pacific histories: Ocean, land, people* (Basingstoke, 2014) and Matt K. Matsuda, *Pacific worlds: A history of seas, peoples, and cultures* (Cambridge, 2012). At the same time, few yet specifically delve into the Pacific Ocean's marginal seas along the Asian coastline. Robert D. Kaplan, *Asia's cauldron: The South China Sea and the end of a stable Pacific* (New York, 2015) provides an overview to various countries' historical contestation over this sea; Tim F. Liao, Kimie Hara and Krista Wiegand, *The China-Japan border dispute: Islands of contention in multidisciplinary perspective* (Burlington, VT, 2015) examine similar matters in the East China Sea. Historical and historiographical consideration of the East Sea/Sea of Japan in underdeveloped not least because it is embroiled in issues of decolonisation. From a Japanese perspective, therefore, the most balanced and broad-minded approach lies first in considering the question of Japan itself. Paramount in this vein is Amino Yoshihiko, *Rethinking Japanese history*, trans. Alan Christy (Ann Arbor, MI, 2012); and for interpretive understanding of early modern Japanese visions of the world around them, David L. Howell, *Geographies of identity in nineteenth-century Japan* (Berkeley, CA, 2005). A path-breaking consideration of the Japanese move to its northern territories is Brett L. Walker, *The conquest of Ainu lands: Ecology and culture in Japanese expansion, 1590–1800* (Berkeley, CA, 2006). Also important is Kären Wigen, Sugimoto Fumiko and Cary Karacas, eds., *Cartographic Japan: A history in maps* (Chicago, IL, 2016). For consideration of this sea through the lens of Korean history and historiography, see Soh Jeong-Cheol and Park Young-Min, eds., *East Sea or Sea of Japan: History and truths* (Seoul, 2015). In addition, Peter E. Raper, Kim Jin Hyun, Lee Ki-suk and Choo Sung-jae, eds., *Geographical issues on maritime names: Special reference to the East Sea* (Seoul, 2010) places similar historical issues on a broader, transnational scale. Also important is William Wayne Ferris, 'Ancient Japan's Korea connection', *Korean Studies*, 20 (1996): 1–22,

208   A. Dudden

to parse histories of the transfer of knowledge and material culture. Equally important, moreover, is consideration of indigenous views in Michael Ashkenazi, *Handbook of Japanese mythology* (New York, 2008); and for broader, comparative understanding, see Josh Reid, *The sea is my country: The maritime world of the Makahs, an indigenous borderlands people* (New Haven, CT, 2015); finally, Nancy Shoemaker, *Native American whalemen and the world: The contingency of race* (Chapel Hill, NC, 2015) introduces an entirely new understanding of ocean transfer and contact during the modern era.

8   The Baltic Sea

*Michael North**

From prehistoric times the Baltic Sea region has witnessed a closely connected settlement of different ethnic and linguistic communities, for example of Germanic, Slavonic, Baltic or Finno-Ugric origin. These societies developed during the Middle Ages and the modern era into nations and states. In several cases (notably in Finland and the Baltic countries) state-building took place only in the twentieth century. Moreover, due to the changing dominion exerted by different powers over the Baltic Sea, the political pertinence of the coastal areas shifted regularly. For many historians therefore, the history of the Baltic seems to be a history of warfare and struggle for dominion: between Poland and the Teutonic Order, among Denmark, Sweden and Poland; between Russia and Sweden.[1] Those struggles and tensions produced enduring stereotypes. These ethnic stereotypes were – or still are – so effective that historians overlooked the fact that the Baltic Sea region was an area of cultural exchange. Here burgeoning communication by shipping, migration and integration of foreigners fostered the emergence of supra-national cultures in the Baltic Sea region; for example, the Viking culture, the culture of the Hanse, Netherlandisation and Sovietisation.[2]

The political upheavals of 1989 with the fall of the Berlin Wall, the collapse of the Soviet Union and the independence of the Baltic States were far-reaching and stimulated a new perception of, and perspective on, the Baltic Sea region. And these changes gained momentum with the eastern enlargement of the European Union. The new situation stimulated

---

[*] Portions of this chapter appeared previously in Michael North, *The Baltic: A history*, trans. Kenneth Kronenberg (Cambridge, MA, 2015). Copyright © 2015 by the President and Fellows of Harvard College.

[1] David Kirby, *Northern Europe in the early modern period: The Baltic world 1492–1772* (London, 1990); Kirby, *The Baltic world 1772–1993: Europe's northern periphery in an age of change* (London, 1995); Matti Klinge, *Die Ostseewelt* (Helsinki, 1995); Alan Warwick Palmer, *Northern shores: a history of the Baltic Sea and its peoples* (London, 2005).

[2] Karl Schlögel, *Im Raume lesen wir die Zeit: über Zivilisationsgeschichte und Geopolitik* (Munich, 2003), p. 68f.; Schlögel, *In space we read time: On the history of civilization and geopolitics*, trans. Gerrit Jackson (Chicago, IL, 2016).

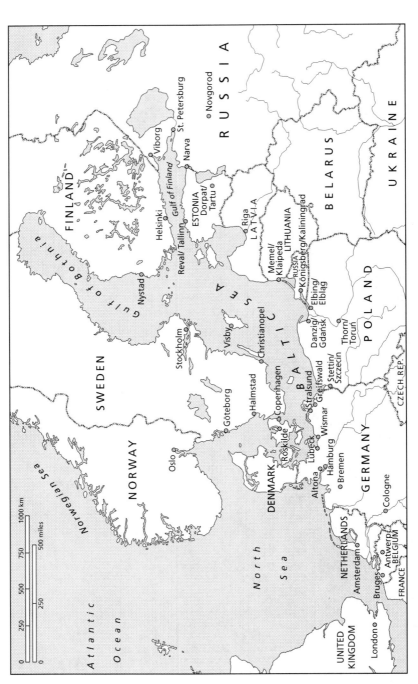

Map 8.1 The Baltic Sea

The Baltic Sea   211

research as well.[3] Although historians from the countries of the Baltic Sea region have been writing from their different perspectives, a synthesis like Fernand Braudel's concept of the Mediterranean has been demanded.[4] However, syntheses along Braudel's model are limited, because they are dominated by the physical setting in which its inhabitants were forced to make a living. In the meantime, concepts of space and regions have developed. For example, regions are no longer viewed as natural entities but as the constructs of a multiplicity of actors. There is, then, not only an unchangeable physical setting of the 'Baltic Sea' that determines the region, but also people and powers interacting continuously to reinvent the Baltic Sea region. In this chapter I shall first focus on the different notions of the Baltic Sea region from the Middle Ages up to now. The central part of this essay will examine the Baltic Sea as trading region and cultural contact zone. In the conclusion I will focus on the relationships between the Baltic Sea and other seas and oceans.

Medieval and Modern Notions of the Baltic Sea

The first notion of a 'Baltic Sea region' was created in the eleventh century by Adam of Bremen in his chronicle on the History of the Church of Hamburg (*Gesta Hammaburgensis Ecclesiae Pontificum*). He wrote about the successful mission of the archbishopric of Hamburg-Bremen in the North, thus designating the Baltic Sea region as a religious and missionary zone. He described the travels of archbishop Unni on the track of St Ansgar across the Baltic Sea to Birka in Sweden with the words 'travelling over the Baltic Sea' (*mare balticum remigans*). In the fourth book of his history, Adam of Bremen characterised the nature of the Baltic as follows: 'Now, to say something about the nature of the Baltic Sea [. . .] this gulf is called Baltic by the inhabitants because it stretches like a belt (*balteus*) to the regions of the Scythians' (*Nunc autem, . . ., aliquid de natura Baltici maris dicere . . . Sinus ille ab incolis appellantur "Balticus" eo quod in modo baltei longo tractu per Sciticas regiones tendatur . . .*).[5] Adam

---

[3] Kirby, *Northern Europe in the early modern period*; Kirby, *The Baltic world*; Klinge, *Die Ostseewelt*; Palmer, *Northern shores*.

[4] Fernand Braudel, *La mediterranée et le monde mediterranéen a l'époque de Philippe II* (Paris, 1949); David Abulafia, 'Mediterraneans', in William V. Harris, ed., *Rethinking the Mediterranean* (Oxford, 2005), p. 65. See also Abulafia, *The great sea: A human history of the Mediterranean* (London, 2012). For a natural-geographical focus on the Baltic Sea, see Hansjörg Küster, *Die Ostsee: Eine Natur- und Kulturgeschichte* (Munich, 2002). For an economic and cultural history, see North, *The Baltic*.

[5] 'Sinus ille ab incolis appelatur Balticus, eo quod in modum baltei longu tractu per Scithicas regiones tendatur usque ad Grecium idemque mare Barbarum seu Pelagus Sciticum vocatur a gentibus, quas alluit, barbaris': *Hamburgische Kirchengeschichte*, ed.

212   M. North

also mentioned the Normans, the Slavs, the Estonians and other peoples living along the shores of the Baltic Sea.[6]

In the thirteenth century the Baltic Sea became visible as a region traversed by pilgrims and trade. In 1241, Duke Albert of Saxony granted safe conduct to merchants travelling from the East Sea to the West Sea (*de orientali mari ad occidentale mare*): that is, between the Baltic and the North Sea.[7] In 1266, the papal nuntio Guido exempted the pilgrims on their way from the Baltic Sea to the North Sea – 'De orientali mari ad occidentae mare [que] Osterse et westerse vulgariter nuncupantur' – from the strand law, the wrecking by coastal communities in the case of a ship accident.[8]

Especially with the expansion of Hanseatic trade in the Baltic Sea and in the North Sea, the cities corresponded. For example, in 1294 the city of Zwolle on the River IJssel wrote to the city of Lübeck about the 'Eastern Sea' (*mare orientale*) and the 'Western Sea' (*mare occidentale*).[9] A century later, in 1401 Albrecht of Bavaria, Duke of Holland, Zeeland and Hainaut promised safe conduct for the deputies of the Hanseatic cities, which he described as 'common cities of the East Sea' ('ghemeenre steden bi der osterzee').[10] In the fifteenth- and sixteenth-century Netherlands the terms 'Oostersche zee' and 'Oostzee' or 'mer d'oost' and 'mer d'Oostlande' were increasingly used, whilst humanist writers still spoke about 'Mare Balticum'. The Swedish chronicler Olaus Magnus mentioned in his *Historia de gentibus septentrionalibus*, 'mare Balticum', 'mare Gothicum, seu Finnonicum ac Livonicum' or 'mare Sveticum, mare Bothnicum' and 'mare Germanicum'. When he referred to *mare Balticum*, he meant in this context the southern coast and waters of the Baltic Sea.[11]

Bernhard Schmeidler (Hanover, 1917), pp. 58, 237f.; 'Sinus quidam ab occidentali oceano orientem versus porrigitur, longitudinis quidem incopertae, latitudinis vero quae usquam centum milia passuum excedat, cum in multis locis contractior inveniatur. Hunc multae circumsedent nationes, Dani siquidem ac Suenos, quos Nordmannos vocamus, et septentrionale litus et omnes in eo insulas tenent. At litus australe Sclavi et Aisti et aliae diversae incolunt nationes': *Einhardi Vita Karoli Magni*, ed. Oswald Holder-Egger (Hanover, 1911), p. 15.

[6] Josef Svennung, *Belt und Baltisch, Ostseeische Namenstudien: Mit besonderer Rücksicht auf Adam von Bremen* (Uppsala/Wiesbaden, 1953), pp. 24–50.

[7] *Codex Diplomaticus Lubecensis* (UBStL) 1 (Lübeck, 1976), pp. 92f.

[8] UBStL 1, pp. 267f.

[9] *Hansisches Urkundenbuch*, Bd. 1: *Urkunden von 975 bis 1300*, ed. Verein für Hansische Geschichte, rev. Konstantin Höhlbaum (Halle an der Saale, 1876), p. 399.

[10] Geleitbrief des Herzogs Albrecht von Bayern für die Hansestädte, 10 April 1401, in Huibert Antoine Poelman, ed., *Bronnen tot de geschiedenis van den Oostzeehandel, eerste deel 1122–1499, eerste stuk, Grote Serie 35* ('s-Gravenhage, 1917), p. 182. I am indebted to Hielke van Nieuwenhuize for his overview on the Dutch sources.

[11] Jörg Hackmann, 'Was bedeutet "baltisch"? Zum semantischen Wandel des Begriffs im 19. und 20. Jahrhundert: Ein Beitrag zur Erforschung von *mental maps*', in Heinrich

The Baltic Sea

In the sixteenth and seventeenth centuries a new notion of the Baltic Sea emerged. Battles for military and economic interests, in particular, led to the notion of 'dominion over the Baltic Sea' (*dominium maris Baltici*). Since Denmark attempted to monopolise access to the Baltic Sea via the Danish Sound, other seafaring neighbours in the Baltic Sea, such as Sweden and Poland, opposed the claim militarily and justified this *dominium maris Baltici* in their propaganda. The Dutch Republic, however, tried to secure free passage to the Baltic Sea to promote their trading interests. In this context, matters of the Baltic Sea ('saken van de Oostzee') became prominent in the correspondence of Dutch politicians such as Johan de Witt, Coenraad von Beuningen and Anthonie Heinsius. In the early eighteenth century a special committee '*Directie van de Oostersche Handel en Rederijen*' was established for this trading and shipping area, while the Russian trade was supervised by the '*Directie van den Moscovische handel*'.

During the Enlightenment, academic and scientific interest in the Baltic Sea intensified. For example, Johann Heinrich Zedler's *Encyclopedic dictionary* (1732) includes an article on the Baltic Sea. In 1845, the Berlin linguist Georg Heinrich Ferdinand Nesselmann coined the term 'Baltic languages' (*Baltische Sprachen*) for Lithuanian, Curonian, Old Prussian and Latvian.[12] Nesselmann linked the names of the languages to the particular areas of settlement along the sea coast, thus, for the first time, using the sea as linguistic and ethnic identifier. This interest coincided with a shift of the political significance of the Baltic provinces from Sweden to Russia due to the Peace of Nystad (1721). Initially, Russia named its new provinces '*ostzejskij*' (after the German *Ostsee)*, designating them as Baltic Sea Provinces. In the later nineteenth century, the official name became '*pribaltijskij*', which means located at the Baltic Sea: the Baltic provinces were now perceived as the coastal provinces of the Russian Empire. '*Baltic*' (Baltisch) became at the same time a label for the Baltic Germans.

Bosse, O. H. Elias and Rorbert Schweitzer, eds., *Buch und Bildung im Baltikum (Festschrift für Paul Kaegbein zum 80. Geburtstag)* (Münster, 2005), p. 21. The various notions are *Oostersche Zee, Ostersche Zee, Oestersche Zee, Oistersche Zee. Niederländische Akten und Urkunden zur Geschichte der Hanse und zur deutschen Seegeschichte, I, 1531–1557*, ed. Rudolf Häpke (Munich, 1913), p. 105f.; see also the letter of the (High) Court of Holland to Stadtholder Hoogstraten, 18 June 1661, cited in *Niederländische Akten und Urkunden*, ed. Häpke, pp. 116–19.

[12] Johann Friedrich Zedler, *Grosses vollständiges Universal-lexicon der Wissenschafften und Künste*, 62 vols. (Halle, 1732–50), III, cols. 289–90, *s.v.*, 'Baltisches Meer'; G. H. F. Nesselmann, *Die Sprache der alten Preussen: an ihren Ueberresten erläutert* (Berlin, 1845), p. xxix ('Ich werde vorschlagen diese Familie die der Baltischen Sprachen zu nennen').

214 M. North

After the foundation of the new Baltic States in 1918–19, the Western powers took 'Baltic' as a term to designate the new Baltic states. This period saw several attempts to create a 'Baltic' or 'Baltic Sea' identity. Although a 'Baltic League' to coordinate foreign policy from Sweden to Poland failed, a number of initiatives proved effective. Among those were the foundation of the Baltic Institute in Toruń (1925) and the journal *Baltic Countries: A survey of the peoples and states of the Baltic with special regard to their history, geography and economics* (1935).[13] In 1937, historians from the Baltic Sea countries met for the first *Conventus primus historicum Balticorum.*[14]

The Soviet occupation of the Baltic states and their integration into the Soviet Union as well as the loss of the German territories along the Baltic coast reduced international interest in the Baltic Sea and the Baltic Sea region which was only kept alive by emigrants. Only in the 1970s and especially in the 1980s did the process of détente build new bridges. Due to the re-established ferry connection between Helsinki and Tallinn by the end of the 1970s, 90,000 people yearly visited Tallinn – the visitors were largely Finnish Vodka-tourists – yet Estonians and Finns began to familiarise themselves with each other again. Furthermore, scientific exchange in the area increased to some extent. In this context, the debate on a 'New Hansa', stimulated by the Schleswig-Holstein Prime Minister Björn Engholm, gained momentum. Engholm wanted to re-establish Baltic Sea relationships with reference to the old German Hansa. He created cultural initiatives, such as 'Ars Baltica' and 'Jazz Baltica'. However Engholm's program became obsolete due to the fundamental changes of 1989 and the subsequent dissolution of the Soviet Union. The perception of the region changed once more. Cities and countries which had been considered as distant, unfamiliar and foreign, since they belonged to a different political bloc, were suddenly discovered to be neighbours and, despite the visible physical deterioration of the architecture, were seen as culturally similar.

Facing these political changes, politicians designed a new vision for the Baltic Sea region. Scandinavia especially, where only Denmark belonged to the EU, was expecting to be marginalised in the dynamics of European unification. That is why, in 1992, at the initiative of the Danish and German foreign ministers Uffe Ellemann-Jensen and Hans-Dietrich Genscher, the countries of the Baltic Sea region founded the Council

---

[13] The title changed to *Baltic and Scandinavian countries* (1937).
[14] Marta Grzechnik, *Regional histories and historical regions: The concept of the Baltic Sea region in Polish and Swedish historiographies* (Frankfurt am Main, 2012).

The Baltic Sea

of the Baltic Sea States (CBSS).[15] Since the CBSS included Iceland and Norway, the Baltic Sea region was politically redefined. At the same time Finland, Sweden and Norway applied for EU membership, but only Swedes and Finns opted for it, while the Norwegians declined. Apart from EU-integration Finland wanted to preserve its traditional middleman role between East and West and developed a strategy of 'Northern Dimension'. Under this umbrella Finland took the lead in the dialogue with post-Soviet Russia. After Sweden's and Finland's entry into the EU, Estonia, Latvia and Lithuania applied together with Poland, the Czech Republic, Slovakia, Hungary and Slovenia for EU membership. The negotiations took quite some time, since the EU wanted to solve the problems of citizens' rights for the Russian-speaking population. In May 2004, the Baltic States together with Poland, the Czech Republic, Slovakia, Hungary, Slovenia, Cyprus and Malta became members of the EU. The enlargement of the EU, to which all states bordering the Baltic Sea, with the exception of Russia, now belong, and the EU Baltic Sea strategy, with its focus on environment, trade, security and access have changed the image of the Baltic Sea again. With these broad shifts in the perception of the Baltic – as a sea and as a region – in mind, let us now examine it as a zone of commerce and circulation, starting in the twelfth century.

The Baltic Sea as a Contact Zone: The Hanseatic League

The Hanseatic League, originally an ad hoc association of travelling merchants, had since the thirteenth century developed into a mighty alliance of cities, which for about 300 years largely controlled trade, shipping and politics in the North Sea and Baltic regions. The Old High German word *Hanse* meant 'crowd' or 'community', and in the twelfth century it designated a cooperative association of long-distance traders who mostly came from the same region or town. Many local *Hanse* associations existed before the German Hanseatic League of the thirteenth century made its first appearance on the political stage. Merchants from Cologne who operated a branch in London were the first to join together

---

[15] Marko Lehti, 'Possessing a Baltic Europe: Retold national narratives in the European north', in Marko Lehti and David J. Smith, eds., *Northern and Baltic experiences of post-Cold War identity policies* (London, 2003), pp. 11–49; Marko Lehti, 'Paradigmen ostseeregionaler Geschichte: Von Nationalgeschichte zur multinationalen Historiographie', in Jörg Hackmann and Robert Schweitzer, eds., *Nordosteuropa als Geschichtsregion* (Lübeck, 2006), pp. 494–510.

216   M. North

as an association. Their London branch, the Guildhall, and the goods they traded in, were granted a special privilege by the king in 1175.[16] But perhaps more important for the history of the Hanseatic League were the processes that began to play themselves out in the Baltic region during the twelfth and thirteenth centuries. These included the founding of Lübeck and many other cities in the Baltic region as Germans settled there and the founding of the German company of merchants travelling to Gotland (*Gotlandfahrergenossenschaft*).

The founding of Lübeck (1143–59) provided German long-distance Baltic traders with a headquarters and enabled more local merchants from Lower Saxony and Westphalia to access markets in the Baltic region and Russia without having to trade through Scandinavian or Slavic middlemen. For many years, for example, the farmer-merchants on the island of Gotland had dominated trade with Russia. Lübeck, and the advantages it provided for German long-distance traders, represented a real challenge to the Gotlanders. The German merchants were better financed, better trained in the techniques of trade, and better organised, and they possessed a boat – the cog – with a larger carrying capacity than the Gotlanders had at their disposal.

Hanseatic trade proceeded from east to west along a line dotted with their trading centres in Novgorod, Reval, Riga, Visby, Danzig, Stralsund, Lübeck, Hamburg, Bruges and London, and its existence was based on the trade between the suppliers of foodstuffs and raw materials in Northern and Eastern Europe and the commercial producers of finished products in northwestern Europe. Ships and shippers from the coastal cities transported the commodities from the west to the east and vice versa, whereby Lübeck served as entrepôt in this exchange. The merchants, however, went well beyond their function as middlemen between east and west, first by trading in the products manufactured by the Hanseatic cities themselves and then by penetrating deep into the Baltic hinterlands south of the coast. As a result, not only did they open up trade with Bohemia and Silesia by way of the Elbe and Oder Rivers, they also followed the Vistula through Kraków and via Lemberg (Lviv/Lwów) connected with trading partners in the Black Sea.[17]

---

[16] Volker Henn, 'Was war die Hanse?', in Jörgen Bracker, Volker Henn and Rainer Postel, eds., *Die Hanse: Lebenswirklichkeit und Mythos* (Lübeck, 1989), pp. 15–21; review in Rolf Hammel-Kiesow, *Die Hanse* (Munich, 2008).

[17] Philippe Dollinger, *Die Hanse* (Stuttgart, 1989), pp. 275–340; Jörgen Bracker and Rainer Postel, eds., *Die Hanse: Lebenswirklichkeit und Mythos* (Lübeck, 1999), pp. 700–57; Henryk Samsonowicz, 'Die Handelsstraße Ostsee-Schwarzes Meer im 13. und 14. Jahrhundert', in Stuart Jenks and Michael North, eds., *Der hansische Sonderweg? Beiträge zur Sozial- und Wirtschaftsgeschichte der Hanse* (Cologne, 1993), pp. 23–30.

The Baltic Sea

Demand and production determined the specific regions to which merchants travelled and ships sailed. The range of commodities the ships transported was broad, and included both mass-produced goods for daily life and luxury products for a small, wealthy clientele. The most important products were wool, woollen and linen textiles, pelts and furs, herring and dried cod, salt, wax, grain, flax and hemp, wood and forestry products (ash, pitch, tar), and beer and wine. Pelts, wax, grain, flax, wood and beer flowed westward, where they were exchanged for needed textiles, salt, wine, metal products, spices and other luxury goods. Fish was sold throughout the Hanseatic region.

We can identify two interconnected economic regions in the east: on the one hand, the Russian trade region, centred in Novgorod with its pelts and furs; and on the other the Livonian urban region around Reval, Dorpat and Riga along with the Daugava hinterland, which supplied mainly flax and hemp. Demand for furs was heavy throughout Europe, from expensive sable to cheap squirrel, as it was for wax for illumination. Hemp was needed for rope and flax for linen in all ports of the Hanseatic region. In Eastern Europe, Flemish textiles and sea salt were in high demand. Another trade region south of Livonia was controlled by the state of the Teutonic Order and the Prussian Hanseatic cities of Danzig, Elbing and Thorn. They made available to Hanseatic trade the products of the Lithuanian and Polish hinterland by way of the Vistula and Memel Rivers. The Lithuanian regions contributed wax, pelts, wood and flax; Poland produced mainly grain and timber products. The latter supplied shipbuilders with wood for masts and planks; herring fisheries, breweries and salt works needed wood for barrels, while numerous manufacturers were dependent on steady supplies of pitch, tar and ash. The primary export product from the Prussian Hanseatic cities, however, was grain, which nourished the population living in the highly urbanised centres of Western Europe. Luxury products like amber were gathered along the Sambian coast of the Baltic. The Teutonic Order had a monopoly on the amber trade, and they exported amber to Lübeck and Bruges, where amber turners worked them into luxurious rosaries. Salt, herring and textiles were the most important Prussian imports.

In the western part of the Baltic, Sweden contributed iron, copper, butter and cattle and cowhides to the Hanseatic trade, although, with the exception of metals, Sweden stood in the shadow of Denmark. Since the fifteenth century, Denmark had become an important exporter of horses, oxen and butter. Earlier, Hanseatic trade with Denmark had primarily concentrated on Scanian herring, schools of which were in the fourteenth century said to be so thick that the fish could be caught by hand. During the late fifteenth and sixteenth centuries, the decline in

Baltic and North Sea herring amplified the importance of Dutch herring fishers. The other important fish supplier, Norway, which at the time belonged to Denmark, was profoundly dependent on Hanseatic imports. Hanseatic merchants supplied grain, flour, beer, malt, hops, salt and linen, and they exported primarily dried cod and small quantities of cod liver oil, walrus tooth, skins and other goods. When, toward the end of the fifteenth century and during the sixteenth, consumers came to prefer Icelandic dried cod, Hanseatic trade with Norway receded in importance.

Trade with England, the original domain of Hanseatic merchants from the Rhineland and Westphalia, continued to be brisk. They exported Rhine wine, metals and the dyes madder and woad to England and imported tin and English wool for the textile industry in Flanders and Brabant, and later also English textiles. The Hanseatic cities of the Baltic coast, in turn, provided wares typical of the east, including pelts, wax, grain and wood as well as Scandinavian fish and metals. The most important market in Western Europe, however, was the Netherlands. Flanders and later Brabant were not only important textile producers, they also established key trade connections with the Mediterranean basin. The Hanseatic merchants bought goods in Flemish and Brabant cities, primarily woollen textiles of high and medium quality, as well as trousers from Bruges. They also acquired spices, figs and raisins from southern Europe. France contributed oil and wine as well as bay salt. This sea salt, harvested from the Atlantic, became increasingly important as a preservative. Prussian and especially Dutch ships made regular bay salt runs, then used it as ballast on the way to the Baltic, where they traded it for grain and wood for the Western European market. By doing so, they undermined Lübeck's monopoly as an intermediary in trade.[18]

The Baltic as a Dutch Lake

Hanseatic trade suffered setbacks on all fronts at the turn of the sixteenth century. The old trading system based on privileges proved inadequate in the face of growing economic competition and the increasing power of the European monarchies. One particular rivalry existed between the Dutch and Zeelanders, on the one hand, and Hanseatic cities, such

---

[18] North, *The Baltic*, pp. 58–63; Dieter Seifert, *Kompagnons und Konkurrenten: Holland und die Hanse im späten Mittelalter* (Cologne, 1997); Johannes Schildhauer, 'Zur Verlagerung des See- und Handelsverkehrs im nordeuropäischen Raum während des 15. und 16. Jahrhunderts: Eine Untersuchung auf der Grundlage der Danziger Pfalkammerbücher', *Jahrbuch für Wirtschaftsgeschichte*, 4 (1968): 187–211.

The Baltic Sea   219

as Lübeck, Wismar, Rostock, Stralsund and Greifswald, on the other, which saw their position threatened in the intermediary trade and freight transport along the east–west route. One important prerequisite for the expansion of Dutch shipping and Dutch business in general during the fifteenth century was the natural environment itself. Because their mediocre soil and the high cost of drainage made grain cultivation unprofitable, the Dutch concentrated on alternative products. The peasants specialised in livestock husbandry and dairy farming; they also cultivated industrial crops and fodder crops such as flax, madder and rapeseed along with tobacco, hops and turnips. Many of these products were sold mainly to businesses in the cities. Fishing and shipping, which were traditional activities, also expanded. The Dutch traded their own products to finance their continuous need to import grain. Over time, they garnered fairly significant shares of the market for their beer, textiles, North Sea herring and a number of cheaper variants of branded Flemish and Hanseatic products.[19] The increasing demand for freight capacity for the burgeoning trade opened the door to the Baltic for the Dutch and Zeelanders. By 1580, half of all Danzig imports and exports were transported by Dutch ships, and the proportion of Dutch shippers in the Baltic trade grew from 60 percent to 70 percent during the seventeenth century.[20]

Starting in the sixteenth century, the Baltic cities began to limit their assortment of wares, concentrating on the export of bulk products, such as grain and wood. The productive regions in the Baltic hinterlands became ever more closely integrated into the overall European economy. The most important Western European imports included herring and salt. Foreign contemporaries, such as the seventeenth-century English ambassador George Downing, viewed such economic success in the Baltic trade with misgivings. Thus, in a letter he wrote, 'The herring trade [of the Dutch] is the cause of the salt trade, and the herring and salt trade are the causes of the country's having, in a manner, wholly engrossed the trade of the Baltic Sea for they have these bulky goods

---

[19] Wim P. Blockmans, 'Der holländische Durchbruch in der Ostsee', in Jenks and North, eds., *Der hansische Sonderweg*, pp. 49–58; Peter Hoppenbrouwers and Jan Luiten van Zanden, eds., *Peasants into farmers? The transformation of rural economy and society in the Low Countries (Middle Ages–19th century) in light of the Brenner debate* (Turnhout, 2001).

[20] Schildhauer, 'Zur Verlagerung des See- und Handelsverkehrs im nordeuropäischen Raum während des 15. und 16. Jahrhunderts', 205–7; J. Thomas Lindblad, 'Foreign trade of the Dutch Republic in the seventeenth century', in Karel Davids and Leo Noordegraaf, eds., *The Dutch economy in the golden age* (Amsterdam, 1993), p. 232.

220   M. North

to load their ships with thither.'[21] Although herring was praised as the 'golden food' of the Dutch, their Baltic trade and economy generally were not based on it alone.

The Baltic trade was of central significance to the Dutch economy for such a long period of time that they rightly viewed it as the *moedercommercie* (mother of all commerce). The grain imported from the Baltic region fed approximately one-third of the Dutch population and freed up Dutch agriculture for more profitable production. In the end, that trade enabled the Dutch to find a footing in completely different areas of commerce. For example, the Dutch were able to exploit their Baltic grain monopoly when crops failed in Western and Southern Europe toward the end of the sixteenth century. As a result, they came to control not only grain and wood exports from the Baltic, but also the export of Western manufactured and luxury products in the other direction. The Hanseatic cities in the Baltic region had to make do with a small proportion of the east–west trade because of their higher freight tariffs and lower transport capacities, although they continued to dominate trade and shipping within the Baltic itself.[22]

The second important Baltic export, wood, was, like its by-products pitch, tar and ash, used in shipbuilding and other types of production. Dutch shipbuilding was already innovative. But this cheap supply of shipbuilding materials, to which were added flax and hemp for sails and rope, ensured that Dutch shipping rates would be low as well. Herring processing required large quantities of manufactured barrel staves, so-called clapholts, from the Baltic, while other businesses, such as soapmakers, were major consumers of potash from Danzig and Königsberg.

Dutch dominance, which was based on their trade in grain, timber and forest products and the shipping capacity needed to make that trade flow, remained unrivalled until the second half of the seventeenth century, when the English Baltic trade began to surge. Over the course of the sixteenth century, Dutch imports of grain alone grew from approximately

---

[21] George Downing to Earl of Clarendon, 8 July 1661, cited in Charles Wilson, *Profit and power: A study of England and the Dutch Wars* (London, 1957), p. 3.

[22] The literature on Baltic trade in the early modern period is vast. The following anthologies contain the best overviews: Wiert Jan Wieringa, ed., *The interactions of Amsterdam and Antwerp with the Baltic Region, 1400–1800* (Leiden, 1983); W. G. Heeres, L. M. J. B. Hesp, L. Noordegraaf and R. C. W. van der Voort, eds., *From Dunkirk to Danzig: Shipping and trade in the North Sea and the Baltic, 1350–1850* (Hilversum, 1988); Jacques P. S. Lemmink and Hans S. A. M. van Koningsbrugge, eds., *Baltic affairs: Relations between the Netherlands and North-Eastern Europe, 1500–1800* (Nijmegen, 1990); Michael North, *From the North Sea to the Baltic: Essays in commercial, monetary and agrarian history, 1500–1800* (Aldershot, 1996). For more on the Dutch trade specifically, see Jonathan Israel, *Dutch primacy in world trade, 1585–1740* (Oxford, 1989).

The Baltic Sea 221

19,000 lasts in 1500 to 80,000 lasts in 1567. (A last of grain, it should be noted, was approximately two metric tons, varying somewhat from location to location.) The volume of trade, especially grain trade, continued to increase in the waning years of the sixteenth century and the beginning of the seventeenth, but it then diminished during the second half of the century.[23]

The development of a ship called the *fluyt* (flute) or fly-ship, which according to one popular legend was first built in 1590 in Hoorn, is credited with sparking the Dutch boom in the Baltic trade. The fly-ship conferred a number of advantages on Dutch shipbuilders and shippers. It was built of light wood, and it was constructed in large numbers based on a standardised design. It was also suited to many different types of use.[24] The standardisation minimised not only production costs but operational costs as well. In the following century, the fly-ship became the model for Baltic shipbuilders because Dutch shipwrights brought their expertise with them when they were hired by the shipyards of Altona, Copenhagen, Stockholm, Danzig, Riga and later even St Petersburg to modernise the local industry. Hanseatic shipbuilding guilds forbade Dutch shipbuilders from being hired or even presenting their knowledge, which slowed down the adoption of state-of-the-art technology.

The export curves for timber and forest products such as potash, pitch and tar, which served the needs of shipbuilders and businesses in Western Europe, approximated those of grain exports. They had risen since the end of the sixteenth century and reached a high point in the 1630s and 1640s, after which they receded. They then grew continuously after the last quarter of the seventeenth century, which often brought about significant changes in the importance of the various ports and hinterland areas. Although Danzig remained the most important port for the export of grain and wood over the entire period, other ports exceeded it from time to time for certain products. These included the ports of Königsberg (for wood), Riga (wood, flax, hemp) and Narva (wood) as well as smaller Swedish and Finnish ports (for tar).[25]

---

[23] Milja van Tielhof, *The 'mother of all trades': The Baltic grain trade in Amsterdam from the late 16th to the 19th century* (Leiden, 2002). For Holland, see Milja van Tielhof, *De Hollandse graanhandel, 1470–1570: Koren op de Amsterdamse molen* (The Hague, 1995), pp. 97f.

[24] Richard W. Unger, *Dutch shipbuilding before 1800* (Assen and Amsterdam, 1978), pp. 4–9, 24–40.

[25] Michael North, 'The export of timber and timber by-products from the Baltic region to Western Europe, 1575–1775', in North, *From the North Sea to the Baltic*, pp. 1–14.

222   M. North

The Dutch not only imported food and raw materials from the Baltic and exported Western commodities to the area, they also transferred people, knowledge, technology and culture (art, science and life-styles). Among Western European immigrants to the Baltic we may distinguish five groups: peasants, craftsmen, merchants, sailors and artists. While Dutch Mennonite colonists, skilled in land improvement, were settled by landowners in the fertile marshlands of Royal Prussia, Calvinist cloth-makers emigrated from the southern Netherlands into the Baltic, revolutionising the cloth industries of Königsberg and Danzig. Dutch immigrants innovated silk weaving and embroidery in Danzig. Most important were the communities of foreign merchants, who settled in harbour towns. Family ties were key: usually a son or a younger brother was sent from Amsterdam to Danzig to establish his residence there and to manage the family business as a resident or a citizen of Danzig. Other merchants maintained their trade relations with the help of Dutch factors residing in Danzig. Their number rose from around fifty in the mid-seventeenth century to seventy-five in the second half of the century. English and Scottish merchants also settled in these towns and cities. Most of the Scottish immigrants to the Baltic were pedlars, who travelled through Pomerania, Ducal Prussia and Poland as hawkers, selling cloth, metal, tools, salt and other imported goods in the country and at fairs. Furthermore, sailors and captains from the Netherlands with their expertise manned the Danish and Swedish naval fleets. They disseminated also navigation manuals, such as Claes Hendrickszoon Gietermaker's *'t Vergulde licht der zeevaert ofte konst der stuurlieden* (1659) and *Schat-kamer ofte kunst der stuurlieden* (1702) by Klaas de Vries, which were in use in the Baltic until the early nineteenth century.

The last and perhaps most interesting group of Western European immigrants to the Baltic were artisans and artists. Fayenciers introduced the manufacture of delftware, furniture carpenters, embellishing bourgeois and noble houses with dernier cri furniture, and tapestry weavers arrived from the southern Netherlands. Architects such as Antoni van Obberghen, painters such as Jan Vredeman de Vries, and engravers such as Willem Hondius, settled in Danzig and received public and private commissions.[26]

---

[26] Maria Bogucka, *Gdańskie rzemiosło tekytylne od XVI do połowy XVII wieku* (Wrocław, 1956); Maria Bogucka, 'Les relations entre la Pologne et les Pays-Bas (XVIe siècle, premiére moitié du XVIIe siécle)', *Cahiers de Clio*, 78–79 (1984): 14ff.; Maria Bogucka, 'Die Kultur und Mentalität der Danziger Bürgerschaft in der zweiten Hälfte des 17. Jahrhunderts', in Sven-Olof Lindquist, ed., *Economy and culture in the Baltic 1650–1700* (Visby, 1989), pp. 129–40; Maria Bogucka, 'Dutch merchants' activities in Gdańsk in the first half of the seventeenth century', in Lemmink and van Koningsbrugge, eds., *Baltic*

The Baltic Sea   223

The visual arts, especially painting and architecture, were a crucial medium of cultural exchange. The effect of the art of the Low Countries on the Baltic region is reflected in the export of styles, paintings and painters. Paintings by Dutch artists or in Dutch style can be traced in royal, noble, municipal and even bourgeois collections. Dutch artists such as Jan Vredeman de Vries, Willem and Abraham van der Blocke in Danzig or Jacob Coning and Pieter van den Hult in Copenhagen worked for municipal and bourgeois patrons, but not for a public art market as in the Dutch Republic.[27] An example is the Steenwinckel family. Hans van Steenwinckel the Elder, who was born *c.* 1545 in Antwerp, became one of the master bricklayers of Antoni van Obberghen, the great architect of Danzig, who asked van Steenwinckel to assist him in the building of Kronborg castle. From 1585 onwards he lived and worked in Copenhagen. In 1588 the new king Christian IV appointed him government architect. From this moment on his main tasks were modernising the maritime fortifications on the Swedish and Norwegian coasts and laying out a completely new town, Christianopel (1599). He himself was most proud of the fortifications of Halmstad, as is to be read on his gravestone in the Nicolaikirke of this town, where he died in 1601. The work was continued by his sons Hans van Steenwinckel the Younger (1587–1639) and Lourens (c. 1585–1619). The brothers were involved in most of the huge building activities Christian IV started in the first two decades of the seventeenth century (Royal Chapel in Roskilde, 1617 and the Bourse of Copenhagen, 1619).

When we look at the prospect of Copenhagen by Jan Dircksen after a painting by Jan van Wijck from 1611 we see many recently built merchant houses with gables in Dutch renaissance style. When Christian IV 'granted' buildings to the Copenhagen burgers, he showed a preference for the Dutch renaissance style, as can be seen in the city hall, the orphanage, set up after a Dutch model, and the Bourse. Housing projects, again after Dutch models, were started for sailors and textile-workers. 'Dutch' must have symbolised modern government, modern welfare, modern

---

affairs, pp. 19–32; K. Ciesielska, 'Osadnictow „olęnderskie' w Prusach Królewskich i na Kujawach w świetle kontraktów osadniczych', in *Studia i materiały do dziejów Wielkopolski i Pomorza, II* (Poznań, 1958), pp. 219–56; Edmund Kizik, *Mennonici w Gdańsku, Elblągu i na Żuławach wiślanych w drugiej połowie XVII i w XVIII wieku* (Gdańsk, 1994).

[27] Juliette Roding, 'The myth of the Dutch Renaissance in Denmark: Dutch influence on Danish architecture in the 17th century', in Lemmink and van Koningsbrugge, eds., *Baltic affairs*, pp. 343–53; Juliette Roding, 'The North Sea coasts, an architectural unity?', in Juliette Roding and Lex Heerma van Voss, eds., *The North Sea and culture (1550–1800), Proceedings of the international conference held at Leiden, 21–22 April 1995* (Hilversum, 1996), pp. 95–106.

trade and industry. From Holland came the many engineers who laid out new towns and fortifications.

To find Dutch renaissance architecture on a similar scale as in Denmark one has to turn to the southern coast of the Baltic Sea, where Danzig attracted many architects, engineers and artists from the middle of the sixteenth century until the late seventeenth century, among them great names like Anthoni van Obbergen, who moved from Denmark to Poland in 1586, and Jan Vredeman de Vries. The buildings in Danzig were constructed with the bricks which Dutch ships took with them as ballast when they went to this town to load grain.

These architects and engineers were active not only in Danzig but in other coastal towns, and towns along and close to the rivers flowing into the Baltic Sea, as well. East of Danzig, for the period until 1650 we can mention: Elbing, Thorn, Neidenburg, Braunsberg, Pillau, Königsberg, Memel and Riga. In northern Germany we furthermore find their influence in Bremen, Rostock, Lübeck and Stralsund. So we witness indeed a Dutch-influenced Baltic Sea culture in the field of urban planning and architecture.[28]

The Upswing in Baltic Trade

Baltic trade boomed during the eighteenth century. The duties collected for passage through the Øresund may be gauged by the fact that the number of ships passing through the Sound grew steadily throughout the entire century. Even the War of Polish Succession, which weighed heavily on Danzig, and the Seven Years' War caused only minor and brief downturns. Despite short-term fluctuations, Baltic trade remained essentially stable.

The Sound was during this period the busiest waterway of the world. Around 1730, more than 2,000 ships sailed annually through the Sound into the North Sea, carrying freight of c. 400,000 tons. This volume rose by 1750 to more than 500,000 tons, which would be four times the annual tonnage of the Atlantic slave trade.[29]

---

[28] Michał Wardzyński, 'Zwischen den Niederlanden und Polen-Litauen. Danzig als Mittler niederländischer Kunst und Musterbücher', in Martin Krieger and Michael North, eds., *Land und Meer: Kultureller Austausch zwischen Westeuropa und dem Ostseeraum in der Frühen Neuzeit* (Cologne, Weimar and Vienna, 2004), pp. 65–70.

[29] Yrjö Kaukiainen, 'Overseas migration and the development of ocean navigation: A Europe-outward perspective', in Donna R. Gabaccia and Dirk Hoerder, eds., *Connecting seas and connected ocean rims: Indian, Atlantic, and Pacific Oceans and China Seas migrations from the 1830s to the 1930s* (Leiden, 2011), pp. 371–86.

Figure 8.1 Ship passages through the Sound (Øresund), 1503–1850.[30]

Dutch trade with the Baltic during the eighteenth century grew slightly at a time when other sectors, such as herring fishing and commercial production, lagged. If not for the Baltic trade, the Dutch economy overall would have fallen even further behind the expanding English economy than was already the case. Dutch ships continued to dominate the Baltic trade over almost the entire eighteenth century, even though their share declined from 50 percent (1711–29) to 27 percent (1771–80). The English and Scandinavian shares filled the gap: English shipping increased to 26 percent (1771–80) and Scandinavian to 28 percent (1771–80). The English benefited from the structural changes taking place in the Baltic region, where the demand for textiles and colonial products replaced that for herring and salt.[31] Accordingly, English ships now supplied the new Russian port of St Petersburg with English textiles and colonial re-exports

---

[30] Jari Ojala, *Tehokasta liiketoimintaa Pohjanmaan pikkukaupungeissa: Purjemerenkulun kannattavuus ja tuottavuus 1700-1800-luvulla* (Helsinki, 1999); and Sound Toll Registers Online: www.soundtoll.nl/index.php/en/over-het-project/str-online (accessed 31 March 2017). See also Jari Ojala and Antti Räihä, 'Navigation Acts and the integration of north Baltic shipping in the early nineteenth century', *International Journal of Maritime History*, 28 (2016): 1–18; Peter Borschberg and Michael North, 'Transcending borders: The sea as realm of memory', *Asia Europe Journal*, 8 (2010): 279–92.

[31] Johannes A. Faber, 'Structural changes in the European economy during the eighteenth century as reflected in the Baltic trade', in Heeres et al., *From Dunkirk to Danzig*, pp. 89–91.

226   M. North

such as sugar, coffee and tobacco. Swedish ships took over the transport of timber and forestry products from the Baltic region to Great Britain.[32] If we analyse shipping traffic through the Øresund between the Baltic region and the ports of destination, between 1784 and 1795 Amsterdam outstripped all other Western European ports in that regard (including London, Hull, Bordeaux and Lisbon).[33] However, even shipping nations not known for their Baltic trade, such as France, increasingly sent ships there. Not only did they supply Königsberg, St Petersburg, Stockholm, Danzig, Stettin, Copenhagen and Lübeck with wine, salt and colonial products, but also they returned with products important to their own domestic shipbuilding industry, including wood, forestry products and metals.[34] The re-export of French and colonial products (such as coffee, sugar and cotton cloth) through Hamburg to the Baltic region should not be underestimated. This trade was conducted using Dutch and, increasingly, merchant ships sailing out of Hamburg.

To measure the importance of the region to the Dutch and English economies, we must compare Baltic imports with those from other regions. While the entire volume of English trade between 1701 and 1800 grew from £4.37 million to £20.42 million, the individual maritime regions participated unequally. For example, the Atlantic region (West Indies, America and Ireland) registered the most explosive growth, from £1.21 million to £8.94 million, with 43.8 percent of imports coming from the Atlantic region. The proportion of trade with Asia was relatively small at the beginning of the eighteenth century (10.9 percent); by the end of the century this trade made up about a fifth of English imports. The proportion from the Mediterranean region decreased from 21.3 percent (1701–10) to 10 percent (1791–1800). The North Sea–Baltic region is of particular interest. At the beginning of the eighteenth century (1701–10), this trade contributed 40 percent of imports; that figure had decreased to about 25 percent during the ten-year period between 1791 and 1800. If we distinguish between the North Sea region and the Baltic region, we see a long-term decrease in imports from the

---

[32] David Ormrod, *The rise of commercial empires: England and the Netherlands in the age of mercantilism, 1650–1770* (Cambridge, 2003), pp. 284–87.

[33] H. C. Johansen, 'Ships and cargoes in the traffic between the Baltic and Amsterdam in the late eighteenth century', in Wieringa, ed., *The interactions of Amsterdam and Antwerp*, pp. 161–70. This may seem strange since a steep decline in Dutch trade and shipping is generally assumed after the Fourth Anglo-Dutch War; Jan de Vries and Ad van der Woude, *The first modern economy: Success, failure, and perseverance of the Dutch economy, 1500–1815* (Cambridge, 1997), p. 493.

[34] P. Pourchasse, *Le commerce du nord: Les échanges commerciaux entre la France et l'Europe septentrionale au XVIIIe siècle* (Rennes, 2006), pp. 99–110, 115–34.

The Baltic Sea 227

North Sea, which is slightly, but not completely, compensated for by growth in the Baltic trade. English imports from the Baltic region, in comparison to English imports overall, rose significantly more (by five-fold) than total imports (by fourfold).[35]

This trade dynamic is also reflected in shipping traffic. Shipping to the East Indies increased slightly and traffic across the Atlantic more strongly, whereas trade with the Mediterranean region decreased significantly and traffic between the North Sea and the Baltic region decreased slightly. When we look at differences between North Sea and Baltic shipping, we again see a decrease in northwestern Europe and an increase in shipping traffic with the Baltic region. Also clearly visible is the importance of trade in mass-produced goods with the Baltic, which required relatively more shipping capacity than such trade was worth by weight. A reconstruction of Dutch imports in the 1770s yields a comparable picture. At 17 million guldens, the Baltic region ranked just barely behind Great Britain, Asia, French colonial re-exports (each 20 million guldens) and the Western Hemisphere (Atlantic) with 18 million guldens.[36]

The evolving role of the Baltic region in the world economy also reflected structural changes, with the most important Baltic ports belonging to the Russian Empire, especially St Petersburg. Nonetheless, Danzig, not to mention Stockholm, which was privileged by the Swedish state, continued to play an important role. Stockholm's trade was so successful that in 1765 it relinquished its previous monopoly on the tar trade and allowed Finnish ports to traffic in tar, which greatly increased Finnish shipping. Merchants from Stockholm and Gothenburg used credits given to iron producers to stimulate exports to Western Europe through its ports. Gothenburg also grew in importance as a result of the founding of the Swedish 'Ostindiska companiet' in 1731. It was especially active in the tea trade with China and organised tea imports in the Baltic region.[37] The company even smuggled tea to Britain.[38] Ships from Danish ports also increased their trade with the Baltic, although much of the upswing in trade was due to Denmark's neutrality.[39]

---

[35] Figures from 'Provenance of English Imports, 1701–1800', in E. B. Schumpeter, *English overseas trade statistics, 1697–1808* (London, 1960), Table 6.

[36] De Vries and van der Woude, *The first modern economy*, pp. 498–503.

[37] Elisabeth Mansén, 'Resor, kolonier och handel', in Mansén, ed., *Sveriges Historia 1721–1830* (Stockholm, 2013), pp. 70f.

[38] Christian Koninckx, 'The Swedish East Indian Company (1731–1807)', in Jaap R. Bruijn, ed., *Ships, sailors and spices: East Indian companies and their shipping in the 16th, 17th and 18th centuries* (Amsterdam, 1993), pp. 121–38.

[39] Martin Krieger, *Kaufleute, Seeräuber und Diplomaten: Der dänische Handel auf dem Indischen Ozean* (Cologne, 1998); Ole Feldbaek, *Dansk Søfarts Historie*, Vol. 3, *1720–1814: Storhandelens tid* (Copenhagen, 1997), pp. 63–131.

228   M. North

After the 1721 Treaty of Nystad, Danzig once again became a supplier of grain to Europe such that annual grain exports (1721–30) came to about 36,000 lasts. This trade dropped to only 20,000 lasts in the 1740s and 1750s, but in the 1760s it topped 40,000 lasts. Danzig also remained an important exporter of timber products, but it was able to defend its leading role in the Baltic only with respect to potash. Danzig ships were involved in about a tenth of the shipping to Western Europe.[40]

However, ships coming from the west increasingly sailed to Königsberg, Riga, St Petersburg, Narva and Viborg. One advantage of these ports was their specialised assortment of wood products. A snapshot of the Øresund is illuminating. The most valuable export goods were the thick balks (beams) used in both ship and house building, which came from Narva and Riga, and then at the end of the eighteenth century increasingly from Memel and its Lithuanian hinterland. Planks were thinner and were offered at most of the ports. Planks may also be distinguished from the even thinner deals, which were available from ports in the Gulf of Finland, but also from Memel and Danzig. Smaller staves were used primarily to make wine casks; these were prefabricated mainly in the hinterlands of Memel, Danzig and Stettin. In terms of size, masts were the largest timber products, and they came primarily from Riga.[41] The huge Western European demand for shipbuilding materials led in the long run to deforestation and displacements in the Baltic hinterlands. As the resources dwindled in Poland and East Prussia, timber harvesting and tar production shifted to the northeastern areas, such as Finland, which is still one of the largest timber and paper producers of the world.

The ports of destination for timber exports document the demand for timber in Amsterdam, although the traffic to English ports was even greater. In Bordeaux and other French ports, barrel staves for French wine and cognac exports were even bigger sellers. Pitch and tar from Sweden and Finland were important imports as well. Dutch merchants were especially interested in Riga's exports, which included ash, flax, hemp, linseed and hemp seed, while the English shopped for different types of timber. The Dutch dominated the Riga trade into the 1770s, with English merchants and ships catching up with the Dutch in about 1780 as a result of their greater timber imports.[42]

---

[40] Edmund Cieślak and Jerzy Trzoska, 'Handel i żegluga gdańska w XVIII w.', in Edmund Cieślak, ed., *Historia Gdańska, III / 1: 1655–1793* (Gdańsk, 1993), pp. 402–19.

[41] Sven-Erik Åström, *From tar to timber: Studies in Northeast European forest exploitation and foreign trade, 1660–1860* (Helsinki, 1988), pp. 99–103.

[42] Artur Attman, *Dutch enterprise in the world bullion trade, 1550–1800* (Gothenburg, 1983), pp. 65f.

The Baltic Sea 229

After the founding of St Petersburg, Dutch and especially English ships dropped anchor there. No Russian merchant fleet yet existed; at the most Russia had only a few ships, captained mainly by Dutch sailors.[43] The main trade – if we exclude supplying the new court with Western European luxury goods – was in flax and hemp, with hemp export double that of Riga after the 1740s. There was also a demand for tallow in Western Europe, which had mainly been obtained from Arkhangelsk, and for Russian leather. Timber exports were banned by the Russian state in 1754, and it was only after this ban was lifted in 1783 that St Petersburg again became a more important timber exporter.[44] However, the most important export product from St Petersburg was pig iron, whose production had greatly increased since the 1730s and had even outstripped English output. In about the middle of the eighteenth century, before the English Industrial Revolution gained steam, Russia had been the largest European iron exporter, exporting 75 percent of the iron it produced, primarily to England.[45]

Because exports from the Baltic region were worth more than the imports from Western Europe, Western European countries were regularly forced to make up the difference in precious metals. In the eighteenth century, for example, approximately two million reichstaler were transported annually from Western Europe to the Baltic region. These monies went to producers in the hinterland, but they also flowed farther east in the Russia trade. During the expansion of English–Russian trade in the eighteenth century, St Petersburg and Riga registered, without doubt, the largest export surpluses. As a result, much of the precious metal sent to the Baltic ended up in those cities. England paid for most of its purchases with Dutch coins or with bills of exchange drawn in Amsterdam. The bills of exchange, which could be used to make cashless payments in Baltic ports, came due in Amsterdam, and the cash flowed from there to the merchants and then on to the producers in the Baltic region.[46]

---

[43] Jake Knoppers, *Dutch trade with Russia from the time of Peter I to Alexander I* (Montreal, 1976), pp. 146–55.

[44] Åström, *From Tar to Timber*, pp. 90–93.

[45] A. Kahan, 'Eighteenth-century Russian-British trade: Russia's contribution to the Industrial Revolution in Great Britain', in Anthony G. Cross, ed., *Great Britain and Russia in the eighteenth century: Contacts and comparisons: Proceedings of an international conference held at the University of East Anglia, Norwich, England, 11–15 July 1977* (Newtonville, MA, 1979), pp. 181–89.

[46] Artur Attmann, *Dutch enterprise in the world bullion trade, 1550–1800*, trans. Eva and Allan Green (Göteborg, 1983), pp. 45–47; Michael North, 'Ostseehandel: Drehscheibe der Weltwirtschaft in der Frühen Neuzeit', in Andrea Komlosy, Hans-Heinrich Nolte and Imbi Sooman, eds., *Ostsee 700–2000, Gesellschaft – Wirtschaft – Kultur* (Vienna, 2008), pp. 141f.

The Baltic as a Crossroads to Other Seas and Oceans

Baltic trade and shipping led the Hanse, the Dutch and the English into other seas and oceans. For example, by the end of the sixteenth century, the Dutch were able to use their monopoly in the Baltic grain trade to intensify their trade with Southern Europe when the harvests failed in the west and south of Europe. Gradually, the range of goods involved in the Dutch Baltic trade changed. The Baltic countries began to import high-quality goods such as spices, sugar, citrus and southern fruits and textiles as well as they controlled not only the export trade in grain and wood, but also imported finished western goods and luxury products. Following these patterns of trade and shipping, the Dutch gained a foothold in the Mediterranean, famously described by Braudel as 'Northern invasion'.[47] They transported goods – for example, Spanish salt and wool to Italy – and supplied the Mediterranean area with pepper and spices from the East Indies.

Furthermore, without the naval stores (supplied by the Baltic hinterlands) global Dutch and British shipping to the Atlantic or the Indian Ocean would not have been possible. Finally, the Baltic Sea provided the basis for maritime engagements with other seas and oceans. For example, the Russian Empire tried to connect its peripheral provinces on the Baltic and on the Pacific. Behind this attempt was the idea to build up a Russian commercial network across the North Pacific to provide the settlements in the Far East and Alaska with provisions and to link them with Spanish California and Manila as well as the Chinese port of Canton (Guangzhou). For this reason, Baltic German naval officers, such as Adam Johann von Krusenstern and Otto von Kotzebue, were sent out with the ships *Nadežda* (1803) and *Rurik* (1815) from the Baltic via the North Sea and the Atlantic to the Pacific. Although the hopes of establishing a Russian trading empire and creating a Russian Pacific did not unfold, Russian explorations and the travel journals of captains had a long-lasting impact on the European public.

Moreover, it was sailing ships from Finland (which was a province of Russia until 1917) that connected the Baltic with other seas and oceans. Finnish ships had specialised in the transport of timber and tar through the Sound, but then increasingly shipped grain in the Black Sea and the Mediterranean. In the 1870s, Finnish shippers played an important role in the freight and transport revolution across the Atlantic, transporting

---

[47] Fernand Braudel, *The Mediterranean and the Mediterranean world in the Age of Philip II*, trans. Siân Reynolds, 2 vols. (London, 1972–73), I, pp. 615–42.

The Baltic Sea   231

grain from New York, Philadelphia and Baltimore to Ireland and to British ports on the North Sea as well as petroleum to Western Europe and even into the Baltic Sea region. They also handled timber exports (especially pine) from the southern United States and Canada.[48]

Conclusion: The Baltic Sea as a Model Region

Economic, environmental and political issues have put the Baltic Sea area in the late 2000s again on the European agenda. A redefinition of Baltic Sea policy came from the Swedish government, especially the Swedish European minister Cecilia Malmström who prioritised regional policy in the Baltic. She declared that the Baltic Sea region should become the strongest European region of economic growth and in 2008 invited Baltic 'stakeholders' to a conference in Stockholm. At the conference the eight EU states of the Baltic Sea region, the non-EU members Russia, Belarus and Norway, thirty-one regional institutions, forty-eight inter-governmental and non-governmental organisations as well as private individuals (entrepreneurs and academics) took part.[49] In a bottom-up process, suggestions for the future development of the Baltic Sea region were put forward that cohered into the formulation of the Baltic Sea Strategy. This aims to make the Baltic Sea region a model for European integration with the following characteristics:

1. An environmentally sustainable region.
2. A prosperous region.
3. An accessible and attractive region.
4. A safe and secure region.[50]

This strategy was agreed during the Swedish presidency of the European Council in October 2009. The implementation of the strategy will take

[48] Yrjö Kaukiainen, *Sailing into twilight: Finnish shipping in an age of transport revolution, 1860–1914* (Helsinki, 1991), pp. 150–74.
[49] Good overviews over governmental and nongovernmental organisation are Michael Karlsson, *Transnational relations in the Baltic Sea region* (Huddinge, 2004); R. Bördlein, 'Regionale und transnationale Zusammenarbeit von staatlichen und nichtstaatlichen Organisationen', *Der Bürger im Staat*, 54 (2004): 147–53; Carmen Gebhard, *Unraveling the Baltic Sea conundrum: Regionalism and European integration revisited* (Baden-Baden, 2009).
[50] For the EU strategy, see Marko Lehti, 'Baltic region in becoming: From the Council of the Baltic Sea States to the EU Strategy for the Baltic Sea Area', *Lithuanian Foreign Policy Review*, 22 (2009): 9–27; Pertti Joenniemi, 'The EU strategy for the Baltic Sea region: A catalyst for what?', DIIS Brief (2009): pp. 1–6: http://pure.diis.dk/ws/files/49041/pjo_eu_strategy_balticsearegion.pdf (accessed 31 March 2017); Carsten Schymik and Peer Krumrey, *EU strategy for the Baltic Sea region: Core Europe in the northern periphery?* (Working Paper FG 1, 2009/08, April 2009, SWP Berlin), pp. 1–21.

232   M. North

place in a number of flagship projects which have either strategic relevance for the whole region or specific importance for individual regions. One project – the replacement of phosphates in detergents – aims to limit the nitrate influx into the Baltic Sea, while the Baltic Energy Market Interconnection Plan (BEMIP) seeks to balance bilateral energy agreements.

Since 2011, the European Council has been receiving annual reports on the implementation of the strategy. These show that the strategy has launched an impressive number of flagship projects, although they will take time to bear fruit. For example, the challenge of limiting the dumping of nitrates into the Baltic Sea is recognised in theory by the farming community. The latest pollution reports, however, have revealed that these effluents have not decreased as expected and the level of eutrophication is still unsatisfactory.[51] Despite these shortcomings the Baltic Sea Strategy offers the potential for overcoming the myriad problems that have plagued cooperation in the Baltic sea region in the past. These efforts could provide a model for other maritime regions in Europe, such as the Mediterranean and the Black Sea, but also for the South China Sea.

Further Reading

In the 1990s political changes in Central, Eastern and Northern Europe triggered interest in the Baltic Sea region. That is why David Kirby and Matti Klinge wrote general surveys then: Kirby, *Northern Europe in the early modern period: The Baltic world, 1492–1772* (London, 1990); Kirby, *The Baltic world, 1772–1993: Europe's northern periphery in an age of change* (London, 1995); Klinge, *The Baltic world*, trans. Timothy Binham (Helsinki, 2010). While Kirby focuses on the peripheral character of the Baltic Sea, Klinge concentrates on the role of empires in the region. In this respect he is followed by Alan Warwick Palmer, *Northern shores: A history of the Baltic sea and its peoples* (London, 2005). A more maritime history that treats the Baltic Sea and the North Sea together has been written by David Kirby and Merja-Liisa Hinkkanen, *The Baltic and the North Seas* (London, 2000). The latest synthesis with a special interest in trade and cultures is Michael North, *The Baltic: A history*, trans. Kenneth Kronenberg (Cambridge, MA, 2015). For a conceptualisation of the Baltic Sea region, see Marko Lehti, 'Possessing a Baltic Europe: Retold national narratives in the European North', in M. Lehti

---

[51] European Commission, Commission Staff Working Paper, Brussels, 13.09.2011.

The Baltic Sea   233

and D. J. Smith, eds., *Post-Cold War identity politics: Northern and Baltic experiences* (London, 2003), pp. 11–49; Michael North, 'Reinventing the Baltic Sea region: From the Hansa to the EU-Strategy of 2009', *The Romanian Journal for Baltic and Nordic Studies*, 4 (2012): 5–17. For histories of the Baltic States, see Andres Kasekamp, *A history of the Baltic states* (Basingstoke, 2010) and Andrejs Plakans, *A concise history of the Baltic states* (Cambridge, 2011).

9 The Black Sea

Stella Ghervas[*]

Located northeast of the Mediterranean Sea, the Black Sea is different from its bigger neighbour, whose sky and water are famed for their hues of blue. Except for days of bright sunshine, the Black Sea is all greens and greys, which gives it a different mood, more melancholy and meditative. This inland body of water also has a distinct formation: according to one theory, its basin might once have been a vast lake, the remnant of a large prehistoric sea that became salinised 50,000 years ago when the Mediterranean suddenly breached the Bosphorus Strait, causing a flood that must have been as majestic as it was devastating.[1] Although this sea has abundant fish with set migration patterns (at least until recent decades),[2] below 1,000 feet the water becomes devoid of oxygen and thus of life. This is a boon for archaeologists, who can find organic material well preserved in the silt of the seabed: ships and artefacts are regularly found along the coasts from Bulgaria to eastern Anatolia in Turkey.[3] That is for the ancient past.

---

[*] This chapter was completed during my term at the Harvard Ukrainian Research Institute and was supported by the Mihaychuk Fellowship 2016–17. A previous version was presented at the Harvard Seminar in Ukrainian Studies under the title 'Calming the waters? Toward a new history of the Black Sea'. I would like to thank the Institute for its generous support, as well as the faculty and fellow members for an intellectually stimulating semester. I am also grateful to Laurent Franceschetti for his patient support, to David Armitage, William Graham, Lubomyr Hajda, Patricia Herlihy, Charles King, George Liber and Serhii Plokhii for their precious comments, as well as to Andrew Bellisari, who translated from French one of my earlier essays on the Black Sea, and to Sait Ocaklı, who reviewed my translations from Turkish.

[1] The thesis of a dramatic flooding of a below sea-level depression is supported in particular by William Ryan and Walter Pitman, *Noah's flood: The new scientific discoveries about the event that changed history* (New York, 2000); Petko Dimitrov and Dimitar Dimitrov, *The Black Sea, the flood, and the ancient myths* (Varna, 2004). There is, however, no consensus around this idea. For more on this debate, see Valentina Yanko-Hombach, Allan S. Gilbert, Nicolae Panin and Pavel M. Dolukhanov, eds., *The Black Sea flood question: Changes in coastline, climate and human settlement* (Dordrecht, 2007).

[2] Yu. P. Zaitsev and V. Mamaev, *Marine biological diversity in the Black Sea* (New York, 1997); Zaitsev, B. G. Aleksandrov and G. G. Minicheva, eds., *Severo-Zapadnaya chast' Chernogo Morya: Biologiya i Ekologiya* [The northwestern part of the Black Sea: Biology and ecology] (Kiev, 2006).

[3] See Robert D. Ballard, Fredrik T. Hiebert, Dwight F. Coleman, Cheryl Ward, Jennifer S. Smith, Kathryn Willis, Brendan Foley, Katherine Croff, Candace Major and Francesco

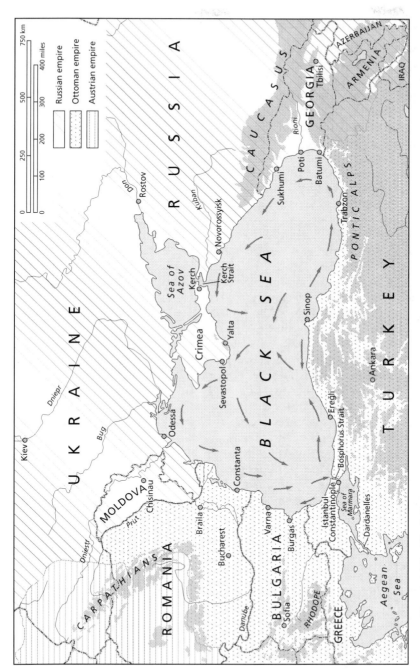

Map 9.1 The Black Sea

236   S. Ghervas

The Role of the Environment

As for the present, how could one envision the current political and social vicissitudes of this sea and its hinterland without also comprehending its geography and its history? The Black Sea belongs to the category of enclosed seas of moderate size, a feature that implies that the sea routes crossing it and the land routes circling it complement and extend each other. In such a configuration, the sea is not the exclusive medium of travel: it is primarily a crucial bridge that cuts down travel time and effort. It can be circumvented and, on occasion, even be dispensed with. Jules Verne wrote, in 1883, a humorous novel entitled *Kéraban-le-Têtu* (*Keraban the Inflexible*) that took this idea to the extreme: this denizen of Constantinople, who wanted to cross the Bosphorus from Galata to Scutari for an evening, was asked to pay a new crossing tax. After the chief of police threatened to arrest Keraban should he attempt to pass without paying his due, the latter set out for a land journey around the whole Black Sea through Odessa, Crimea, the Kuban and Georgia, heading back to Constantinople via the coast of Anatolia. The obvious conclusion was that travelling the circumference of the Black Sea in the age of railways (which Keraban even declined to use) proved to be time-consuming, but very feasible.[4]

Unlike in the case of oceans, there is thus an overlap and entanglement between maritime and land histories of the Black Sea that cannot be avoided. A central question is how well such a body of water has been connected to other seas and lands, in various periods of time, notably through its straits (its relative *enclosure* versus *openness*). Indeed, the repeated clashes of empires over inlets to the Black Sea played a central role in its vicissitudes. The inextricable interplay between geopolitical and maritime factors is what, in fact, gives distinctive flavour and richness to the history of that inland sea.

Nevertheless, the statement by Fernand Braudel about the Mediterranean Sea, that the environment imposed persistent constraints

---

Torre, 'Deepwater archaeology of the Black Sea: The 2000 season at Sinop, Turkey', *American Journal of Archaeology*, 105 (2001): 607–23; C. Ward and R. Horlings, 'The remote exploration and archaeological survey of four byzantine ships in the Black Sea', in Robert D. Ballard, ed., *Archaeological oceanography* (Princeton, NJ, 2008), pp. 148–75. For an overview of the recent literature on the Black Sea archaeology, see Jan Bouzek, Viktoria Čisťakova, Petra Tušlová and Barbora Weissová, 'New studies in Black Sea and Balkan archaeology', *Eirene: Studia Graeca et Latina*, 50 (2014): 298–316. An example of recent discovery of marine archaeology in the Black Sea is William S. Broad, ' "We couldn't believe our eyes": A lost world of shipwrecks is found in the Black Sea', *New York Times*, 11 November 2016: www.nytimes.com/2016/11/12/science/shipwrecks-black-sea-archaeology.html (accessed 31 March 2017).

[4] Jules Verne, *Kéraban-le-Têtu* (Paris, 1883).

The Black Sea   237

on the history of humankind, is definitely valid in this context.[5] By contrast, the more recent model elaborated by Horden and Purcell for the Mediterranean – as a constellation of distinct and separate micro-environments, where the hazards of subsistence constituted the root cause of sea connections[6] – is less applicable to the Black Sea, which is more of a coherent geographical unit. In the first place, it has a smooth shoreline that is almost devoid of islands, where every point is therefore potentially in contact with all others. Furthermore, each shore could have been largely self-sufficient since the Black Sea's climate allows very productive crops with little risk of failure – the continental north is favourable to grain, while the eastern and southern subtropical climates support the produce typical of the Mediterranean.[7]

The reason why the Black Sea has been so favourable to human circulation is that its basin connects the settled and warm Mediterranean world of the south to the frigid plains of the north, which have been continuously crossed by waves of nomads. Its shape has been aptly compared to an archer's bow: the bow shaft (comprising its grip and two limbs) corresponds to the northern coasts and the bowstring to the southern.[8] In reality, only the left limb of the northern coast is truly open to the remarkably fertile steppe that extends beyond the Urals all the way to Siberia. By contrast, the right limb is a steep coastline, difficult to access by land because it is on the foothills of the Caucasus. The bowstring to the south – the Anatolian and Thracian coasts – is equally narrow because of its mountainous hinterland. Given this topography, the sea has been a much more favourable travel route than the land.[9]

Since the Black Sea is entirely contained inland and captures all rivers around it without allowing any outflow into an ocean, it is known as an *endorheic basin*.[10] While its size is respectable (435,000 square kilometres,

---

[5] Fernand Braudel, *La Méditerranée et le monde méditeranéen à l'époque de Philippe II*, I: *La part du milieu* (Paris, 1949).

[6] Peregrine Horden and Nicholas Purcell, *The corrupting sea: A study of Mediterranean Sea* (Oxford, 2000). On the applicability of Horden and Purcell's model to the Black sea, see Owen Doonan, 'The corrupting sea and the hospitable sea: Some early thoughts toward a regional history of the Black Sea', in Derek B. Counts and Anthony S. Tuck, eds., *Koine: Mediterranean studies in honor of R. Ross Holloway* (Providence, RI, 2010), pp. 68–74.

[7] Doonan, 'The corrupting sea and the hospitable sea', pp. 69–70.

[8] See Anca Dan, 'The Black Sea as a Scythian bow', in Manolis Manoledakis, ed., *Exploring the hospitable sea. Proceedings of the international workshop on the Black Sea in Antiquity held in Thessaloniki, 21–23 September 2012* (Oxford, 2013), pp. 39–58.

[9] Stella Ghervas, 'L'espace mer Noire: conquêtes et dominations, de l'Antiquité à nos jours', *Questions internationales*, 72 (2015): 14–25.

[10] From Ancient Greek: ἔνδον, *éndon*, 'within' and ῥεῖν, *rheîn*, 'to flow'. It is a feature that the Black Sea shares with the Caspian Sea in Asia, as well as the (nearly extinct) Aral Sea.

approximately three times the size of Great Britain), its true dimension stems from its huge hinterland: it drains a substantial part of the rivers of Europe – up to a watershed stretching east from the Swiss Alps, southern Germany and part of Poland, across to the heart of European Russia. Among these rivers is the mighty Danube, the great waterway of *Mitteleuropa*.[11] Not far up from its delta are the mouths of the Dniester and the Dnieper, large rivers that originate in the north, far away beyond the steppes. One should also mention a secondary basin: the Sea of Azov, in the northeast. From the northern steppes, it is easily reachable by descending the River Don. From the Black Sea, it is accessible through the Kerch Strait that separates Crimea from the mountainous mainland to the east (Kuban).

Human settlements on the Black Sea thus differ markedly from those on the Mediterranean Sea, which had seen agricultural civilisations slowly emerge over the centuries and then take to the sea. The Black Sea is a basin that has regularly drawn human immigration from its periphery, just as it has drawn the water of surrounding rivers and the Mediterranean.[12] In every era, nomad invaders arriving by land or river from the northern steppe encountered the same major obstacle: to go farther it would then be necessary for them to cross the sea in ships (something ordinarily alien to horse-mounted tribes), or else head south by land along the western shore to the Danube Delta – only to confront coastal seafarers solidly entrenched in their fortress towns built on cliffs, with their backs against the surrounding mountains. Conversely, southern invaders could easily cross the waters to land on the northern shores and settle there – providing of course they did not find the place already occupied. But as soon as they ventured out farther north, they found themselves up against the formidable threat of the horsemen of the steppes. Much of the strategic history of the Black Sea could thus be summarised by this dynamic north–south equilibrium: northern horse-mounted nomads against southern city-dwellers who were also seafarers. The advent in the nineteenth and twentieth centuries of self-propelled ships, railways and even airplanes only marginally modified this general pattern.

As could be expected, all movement across the Black Sea oscillates around the grip of the bow: the famous Crimean Peninsula, whose

---

[11] See Joseph Wechsberg, *The Danube: 2,000 years of history, myth, and legend* (New York, 1979); Claudio Magris, *Danubio* (Milan, 1986); Andrew Eames, *Blue river, Black Sea: A journey along the Danube into the heart of the new Europe* (London, 2010).

[12] For more on this subject, see Tonnes Bekker-Nielsen and Ruthy Gertwagen, eds., *The inland seas: Towards an ecohistory of the Mediterranean and the Black Sea* (Stuttgart, 2016).

The Black Sea

southern ports are cut off from the northern plain by a mountain range, had a destiny of its own. As a rule, whoever held this strategic area – the fulcrum of the Black Sea – became master of the waters. Indeed, any northern power wishing to extend its control on the Sea of Azov without also holding eastern Crimea (and thus the Kerch Strait) did not draw much benefit, because it remained hopelessly bottled up.

In fact, the Black Sea is also accessible from the west and the east, from both tips of the bow. The Danube is well suited for commerce, although invaders repeatedly followed along its banks from west to east or from east to west, fighting many battles on their way.[13] On the other side, on the eastern shore of the Black Sea, lies the steep valley of the River Rioni (called Phasis by the Greeks). Not a significant waterway by a long stretch, its main merit is that it long ago dug a gash across the otherwise impassable massif of the Caucasus Mountains, neatly dividing it in two parts. The Rioni Valley has been a significant land route for the trade connecting the Black Sea region to the Caspian Sea and then to Central Asia, the only alternative being the caravan route that starts from the eastern Anatolian shore at Trebizond, skirting south of the Caucasus to reach Iran.

No account of the Black Sea can be complete without mentioning the city that guards its southwest passage into the Mediterranean Sea: Istanbul, formerly known as Constantinople (and still earlier, Byzantium).[14] Its colossal walls, its grand monuments, its wealth and population earned it such titles as Miklagaard (the 'Great City') by the Vikings, Tsarigrad (the 'Imperial City') by the Slavs, or simply *Polis*, the 'City'. Indeed the Turkish name Istanbul is said to come from the Greek phrase *eis tin Polin*, 'to the City'.[15] This colloquial antonomasia illustrates how Constantinople has been indeed the city *par excellence*, to match the sea *par excellence*. Istanbul still treats the visitor who arrives from the Sea of Marmara with a spectacular and strikingly beautiful sight: the domes of the Ancient Greek Church of Hagia Sophia and the Blue Mosque.

The two Black Sea straits of the Bosphorus (to the Sea of Marmara and the Mediterranean) and Kerch (to the Sea of Azov), along with half a dozen large and medium-sized rivers are the access routes in and out

---

[13] Klaus Roth, 'Rivers as bridges – rivers as boundaries: Some reflections on intercultural exchange on the Danube', *Ethnologia Balkanica*, 1 (1997): 20–28.

[14] For the geopolitical problems, see Stéphane Yerasimos, 'Istanbul: approche géopolitique d'une mégapole', *Hérodote*, 103 (2001): 102–17.

[15] Necdet Sakaoğlu, 'İstanbul'un adları' [The names of Istanbul], in Türkiye Kültür Bakanlığı, ed., *Dünden bugüne İstanbul ansiklopedisi* (Istanbul, 1994), p. 94; Marek Stachowski and Robert Woodhouse, 'The etymology of Istanbul: Making optimal use of the evidence', *Studia Etymologica Cracoviensia*, 20 (2015): 221–45.

of the sea and a strong geographical constraint; without them, there is no connection with the outside world. Any empire (such as the Persian and Roman empires of Antiquity, the Ottoman empire, or the Russian empire and later the Soviet Union), that managed to control all of these, either directly or through vassal states, was able to turn this inland sea into its own 'lake'. Thus the Black Sea has experienced alternating periods of openness and enclosure, according to the evolving configurations of the states that bordered its shores. Whenever an empire did manage to establish hegemony over these key points, the Black Sea seemed to close up like a clamshell – at least for outsiders. When its grip was loosened, the sea became once more open to general free movement.

These successive periods of relative openness and enclosure, which affected the circulation of people, goods and ideas, also influenced the narratives of the Black Sea: during periods of openness, such as the heyday of the Greek commercial network of Antiquity, the Italian period of the Middle Ages, or the nineteenth century, it attracted more attention from navigators and travellers from outside, who naturally saw it as a maritime unit; while those periods of enclosure generated a different type of narrative, one more focused on the land. The rise, during the second part of the nineteenth century and the early twentieth century, of new nation-states (Romania, Bulgaria, followed by Georgia and Ukraine, as well as Turkey) on the Black Sea's shores confirmed this enclosure and led to a dearth of works that considered the Black Sea either as a maritime or regional unit in the modern period (since land and sea can hardly be disentangled).[16] All littoral states endeavoured to 'reinvent' their identities and give them legitimacy by using a recipe universally applied at the time: nation-centric narratives that extolled a heroic past. While these stories were very different and often conflicting – especially when dealing with contested territories – all had one feature in common: they focused on their respective 'heartland' and inland capital city; in doing so, they resolutely turned their back on the sea. As a result, the Black Sea almost disappeared from the scene as an historical actor, as if its image had been scattered across the pieces of a broken jigsaw puzzle.

On top of this national fragmentation, a second political rift occurred along a north–south line in the first half of the twentieth century: first the establishment of Soviet regimes in Ukraine, Russia and Georgia, as early as 1920, and then the incorporation of Romania and Bulgaria in the Soviet bloc from after World War II turned the Black Sea into a political and ideological line of demarcation during the Cold War. We will return

---

[16] Charles King, *The Black Sea: A history* (New York, 2004), pp. 3–6.

The Black Sea 241

to the consequences of this enclosure at the end of this chapter, but to understand the larger significance of openness and closure in the history of the Black Sea, it is necessary to return to its early history.

The 'Hospitable Sea' of Ancient Times

As the writer Neal Ascherson stated metaphorically, the Black Sea was a 'birthplace for both civilization and barbarism': it acted as a crucible for the disparate human populations that converged there.[17] Among the earliest peoples to have sailed along its shore during the late Bronze Age (around the fifteenth century BCE), were presumably the Kaskians, who lived on the Anatolian coast and are depicted in Hittite records.[18] Passing the Pontic Mountains into the Hittite-controlled heartlands and eventually the Mediterranean, they may have contributed to the constellation of pirate 'sea peoples' that dealt a devastating blow to the ancient civilisations of the Levant, shortly before the general collapse of the Bronze Age civilisation.[19]

The ancient Greeks, at the turn of the first millennium BCE, considered the Black Sea the upper limit of their known world. This expanse of water must have appeared initially boundless to them – an ocean – and confirmed their own mental geography of a world in which the Aegean Sea separated the cities of 'Europe' (mainland Greece), from those of Asia (Anatolia), and which remains a foundation of our geographical conception of Eurasia.[20] Before their sea travels, the Greeks had conceived of the 'Straits' as a narrow passage between the two 'continents', both supposedly surrounded by water.[21]

These Straits were a strategic location from the outset.[22] Two of the earliest texts to have survived, the *Iliad* and the *Odyssey* attributed to

[17] Neal Ascherson, *Black Sea: The birthplace of civilisation and barbarism* (London, 1995), pp. 12–27.
[18] For the prehistory of the Black Sea, see Mariya Ivanova, *The Black Sea and the early civilizations of Europe, the Near East, and Asia* (Cambridge, 2013); on the Kaskian people, see in particular Claudia Glatz and Roger Matthews, 'Anthropology of a frontier zone: Hittite-Kaska relations in late Bronze Age north-central Anatolia', *Bulletin of the American Schools of Oriental Research*, 339 (2005): 47–65.
[19] M. I. Maksimova, 'Hittites in the Black Sea region', *Journal of Near Eastern Studies*, 10 (1951): 74–81.
[20] See Marianna Koromila, ed., *The Greeks and the Black Sea: from the Bronze Age to the early twentieth century* (Athens, 2002), pp. 34–48.
[21] This term is used to designate the area comprising the Dardanelles (Hellespont), the Sea of Marmara and the Bosphorus. See Viktor Burr, *Nostrum Mare. Ursprung und Geschichte der Namen des Mittelmeeres und seiner Teilmeere im Altertum* (Stuttgart, 1932), p. 24.
[22] See George I. Brătianu, *La Mer Noire: Des origines à la conquête ottomane* (Paris, 2009 [1949; 1st edn, Munich, 1969]), pp. 37–39. Brătianu advisedly insists on the two 'key-strongholds' controlling the access to the Black Sea (the Straits and eastern Crimea).

242   S. Ghervas

Homer, recount the famous war fought by a coalition of Greek city-states against Ilion (Troy), located on the Asian coast at the mouth of the Dardanelles (thus controlling the entrance to the Straits). Archaeological excavations have uncovered a site overlooking the Aegean Sea, five kilometres from the southern entrance to the Dardanelles composed of nine cities successively built on top of each other, the first dating from 3000 BCE and the latest 500 CE.[23] They do not, however, establish a certain connection between the Homeric myth and history.

The Greeks originally called the Black Sea *Pontos Axeinos*, the 'inhospitable sea', or simply *Pontos*. The dual valence of the sea – as both a fearsome obstacle and an essential means of travel – is contained in the double meaning of the word *Pontos*: while it signifies '(high) sea' and 'hostile space' in poetic language, it is also related to the Indo-European root meaning 'bridge' or 'path', hence 'navigable waterway for boats'. Over the course of various migrations, the negative connotation waned and reversed, as it came to be called *Pontos Euxinos*: the 'hospitable sea'.[24]

The Greek colonisation of the region was well under way by the eighth century BCE, beginning with Anatolia and the western coast. A century later, Greek ships reached the northern coast, founding the colony of Olbia at the mouth of the Dniester before continuing on to Crimea and finally reaching the mouth of the Don beyond the Sea of Azov.[25] Two cities, Miletus in Asia and Megara near Athens, led a race for settlement that was concluded within two centuries. In the seventh century BCE the city of Byzantium – distant ancestor of Istanbul – was founded on the European side of the Straits, on a strategic finger of land extending eastward between the Sea of Marmara and the Golden Horn, a curving estuary at the mouth of Bosphorus. The economy of the Black Sea's

[23] So-called Mound of Hisarlık, on the Asian shore, 30 kilometres south of Çanakkale Boğazı. It was discovered by Heinrich Schliemann in 1868. See Jorrit Kelder, Günay Uslu and Ömer Faruk Şerifoğlu, eds., *Troy: City, Homer, Turkey* (Zwolle, 2012).

[24] See Brătianu, *La Mer Noire*, pp. 34–36; Alessandro Baccarin, 'Il "Mare Ospitale": L'arcaica concezione greca del Ponto Eusino nella stratificazione delle tradizioni antiche', *Dialogues d'histoire ancienne*, 23 (1997): 89–118; François de Blois, 'The name of the Black Sea', in Maria Macuch, Mauro Maggi and Werner Sundermann, eds., *Iranian languages and texts from Iran and Turan* (Wiesbaden, 2007), pp. 1–8.

[25] Jurij G. Vinogradov and Sergej D. Kryickij, *Olbia: Eine Altgriechische Stadt Im Nordwestlichen Schwarzmeerraum* (Leiden, 1995). For more on the archaeological sites of Greek colonisation in the Black Sea, see Robert Drews, 'The earliest Greek settlements on the Black Sea', *The Journal of Hellenic Studies*, 96 (1976): 18–31; Gocha R. Tsetskhladze, ed., *The Greek colonisation of the Black Sea area: Historical interpretation of archaeology* (Stuttgart, 1998); Owen P. Doonan, *Sinop landscapes: Exploring connection in a Black Sea hinterland* (Philadelphia, PA, 2004), pp. 23–50; Christel Müller, *D'Olbia à Tanaïs. Territoires et réseaux d'échanges dans la mer Noire septentrionale aux époques classique et hellénistique* (Bordeaux, 2010).

The Black Sea 243

north coast was thus established: ports in the north exported grain and slaves, importing agricultural produce from the south, in particular olive oil, as well as manufactured goods. In what is today Georgia, they met with the Kingdom of Colchis around the River Phasis (Rioni), leading to its disappearance. Greek ships, by meeting the northern and eastern shores, had done away with the fancy of Europe and Asia as two 'continents' surrounded by water: in the fifth century BCE, Herodotus noted that the division between Europe and Asia north of the Black Sea was conventionally placed on what is today River Rioni in Georgia, or sometimes at the River Don and the Kerch Strait (in other words, it crossed the Sea of Azov).[26] It was a *topos* that Colchis was 'the farthest voyage' and it is no wonder that the mythical Argonauts went to seek the golden fleece in that land.[27]

The region around the Black Sea was unified for the first time under the Persian empire at the turn of the fifth century BCE and remained so until Alexander the Great defeated the Persians. In the first century BCE, Mithridates VI, King of Pontus, unified that sea once again taking the whole of Anatolia in the bargain. His kingdom became one of the great powers of the time.[28] This saga was, however, short-lived: Rome, troubled by his sudden and unexpected success, reacted by sending its legions into the region. Eventually, Gnaeus Pompeius Magnus (Pompey) decisively crushed Mithridates who later committed suicide.

The Romans then established lasting control over the west coast of the Black Sea to the Danube and over Anatolia to the Caucasus, with Tomis (modern Constanța in Romania) as the main port city,[29] not far from the delta of the great river.[30] Yet this was at the cost of dividing the sea

---

[26] The Greek names were the Phasis and Tanais Rivers, as well as the Cimmerian Strait (also known as Cimmerian Bosphorus). The Ancient name of the Sea of Azov was Maeotic Lake (Herodotus, *History*, 4:45). See Denis Zhuravlev and Udo Schlotzhauer, eds., *Drevnie Elliny mezhdu Pontom Evksinskim i Meotidoi* [Ancient Greeks between Pontos Euxeinos and Maiotis] (Moscow, 2016); Anca Dan, 'The rivers called Phasis', *Ancient West & East*, 15 (2016, Festschrift Alexandru Avram): 245–77: DOI: 10.2143/ AWE.15.0.3167476; C. J. Tuplin, ed., *Pontus and the outside world: Studies in Black Sea history, historiography and archaeology* (Leiden, 2004).

[27] As recounted in the *Argonautica* of Apollonius of Rhodes (third century BCE). See Francis Vian, 'Légendes et stations argonautiques du Bosphore', in Raymond Chevallier, ed., *Mélanges offerts à Roger Dion. Littérature gréco-romaine et géographie historique* (Paris, 1974), pp. 93–99.

[28] Appian of Alexandria (c. 95–c. 165), *The Mithridatic Wars*, 119. See B. C. McGing, *The foreign policy of Mithridates VI Eupator, King of Pontus* (Leiden, 1986), pp. 89–167.

[29] The Roman poet Ovid famously wrote about being exiled to Tomis in 8 CE to the end of his life (where he likely wrote his works *Tristia* and *Epistulae ex Ponto*).

[30] Jean Rougé, *Recherches sur l'organisation du commerce maritime en Méditerranée sous l'Empire romain* (Paris, 1966); Octavian Bounegru and Mihail Zahariade, *Les forces*

244   S. Ghervas

in two. The emperor Trajan (97–117), who extended Rome's frontiers up to Dacia (modern Romania), briefly entertained the ambitious idea of invading the Black Sea's entire northern coast. But the vast steppe, easily traversed by horse-mounted warriors, was never favourable terrain for Rome's legions. The Romans therefore contented themselves with southeastern Crimea, easily reachable by sea, which they maintained as a client kingdom. Unsurprisingly, they placed their naval base at Korsun, near modern Sevastopol.

At the beginning of the fourth century, the emperor Constantine decided to found a new capital for the Eastern Empire, Constantinople, designed as a counterpart to Rome. For this he chose the site of Byzantium, which he completely reconstructed from top to bottom. Occupying the entire peninsula, the city was nearly impregnable: it was surrounded by water on three sides, a ring of double walls defending the fourth (the outer line was built under the reign of Theodosius, 408–50) making it impassable with the siege technologies of the time. Even today, the vestiges of these fortifications impress the onlooker with their sheer size and the quality of their anti-seismic construction. With such a location, a large population and a vast array of port installations to ensure its supply from the Aegean and Black Seas, complemented by a network of major land routes converging from Europe and Anatolia, the city became the trade hub of that part of the world during the high Middle Ages. Holding Constantinople and both sides of the Straits was a guarantee of safety but holding the shores did not allow the Empire to prevent passage of unwanted vessels through the Straits; that task had to be delegated to a fleet of galleys and thus the need for naval supremacy remained paramount. Without it, the Byzantine Empire would be unable to prevent enemies or economic competitors from sailing to and fro between the Mediterranean Sea and the Black Sea.

A Sea at the Crossroads of the Middle Ages

If the arrival of the Goths in the third century brought a period of decline for the cities on the northern and western coasts of the Black Sea, the invasion of the Huns, a few decades later, brought disaster. The Western Roman Empire perished in the storm, but the Eastern part managed to recover. Arbitrarily called the 'Byzantine' empire in modern historiography, even though Europeans and Arabs alike called it unequivocally

---

navales du Bas Danube et de la mer Noire au Ier–VIe siècles (Oxford, 1996); Octavian Bounegru, 'The Black Sea area in the trade system of the Roman empire', *Euxeinos*, 14 (2014): 8–16.

The Black Sea

'Roman',[31] it restored its sovereignty by summarily eliminating its Gothic mercenaries in 400 BCE. It progressively reasserted control over its traditional territories in the Black Sea region, while the nomadic Khazars dominated the north of Crimea and the Kerch Strait. For the Byzantines, however, the area held a different importance altogether, since it formed, according to Braudel, 'Constantinople's backyard' or its 'preserve' and provided a vital source of supply for its inhabitants.[32]

Reality was slightly more complicated. Confronted by the arrival of successive waves of new settlers in the region – most notably the Slavs – the Byzantine Empire practised the shrewd strategy of establishing alliances and counter-alliances that permitted its rulers to use its army and navy with great parsimony,[33] while keeping direct control of the Crimean coast.[34] And even though the Eastern Roman Empire lost control of the Black Sea's western coastline up to the Danube following the arrival of the Bulgars, Constantinople – a metropolis at a time when Western 'cities' were little more than large villages – nonetheless continued to inspire awe and admiration.[35]

In what is modern-day Ukraine, the Rus' principality of Kiev prospered under the authority of the Vikings, whereas to the east the Christian kingdom of Georgia governed an area from the Kuban (east of Crimea) to Caucasia. It was a golden age in which cities and urban civilisation underwent a renaissance, as they did elsewhere in the Middle East and Europe. The Byzantine Empire itself enjoyed a new apogee under the reign of Emperor Basil II (960–1025) who, after conquering the Bulgars in the west, even extended his control southward towards Palestine.

Byzantium's decline came in part from the invasion of the Seljuk Turks who established an Islamic sultanate in the heart of Anatolia, as well as from the competition of the merchant city-states of Venice and Genoa. The impoverished empire could no longer maintain a sufficient army as

---

[31] The invention of the term is credited to the German Hieronymus Wolf (1516–80) in *Corpus Historiae Byzantinae* (1557). It appears to us as an attempt to retrospectively create an ideological break between the Roman Empire of Antiquity (with its capital in Rome) from the one Middle Ages (Constantinople). Enlightenment authors like Montesquieu and Voltaire also used the term 'Byzantine Empire', painting a dismal image of it.

[32] Fernand Braudel, *La Méditerranée et le monde méditerranéen*, pp. 128–29.

[33] See Edward N. Luttwak, *The grand strategy of the Byzantine Empire* (Cambridge, MA, 2009), pp. 95–144.

[34] See Aleksandr I. Aibabin, 'Written sources on Byzantine ports in the Crimea from the fourth to the seventh century', in Flora Karagianni, ed., *Medieval ports in North Aegean and the Black Sea: Links to the maritime routes of the East* (Thessaloniki, 2013), pp. 57–67.

[35] For more on the medieval port-cities of the Black Sea, see Karagianni, ed., *Medieval ports in North Aegean and the Black Sea*.

246   S. Ghervas

well as a crucially important navy. Venice, in particular, profited from the
Fourth Crusade, which saw Constantinople sacked in 1204 (the city, still
technically impregnable, was captured by treachery). This tragic event
occurred at the same moment that Georgia enjoyed great power and
prosperity; it was under its aegis that the Greek empire of Trebizond was
founded at the western end of the route to Persia. The Byzantine Empire
managed somehow to recover and (although a shadow of itself) to restore
its control over Thrace and western Anatolia.

Every era brought its own collection of invaders, some more devastating than others. In the 1230s, the Mongols conquered and subjugated
both the Seljuk and Georgian kingdoms. Their extraordinary military
capabilities supported unlimited ambitions and fierce methods. For the
principality of Kiev, already weakened by political divisions, their arrival
spelt worse than disaster: it was obliteration. Furthermore, the Mongols
did not capture this land in order to develop it: they merely collected
war spoils and tribute. The area north of the Black Sea was once more
reduced for a long period to a near-deserted countryside. Apart from
the Thracian coast and pockets of coastal Anatolia still controlled by the
Byzantines, the Black Sea thus largely came under Mongol domination.[36]

Yet these misfortunes also afforded new opportunities. The unification
of Asia under the Mongol Empire brought more security to the great
commercial routes from China to Europe, opening an 'Italian era' that
lasted from the thirteenth to the fifteenth centuries.[37] Taking advantage
of this development, Genoa extended its network of trading posts to the
Black Sea, or as the Genoese called it, *Mare Maggiore* – the Greater Sea –
largely winning the competition against its rival Venice.[38] Varna (formerly
Odessos) became the largest seaport on the western coast south of the
Danube, while the port city of Kaffa prospered on the site of ancient

---

[36] For this period, see Nicola di Cosmo, 'Mongols and merchants on the Black Sea frontier
(13th–14th c.): Convergences and conflicts', in Reuven Amitai and Michal Biran, eds.,
Turco-Mongol Nomads and sedentary societies (Leiden, 2005), pp. 391–424; di Cosmo,
'Black Sea emporia and the Mongol empire: A reassessment of the *Pax Mongolica*', in
Jos Gommans, ed., *Empires and emporia: The Orient in world historical space and time*,
Jubilee issue, *Journal of the Social and Economic History of the Orient*, 53, 1–2 (2010):
83–108; Victor Ciocîltan, *The Mongols and the Black Sea trade in the thirteenth and four-
teenth centuries*, trans. Samuel Willcocks (Leiden, 2012).

[37] On the Italian period of the Black Sea, see Nicolae Iorga, *Studii istorice asupra Chiliei și
Cetății Albe* (Bucharest, 1899), pp. 44–53; Iorga, *Veneția în Marea Neagră* (Bucharest,
1914); George I. Brătianu, *Recherches sur le commerce génois dans la mer Noire au XIIIe
siècle* (Paris, 1929); Maria G. Nystazopoulou-Pélékidis, *Venise et la mer Noire du XIe au
XVe* (Venice, 1970).

[38] For more on this subject, see Sergej P. Karpov, *La navigazione veneziana nel Mar
Nero: XIII–XV sec.* (Ravenna, 2000); Andreea Atanasiu, *Veneția și Genova în Marea
Neagră: nave și navigație (1204–1453)* (Brăila, 2008).

The Black Sea   247

Theodosia in Crimea (today's Feodosia).[39] Beside its initial function as
a slave trade post, it became the starting point of the maritime Silk Road
and with a population of 80,000 it was the largest trading colony of the
Genoese Empire.[40]

The Crimean Tatars meanwhile held the hinterland. These were a new
people formed from the Mongol elite, who had brought in their wake
Turkic tribes from Central Asia.[41] In 1347, the Tatars, attempting to take
Kaffa from the Genoese, transmitted the bubonic plague to the besieged
population, who in turn likely spread the terrible epidemic to the West
through the ships that sailed back to northern Italy.[42] A sizable proportion of the European population died from the Black Death precipitating
a demographic crisis from which the continent would take centuries to
emerge.

The 'Ottoman Lake'

The history of the Black Sea was permanently influenced by the extraordinary rise of a small Turkic tribe that formed at the end of the thirteenth
century in western Anatolia at a stone's throw from Constantinople: the
Osmanlis, better known as the Ottomans. Their unity, competence and
organisation, compared to the bickering Greeks and Slavs, led to a phe-
nomenal expansion beyond the Bosphorus, quickly making them masters
of the Balkans.[43] The king of Poland, Wladyslaw III, rallied a European
coalition (a 'crusade') to check it, but was crushed in 1444, at Varna (in

---

[39] Geo Pistarino, 'Genova e i Genovesi nel Mar Nero', in *I Gin dell'Oltremare* (Genova,
1988); Serban Papacostea, *La Mer Noire carrefour des grandes routes intercontinentales
1204–1453* (Bucharest, 2006), pp. 47–63; Şerban Papacostea and Virgil Ciocîltan, *Marea
Neagră, răspântie a drumurilor intercontinentale, 1204–1453* [The Black Sea, crossroad of
great intercontinental routes, 1204–1453] (Constanța, 2007); Ovidiu Cristea, *Veneția și
Marea Neagră în secolele XIII–XIV: Contribuţii la studiul politicii orientale veneţiene* [Venice
and the Black Sea, XIIIe–XIVe] (Brăila, 2004); Cristea, ed., *Marea Neagră: Puteri
maritime – Puteri continentale* [The Black Sea: Naval powers – continental powers]
(Bucharest, 2006).

[40] Mikhail B. Kizilov, 'The Black Sea and the slave trade: The role of Crimean mari-
time towns in the trade in slaves and captives in the fifteenth to eighteenth centuries',
International Journal of Maritime History, 17 (2005): 211–35. On the trade routes in the
Black Sea during this period, see Serban Papacostea, *La Mer Noire carrefour des grandes
routes intercontinentales 1204–1453* (Bucharest, 2006), pp. 47–63; Cristea, ed., *Marea
Neagră*, pp. 21–158.

[41] See Alan W. Fisher, *The Crimean Tatars* (Stanford, CA, 1978).

[42] Nükhet Varlık, *Plague and empire in the early modern Mediterranean world: The Ottoman
experience, 1347–1600* (Cambridge, 2015), pp. 178–79.

[43] For an overview of this expansion, see Nihat Çelik, 'The Black Sea and the Balkans
under Ottoman rule', *Karadeniz Araştırmaları*, 6, 24 (2010): 1–27.

248   S. Ghervas

today's Bulgaria) on the western coast of the Black Sea; after this nothing could prevent the conquest of the northern shore.[44]

For the last shreds of the Eastern Roman Empire, the end drew near: the Ottomans already held the Straits north and south of Constantinople.[45] A new factor completely changed the naval history of the Black Sea: the progress of artillery.[46] Thanks to the range of their coastal cannons, the Ottomans were now able to forbid the passage of enemy vessels between the Mediterranean and the Black Sea, effectively severing the connection between the two. The crumbling walls of the isolated great city eventually fell to the siege cannons of the Sultan Mehmed the Conqueror in 1453, as did those of Trebizond in 1461, and finally those of Kaffa in 1473. Georgia, fragmented and made an imperial vassal, disappeared as an independent state. Constantinople, by contrast, experienced a revival under its new masters and a new economic system took root. The Black Sea commerce hitherto in the hands of Italians was reorganised into a coherent system whose centre was again Constantinople, and which provided tax revenue to the central administration. Seen from the south, it was as if the city 'had monopolized the long-distance and the short-distance trade of the Black Sea, shielding this Mediterranean extremity from the rest of the sea'.[47] On the left, European shore, the direct provincial administration of the Sultan stopped at the Danube not unlike in Roman times; beyond, the two Danubian principalities of Wallachia and Moldavia continued to exist as vassal states with their own institutions and Christian religion. In Crimea the Ottomans oversaw the lasting establishment of a Tatar khanate affording it a large measure of autonomy. Kaffa – dubbed 'Little Istanbul' – continued its life as a trade hub, particularly for slaves.[48] The Tatars, accustomed to raids through Polish and Russian lands, would long represent a threat to the northern states of Europe.[49]

[44] George I. Brătianu, *Chestiunea Mării Negre: Curs 1941–1942* [The question of the Black Sea: Lectures 1941–1942], ed. Ioan Vernescu (Bucharest, 1942), pp. 4–10.

[45] Gilles Veinstein, 'From the Italians to the Ottomans: The case of the northern Black Sea coast in the sixteenth century', *Mediterranean Historical Review*, 1 (1986): 221–37.

[46] See Gabor Agoston, *Guns for the Sultan: Military power and the weapons industry in the Ottoman empire* (Cambridge, 2005), pp. 29–60.

[47] Braudel, *La Méditerranée et le monde méditerranéen*, p. 129. See also Suraiya Faroqhi, *Towns and townsmen of Ottoman Anatolia: Trade, crafts and food production in an urban setting, 1520–1650* (Cambridge, 1984).

[48] See Halil İnalcık, *Sources and studies on the Ottoman Black Sea*, I: *The customs register of Caffa, 1487–1490* (Cambridge MA, 1997); Yücel Öztürk, *Osmanlı Hâkimiyetinde Kefe, 1475–1600* [Kaffa under Ottoman rule, 1475–1600] (Ankara, 2000).

[49] Victor Ostapchuk, 'Long-range campaigns of the Crimean Khanate in the mid-sixteenth century', in Brian Davies, ed., *Warfare in Eastern Europe, 1550–1800* (Leiden and Boston, MA, 2011), pp. 147–72.

The Black Sea 249

It is thanks to the Turks that the term 'Black Sea' (*Karadeniz* in Turkish) entered into Western usage: the sea was located to the north of the Ottoman Empire, a direction represented by the black colour in Turkish culture. In the eighteenth century, Diderot's *Encyclopédie* noted soberly: 'The people who inhabit the shores of this sea are subjects or tributaries of the Ottoman Empire.'[50] Thanks to the military capability of the Ottomans to control effectively every passage of the Straits, this period of the 'Turkish' lake was portrayed as one of enclosure as far as Europe was concerned;[51] only the Poles retained a tenuous access to it thanks to the Bug and Dnieper rivers. That may be a partial view, however, since the peoples who inhabited its shores continued to trade with Istanbul, with the northern steppe and beyond the Caucasus with Persia;[52] furthermore, the trade was still functioning with Central Europe along the Danube, as well as with the Mediterranean Sea through the Straits.[53] The seventeenth and eighteenth centuries saw an expansion of the merchant marine.[54] As was the case on other seas, Ottoman control of the water was however undermined by a nation of fearsome seafarers who practised piracy all the way across the Black Sea to Anatolia: the Cossacks.[55] Ironically, history would better remember them for their exploits on land, in the service of the Russian cavalry.[56]

[50] [Louis de Jaucourt], 'Mer Noire' (1765), in Denis Diderot and Jean Le Rond d'Alembert, eds., *Encyclopédie ou dictionnaire raisonné des sciences, des arts et des métiers*, 28 vols. (Paris and Neuchatel, 1754–72), X, p. 366.

[51] King, *The Black Sea*, pp. 132–34; Cemal Tukin, *Boğazlar Meselesi* [The Straits' Question] (Istanbul, 1999); Anca Popescu, 'La mer Noire ottomane: mare clausum? Mare apertum?', in Faruk Bilici, Ionel Cândea and Anca Popescu, eds., *Enjeux politiques, économiques et militaires en mer Noire (XIVe–XXIe siècles). Etudes à la mémoire de Mihail Guboglu* (Brăila, 2007), pp. 141–70.

[52] Halil İnalcık, 'The question of the closing of the Black Sea under the Ottomans', *Archeion Pontou*, 35 (1979): 74–110; Kemal Beydilli, 'Karadeniz', in Kapalılığı Karşısında Avrupa Küçük Devletleri ve "Mîrî Ticâret" Teşebbüsü' [Facing the closure of the Black Sea: Small European states and imperial trade initiatives], *Belleten*, 55, 214 (1991): 687–755.

[53] Tufan Turan, 'Osmanlı-İspanyol Karadeniz Ticaret Müzakereleri ve İspanya'nın Karadeniz Ticaretine Girişi' [Ottoman-Spanish Black Sea trade negotiations and the entry of Spain into the Black Sea trade], *Uluslararası Sosyal Araştırmalar Dergisi / The Journal of International Social Research*, 7, 32 (2014): 252–71.

[54] İdris Bostan, *Osmanlı Bahriye Teşkilatı: XVII. Yüzyılda Tersâne-i Âmire* [The Ottoman naval administration and the imperial maritime arsenal in the seventeenth century] (Ankara, 1992); Bostan, *Kürekli ve Yelkenli Osmanlı Gemileri* [Ottoman rowing and sailing galleys] (Istanbul, 2005).

[55] Marina A. Tolmacheva, 'The Cossacks at Sea: Pirate tactics in the frontier environment', *East-European Quarterly*, 24 (1991): 483–512; Victor Ostapchuk, 'The human landscape of the Ottoman Black Sea in the face of the Cossack naval raids', *Oriente Moderno*, 20 (2001): 28–33.

[56] For more on this aspect, see Serhii Plokhy, 'Revisiting the Golden Age: Mykhailo Hrushevsky and the early history of the Ukrainian Cossacks', introduction to Mykhailo Hrushevsky, *History of Ukraine-Rus'*, VII: *The Cossack Age to 1625*, ed. Serhii Plokhy and Frank A. Sysin (Edmonton and Toronto, 1999), pp. xxvii–lii. For criticism of Hrushevsky's views, see Andrei Pippidi, 'Cazacii navigatori, Moldova și Marea Neagră la începutul secolului al XVII-lea', in Cristea, ed., *Marea Neagră*, pp. 260–82.

250   S. Ghervas

From the Opening of the Straits to Steam Navigation

The war of the Holy League (1683–99), which united Austria, Poland and Venice in a coalition against the Turks, brought the Ottoman advance toward Central Europe to a final halt. For the first time the Russian Empire participated in a European military coalition, in a war against the Turks. For all this, the Ottoman Empire remained a formidable power and tsar Peter the Great famously failed in his attempts to seize Crimea. Instead, he contented himself with the establishment of a small bridgehead in the Sea of Azov (where Russian ships remained bottled up), and even that he was unable to keep for very long.

Yet the Ottomans' days of dominance over the Black Sea were numbered. Following another war against the Russians, they were forced to sign the Treaty of Küçük Kaynarca in 1774, which at long last gave control of Crimea to the Russian Empire along with the estuaries of the Bug and Dnieper.[57] Russia finally had its access to the open sea and the sky seemed the limit. Most importantly, the Russians also obtained right of passage through the Straits and thus could conduct long-distance trade with the Mediterranean.[58] The Black Sea was open again to a foreign power.[59]

The empress Catherine the Great was now dreaming of Greek glory, which required nothing less than the destruction of the Ottoman Empire and the reconstruction of an Eastern Roman Empire with Constantinople as its capital. It implied the building of Russian maritime power in the Black Sea.[60] This new expansion also signalled a race

---

[57] Today Kaynardzha (often transliterated as Kaynardja) in northern Bulgaria, close to the city of Silistra and the Romanian border. For more on this subject, see Ekaterina I. Druzhinina, *Kyuchuk-Kaynardzhiyskiy mir 1774 goda: Ego podgotovka i zaklyuchenie* [The treaty of Küçük Kaynarca of 1774: Its preparation and results] (Moscow, 1955).

[58] L. N. Nezhinskiy and A. V. Ignat'ev, eds., *Rossiya i Chernomorskie Prolivy (XVIII–XX stoletiya)* [Russia and the Straits, 18th–20th century] (Moscow, 1999).

[59] See Irina M. Smilianskaya, Elena B. Smilianskaya and Mikhail B. Velizhev, *Rossiya v Sredizemnomor'e: Arkhipelagskaya ekspeditsiya Ekateriny Velikoy* [Russia in the Mediterranean region: The archipelago expedition of Catherine the Great] (Moscow, 2011); Constantin Ardeleanu, 'The opening and development of the Black Sea for international trade and shipping (1774–1853)', *Euxeinos*, 14 (2014): 30–52.

[60] See Aleksey A. Lebedev, *U istokov Chernomorskogo Flota Rossii: Azovskaya Flotiliya Ekateriny II v bor'be za Krym i v sozdanii Chernomorskogo Flota, 1768–1783 gg.* [At the origins of the Russian Black Sea fleet: The Azov flotilla of Catherine II in the struggle for Crimea and in the creation of the Black Sea fleet, 1768–1783] (St Petersburg, 2011); Faruk Bilici, 'Navigation et commerce en mer Noire pendant la guerre ottomano-russe de 1787–1792: Les navires ottomans saisis par les Russes', *Anatolia Moderna*, 3 (1992): 261–77; Adrian Tertecel, 'Marea Neagră Otomană şi ascensiunea Rusiei (1654–1774)' [The Ottoman Black Sea and the rise of Russia], in Cristea, ed., *Marea Neagră*, pp. 325–46; Julia Leikin, 'Across the seven seas: Is Russian maritime history more than regional history?', *Kritika: Explorations in Russian and Eurasian History*, 17 (2016): 635–37.

The Black Sea

to colonise the northern coast, which had been hitherto sparsely inhabited. Settlers from Russia as well as from the rest of Europe were invited, and incentivised by tax exemptions and grants of land. Many new cities were founded.[61] Significantly, most were given Greek-sounding names meant to evoke the first wave of Greek settlement in Antiquity: Kherson at the mouth of the Dnieper (1778), Sevastopol (1783) and Simferopol (1784) in Crimea (the suffix -pol meaning 'city' in Greek, as in 'Constantinople').[62]

For the northern shore, it was a period of accelerated Westernisation as a new form of urbanism, social organisation, architecture and dress; more generally, culture began to overlay and often to erase the Oriental substrates of earlier times. The commercial port city of Odessa, overlooking the Dnieper estuary on the northwestern coast, was founded in 1794; its name was borrowed from the ancient Greek city of Odessos.[63] Located in healthier climes and better positioned than Kherson, Odessa – with gridded streets, stone buildings and French governors – was a city conceived as a testament to Enlightenment Europe.[64] Its status of a new port city, founded in modern history as a trading outlet for a newly settled hinterland makes it a particularly rich case study, almost a paradigm for maritime history, which presents some analogies with the development of American port cities and their imagery of a 'new world'; at the same time it also has features similar to those of the ancient multicultural port cities that dot the Mediterranean Sea. The region of New Russia (*Novorossiya*) became the granary of Europe, thanks to its exceptionally

---

[61] King, *The Black Sea*, pp. 162–65.

[62] See Boris Unbegaun, 'Les noms des villes russes: la mode grecque', *Revue des études slaves*, 16 (1936): 214–35; John A. Mazis, *The Greeks of Odessa: Diaspora leadership in late Imperial Russia* (Boulder, CO, 2004), pp. 1–16.

[63] While the reference to Odessos is certain, its origin remains open to question. The empress Catherine II may have christened the new town after a small ancient Greek town that might have existed in the area. In any event, there did in fact exist a Greek city called Odessos, but much further south at present-day Varna in Bulgaria. It is now accepted that the name means 'city of water' in a pre-Greek language. However, the idea that the name Odessos came from the name of Odysseus had been invoked since the city's founding. Although this explanation is incorrect from an etymological point of view, one cannot exclude the fact that this perceived connection may have helped capture Catherine the Great's imagination. For more, see Ghervas, 'L'espace mer Noire', pp. 19–20; Charles King, *Odessa: Genius and death in a city of dreams* (New York, 2011), pp. 50–52.

[64] See Frederick William Skinner, 'City planning in Russia: The Development of Odessa, 1789–1892' (PhD diss., Princeton University, 1973), pp. 29–57; Patricia Herlihy, *Odessa: A History 1794–1914* (Cambridge, MA, 1986), pp. 6–17; King, *Odessa*, pp. 53–70; Stella Ghervas, 'Odessa et les confins de l'Europe: un éclairage historique', in Ghervas and François Rosset, eds., *Lieux d'Europe. Mythes et limites* (Paris, 2008), pp. 107–24.

252   S. Ghervas

fertile hinterland, with Odessa and Taganrog (on the Sea of Azov) being the two major ports.[65]

Russia's expansion continued: in 1812, following yet another war against the Ottomans, Russia annexed part of the Danubian principality of Moldavia north of the River Prut, renaming this land Bessarabia. The Congress of Vienna (1814–15) maintained the status quo in the Black Sea and the Ottoman Empire enjoyed a brief respite – though, by now, Western, Greek and Russian ships were plying its waters, taking a sizable share of the long-range traffic (Marseille and Trieste being two key outlets for exports to respectively France and Austria).[66] At that time, Odessa had a significant and prosperous Greek population, so much so that it would serve in 1822 as the base from which Hellenic patriots would launch their uprising against the Turks, much to the chagrin of tsar Alexander I.[67] Following the accession of his brother Nicholas I to the throne, the Westernised and liberal atmosphere that reigned in New Russia was progressively replaced by a policy of centralisation and Russification. While Britain and France fought to support Greek independence, Russia extended its influence over the principalities of Moldavia and Wallachia (located in modern-day Romania). After the Treaty of Adrianople of 1829, and Greece gaining its independence the next year, the northern Black Sea region continued to grow economically. In that era, everything seemed possible in the rapidly expanding territories recently acquired by Russia and optimism reigned supreme. Indeed, in the novel *Père Goriot* (1835) of the French author Honoré de Balzac, the main character Goriot, who had made his fortune in Ukrainian grain, still dreamt on his deathbed of going to Odessa to start a pasta factory, a processed product that would evidently be loaded onto ships for the consumption of the French.[68]

[65] 'Novorossiya' comprised the territories to the north of the Black Sea conquered by Russia from the Ottoman Empire following the Russo-Turkish wars that took place during the second half of the eighteenth century. See Mose Lofley Harvey, 'The development of Russian commerce on the Black Sea and its significance' (PhD diss., University of California, Berkeley, 1938); Patricia Herlihy, 'Russian grain and Mediterranean markets, 1774–1861' (PhD diss., University of Pennsylvania, 1963).

[66] For a sampling of the wide literature on this topic, see Vassilis Kardasis, *Diaspora merchants in the Black Sea: The Greeks in southern Russia, 1775–1861* (New York, 2001); Patricia Herlihy, 'Greek merchants in Odessa in the nineteenth century', *Harvard Ukrainian Studies*, 3–4 (1979–80): 399–420.

[67] See, in particular, Theophilus C. Proussis, *Russian society and the Greek Revolution* (DeKalb, IL, 1994), pp. 11–24; Stella Ghervas, *Réinventer la tradition: Alexandre Stourdza et l'Europe de la Sainte-Alliance* (Paris, 2008), pp. 84–88; Lucien J. Frary, *Russia and the making of modern Greek identity, 1821–1844* (Oxford, 2016), pp. 242–49.

[68] Honoré de Balzac, *Le Père Goriot*, in *Comédie humaine* (Paris, 1835).

The Black Sea

This renewed interest from the West in this pioneering time generated a flowering of literature from the angle of geography (including land and sea maps), trade and history as well as synthetic studies.[69] It shows that during that era, it was self-evident in Western Europe, Russia and the US that the Black Sea was a coherent geographical unit.[70] Steamships were already providing regular service from Odessa to Yalta in Crimea, allowing regular travel. The first known tourist guide for Crimea, written in French, published in Odessa in 1834, symbolises the opening of this region to travel and discovery.[71]

In contrast to this bold prosperity, the economically weakened Ottoman Empire was now labelled the 'sick man of Europe'. Nevertheless, the Ottomans initiated a series of reforms beginning in the 1840s (known as *Tanzimat* in Turkish).[72] Gradually, equality between Ottoman citizens, regardless of their religion, was established and slavery abolished. Around the Black Sea, economic development accelerated further still with the development of the railroads. The Anatolian coast saw the development of coal mining activities in 1849 at Zonguldak, not far from Sinope (Sinop) exploited by French and Belgian companies, while the city of Trebizond (Trabzon) experienced a revival as an outlet for commerce with Persia.[73] Those products were not only destined to the markets of the Ottoman Empire; ships carried them beyond the Strait of Gibraltar to European ports, to meet the needs of the Western economies during the Industrial Revolution.[74]

[69] See Henry A. S. Dearborn, *A memoir of the commerce and navigation of the Black Sea, and the trade and maritime geography of Turkey and Egypt*, 2 vols. (Boston, MA, 1819); Marquis Gabriel de Castelnau, *Essai sur l'histoire ancienne et nouvelle de la Nouvelle Russie. Statistique des provinces qui la composent* (Paris, 1820); Antoine-Ignace de Saint-Joseph, *Essai historique sur la navigation de la mer Noire* (Paris, 1820); François Elie de la Primaudaie, *Histoire du commerce de la mer Noire et des colonies génoises de la Krimée* [sic] (Paris, 1848).

[70] See Andrew Robarts, *Migration and disease in the Black Sea region: Ottoman-Russian relations in the late 18th and early 19th centuries* (London, 2017), pp. 1–32.

[71] C. H. Montandon, *Guide du voyageur en Crimée* (Odessa, 1834).

[72] Halil İnalcık, *Tanzimat ve Bulgar Meselesi kitabı* [The Tanzimat and the Bulgarian Question] (Istanbul, 1942); Edouard Engelhardt, *La Turquie et le Tanzimat ou histoire des réformes dans l'Empire Ottoman depuis 1826 jusqu'à nos jours*, 2 vols. (Paris, 1882–84); Donald Quataert, *The Ottoman empire, 1700–1922* (Cambridge, 2000); Tunay Sürek, *Die Verfassungsbestrebungen der Tanzimât-Periode* (Frankfurt, 2015).

[73] Donald Quataert, *Miners and the state in the Ottoman empire: The Zonguldak coalfield, 1822–1920* (New York, 2006); A. Üner Turgay, 'Trabzon: Trade and society in the nineteenth century' (MA thesis, University of Wisconsin, Madison, 1972).

[74] See Gelina Harlaftis, *A history of Greek-owned shipping: The making of an international tramp fleet, 1830 to the present day* (London and New York, 1996), pp. 8–37; Vedit İnal, 'The eighteenth and nineteenth century Ottoman attempts to catch up with Europe', *Middle Eastern Studies*, 47 (2011): 725–56.

254   S. Ghervas

Maritime Circulations in the Twilight of Empires

Clouds gathered once more as renewed Russian expansion towards Constantinople, coupled with a policy of intervention in the eastern Mediterranean, threatened the very survival of the Ottoman Empire. Thus, the seemingly inevitable distribution of Ottoman spoils and notably the Straits – the so-called 'Eastern Question' – became again the major concern of the great powers.[75] During a course on the Black Sea given at the University of Bucharest in the middle of the Second World War, George I. Brătianu synthesised the period of the nineteenth to the mid-twentieth centuries as a 'struggle between Russia and Europe for the Black Sea'.[76] It is a fact that Russia aimed to conquer new lands around the Black Sea, while France and Britain's economic interests (mainly of a maritime nature) led them to oppose that expansion. Compared to the consequences of the Straits falling in Russian hands – which would have changed drastically the balance of power in the region – European powers saw the Ottoman Empire as a lesser evil.

A situation that might have remained diplomatically manageable under diplomats of the generation of the Congress of Vienna descended into war in 1853. Britain and France came to the rescue of the Turks, forcing the Russian army to retreat back into its own territory. Things might have remained at that, but for obscure reasons that are still debated, the Western Allies decided to make a landing in Crimea, effectively starting the Crimean War (1853–56).[77] This anomalous and cruel siege of the naval base of Sevastopol ended with an orderly retreat of the defenders through Crimea (the land road having never been cut) – and their prompt return after the expeditionary force had re-embarked on its transport ships.

On the level of the *imaginaire*, the Crimean War popularised the Black Sea and its region in Western European culture. Its landmarks (the cities of Sevastopol, Eupatoria and Balaklava, the River Alma and the fortress of Malakoff) became household names in Western Europe.[78] By

---

[75] M. S. Anderson, *The Eastern Question, 1774–1923* (London, 1966); Richard Millman, *Britain and the Eastern Question, 1875–1878* (Oxford, 1979). For a discussion of the historiography on the Eastern Question, see Lucien Frary and Mara Kozelsky, eds., *Russian Ottoman borderlands: The Eastern Question reconsidered* (Madison, WI, 2014), pp. 3–34.

[76] Brătianu, *Chestiunea Marii Negre*, p. 27.

[77] Among the recent publications on the Crimean War, see Olga V. Didukh, *Donskie kazaki v Krymskoy voyne 1853–1856 gg.* [Don Cossacks in the Crimean War, 1853–1856] (Moscow, 2007); Candan Badem, *The Ottoman Crimean War (1853–1856)* (Leiden and Boston, MA, 2010); Orlando Figes, *The Crimean War: A History* (New York, 2011).

[78] See Gavin Hughes and Jonathan Trigg, 'Remembering the Charge of the Light Brigade: Its commemoration, war memorials and memory', *Journal of Conflict Archaeology*, 4 (2008): 39–58. This charge took place in Balaklava.

The Black Sea   255

contrast, it was a traumatic blow for the Russians, not only for the city of Sevastopol, which according to Mark Twain (who saw it a decade later) was 'probably the worst battered town in Russia or anywhere else'.[79] The Russians had lost, together with their painfully obsolete fleet, their naval domination of the Black Sea;[80] the Greek dream of Catherine the Great was badly hurt. In the Russian imagination, it stands as one of the few lost wars that was never vindicated, a moral wound that still fosters a strong desire of military revenge against the 'West'.[81]

The Treaty of Paris of 1856, which concluded the conflict, prohibited the navigation of warships on the Black Sea and the construction of fortresses around its shores. As a reaction, the policies of the Russian Empire started turning inwards, toward a tighter integration of the region, particularly the northeast shore of Black Sea. The Russians had already established nominal control of the mountainous east coast, bounded by the Kuban River (then called Circassia). Unlike the Georgians, who were annexed in 1801, the Circassians were Muslims and without a proper state. Between 1864 and 1867, the Russian army unceremoniously occupied their territory and practised a determined policy of expulsion. Nearly half a million people were deported to the Ottoman Empire under appalling conditions.[82] Tens of thousands of Crimean Tatars also took the same path of exile.

The Black Sea also became a secondary theatre in the 'Great Game' between Great Britain and Russia for control of the trade routes to Central Asia, and to Persia in particular. This competition is key to understanding the development of transport infrastructures in the eastern part of the Black Sea: in addition to Odessa, the Russians developed the port of Novorossiysk on the shore across the Kerch Strait (reachable by train from the north) and controlled the Transcaucasian corridor that leads to the Caspian Sea through the Caucasus.[83] The British exploited for their part – with Ottoman permission – the route through the south Caucasus: ships crossing the Bosphorus unloaded in Trebizond,

---

[79] Mark Twain, *The innocents abroad or the new Pilgrims' Progress* (San Francisco, CA, 1869), p. 381.

[80] Evgeniy A. Myazgovskiy, *Istoriya Chernomorskogo Flota, 1696–1912* [The history of the Black Sea navy, 1696–1912] (St Petersburg, 1912), pp. 74–88.

[81] See Serhii Plokhy, 'The city of glory: Sevastopol in Russian historical mythology', *Journal of Contemporary History*, 35 (2000): 373–7; Yuliya A. Naumova, *Ranenie, bolezn' i smert': Russkaya meditsinskaya sluzhba v Krymskuyu voynu, 1853–1856 gg.* [Injury, disease, and death: Russian medical service in the Crimean War, 1853–56] (Moscow, 2010), pp. 259–94.

[82] Irma Kreiten, 'A colonial experiment in cleansing: The Russian conquest of Eastern Caucasus, 1856–65', *Journal of Genocide Research*, 11 (2009): 213–41; Walter Richmond, *The Circassian genocide* (New Brunswick, NJ, 2011), pp. 54–97.

[83] Gelina Harlaftis, 'Trade and shipping in the nineteenth-century Sea of Azov', *International Journal of Maritime History*, 22 (2010): 244–45.

256   S. Ghervas

bridgehead of the caravans to Persia. At the turn of the twentieth century, with the development of oil wells in the Caspian Sea, Russia built a railway through the Transcaucasian corridor. At the port of Batumi on the Black Sea, oil was shipped and brought to Novorossiysk and again loaded onto trains heading north to the Russian heartland.

In 1877–78 Russia tried once again to end the Ottoman Empire, which was saved *in extremis* by the arrival of the British navy in the Straits. The 1878 Treaty of Berlin led to a new configuration of the Black Sea's western coast with the recognition of Romanian sovereignty and the creation of modern Bulgaria. The withdrawal of the Turks saw massacres committed against the civilian population by each side and the Balkans became the scene of deportations and population transfers. With the accession of tsar Alexander III in 1881, a highly conservative monarch, the russification policies in the Empire took on an entirely new scale: a wave of repression befell non-Orthodox Christians and Muslims. In the case of Jews, segregation and violence became institutionalised, leading to pogroms committed by the locals, on which the authorities turned a blind eye. The situation on the western shore of the Black Sea remained tense: the two Balkan Wars of 1912–13, which took place largely in Bulgaria and Thrace, were only the prelude to the coming storm.

Glacial Period: Conflicts and the Collapse of Circulations

For the Balkans and the Black Sea, the First World War (1914–18), fought primarily on land with minor sea engagements, was but another episode in a series of unending upheavals, and the region fell into a nightmare: in Anatolia, a million or more Armenians were massacred;[84] the Russian and Ottoman Empires, both exhausted, ultimately collapsed and splintered into a galaxy of small states. A 'de-hellenisation' of Asia Minor brought about the resettlement of millions of Christians into mainland Greece, and conversely the expulsion of Turks from Greece.[85] In Ukraine, pogroms continued in the context of the Russian civil war,[86] while Muslim populations disappeared almost entirely from Romania and Bulgaria. A process of ethnic and religious homogenisation took place across the entire region on an epic scale. Most of the political and social troubles or controversies occurring today in the Black Sea region can be traced back to that period of extreme human suffering. This contributed to changing

---

[84] See notably Ronald Grigor Suny, *'They can live in the desert but nowhere else': A history of the Armenian genocide* (Princeton, 2015), pp. 281–327.

[85] 'Convention concerning the exchange of Greek and Turkish populations', signed at Lausanne on the 30th of January 1923 (appendix VI to the Peace Treaty of Lausanne between the victorious powers and Turkey).

[86] Henry Abramson, *A prayer for the government: Ukrainians and Jews in Revolutionary Times, 1917–1920* (Cambridge, MA, 1999), pp. 109–40.

The defeat of the White Russians in Crimea (November 1921) occasioned a new exodus of nearly a hundred thousand refugees from Sevastopol, thanks to the ships of the Black Sea fleet. The new order of the interwar period led to the reincorporation of the successor states of the Russian Empire into the Soviet Union and the birth of a Turkish nationalist state (the Republic of Turkey). To the west, Romania recovered Bessarabia – the part of the principality of Moldavia lost in 1812.

By contrast, a radical change in the regime of the Black Sea came with the Treaty of Lausanne of 24 July 1923 in which the Western Allies of World War I recognised the new Republic of Turkey as the successor state to the Ottoman Empire. The former system of bilateral treaties of foreign countries for the passage of the Straits was replaced by a multilateral agreement with Turkey: the Convention relating to the Regime of the Straits. It established the principle of 'freedom of transit and of navigation, by sea and by air, in time of peace as in time of war' through the Straits. With the Straits demilitarised and under an International Commission, Turkey no longer had the power to impede any traffic at any time, with the only exception of wars in which it would be itself belligerent – in which case, it would have to grant right of passage to neutral ships, whether merchant or military. The Montreux Convention on the Regime of the Straits of 1936 made a compromise that was more favourable to Turkey: it brought the Straits back under its military control and allowed a refortification of the Dardanelles. The clauses for merchant ships remained more or less the same including in case of war; the greatest change was for vessels of wars, whose right of passage was more strictly regulated. In time of war, when Turkey was neutral, belligerent powers would be denied passage, while if Turkey was involved, it would do as it pleased.

One might think that largely opening access to commerce in the Black Sea would have been the end of the region's trials, yet it was not to be: sea commerce plummeted on the northern shore, now under the control of the Soviet Union. In the 1920s, Russia and Ukraine suffered a terrible shortage of food that killed millions as a consequence of war and droughts: the bread basket of Russia suddenly failed to feed itself, but the traditional solution of bringing relief supplies by sea was applied. A new famine known as the Holodomor occurred again in the 1932–33 under Joseph Stalin; this time, there was no relief from the sea and the death toll was staggeringly high.

A secret clause in the non-aggression pact between Hitler and Stalin in 1939 (the Molotov-Ribbentrop pact) conceded Bessarabia back to the Soviet Union, as part of its 'sphere of influence'. After the country was annexed (and rebranded as the Republic of Moldova), tens of thousands of Romanian-speaking inhabitants were deported or massacred and the German population expelled.

The subsequent war between Germany (with its allies Romania and Bulgaria) and the USSR had the effect of closing the Straits to the belligerents of both sides, as Turkey remained neutral. This not only prevented the British navy from assisting the Russians; it effectively prevented Italy and Germany sending their own war vessels into the Black Sea. As a result, naval warfare on the Black Sea was almost non-existent during World War II, in comparison to the enormous land operations. Extreme violence seems to have been a hallmark of the region: the occupation of Ukraine provided another opportunity for mass carnage, with the killing or deportation of nearly two-thirds of the Jewish population from the region by the Germans and their allies.[87] Crimea, for its part, was the scene of fierce land fighting that gave rise to particularly cruel episodes (for the Russians, the defence of Sevastopol built its patriotic significance on the defeat of the Crimean War). Finally the Battle of Stalingrad (September 1942–February 1943), one of the deadliest in recorded history, took place halfway between the Black Sea and the Caspian Sea. In the contest for pre-eminence between land and sea in the region, the first was definitely winning.

As if finally to accomplish the ambitions of Tsarist Russia, the defeat of Germany allowed the USSR to expand its control over the western shore of the Black Sea: it brought the Soviets back to Bessarabia, which they re-annexed. The coastline of the Black Sea between Odessa and the River Prut, which had belonged so far to Bessarabia was ceded to Ukraine, making the new Republic of Moldova landlocked; it also placed Romania and Bulgaria under Soviet domination. The Crimean Tatars, accused *en masse* of collaborating with the Nazis were deported to Central Asia. The Western Allies staunchly supported Turkey against a Soviet seizure of the Straits and the Anatolian land routes to Persia and the Middle East, pursuing a similar geostrategic policy as with the Ottoman Empire a century earlier. (Turkey joined the US-led NATO in 1952.)

The Cold War therefore closed the Black Sea, dividing it in two: a communist north under the Warsaw Pact, and Turkey to the south

---

[87] King, *Odessa*, pp. 201–27; George Liber, *Total wars and the making of modern Ukraine, 1914–1954* (Toronto, 2016), pp. 131–97.

The Black Sea   259

within NATO.[88] Most sea connections between the two 'worlds' were interrupted, with the notable exception of long-distance trade through the Straits (especially from the port of Novorossyisk). To make things more complicated, an awkward redistribution of territory occurred in the Black Sea in the early 1950s, the consequences of which are felt to this day: Nikita Khrushchev gave Crimea to the Ukrainian Soviet Republic (1954). What had merely been an administrative division became a serious issue when the Soviet Union split apart in 1991.[89]

The Thawing of the Black Sea

The fate of the Black Sea was once more influenced by events occurring thousands of kilometres away in Moscow. The Soviet Union, ideologically weakened and economically bankrupt, collapsed into a *smuta* (social and political chaos) reminiscent of the fall of the Tsarist Empire in 1917, albeit less bloody. By the end of 1991, in place of a Soviet Union stretching from the Prut River in the west to the Turkish border in the east, there were now three countries: Ukraine, Georgia and Russia, or four counting the (by then) landlocked Republic of Moldova.

Liberation from Soviet domination and the introduction of a market economy brought new hope and a period of openness on the Black Sea. During the 1990s, traffic in the Romanian port of Constanța soared to unprecedented levels; the port of Odessa also experienced a remarkable growth. The period also brought a wave of raw nationalisms that had been hitherto suppressed. Pro-Russian dissidences along the northern part of the Black Sea resulted in breakaway states still locked in frozen conflicts: Transnistria seceded from Moldova; in 2008 the Russian army intervened in Abkhazia in the revolt against Georgia (which provided yet another opportunity for population expulsion). Compounding these political confrontations was the struggle for the transport of oil and gas resources from the Caspian Sea through the Caucasus: the so-called 'geopolitics of pipelines'.[90] Not unlike in the nineteenth century, the competition is between northern routes under Russian control and southern corridors under the control of other powers (all of which involve a mix of pipeline, rail, ships and even trucks).

---

[88] Melvyn P. Leffler, 'Strategy, diplomacy, and the Cold War: The United States, Turkey, and NATO, 1945–1952', *The Journal of American History*, 71 (1985): 807–25.

[89] Gwendolyn Sasse, *The Crimea question: Identity, transition, and conflict* (Cambridge, MA, 2014), pp. 107–26.

[90] See Ernest Wyciszkiewicz, ed., *Geopolitics of pipelines: Energy interdependence and interstate relations in the post-Soviet area* (Warsaw, 2009).

260   S. Ghervas

In the early twenty-first century, the balance of power seems to have shifted and altered in nature.[91] The political contentions concerning Moldova, Ukraine and Georgia are now conceived of as taking place between 'Europe' ('the West') and 'Russia'. In reality, the source of tension is another: Russia's perceived threat that NATO could now expand its membership to ex-members of the USSR north of the Black Sea. Indeed, Romania and Bulgaria had joined the alliance in 2004.

Turkey is a particular case: torn between Europe and the Middle East, it has been a candidate for membership to a reluctant EU since 1987 while it has been experiencing its own identity crisis.[92] On the other hand, the Anatolian coast, which had once struck visitors as undeveloped and backwards, is bustling today with economic activity and the building of modern infrastructure, in a stark contrast to the Black Sea's northern coast of Ukraine and Russia. As for Istanbul, it is a rapidly expanding modern metropolis and an international trade hub that ranks among the world's major international capitals. The amount of traffic that passes through the Straits has been steadily growing; so much so that the Turkish government announced in April 2011 the construction of a 50 km-long sea-level waterway (Kanal İstanbul) that should run west of the Bosphorus, connecting the Sea of Marmara to the Black Sea. The consequences for the region may be considerable, both in terms of the volumes of sea traffic, but also geopolitically: since the Convention of Montreux obviously applies to the Bosphorus, this new channel between two seas might also provide greater leeway to Turkey for military purposes.

Sailing between a Lull and Storm Clouds

The fall of the Soviet Union in 1991 (which allowed sea commerce to resume between the northern and southern shores of the Black Sea) also allowed the birth of a new type of unitary narrative, which includes lesser known periods such as the Ottoman era and the twentieth century. This development was facilitated by greater freedom of speech, the opening of Russian and Ukrainian archives, the circulation of scholars and a period of relative peace for two decades on the shores of that sea. Similarly, the concept of the Black Sea as a unit came back in vogue in contemporary geopolitical studies, under the name of the 'Wider Black

---

[91] Duygu Bazoğlu Sezer, 'Balance of power in the Black Sea in the post-Cold War era: Russia, Turkey, and Ukraine', in Maria Drohobycky, ed., *Crimea: Dynamics, challenges, and prospects* (Boston, MA, 1995), pp. 157–94.

[92] On the Turkish identity crisis, see Orhan Pamuk's novels *The black book* (1994) and *Snow* (2004).

The Black Sea
261

Sea Region' (or 'Greater Black Sea Area').[93] There are least three reasons for this: first, the Black Sea is a whole in the perspective of international law, by reason of the agreements on the free passage of ships through the Straits. Second, a number of littoral countries share common issues, such as being located at the frontier of Russia and the European Union, social and political instability, economic woes and as a conduit of energy resources. Finally, the 'Black Sea region' is a commodious concept, serving as a link between geographical appellations such as 'Europe' and 'Middle East' or between 'Balkans' and 'Caucasus'.[94]

Cooperation initiatives (such as the Organisation of the Black Sea Economic Cooperation or BSEC, founded in 1997) have led to working papers and publications.[95] The European Union,[96] NATO[97] and the Russian-led Commonwealth of Independent States (CIS)[98] are also abundant sources of political literature. In the Russian context, however, 'Black Sea' is generally understood in a restricted way: as the northern coast formerly controlled by the Russian Empire and the Soviet Union, from the left bank of the Danube all the way to the Turkish border in eastern Anatolia. In Turkey, the end of the Cold War and the reconnection of the shores, as well as the debate about the 'Europeanness of Turkey' prompted a new wave of historical research on the Black Sea.[99] Yet interest in the Black Sea *region* is not necessarily interest in the sea itself.

At the same time, the Black Sea is also at risk of heading again for a period of partial enclosure. In 2014, following the fall of the

[93] The phrase 'Wider Black Sea Region' was used officially in the reports of NATO at the Istanbul Summit of 2004 and was popularised, in particular, by Ronald Asmus, 'Developing a new Euro-Atlantic strategy for the Black-Sea region', *Istanbul Papers*, 2 (25–27 June 2004). See also Gavriil Preda and Gabriel Leahu, eds., *Black Sea: History, diplomacy, policies and strategies* (Bagheria, 2012); Andrew Robarts, *Black Sea regionalism: A case study* (Washington, DC, 2015).

[94] Mustafa Aydın, *Europe's next shore: The Black Sea region after EU enlargement*, Occasional Paper, EU Institute for Security Studies, 53 (2004); Oleg Serebrian, *Geopolitica spaţiului pontic* (Chisinau, 2006).

[95] This organisation comprises the riparian states, Moldova, Armenia, Azerbaijan, as well as three Balkan countries (Greece, Serbia and Albania).

[96] See, notably, *Black Sea synergy – A new regional cooperation initiative*, Communication from the Commission to the Council and the European Parliament, 11 April 2007. For a clarification, see Dimitrios Triantaphyllou, ed., *The security context in the Black Sea region* (London, 2010); Baptiste Chartré and Stéphane Delory, eds., *Conflits et sécurité dans l'espace mer Noire: L'Union européenne, les riverains et les autres* (Paris, 2009).

[97] Ronald Asmus, ed., *Next steps in forging a Euroatlantic strategy for the wider Black Sea* (Washington, DC, 2006).

[98] See for example the recent collective volume *Prichernomor'e: Istoriya, politika, geografiya, kul'tura* [The shores of the Black Sea: History, politics, geography, culture] (Sevastopol, 2010).

[99] Atila Eralp and Çiğdem Üstün, eds., *Turkey and the EU: The process of change and neighbourhood* (Ankara, 2009).

262   S. Ghervas

pro-Russian government in Ukraine, Russia forcibly annexed Crimea, in violation of pre-existing international agreements, while an insurrection broke out in the Donbass (the eastern part of the country). As a result of the embargo on Russia, the sea trade of Crimea and the Russian shore (particularly Novorossiysk) with the rest of the world was severely reduced.[100] Today European cruise liners are no longer allowed to call at Yalta or Sevastopol (at the same time the port cities of Constanța in Romania and Odessa in Ukraine are experiencing a corresponding expansion). There has been little commerce from the Crimean ports since the 1990s and even less since the Russian annexation; most of the regional traffic goes by land. The bridge currently under construction that will connect Crimea to the Russian mainland across the Kerch Strait will only reinforce that trend.[101] In that case, circulation across the Black Sea seems indeed to have evolved in inverse ratio to nationalism.

A recent authoritarian turn in Turkey and a resulting resolution of the EU parliament in November 2016 to freeze its membership application process seem to have checked this country's integration into the European system. On the other hand, coastal shipping on the Anatolian Black Sea coast is still vibrant. The second decade of the twenty-first century is undoubtedly one of instability, when the balance of power in the region is shifting and could evolve in several possible directions. Russia and Turkey, unsurprisingly, are attempting a rapprochement that needs, however, to overcome a territorial rivalry that traces back to the Russian and Ottoman Empires, especially over influence over eastern Anatolia. Whether this could result in an increase of sea connections between Russia and the Anatolian coast remains to be seen.

Calming the Waters: For a New Narrative of the Black Sea

All in all, writing a coherent maritime history of the Black Sea presents at least four challenges or paradoxes: the dual valence of the land and the sea; the largely geopolitical issue of openness versus closedness (especially in relation to the Straits); the prevalence of micro-history over

---

[100] See 'Council Regulation (EU) No 692/2014, concerning restrictive measures in response to the illegal annexation of Crimea and Sevastopol'.

[101] Daria Litvinova, 'Why Kerch may prove a bridge too far for Russia', *The Moscow Times*, 17 June 2016: https://themoscowtimes.com/articles/why-kerch-may-prove-a-bridge-too-far-for-russia-53309 (accessed 20 July 2017); Céline Bayou, 'Le pont de Kertch: Derrière la prouesse technique, le geste politique', *Regard sur l'Est*, 20 September 2016: www.regard-est.com/home/breve_contenu.php?id=1659 (accessed 20 July 2017).

The Black Sea 263

macro-history in the existing literature; and (last but not least) the difficulty of writing a narrative escaping the inertia of imperial and national histories.

Indeed, while the nineteenth century had presaged a new era of modernity, the creation of new states bordering that sea bequeathed a string of problematic national identities, marred by a memory of wars, massacres and deportations. Nationalist ideologies (an essentially land-oriented form of thought) are threatening to relegate the sea to the background again and to reduce its circulations. Particularly in Russia, Ukraine and Turkey, the dominant narratives remain those of ethnically homogeneous nations, oriented to the land (i.e. turning their backs on the sea), afflicted by essentially hostile neighbours and misfit 'minorities'. Reality is different: in spite of everything, family ties still create intricate webs of local and regional identities, bringing together people in a constellation of social and religious affiliations; and the sea remains a connecting medium between the shores.

In general, attempting to write a maritime history of the Black Sea as a whole in the perspective of the 'new thalassology', remains a risky business, and not only by reason of its human complexity. In a region where historical 'truth' is still a matter of territorial stakes among rival nation-states, national narratives (which largely continue to ignore that diversity) persist to feed controversy. The recent falling out between Ukraine and Russia and generally the fierce exploitation of historical biases in littoral states toward legitimising political standpoints (not to mention laws curbing free speech), are making the task of historians increasingly difficult. Accounts of atrocities suffered are still too often used to minimise those previously committed or justify new ones perpetuating an endless cycle of revanchism, irredentism and violence.

Writing a new regional narrative where the sea plays a foreground role may require that all states admit that they played a guilty part in the immense tragedy that disconnected the coastlines from the late nineteenth century forward. A new generation of historians is recognising the need to rewrite a history of the Black Sea that moves beyond political partisanship and parochial interests in order to bring together populations forcibly divided by 'national identities'. This process, which also includes collecting the confessions of perpetrators alongside the testimonies of victims, is occasionally a painful one. Those who undertake this path of intellectual pacification are likely to expose themselves to vehement criticism by those who believe that historians should be subservient to self-righteous political agendas. Yet reconciliation among the littoral states of the Black Sea could be envisioned if all states involved abandoned desires of self-aggrandisement and instead turned to 'concrete achievements

264   S. Ghervas

which first create a *de facto* solidarity',[102] a method that paid dividends for France and Germany after the Second World War.

In the long term, the hostilities that have existed between the states bordering the Black Sea are but a brief moment in the history of the region. Empires and nation-states, together with their ideologies, appear as transient actors that enter, perform their act and exit against a slowly moving backdrop. Indeed, geopolitical stakes, national ambitions and past military glories appear ephemeral when placed next to the relative permanency of the grey-green waves of the Black Sea – 'the most marvellous of seas', according to Herodotus. Despite the advent of rail, motorcars and airplanes, sea shipping will continue to be a cheap and effective transportation method. The *Pontos Euxeinos*, the 'hospitable sea' remains the true lord and the main actor of this region in the *longue durée*: it existed long before empires and nation-states and will likely outlast them. Indeed, it might be up to the Black Sea's inhabitants to bring it honour by establishing a lasting peace by favouring the circulation of people, goods and ideas along its shores, while protecting and perpetuating its precious environment.

Further Reading

Few historians have attempted to write comprehensive accounts of the Black Sea over the *longue durée*. The two reference books in English are Neil Ascherson, *Black Sea: The birthplace of civilisation and barbarism* (London, 1995) and Charles King, *The Black Sea: A history* (Oxford, 2004); the former is an evocative book of historical nonfiction and a good travelogue; the latter represents the most extensive overview of the Black Sea history to this day. We could not leave out George I. Brătianu's *La mer Noire: des origines à la conquête ottomane* [The Black Sea, from the origins to the Ottoman conquest] (Munich, 1969): it is a pioneering synthesis that covers the period beyond the end of Antiquity, alas never translated into English. Some recent journal issues cover the history of the Black Sea (albeit limited in their temporal or spatial scope), such as 'Nations, nation-states, trade and politics in the Black Sea', *Euxeinos*, 14 (2014). There are, however, very few historiographically oriented articles attempting to consider critically the Black Sea as a unit of research (an issue still subject of debate): on this, see Eyüp Özveren, 'The Black Sea as a unit of analysis', in Tunc Aybak, ed., *Politics of the Black Sea: Dynamics of cooperation and conflict* (London, 2001),

---

[102] 'Schuman Declaration' (9 May 1950). For more, see Stella Ghervas, *Conquering peace: From the Enlightenment to the European Union* (Cambridge, MA, 2018), ch. 5.

The Black Sea

pp. 61–84, and Owen Doonan, 'The corrupting sea and the hospitable sea: Some early thoughts toward a regional history of the Black Sea', in Derek B. Counts and Anthony S. Tuck, eds., *Koine: Mediterranean studies in honor of R. Ross Holloway* (Providence, RI, 2010), pp. 68–74.

On the environment of this sea, and particularly the controversy about the great flood, see Petko Dimitrov and Dimitar Dimitrov, *The Black Sea, the flood, and the ancient myths* (Varna, 2004) and Valentina Yanko-Hombach, Allan S. Gilbert, Nicolae Panin and Pavel M. Dolukhanov, eds., *The Black Sea flood question: Changes in coastline, climate and human settlement* (Dordrecht, 2007). On its biology and ecology, consult Yu. P. Zaitsev and V. Mamaev, *Marine biological diversity in the Black Sea* (New York, 1997) and Zaitsev, *An introduction to the Black Sea ecology* (London, 2001). The maritime archaeology of the Black Sea is detailed by Robert D. Ballard, Fredrik T. Hiebert, Dwight F. Coleman, Cheryl Ward, Jennifer S. Smith, Kathryn Willis, Brendan Foley, Katherine Croff, Candace Major and Francesco Torre, 'Deepwater archaeology of the Black Sea: The 2000 season at Sinop, Turkey', *American Journal of Archaeology*, 105 (2001): 607–23. It is only recently that historians have started to give attention to the environment of that sea and its region: see, for example, Carlos Cordova, *Crimea and the Black Sea: An environmental history* (London, 2016).

As for historical literature, contemporary works on the Black Sea reflect the successive periods of openness and closedness. In particular, historians and archaeologists devoted considerable research to proto-historic and Ancient times, with the first settlement of nomadic tribes, the process of maritime colonisation by the Greeks, as well as the incorporation of that region into the Roman civilisational sphere; see in particular: Gocha R. Tsetskhladze, ed., *The Greek colonisation of the Black Sea Area: Historical interpretation of archaeology* (Stuttgart, 1998); Mariya Ivanova, *The Black Sea and the early civilizations of Europe, the Near East, and Asia* (Cambridge, 2013). Among the works on later times spanning the Hellenistic period to the Ottomans (Roman, Italian, Mongol), with a focus on the trade and economic/social developments of the Black Sea, see Alan W. Fisher, 'Muscovy and the Black Sea trade', *Canadian-American Slavic Studies*, 6 (1972): 575–94; Nicola di Cosmo, 'Mongols and merchants on the Black Sea frontier (13th–14th c.): Convergences and conflicts', in Reuven Amitai and Michal Biran, eds., *Turco-Mongol nomads and sedentary societies* (Leiden, 2005), pp. 391–424; Victor Ciocîltan, *The Mongols and the Black Sea trade in the thirteenth and fourteenth centuries*, trans. Samuel Willcocks (Leiden, 2012); Mikhail B. Kizilov, 'The Black Sea and the slave trade: The role of Crimean maritime towns in the trade in slaves and captives in the fifteenth to eighteenth centuries', *International Journal of Maritime*

History, 17 (2005): 211–35. For the Ottoman era, see Gilles Veinstein, 'From the Italians to the Ottomans: The case of the northern Black Sea coast in the sixteenth century', *Mediterranean Historical Review*, 1 (1986): 221–37; Halil İnalcık, 'The question of the closing of the Black Sea under the Ottomans', *Archeion Pontou*, 35 (1979): 74–110; Carl M. Kortepeter, 'Ottoman imperial policy and the economy of the Black Sea region in the sixteenth century', *Journal of the American Oriental Society*, 86 (1966): 86–113. The opening of the Black Sea region to foreign powers during the modern period was researched in Vassilis Kardassis, *Diaspora merchants in the Black Sea: The Greeks in southern Russia, 1775–1861* (Lanham, MD, 2001); Gelina Harlaftis, 'The role of Greeks in the Black Sea trade, 1830–1900', in Lewis R. Fischer and Helge W. Norvik, eds., *Shipping and trade, 1750–1950: Essays in international maritime economic history* (Rotterdam, 1990), pp. 63–95; Andrew Robarts, *Migration and disease in the Black Sea region: Ottoman-Russian relations in the late 18th and early 19th centuries* (London, 2017). On the port-cities of the Black Sea, see Flora Karagianni, ed., *Medieval ports in North Aegean and the Black Sea: Links to the maritime routes of the East* (Thessaloniki, 2013); Patricia Herlihy, *Odessa: A history, 1794–1914* (Cambridge, MA, 1986); Charles King, *Odessa: Genius and death in a city of dreams* (New York, 2011); and Constantin Ardeleanu and Andreas Lyberatos, eds., *The port-cities of the Black Sea, port cities of the western Black Sea coast and the Danube* (Corfu, 2016). Finally, for a few more works on the issue whether the Black Sea should be considered at all as a region and a unit of research, see Charles King, 'Is the Black Sea a region?', in Oleksander Pavliuk and Ivana Klympish-Tsintadze, eds., *The Black Sea region: Cooperation and security building* (London, 2004), pp. 13–26; Daniel S. Hamilton and Gerhard Mangott, eds., *The wider Black Sea region in the 21st century: Strategic, economic, and energy perspectives* (Washington, DC, 2008); as well as Ruxandra Ivan, ed., *New regionalism, or no regionalism? Emerging regionalism in the Black Sea area* (London, 2012). This debate would benefit from more interaction between historical research and geopolitical studies on the Black Sea.

Part III

Poles

10 The Arctic Ocean

Sverker Sörlin

The Arctic Ocean is an unusual part of the world of seas. As oceans have entered an historiographical centre stage in recent years, part of what has been called the 'new thalassalogy',[1] the Arctic Ocean has remained to a large extent on the margins. Historical scholarship on the oceans has importantly noted that meta-geographical entities such as the Pacific, the Atlantic, the Caribbean and others are of relatively recent date and that such 'basin thinking' can be seen as a product of high imperialism of the post-Enlightenment period and in some cases has gained real currency even later.[2] This is true for the Arctic Ocean as well, perhaps to the extent that this region stands out as a case of ocean exceptionalism. It is a sea which until the twentieth century almost no one had crossed, that was not used for trade or contact, and that was more or less inaccessible apart from very small groups of local inhabitants – who furthermore knew nothing of the extent of their northern ocean, beyond what they could reach on their hunting and fishing tours. After millennia of human occupation on its shores, its ice-covered core areas were still quite unreachable for Western explorers as well, although hunters and whalers visited frequently, and cruise ship tourism was emerging from the latter half of the eighteenth century.

Hence, as a meta-geographical *ocean project* it arrived very late and with a number of peculiar features, including the very opposite of the core notion of Fernand Braudel's vision of the Mediterranean, despite its many boundaries and divisions, as a common space marked by trade and relations. Since the late Middle Ages, the Arctic Ocean was an ocean mostly in a figurative and imaginary fashion. It was brought into the globalising meta-geography of oceans only with the geopolitics of the twentieth century and especially the tensions of the Cold

---

[1] Peregrine Horden and Nicholas Purcell, 'The Mediterranean and the "new thalassology"', *American Historical Review*, 111 (2006): 722–40.

[2] Kären Wigen, 'Introduction' [to a special issue on oceans and history], *American Historical Review*, 111 (2006): 717–21.

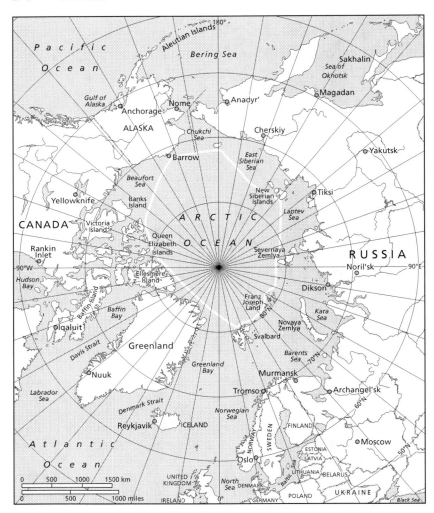

Map 10.1 The Arctic Ocean

War, when the Arctic finally entered a broader discourse as an entire ocean, with a spatial and political significance. It was formally recognised as an ocean by the International Hydrographic Organisation, founded in Monaco in 1921. In 1953 it was further delineated from northern coastal seas in an elaborate remaking of the 1937 map of 'Limits of oceans and seas' to make up only the sea north of any land, including islands, extending from continental territories and of the

The Arctic Ocean   271

lines connecting these points.[3] In further revisions of these limits the
Arctic Sea was joined with the smaller northern seas, then called 'sub-
divisions', into an extended Arctic Ocean space in 1986.[4] In practice,
the waters surrounding all shores of the region are called 'the Arctic',
yet another phenomenon that gained currency around and after the
Second World War, especially in North America, although it had an
older history as well.[5] Despite no human being crossing the ice-clad
waters, the Arctic Ocean was neither an empty space, nor a silent one.
It was a more-than-human world with a more-than-human world's history of subtle changes over epochs and aeons, recordable only through
layers left behind for latecomers to register if we can. Even in our time,
recording this fine-tuned 'cacophony' requires a hydrophone, as the
one lowered on a summer day, seemingly 'utterly silent', but far from
it:

The tremolo moans of bearded seals. The baritone boom of walrus. The high-
pitched bark and yelp of ringed seals. The clicks, pure tones, birdlike trills, and
harmonics of belukhas and narwhals [. . .] the whine and fracture of sea ice, and
the sound of deep-keeled ice grounding in shallow water.[6]

The Arctic Ocean 'before history' had its own history of life.

An Ocean of High Modernity

As a project of historiography, then, the Arctic Ocean becomes almost
a non-entity, a void in between the Arctic nations, with few sources,
and with little connection, and recognised as an integrative space by an
extremely small number of people. If it does not fit conventional histories, or emerging world and global histories (where the Arctic as a
whole has been largely absent), one may say that it belongs at least to
international or transnational history, or what Patricia Seed has called
'a world of comparative possibility'. But even such a history is hard
to undertake for an entity which so poorly accords with the common
definition of transnational history, with its focus 'on a whole range of
connections that transcend politically bounded territories and connect
various parts of the world to one another. Networks, institutions, ideas,

---

[3] International Hydrographic Bureau, *Limits of oceans and seas*, 3rd edn. (Monte Carlo,
1953), pp. 11–12, map on p. 43.
[4] International Hydrographic Bureau, *Limits of oceans and seas*, 4th edn. (Monte Carlo,
1986), pp. 189–215, map on p. 5.
[5] E. C. H. Keskitalo, *Negotiating the Arctic: The construction of an international region*
(New York, 2004).
[6] Barry Lopez, *Arctic dreams: Imagination and desire in a northern landscape*, new edn.
(London, 1987), p. 138.

272 S. Sörlin

and processes constitute these connections, and though rulers, empires, and states are important in structuring them, they transcend politically bounded territories.'[7]

This is particularly true for the Arctic Ocean space since the first half of the twentieth century. Elements of such a reading existed from an early Arctic imperial phase from circa 1870, but to define its history as 'transnational' at all before, say, 1918 is possible only because it *lacked* comprehensive and spatially covering national histories, not because it did actually transcend the national. On the contrary, nations tried as best they could to claim their own slices of it, a practice that has only been reinforced after the end of the Cold War. It was during and after World War I that more serious modern diplomacy and politics entered the Arctic Ocean with the Svalbard Treaty, decided at Versailles in 1920, and the sector principle as a foundation for claims on the Arctic Ocean up to the North Pole that were put forth by Arctic coastal states, starting with Canada in 1925 and followed by the Soviet Union in 1926.

It may be useful to think of the Arctic Ocean, despite its relative smallness and its position in between three major continents and the world's largest island (Greenland), as in fact the opposite of a 'mediterranean' such as the Baltic or the Black Sea.[8] Rather it stands out as what we may wish to call a barrier region, a black hole, despite its whiteness. Such regions have drawn a lot of interest in recent years. The Amazon, the Sahara, Antarctica, Siberia, the wider Himalaya/ Pamir are examples of regions with relatively limited access, sparse and scarce communication, internal and external. They are also meta-geographical projects, with contested borders but each with their particular significance, economic, political, environmental, cultural and with a set of structured narratives that could be mobilised as evidence in the meta-geographical work at different points in time. Nonetheless, these regions are typically read as lands 'without history'. The Amazon region for example, has been validated for its natural exuberance rather than as a place of dynamic political change, as wild, not modern.[9] They have been perceived as outside of R. G. Collingwood's definition of

---

[7] C. A. Bayly, Sven Beckert, Matthew Connelly, Isabel Hofmeyr, Wendy Kozol and Patricia Seed, '*AHR* conversation: On transnational history', *American Historical Review*, 111 (2006): 1441–64; quotes on 1444 (Seed), and 1446. See also Akira Iriye, *Global and transnational history: The past, present, and future* (Basingstoke, 2012).

[8] Despite the fact that to many oceanographers that is precisely how it should be defined: as a Mediterranean sea; see, for example, Günther Dietrich, *General oceanography: An introduction* (Oxford, 1980).

[9] Susanna Hecht, *The scramble for the Amazon and the lost paradise of Euclides da Cunha* (Chicago, IL, 2013).

The Arctic Ocean 273

'human affairs' as the criteria for history, hence the place of 'events' rather than 'actions'.[10] These are also spaces which have become state spaces only recently, thus fulfilling John Agnew's point that modernity often appears as a set of spatial binaries where certain geographies represent the past, while others appearing as fully integrated state territories represent the normal present.[11]

But not even these binaries tend to work all that well for the Arctic Ocean space. True, it is the object of intensified interest from all five current coastal states – Canada, the United States, Russia, Norway and Denmark – that in the UNCLOS (United Nations Convention on the Law of the Sea) process have launched claims for extended coastal zones based on the sea floor principle. Indeed, these claims now cover almost the entire Arctic Ocean. There are also increasing attempts among many states, not just the Arctic coastal states, but also states that have status as observer states of the Arctic Council (for example, China, India, Korea, Japan), to claim access to trade, traffic, services and sometimes resources, in the region.[12] In this ambition they make active use of history and precedent, claiming past Arctic presence through research or resource use.[13]

While certainly part of the history of colonialism, the exceptional feature of the Arctic Ocean seems to be that it emerges as a historical and meta-geographical entity through high modernity rather than high imperialism. As a strategically important region it is more contemporary with the atomic bomb, the computer, long-distance missiles, space stations and issues of human survival, including Arctic warfare, climate change and environment, than with trade, colonies, the allure of temperate wilderness and emerging consumer markets of food, spices and fabrics, the traditional luxuries of overseas cultures. Even in terms of goods, cultural and material, the relative contribution of exotic goods from the Arctic Ocean and its 'rims' tended to be sparse and relatively recent. Hans Sloane's vast private eighteenth-century collection in London included Inuit artifacts from west Greenland and eastern Canada (barely parts of a strictly defined Arctic Ocean), including snow goggles, ivory tools, a snow knife, harpoons, a kayak model, walrus

[10] R. G. Collingwood, *The idea of history* (Oxford, 1946).
[11] John Agnew, *Geopolitics: Re-visioning world politics*, 2nd edn. (London, 2003).
[12] Timo Koivurova, 'Limits and possibilities of the Arctic Council in a rapidly changing scene of Arctic governance', *Polar Record*, 46 (2010): 146–48.
[13] Erica Paglia, 'The northward course of the Anthropocene: Transformation, temporality and telecoupling in a time of crisis' (PhD diss., KTH, Division for History of Science, Technology and Environment, Stockholm, 2016).

274   S. Sörlin

teeth, a decorated belt. But numbers were unimpressive, only forty from Hudson Bay, Hudson Strait, Davis Strait and Greenland.[14] Although some of this ethnographic collecting started to appear in early modern colonial coffee-table books and collections (tusks of walrus, Inuit art objects, seal fur), and despite occasional shows by Inuit in the Danish imperial capital, it was marginal compared to other ocean colonial exotica and became more common only in the nineteenth and especially the twentieth centuries.[15]

This is to some extent countered by the role of certain parts of the Arctic Ocean in early modern resource economies, for example the Barents region (again a boundary zone to current definitions of the Arctic Ocean) where trade and technology transfer included not only Russians and the neighbouring Scandinavians but also the Dutch and the British. By the seventeenth and eighteenth centuries there was a massive export of fish and marine mammals' blubber from the Russian port of Arkhangelsk and the Kola peninsula to Europe. If we include the White Sea, this chronology might be stretched even further back and linked to Russian colonisation that became significant from at least the fifteenth century.[16] But again, in order to do full justice to these important early developments it is necessary to compromise on the definition of the Arctic Ocean and extend it to what is today rather considered the North Atlantic or the northern Pacific, including the Aleutians and southern Alaska. One might say that whereas other oceans have become appropriated by continents, empires and cultures over long periods of time, the process of appropriation of the Arctic Ocean started recently and tended to focus on a fairly narrow set of elements, to do with natural resources, security and indigenous status and rights. In this sense its exceptionalism also has to do with its comparative youth, its recent and still emerging character as a meta-geographical space, where it remains an open question as to what thalassological properties will stand out as characteristic.

[14] Angela Byrne, *Geographies of the Romantic North: Science, antiquarianism, and travel, 1790–1830* (New York, 2013), p. 88.

[15] Michael Harbsmeier, 'Bodies and voices from Ultima Thule: Inuit explorations of the Kablunat from Christian IV to Knud Rasmussen', in Michael T. Bravo and Sverker Sörlin, eds., *Narrating the Arctic: A cultural history of Nordic scientific practices* (Canton, MA, 2002), pp. 37–71; Jørgen Ole Bærenholdt, *Coping with distances: Producing Nordic Atlantic societies* (Oxford, 2007). For a case of early modern Arctic collecting, see Ole Worm's comprehensive, *Musei Wormiani Historia* (Leiden, 1655), which included maritime antiquities and specimens.

[16] Julia Lajus, 'Colonization of the Russian North: A frozen frontier', in Christina Folke Ax, Niels Brimnes, Niklas Thode Jensen and Karen Oslund, eds., *Cultivating the colonies: Colonial states and their environmental legacies* (Athens, OH, 2011).

The Arctic Ocean 275

Arctic Ocean – Arctic or Ocean?

The exceptionalism in historical terms is borne out in geographical features as well. The Arctic Ocean is the smallest of the world oceans, with less than three per cent of the world's saltwater surface and even less of its saltwater volume, and the shallowest, with an average depth of 1,200 metres. Its deep regions, reaching a maximum depth of little more than 5,000 metres are separated by undersea ridges, three of the largest, Lomonosov, Gakkel and Mendeleyev named after Russian scientists, at the same time indicating where some of the formative oceanographic science has taken place. It has major tributaries from all directions: the Pechora, Ob, Yenisey and Lena in Russia, the Tana from Finland and Norway, the Coppermine and the Mackenzie in North America, and many smaller ones, plus a sprinkling from the melting Greenland ice cap. Given the drastic seasonality of the region and the slow gradient between coastal regions and the deep sea, salinity and temperatures vary considerably between the ocean's sub-regions, and hence fauna and flora.

The Arctic Ocean is semi-closed and has a very irregular extent. It is commonly defined as including both the Davis Strait west of Greenland and the Hudson Bay, extending as far south as the 57th Parallel, but is otherwise far from congruent with the extent of the Arctic region. The modern orthodoxy is that the sea ice cover, with seasonal variations, has existed for at least 800,000 years. Although still standing, this claim has been questioned by recent research and it is now also challenged by projections of the future extent of summer sea ice.

Arctic Ocean coastal populations are, and have always been, very small. The Arctic, commonly defined as the territory north of the Arctic Circle at latitude 66° 33′ N, holds little more than four million inhabitants, many of whom are concentrated in several inland cities and communities and the large majority at considerable distance from the Arctic Ocean proper. The Arctic as a whole has a much wider expanse than the Arctic Ocean, although the terrestrial Arctic, circumscribing the ocean, is only a small portion of the whole. The total and integrated region comprises parts of the North Atlantic and adjacent seas around Greenland and northwestern Russia, and parts of the north Pacific. Contact with European whalers, traders and missionaries introduced indigenous populations to a range of diseases and changed their traditional nomadic lifestyle.[17] Inhabitants are largely sedentary or semi-nomadic and, if they

---

[17] D. Bogoyavlenskiy and A. Siggner, 'Arctic demography', in N. Einarsson, J. N. Larsen, A. Nilsson and O. R. Young, eds., *Arctic human development report* (Copenhagen, 2004), pp. 27–41.

276   S. Sörlin

belong in certain communities, practise traditional methods of hunting, fishing, reindeer herding and arts and crafts, and are distributed across the territories of eight nation-states.

Yet another special feature of the Arctic Ocean is that it is, through the thermohaline circulation, fed by warm waters from the mid- and western Atlantic (the Caribbean, hence 'the Gulf Stream') which makes the boundary to the North Atlantic a zone of unusually northerly agriculture, especially affecting Scandinavia which had sizable populations since the Bronze Age and through the Middle Ages. Norse colonisation took place from the ninth century, a lasting one to Iceland and, not lasting, to Greenland and northeastern 'Vinland', now the northern coast of Newfoundland. The Gulf Stream also warms the coast of eastern Greenland, the Svalbard archipelago (under Norwegian jurisdiction following the 1925 Svalbard Treaty) and northwestern Russia with the Barents Sea, named after the Dutch sixteenth-century explorer Willem Barents, and Franz Josef Land and the eastern coasts of Novaya Zemlya islands.

With these conditions it is obvious that much of the history of the Arctic Ocean is both one of the life and cultures of sparse northern populations over long periods of time and one of forays into the ocean from European nations. This pattern is not dissimilar from colonial ocean encounters elsewhere in the world but with the major difference that non-indigenous Arctic colonisation was small in absolute numbers and large in relative terms.

Perhaps more importantly, it is an ocean that has not been sailed across as part of trade, travel, migration or happenstance; only research vessels and icebreakers have done so. While for centuries there had been extensive coastal sea-ice navigation among Inuit in the Canadian archipelago,[18] there was never any trans-oceanic travel on the ice. The shores of the Arctic Ocean have therefore not stood in relation to each other before the era of air travel, and even then to a very limited extent given the sparsity of population and the political divides across this ocean that during the Cold War was literally the closest boundary between the North American part of the West and the Eastern bloc, and also a potential theatre of war. The first Arctic Ocean crossing was done with the Norwegian ship *Fram* on an expedition, which lasted from 1895 to 1897, led by explorer-scientist and later Nobel Peace Prize winner Fridtjof Nansen. It demonstrated empirically that there was a major east to west current that

---

[18] As has recently been reconstructed in a 'Pan Inuit Trail Atlas' based on archival, field and oral history sources; see Claudio Aporta, Michael Bravo and Fraser Taylor: http://paninuittrails.org (2014) (accessed 2 May 2017).

The Arctic Ocean 277

transported ice towards Greenland and the western Arctic. The first surface crossing of the ocean was led by Wally Herbert in 1969, in a dog sled expedition from Alaska to Svalbard, with air support. The first nautical transit of the North Pole was made in 1958 by the submarine USS *Nautilus* (the first on foot was claimed by Frederick Cook (1908) and Robert Peary (1909); a dispute that has been lingering ever since),[19] and the first surface nautical transit occurred in August 1977 by the 23,400 ton Russian icebreaker NS *Arktika* propelled by its 75,000 horsepower engines.

The first flight to reach the North Pole was claimed by US Admiral Richard F. Byrd in 1926, but not documented and much doubted (Byrd also made the first flight to the South Pole). Even today, with the polar air route established by Scandinavian Airlines in 1950, there are literally no connections between the shores of this major ocean. To get from Iqaluit on Baffin Island, a mere 400 miles from the Greenland capital of Nuuk, it is necessary to fly to Ottawa, then to a major hub in the US or Canada, from there to Copenhagen, only to fly all the way back across the North Atlantic to Nuuk, a trip hard to complete in less than thirty-six hours. Other Arctic destinations are in real terms even farther apart. Oceans typically connect continents, islands and people but the Arctic Ocean has traditionally divided east from west, north from south, and major industrial and energy resources from their potential users, possibly more than in any other oceanic part of the world.

Recent geopolitics of the Arctic Ocean remain a feature of distinction. With its natural resources such as minerals, oil and gas for a long time unattainable for climatic, technical or economic reasons they have become more accessible through new technologies, the end of the Cold War and climate change which makes offshore activities and all-year open sea routes more likely. After a long period of relatively stable geopolitics the general situation has turned more dynamic and a new scramble for resources and political turf-holding has arisen, involving new Arctic interests from countries such as China, Korea, India and several European states.

The Non-Historical Ocean

The first general history of the Arctic was published as late as 2012 and treats the Arctic Ocean parsimoniously, mostly as an environmental

---

[19] Bruce Henderson, *True North: Peary, Cook and the race to the Pole* (New York, 2005).

278   S. Sörlin

and climatic phenomenon.[20] The late arrival of an historiography of the Arctic can be explained as a default outcome of its largely colonial status and its peripheral relations to major states and powers, partly by the absence of the standard actors with whom historians associate methodological relevance. Arctic territories, populations and events have, in some exceptional cases, been counted as legitimate elements of the histories of states, especially Russia/USSR, where the northeastern sea route to Asia has become a national priority under Soviet power and especially since the 1930s when the special institution to govern the route and a large adjacent territory of the Arctic, *Glavsevmorput*, had been organised along with considerable research facilities. The Arctic Ocean has to some extent been part of the history of companies, such as the Hudson's Bay Company or the London Muscovy Company. In particular, it has become part of the history of exploration or woven into Arctic sub-fields such as Arctic anthropology, archaeology, religious studies or the Danish sub-specialty of Eskimology or elsewhere Inuit studies.[21] Very rarely, if at all, have historians felt inclined to research and write, or even compile comprehensive pan-Arctic histories. When some attempts in this direction were started only quite recently they appeared in sub-specialties focusing on science, environment, geography, geopolitics or other fields where the Arctic was considered a more relevant category than it was in more general histories of, for example, power, legislation, war, political and social life.[22]

This is, hence, even more true for the Arctic Ocean, which, it may be argued, has not yet been made the subject of a historical analysis or narrative in its own right. This does not exclude that there are many historical events and structural processes that have occurred in, on, or in relation to the Arctic Ocean – only that they have not been organised into any template narrative. Historiography of the Arctic Ocean has to some extent arisen, or come in demand, in relation to the interest in 'new mediterraneans' where multiple states find themselves sharing certain common interests or predicaments around a particular sea. This is a policy-related interest stemming from changing geopolitics post-1989. The history that has just started to emerge has sometimes been told from a 'territorial political economy' lens, with influence from world-systems

---

[20] John McCannon, *A history of the Arctic: Nature, exploration and exploitation* (London, 2012).

[21] Igor Krupnik, ed., *Early Inuit studies: Themes and transitions, 1850s–1980s* (Washington, DC, 2016).

[22] Dolly Jörgensen and Sverker Sörlin, 'Making the action visible: Introduction', in Jörgensen and Sörlin, eds., *Northscapes: Science, technology, and the making of northern environments* (Vancouver, BC, 2013), pp. 1–14; Bravo and Sörlin, eds., *Narrating the Arctic*.

The Arctic Ocean 279

theory, the spatiality of capitalism and political-geographic work on the history of territoriality.[23]

It is not the first time that there has been a search for Arctic narratives in phases of territorialisation. When they occasionally did include the Arctic Ocean, they were commonly starkly nationalist. The quintessential example is Fridtjof Nansen, who had barely embarked upon his heroic journeys in Norway, Greenland and in the Polar Sea, when he started collecting paraphernalia on exploration and seafaring, including charts, and published widely on the subject of polar travel, especially the comprehensive *In northern mists*.[24] Knud Rasmussen, the Danish explorer-hero, performed similar nationalist work for the Danish Greenland colony.[25] Based partly on his own extensive dogsled Thule expeditions, which touched on coastal cultures of the North American Arctic and vernacular knowledge compiled from them in the 1920s, he published *Polarforskningens Saga* [The saga of polar exploration] as volume six of 'The Conquering of the World' book series in 1932.[26] In Sweden Adolf Erik Nordenskiöld also collected books, manuscripts and maps, and then wrote himself into the great tradition. His facsimile-atlas to the early history of cartography with reproductions of the most important maps printed in the fifteenth and sixteenth centuries was co-translated by his polar explorer colleague Clements Markham at the British Admiralty.[27] In the Canadian context one could think of Vilhjalmur Stefansson, leader of controversial expeditions, and maker of a Canadian northern mythology, especially with his book *The northward course of empire* (1922), which launched the prospect of massive development on the Arctic northern rim with bustling ports, trans-Arctic sea and air routes, and Alaskan agriculture.[28]

[23] See multiple contributions by Philip Steinberg, including 'Mediterranean metaphors: travel, translations, and oceanic imaginaries in the "new mediterraneans" of the Arctic Ocean, the Caribbean, and the Gulf of Mexico', in J. Anderson and K. Peters, eds., *Water worlds: Human geographies of the ocean* (Farnham, 2014), pp. 23–37; Steinberg, 'U.S. Arctic policy: Reproducing hegemony in a maritime region', in Robert W. Murray and Anita Dey Nuttall, eds., *International relations and the Arctic: Understanding policy and governance* (Amherst, NY, 2014), pp. 165–90.

[24] Fridtjof Nansen, *In northern mists: Arctic exploration in early times*, trans. Arthur G. Chater, 2 vols. (London, 1911).

[25] Igor Krupnik, Claudio Aporta, Shari Gearheard, Gita J. Laidler and Lene Kielsen Holm, eds., *SIKU: Knowing our ice* (Heidelberg, 2010).

[26] Knud Rasmussen, *Polarforskningens saga* [The saga of polar exploration], in Aage Krarup Nielsen, ed., *Jordens Erobring* [The conquering of the world], VI (Copenhagen, 1932).

[27] Adolf Erik Nordenskiöld, *Facsimile-Atlas to the early history of cartography with reproductions of the most important maps printed in the XV and XVI centuries*, trans. Johan Adolf Ekelöf and Clements R. Markham (New York, 1889); Adolf Erik Nordenskiöld, *Periplus: An essay on the early history of charts and sailing directions*, trans. Francis A. Bather (Stockholm, 1897).

[28] V. Stefansson, *The northward course of empire* (New York, 1922); Gísli Pálsson, *Travelling passions: The hidden life of Vilhjalmur Stefansson*, trans. Keneva Kunz (Winnipeg, MB, 2005).

280   S. Sörlin

The history of Arctic maritime exploration makes up a library of something that is almost a genre of its own.[29] Add to this the travelogues and the memoirs, and polar self-chronicling easily outstrips that of scientists in general, chiefly because of the conditions of the book market, where, still-rare polar books and charts became collector's items already in the seventeenth and eighteenth centuries, and were a major trade in the nineteenth. The country where the Arctic Ocean meant the most was Russia, given the long trading distance for Russian export products, and consequently oceanography and research on fisheries was very active there since the nineteenth century. It also stimulated works of geography and fiction and the Arctic Ocean was from a fairly early stage a central element in the emerging national narrative and passed on as such from Tzarist to Soviet Russia. The Arctic sea served as a projection of national imaginaries and the stage for past achievements and future visions.[30] As late as 1926 a reputable Russian geologist working in Siberia, Vladimir A. Obruchev, used a paradise myth on earth beyond the Arctic ice in his science fiction novel *Sannikov's land.* He based the novel on scientific hypotheses from geology and anthropology and proclaimed the possibility of indigenous people living on a warm volcanic island beyond the ice. He symbolically pushed Siberia into the Arctic Ocean and in his own way justified Soviet territorial claims for Arctic islands.[31]

Since 1989, and increasingly since the formation of the Arctic Council in 1996 – with eight member states, all sharing territory within the Arctic circle – work on Arctic Ocean imaginaries has, almost by force, turned their interest towards more integrative and less nationalist approaches, although underlying national interests have remained strong. It could certainly be questioned whether the Arctic Ocean can be fully compared to other new mediterraneans. This has coincided with the rise of interest from geographers and historians and environmental humanists in the sea as a space with a history. Just as the modern era has been characterised by a conflicting set of dynamic and contested spatiality on lands, so has it been marked by a conflicting set of spatial functions at sea. Evidence is marshalled from legal texts, literary and artistic creations, cartographic representations,

[29] An early and emblematic example is E. Sargent, *The wonders of the Arctic world: A history of all the researches and discoveries in the frozen regions of the North* (Philadelphia, PA, 1873).

[30] Eva Marie Stolberg, ' "From icy backwater to nuclear waste ground": The Russian Arctic Ocean in the twentieth century', in Charlotte Mathieson, ed., *Sea narratives: Cultural responses to the sea, 1600–present* (London, 2016), pp. 111–33.

[31] S. K. Frank, 'Arctic science and fiction: A novel by a Soviet geologist', *Journal of Northern Studies*, 1 (2010): 67–86.

The Arctic Ocean 281

advertisements, commercial and military history and policy debates. It has been proposed that lessons learned from the history of the ocean may be applied to other emerging spaces, such as cyberspace, which are also characterised by difficulty in adapting to the institutions of state governance.[32]

Prehistoric Coastal Settlements

Human use of the Arctic Sea is known throughout the Holocene (since the last glaciation) and may have also occurred in the Pleistocene. The drowning of Beringia at the end of the last Ice Age, a formative event in the history of the Arctic Ocean, meant the loss of some of the sites of the migrating first populations into North America. The remaining sites of the Palaeo-Arctic culture are the earliest evidence of a coastal Arctic culture in the western hemisphere in current Alaska since 11,000 BP.

Migrating slowly to the east over many centuries there have been human coastal activities. Coastal settlements were rare and likely seasonal in the North American Arctic as part of the so called Small Tools Culture, a common name for the Dorset and Thule Cultures covering the period from c. 4,500 BP up to European contact. Hunting of large mammals was common to provide protein. The population used harpoons and breathing holes for sealing. Dwellings close to the shores went low into the surface in contrast to more permanent inland dwellings which were dug deep for protection. Temporary houses of snow were also built on the sea ice for which snow knives of stone and bone have been preserved. These cultures may also have used boats, both from Canadian and Greenland coasts. They may also have been expanding and retreating with natural climate variation that affected the length of seasonal ice-free conditions.[33]

In the eastern Arctic, current Scandinavia and Russia, coastal communities are likewise known for several thousand years. The Norwegian Komsa culture, in evidence from approximately 12,000 BP, was mainly oriented towards the sea for fishing and sealing.[34] A theory of Stone Age

---

[32] Philip E. Steinberg, *The social construction of the ocean* (Cambridge, 2010).

[33] Robert Park, 'Adapting to a frozen coastal environment', in Timothy Pauketat, ed., *The Oxford handbook of North American archaeology* (Oxford, 2012), pp. 113–23; S. Funder and K. Kjær, 'Ice free Arctic Ocean, an early Holocene analogue', *Eos, Transactions of the American Geophysical Union*, 88 (2007): 52; Peter Rowly-Conwy, ed., 'Arctic archaeology', special issue of *World Archaeology*, 30 (1999): 3.

[34] Bjørnar Olsen, *Bosetning og samfunn i Finnmarks forhistorie* (Oslo, 1994); Grahame Clark, *The earlier stone age settlement of Scandinavia* (Cambridge, 2009).

282   S. Sörlin

settlements in Svalbard since c. 5000 BP, based on alleged stone tool findings, remains unsupported.[35]

Establishing the Ocean

Encounters between Arctic Ocean coastal communities and temporary settlements and cultures and people from elsewhere are not known until historical times. In Antiquity there are tales of travels to vaguely described northern lands, for example that of Pytheas of Massalia in 325 BCE to 'Thule', which may have been Norway or the Shetland Islands. The Norse settlements in the North Atlantic were on the fringes of an Arctic Ocean history but provided most of the early Arctic Ocean encounters that helped draw the contours of the ocean for European elites. In the European Middle Ages Norse colonisers sailed to places such as Ellesmere Island, Skraeling Island and Ruin Island for hunting expeditions and trading with the Inuit and people of the Dorset culture.[36] The local Inuit, or *skraeling* population (so called by the Norse), were in several skirmishes with the colonisers and added to their weakening and final abandonment of their Greenland colony which coincided with the onset of a long cooling period from the late Middle Ages.[37] The accessible entry point to the Arctic Ocean was through the thermohaline warming Atlantic, and as geographical interest and seafaring skills grew in Europe in the late Middle Ages and the early modern period the Arctic Ocean drew increasing attention and curiosity. Cartographers, lacking information, rendered the region – still known under names such as *Septentrionalis*, or *Boreas* – 'Arctic'. It had long been a mythical place.

Renaissance and early modern speculation got most of its visions from Greek sources. Tales of the northern 'Thule' and of a 'Hyperborean' people, living north of Boreas, the northern wind, by Herodotus and many other authors, were surprisingly merry, presenting an exuberant and liveable region of remarkable beauty. The trope lived on all through to Linnaeus in the eighteenth century, who praised the virtues of winter, with ice skating and the friction free logistics of sled travel, and to Vilhjalmur Stefansson in the twentieth, whose imaginary of the Arctic

---

[35] Hein B. Bjerck, 'Stone Age settlement on Svalbard?: A re-evaluation of previous finds and the results of a recent field survey', *Polar Record*, 36 (2000): 97–112.

[36] P. Schledermann and K. M. McCullough, 'Inuit–Norse contact in the Smith Sound region', in James H. Barrett, ed., *Contact, continuity, and collapse: The Norse colonization of the North Atlantic* (Turnhout, 2003), pp. 183–205.

[37] Alfred Crosby, *Ecological Imperialism* (Cambridge, 1985); Gustaf Utterström, 'Climatic fluctuations and population problems in early modern history', *Scandinavian Economic History Review*, 3 (1955): 3–47.

The Arctic Ocean 283

Ocean turned it into a domesticated Polar Mediterranean of trade and exchange.[38] Yet for some time there was little consensus on what existed so far north. Was it land or sea? Some cartographers, for example Johannes Ruysch in 1507 and Gerardus Mercator in 1595, drew it as land, or a set of islands, keeping with interpretations of the vague Hyperborean geography that could be drawn from ancient sources. The 1539 *Carta Marina* map by Swedish Catholic chronicler Olaus Magnus, published in Rome, used the typical *miracula* and *mirabilia* in the shape of sea monsters to impress the Church and draw attention to the North and possibly return it from Protestant reformation to the pope. Olaus Magnus had good information of the terrestrial North, but lacking information on the Arctic Ocean there was not much he could insert there. He did, however, include the phrase *Mare glaciale* and depicted appropriate ice floes close to what must be Greenland, where he had pencilled in some armoured cavalry.[39] Others followed Olaus Magnus and preferred to regard it as sea, like Willem Barents and Martin Waldseemüller, arguably the most influential of Renaissance mapmakers.

By the late sixteenth century the perception that the far north consisted at least to a large extent of open sea became dominant, chiefly informed by explorers navigating to Spitsbergen and encountering only sea, much of it covered with ice (see below). The recurring speculations of northern sea routes to the East maintained the interest in an Arctic Ocean. Early expeditions to discover the Northwest Passage were undertaken in 1497 by John Cabot, dispatched by Henry VII; in 1524 by Estêvão Gomes on the commission of emperor Charles V; and in 1576 by Martin Frobisher, travelling through what is now the Canadian Arctic.[40] Only later did explorers enter the Arctic Ocean proper. Alexander McKenzie, travelling in 1789 down the river that now carries his name all the way to the Arctic Ocean, repeated the Arctic paradise trope: 'Set nets and catch the Tickameg, Carp-Perch-Pike-and the Unknown Fish-Geese, Ducks, Swans and breed here in great numbers-Water not least Salt-quite fresh-Owls found here-and Sacuttim berries.'[41]

---

[38] Timothy P. Bridgman, *Hyperboreans: Myth and history in Celtic-Hellenic contacts* (New York, 2005). Linnaeus's winter lore is in his foreword to Carl Renmarck, *De praestantia orbis Sviogothici* (Uppsala, 1747).

[39] The best analysis of the Arctic Ocean lore of Olaus Magnus is Kurt Johannesson, *Götisk renässans: Johannes och Olaus Magnus som politiker och historiker* (Uppsala, 1982). See also Michael Roberts, *The Early Vasas* (Cambridge, 1969).

[40] Samuel Morison, *The European discovery of America: The northern voyages* (New York, 1971).

[41] McKenzie's journal cited in Byrne, *Geographies*, pp. 106–7.

284   S. Sörlin

Entering the Polity

The first major economic and political activity in the Arctic Ocean concerned resource extraction, a pattern that has remained largely unchanged to this day. After the discovery of Spitsbergen in 1596 by Willem Barents, who also drew a map of the Arctic Ocean in 1599, and eyewitness reports in the following years of the excess availability of whales, walrus and seals a bonanza of whaling expeditions to harvest maritime resources was triggered. These expeditions were first summer campaigns, only from the 1630s occasionally including wintering, and initially with Basque expert whalers hired by the participating nations. At its peak the Svalbard whaling was a major operation. The Dutch set up the Smeerenburg station which was sometimes called a 'city', employing 200 people, with bars and restaurants. By the late seventeenth century there were, in peak years, several hundred ships and in excess of 10,000 whalers around Spitsbergen.

Claims were made on the islands, first by the Danish crown in 1616, including Jan Mayen, which was before the Danes founded their colony in Greenland in 1721. Denmark, which until 1814 included Norway, founded their position on the fact that the entire North Sea had always been Norwegian tax land. A few years earlier, in 1613, the English Muscovy Company had also claimed ownership based on their charter from the English Crown granting a monopoly on whaling in Spitsbergen, based on the (erroneous) claim that Hugh Willoughby had discovered the land in 1553 and discoveries made by Henry Hudson during his first Arctic voyage in 1607.[42] Initially the English tried to drive away competitors; but after disputes with the Dutch (1613–24), they claimed only the bays south of Kongsfjorden. The Dutch rejected the English exclusive rights, claiming the *mare liberum* principle.

The perceived value of the resource, and this northern ocean, manifested in the events that unfolded. First, England offered to purchase the rights from Denmark–Norway in 1614, but the Danes refused and instead sent warships to collect taxes from English and Dutch whalers. The English also sent warships to Spitsbergen and for a few years European powers were on the brink of a resource war in the Arctic Ocean. An interesting situation occurred, namely that some countries

---

[42] Joost C. A. Schokkenbroek, *Trying-out: An anatomy of Dutch whaling and sealing in the nineteenth century, 1815–1885* (Amsterdam, 2008); Thor Bjorn Arlov, *A short history of Svalbard* (Oslo, 1994). On Hudson's first Arctic voyage, Dagomar Degroot, 'Exploring the North in a changing climate: The Little Ice Age and the journals of Henry Hudson, 1607–1611', *Journal of Northern Studies*, 9 (2015): 77–79.

The Arctic Ocean

(Denmark and England) claimed sovereignty whereas France, the Netherlands and Spain claimed it a free zone under *mare liberum*. A certain partition of the whaling also took place with the French in the northeast, the English further south, and the Dutch, who had started their own Noordsche Compagnie were active in the northwest with the Danes. This arrangement gradually lowered the tension and from the 1630s incidents of conflict were rare. Whaling and sealing continued, although with fewer participating countries and was dominated by the British during the eighteenth century.[43] There were also hunting of walrus conducted by the northwest Russian hunting and fishing Pomor population.[44]

The Spitsbergen whaling wars, marginal as they turned out to be, were the more important as they initiated the period of Danish colonialism. It had outliers in Africa (the Guinea Coast), India (Tranquebar, now Tharangambadi) and the Caribbean (Virgin Islands), but essentially it was a North Atlantic and Arctic Ocean empire with Norway, Iceland and Greenland as the main assets along with the smaller Faroe Islands.[45] This development could also be seen as an opening phase of a more general Scandinavian colonial relationship with the northern oceans.

Norway, assuming semi-autonomy in a union with Sweden from 1814, largely continued the Danish colonial resource expansionism in the north and this became a central theme of Norwegian foreign policy after full independence in 1905, then including Antarctica and the South Seas. Sweden, similarly, made colonialist forays to Spitsbergen based on mineral deposits there, often spearheaded by entrepreneurially minded scientists and explorers. Sweden also started new mines, but gave this up after World War I when coal prices dropped in the 1920s recession and the Svalbard Treaty fundamentally changed the rules of the resource game and gave most of the authority to Norway.[46]

---

[43] The standard account of Svalbard whaling is Arlov, *A short history of Svalbard*.

[44] On Russian hunting, see Margarita Dadykina, Alexei Kraikovski and Julia Lajus, 'Mastering the Arctic marine environment: Organizational practices of Pomor hunting expeditions to Svalbard (Spitsbergen) in the eighteenth century', *Acta Borealia* (2017), in press, online 8 May 2017 DOI: 10.1080/08003831.2017.1322265 (accessed 31 May 2017).

[45] Pernille Ipsen and Gunlög Fur, 'Introduction to Scandinavian colonialism', *Itinerario*, 33 (2009): 7–16.

[46] Dag Avango, Louwrens Hacquebord and Urban Wrakberg, 'Industrial extraction of Arctic natural resources since the sixteenth century: Technoscience and geo-economics in the history of northern whaling and mining', *Journal of Historical Geography*, 44 (2014): 15–30; Dag Avango, Louwrens Hacquebord, Ypie Aalders, Hidde De Haas, Ulf Gustafsson and Frigga Kruse, 'Between markets and geo-politics: Natural resource exploitation on Spitsbergen from 1600 to the present day', *Polar Record*, 47 (2010): 29–39.

286   S. Sörlin

Knowing the Ocean

Knowing the Arctic Ocean has to a large extent been about knowing Arctic sea ice, both in Western science and by indigenous populations. Knowing sea ice is a deeply sensory, tactile experience that cannot be treated separately from one's life world, personal or local temporalities or from society.[47] It is an element where everyday space and time not only change but have also undergone processes of what we might call inadvertent scaling and synchrony. Globalisation and modernity have brought a common frame; the realities of Earth system science and climate change are as well known here as anywhere else. Things happen in Arctic communities in close relationship with things happening elsewhere in the world.[48]

Early scientific study was supported by the British Admiralty, as in so many other oceans. Sir John Ross and his nephew John Ross made deepsea soundings to a depth of possibly 600 fathoms in 1818.[49] A decade later, William Parry conducted his 'crusade' for the magnetic North Pole, and indirectly made a strong case for a science of the northern ocean. Indeed, the rise of Arctic exploration in the nineteenth century coincided with the rise of oceanography, mountaineering and meteorology; they were all linked to the scientific underpinning of Western imperial hegemony that became increasingly interested in navigation and the geographical knowledge and political control of natural resources.[50]

Glaciology belonged in the same group of sciences, and the object of its study covered most of the Arctic Ocean, and was the object of measurement and noted in logs by whaling vessels during the nineteenth century. Even longer historical records of ice cover exist from coastal seas bordering on the Arctic Ocean, for example the Barents Sea, where a record has been compiled covering four centuries.[51] Systematic records of the position of the sea-ice margin around the Arctic Ocean have been compiled for the period since 1870.[52] Although there was a widespread

---

[47] Shari Fox Gearheard, Lene Kielsen Holm, Henry Huntington, Joe Mello Leavitt, Andrew R. Mahoney, Margaret Opie, Toku Oshima and Joelie Sanguya, eds., *The meaning of ice: People and ice in three Arctic communities* (Hanover, NH, 2013).

[48] Paglia, 'The northward course of the Anthropocene'.

[49] A. L. Rice, 'The oceanography of John Ross' Arctic Expedition of 1818: A reappraisal', *Journal of the Society for the Bibliography of Natural History*, 7 (1975): 291–319.

[50] Helen M. Rozwadowski, *Fathoming the ocean: The discovery and exploration of the deep sea* (Cambridge, MA, 2005), pp. 30–32, 94.

[51] T. Vinje, 'Barents Sea ice edge variation over the past 400 years', *Extended Abstracts, Workshop on Sea-Ice Charts of the Arctic* (Seattle, WA, 1999); Dimitry V. Divine and Chad Dick, 'Historical variability of sea ice edge position in the Nordic seas', *Journal of Geophysical Research – Atmospheres*, 111(C01001) (2006).

[52] J. E. Walsh and W. L. Chapman, 'Twentieth-century sea ice variations from observational data', *Annals of Glaciology*, 33 (2001): 444–48.

The Arctic Ocean   287

opinion in the nineteenth and twentieth centuries that the Arctic was always covered by perennial ice, both on large parts of its land mass and on the Arctic sea, it was an idea with some significant exceptions.[53]

The systematic study of sea ice in the Western science tradition is comparatively late. Observations and skilful reflection on sea ice was started as some nations, notably the United Kingdom, were searching for the Northwest Passage. British whaler-scientist William Scoresby was a notable presence in the period after the Napoleonic wars, combining economic (whaling) and strategic (Northwest Passage) interests with methodological rigour, and making productive use of vernacular knowledge as scientific data collection had scarcely begun.[54]

The Arctic ice may have its gaps and holes. There was, for example, until the 1880s still some belief in the notion of a green central Greenland, fuelled by observations of floating timber in the waters near the big island.[55] Ideas of an ice-free Arctic were presented in the leading geographical journals and magazines in the latter decades of the nineteenth century such as *Petermann's Geographische Mitteilungen.* The trope had been increasingly present already in the nineteenth century and became interesting again when the period of interwar Arctic warming had begun to be noticed in the 1920s and 1930s.[56]

The Bellwether Ocean

The modern history of the Arctic Ocean is marked by its increasing role as an indicator, or bellwether, of global climate and environmental change.[57] This is a remarkable position for a region that only a few generations before was seen from the south as marginal and isolated from

---

[53] Leonid Polyak, Richard B. Alley, John T. Andrews, Julie Brigham-Grette, Thomas M. Cronin, Dennis A. Darby, Arthur S. Dyke, Joan J. Fitzpatrick, Svend Visby Funder, Marika Holland, Anne E. Jennings, Gifford H. Miller, Matt O'Regan, James Savelle, Mark Serreze, Kristen St John, James W. C. White and Eric Wolff, 'History of sea ice in the Arctic', *Quaternary Science Reviews*, 2 (2010): 1757–78.

[54] M. T. Bravo, 'Preface: Legacies of polar science', in Jessica M. Shadian and Monica Tennberg, eds., *Legacies and change in polar sciences: Historical, legal and political reflections on the International Polar Year* (Aldershot, 2009), pp. xiii–xvi.

[55] A. E. Nordenskiöld, *Den andra Dicksonska expeditionen till Grönland: Dess inre isöken och dess ostkust: Utförd år 1883 under befäl af AE Nordenskiöld* (Stockholm, 1885); T. Örtenblad, 'Om Sydgrönlands drifved', *Bidrag till Kungl. Vetenskapsakademiens Handlingar*, 6 (1881).

[56] J. K. Wright, 'The open Polar Sea', *Geographical Review*, 43 (1953): 338–65; S. Sörlin, and J. Lajus, 'An ice free Arctic sea?: The science of sea ice and its interests', in M. Christensen, A. E. Nilsson, and N. Wormbs, eds., *Media and the politics of Arctic climate change: When the ice breaks* (New York, 2013), pp. 70–92; B. Luedtke, 'An ice-free Arctic Ocean: History, science, and scepticism', *Polar Record*, 51(2) (2015): 130–39.

[57] N. Wormbs, R. Döscher, A. E. Nilsson and S. Sörlin, 'Bellwether, exceptionalism, and other tropes: Political coproduction of Arctic climate modeling', in Matthias Heymann, Gabriele Gramelsberger and Martin Mahony, eds., *Cultures of prediction: Epistemic and cultural shifts in computer-based atmospheric and climate science* (New York, 2017), pp. 133–55.

288   S. Sörlin

the rest of the world. This reflects a new scientific understanding, both of the Earth system and the role of the Arctic in it. Sea ice is a central component of that change. If cold, ice and snow were always in play as determinants of anthropology and history, we now also have a literature on the retreat of ice, especially a discourse of the warming Arctic.[58] What used to be an Arctic trope, the coming and going of ice and snow, the capricious play of climate with culture in that remote stretch of human presence, has expanded to become a global predicament in which the Arctic Ocean is an indicator of global climates and a factor in global anxieties.

The waning ice of the Arctic Ocean links excesses of modern consumer society and industrialism to disastrous impacts on the innocent original populations, whose vulnerability, despite a long history of successful adaptation, is aggravated when the ice melts.[59] At the same time the question can be asked where the authority of knowledge about this elusive material rests. Local communities – carriers of traditional knowledge and technology – are increasingly living alongside scientifically trained ice and glacier experts.[60] The latter have made direct observations on ice concentrations spanning the Arctic since the middle of the twentieth century. Since the arrival of satellites for monitoring of the global cryosphere from around 1970 there has been a comprehensive record of sea-ice data from the Arctic Ocean with the modern satellite records starting in 1979.[61] Since the 1990s, data show a consistent co-variation with the increased rates of atmospheric CO_2, only that the effects on sea ice are disproportionately big. The same goes for Arctic temperatures that exceed the global average. This 'Arctic amplification' of global climate change has a strong ocean component.[62] Today it has to a large extent taken over the narrative of the Arctic, which is commonly linked to threatened polar bears and economic opportunities following

[58] Stefansson, *Northward course of empire*; S. Sörlin, 'Cryo-history: Ice, snow, and the great acceleration', in Julia Herzberg, Christian Kehrt and Franziska Torma, eds., *Snow and ice in the Cold War: Histories of extreme climatic environments* (New York and Oxford: Berghahn Books, in press).

[59] Krupnik et al., *SIKU: Knowing our ice*; Kirsten Hastrup, 'The icy breath: Modalities of climate knowledge in the Arctic', *Current Anthropology*, 53 (2012): 226–44; Hastrup, 'Anticipation on thin ice: Diagrammatic reasoning', in Hastrup and M. Skrydstrup, eds., *The social life of climate change models: Anticipating nature* (New York, 2013), pp. 77–99.

[60] Kirsten Hastrup, *Thule: Paa tidens rand* (Copenhagen, 2015).

[61] D. J. Cavalieri, C. L. Parkinson and K. Y. Vinnikov, '30-year satellite record reveals contrasting Arctic and Antarctic decadal sea ice variability', *Geophysical Research Letters*, 30 (2003): 18. Nina Wormbs, 'Eyes on the ice: Satellite remote sensing and the narratives of visualized data', in Miyase Christensen, Annika E. Nilsson and Nina Wormbs, *Media and the politics of Arctic climate change*, pp. 52–69.

[62] R. V. Bekryaev, I. V. Polyakov and V. A. Alexeev, 'The role of polar amplification in long-term surface air temperature variations and modern arctic warming', *Journal of Climatology*, 23 (2010): 3888–906.

The Arctic Ocean   289

the waning ice, putting at peril a more integrated, historically informed understanding including local populations and issues of power, voice and social context.[63]

The bellwether trope of the Arctic Ocean has co-evolved with broader changes in the scientific description of the Earth system. But an essential component was a rapidly growing body of knowledge from the ocean itself. During the nineteenth century there had been several expeditions, some motivated by the search for the Northwest Passage or the North Pole and their scientific findings transformed the understanding of the Arctic Ocean from a basin of low diversity and few species to one of rich marine fauna. Towards the end of the century Russian scientists and marine officers initiated sea-ice observations and started to accumulate the data that provide the baselines for later changes, assisted by the mighty Arctic icebreaker *Yermak* from 1899. Oceanographers Nikolai Knipowitsch and Nikolai Zubov could establish a warming trend in the Barents Sea in the interwar period and a persistent pattern of diminishing sea ice.[64] The interest in melting and strangely behaving sea ice resulted in a significant growth of publications in several countries, not least on research methods and terminological issues; the trope of the ice-free Arctic Ocean required technologies and research infrastructures, and became increasingly linked to security and national economic interest.[65]

In the 1930s Soviet scientists stood out as exceptionally active and skilled, playing a key role in the Second International Polar Year, and in 1937 the USSR opened its longstanding program of ice floe research which was to last throughout the Cold War. The first base was set up on 3-metre thick ice close to the North Pole in March 1937, furnished by several airplanes and boasting measuring instruments in the air, the

---

[63] Andrew Stuhl, *Unfreezing the Arctic: Science, colonialism, and the transformation of Inuit lands* (Chicago, IL, 2016).

[64] N. M. Knipowitsch, 'O termicheskikh usloviiakh Barentseva moria v kontse maia 1921 goda', *Bulleten' Rossiiskogo gidrologicheskogo instituta*, 9 (1921): 10–12; N. N. Zubov, "The circumnavigation of Franz Josef Land', *Geographical Review*, 23 (1933): 394–401, 528. Terence Armstrong, *The Russians in the Arctic* (London, 1958); J. Lajus and S. Sörlin, 'Melting the glacial curtain: The politics of Scandinavian-Soviet networks in the geophysical field sciences between two Polar Years, 1932/33–1957/58', *Journal of Historical Geography*, 42 (2014): 44–59.

[65] Lauge Koch, *The East Greenland ice, Meddelelser om Grønland*, 103, 3 (Copenhagen, 1945); Aleksandr Kolchak, 'The Arctic pack and the polynya', in American Geographical Society of New York, *Problems of Polar research* (New York, 1928), pp. 125–41; F. Malmgren, 'On the properties of sea-ice', in H. U. Sverdrup, ed., *Norwegian North Polar expedition with the 'Maud' 1918–1925: Scientific results* 1, 5 (Bergen, 1927); E. H. Smith, 'Ice in the sea', chapter 10 of *Physics of the Earth V: Oceanography* (Washington, DC, 1932), pp. 384–408; N. A. Transehe, 'The ice cover of the Arctic Sea, with a genetic classification of sea ice', *Problems of polar research* (New York, 1928), pp. 91–123. A. Maurstad, *Atlas of sea ice: Geofysiske publikasjoner*, 10, 11 (Oslo, 1935).

290   S. Sörlin

ice and the ocean beneath. In February 1938 the 'North Pole' station drifted out to the Greenland Sea, and after several attempts, the camp was evacuated successfully with the help of an icebreaker. The lingering ideas about the lifeless deep Arctic Ocean were disproved. It was also discovered that rain, fog and unstable weather were typical for the central Arctic Ocean. After 1954, Soviet field work on the drifting ice became regular; every year one, two or sometimes even four ice camps operated in the Arctic Ocean.[66] In the early 1950s the US initiated a similar, but more short-lived, programme on massive concentrations of ice, so called ice islands, north of Barrow, Alaska.[67] The US Navy began charting sea-ice conditions from reconnaissance flights in 1947 and began a sustained ice observing and forecasting programme a few years later.[68] Canadian agencies were asked to contribute with station-based monitoring data.

Alongside the major powers, oceanographic research grew in scope and intensity, and was increasingly based on permanent research stations and long-term programmes; availability of data grew. Among those who attempted to predict future ice conditions was the head of the Canadian Defence Research Board's Arctic division, Graham Rowley, who suggested in 1952 that 'an open polar sea' was a possibility in less than thirty years.[69] Rowley's US Army counterpart, the bio-geographer Paul A. Siple, likewise predicted, in 1953, a possible ice-free Arctic Ocean in half a century. Both Rowley and Siple related the vanishing of summer sea ice to (likely natural) climate variation, that now rose to the status of national security concern.[70]

Becoming a Meta-Geographical Space

The transformation into the bellwether Arctic Ocean came through an interplay between the growing oceanographic knowledge and the changes in global understanding of environmental issues. It was especially the understanding of anthropogenic climate change, established

---

[66] 'North Pole Drifting Stations (1930s–1980s): History', website published by the Woods Hole Oceanographic Institute, Massachusetts, USA: www.whoi.edu/beaufortgyre/history/history_drifting.html (accessed 31 May 2017). See also A. F. Treshnikov, 'Results of the oceanological investigations by the "North Pole" drifting stations', *Polar Geography*, 1 (1977): 22–40.

[67] J. E. Sater, *Arctic drifting stations* (Washington, DC, 1964).

[68] *Report of the ice observing and forecasting program, 1958* (Washington, DC, 1958), p. 2.

[69] Peder Roberts, 'Scientists and sea ice under surveillance', in S. Turchetti and P. Roberts, eds., *The surveillance imperative: Geosciences during the Cold War* (New York, 2014), pp. 125–45.

[70] P. A. Siple, *Proposal for consideration by the US National Committee (IGY)*. 1 May 1953, C1, *USNC-IGY* (Washington, DC, 1953).

The Arctic Ocean

291

in the two last decades of the twentieth century that provided a new rationale for an Arctic dimension. The result was a 'new north' or 'future Arctic' narratives in which concepts such as vulnerability, adaptation and sustainability became paramount.[71] The transformation was fundamental. Up until World War II the central Arctic Ocean was seen as largely frozen and potentially next to lifeless and with no significance for the rest of the world (which is not to say that near-terrestrial parts of the ocean were not of high interest for Arctic countries including the Nordic countries). It was not a dead zone, but not far from it. Yet in just a brief period the Arctic Ocean became precisely the opposite: full of life, with a sensitive environment and the world's most drastically changing climate.

It is necessary to acknowledge here the co-existence of the history of the Arctic Ocean as a physical entity and the history of the images and readings of it. These histories should be understood as co-evolving, but there is also a reason to see an independent logic in each of them. The natural history of the Arctic Ocean has provided a geophysical underpinning of future narratives that serve certain geopolitical interests. Business and industrial interests, and many states, from the US and Russia to China and India – leading powers of the world – share an interest in the accessibility of resources following from reduction of sea ice, opening of seaways and a historical framing that glosses over the permanent presence of, albeit small, Arctic populations and presents the Arctic Ocean as a blank, white slate, open for adventure and resource exploitation. This narrative relies heavily on natural knowledge since it seems as if it is through a climate intervention that the change happens. The modern history of the Arctic Ocean is hence presented through climate as 'a driver'. This is a history with very little agency and most of it located outside of the region itself.

A history which brings the narrative closer to experiences inside the region needs to take a more selective and integrative view of outside 'drivers'. One thing to consider, then, is to balance the natural history (or 'species history', to use Dipesh Chakrabarty's thought-provoking concept),[72] with the political histories of the Arctic Ocean. These have yet to be fully analysed, but one part of them is clearly the growth of legislation and institutions. The recent reframing of the history of the Arctic Ocean, its geophysical and environmental turn, has offered a rationale to institutions such as the Inuit Circumpolar Council, and the Arctic Council, both founded in the mid-1990s. The Arctic Council works to establish

---

[71] Marcus Carson, ed., *Arctic Resilience Report* (Stockholm, 2016).
[72] Dipesh Chakrabarty, 'The climate of history: Four theses', *Critical Inquiry*, 35 (2009): 299–327.

292   S. Sörlin

evidence for action but has no political decision-making power. It works through assessments and other knowledge-based documents on issues that the eight member states have been able to agree on. It could be argued that this is in practice a post-political turn of Arctic affairs, pushing back issues of power, human rights and environmental concern.[73]

The notion that local people are impacted by the reduction of sea ice was not much in circulation until the anthropogenic climate change narrative was established on a broad basis.[74] This should come as no surprise. In the Western perspective sea ice has for hundreds of years, and not just since the sinking of the *Titanic* in 1912 (a year of unusual southern spread of sea ice in the Newfoundland area),[75] been regarded as a risk and an obstacle to the economic value of the Arctic, which lay in whaling, sealing, shipping and mineral and fossil-fuel extraction.[76] This is the opposite of the value ice represents to Arctic populations like the Inuit, for whom the sea ice – hunting ground, livelihood, medium of travel, play and wayfaring – is awaited with expectation, and where November, the usual first month of sea ice, is called *Tusaqtuut*, 'the news season'.

But equally important is to write local populations and cultures into the history of the Arctic Ocean. Interestingly this work has for a long time been done mostly by geographers, anthropologists and scholars of religion, who have felt compelled to navigate the past as they have made sense of the present.[77] Perhaps this is a natural effect of the unconventional history that unfolds for those who wish to unpack the Arctic Ocean; the histories and narratives produced are often insightful and impressive. However, as the Arctic Ocean is now, finally, becoming a meta-geographical project and drawn into global environmental, human rights and geo-politics, we can see how, correspondingly, a professional historiography is gradually emerging. It is timely and is, in and of itself, evidence of the silent patience of history as an enterprise: slowly but surely covering every space of the globe with some kind of meaningful narrative, which will surely be immediately contested.

---

[73] Nina Wormbs and Sverker Sörlin, 'Arctic futures: Agency and assessing assessments', in Lill-Ann Körber, Scott MacKenzie and Anna Westerståhl Stenport, eds., *Arctic environmental modernities: From the age of polar exploration to the era of the Anthropocene* (London, 2017), pp. 263–85. For the concept, see E. Swyngedouw, 'Depoliticized environments: The end of nature, climate change and the post-political condition', *Royal Institute of Philosophy Supplement* (2011): 69.

[74] Krupnik et al. *SIKU: Knowing our ice*, bears evidence to this.

[75] Smith, 'Ice in the sea', 404.

[76] M. T. Bravo, 'The humanism of sea ice', in Krupnik et al, *SIKU: Knowing our ice*, pp. 447–48.

[77] For example, Michael Bravo, Kirsten Hastrup, Igor Krupnik, all cited above.

The Arctic Ocean   293

Further Reading

The closest one gets to a general description of the Arctic Ocean as a common space is through literature from the geophysical sciences. A good place to start is chapter 1 of Rüdiger Stein and Robie W. Macdonald, eds., *The organic carbon cycle in the Arctic Ocean* (Berlin, 2004), which offers a comprehensive view of the geographic, oceanographic and climatic changes in the Arctic ocean over the last several glaciation cycles, based on the state of knowledge at the beginning of the new millennium. Two state of the art reports from the Arctic Council provide a review in accessible form of several trends and issues mainly to do with recent and ongoing, and threatening, change in the Arctic environment. *The Arctic resilience report* (Oslo and Stockholm, 2016) has a broad remit and discusses the Arctic Ocean only parsimoniously, which is a good indicator of how terrestrial, and possibly atmospheric, the geographical concept of the Arctic has become. The other report, *Arctic Ocean review – final report* (Oslo and Akureyri, Iceland, 2015), puts the Arctic Ocean centre stage and is focused especially on maritime governance. Still useful for its comprehensive coverage of climate effects on both terrestrial and coastal Arctic communities is the *Arctic climate impact assessment report* (Cambridge, 2004). A brief, general background to latter day concerns is offered by Paul Arthur Berkman's book-length Whitehall Paper series report, *Environmental security in the Arctic Ocean: Promoting co-operation and preventing conflict* (London, 2010) with separate chapters on governance, security and the legal regime wrapped in a largely contemporary framing with forays into the Cold War era. Also focusing on legal regimes is Suzanne Lalonde and Ted L. McDorman, eds., *International law and politics of the Arctic Ocean: Essays in honor of Donat Pharand* (Leiden, 2015), although with a special focus on the Canadian Arctic archipelago and the disputes between the US and Canada over access to the Northwest Passage. It has a solid coverage of the last one hundred years, for example in an essay by P. Whitney Lackenbauer and Peder Kikkert, 'The dog in the manger – and letting sleeping dogs lie: The United States, Canada and the sectoral principle, 1924–1955', pp. 216–39. Also focusing on legal issues are Klaus Dodds and Richard C. Powell, eds., *Polar geopolitics: Knowledges, resources and legal regimes* (Cheltenham, 2014), and Leif Christian Jensen and Geir Hønneland, eds., *Handbook of the politics of the Arctic* (Cheltenham, 2015), with several contributions probing into the historical background to current territorial treaties and disputes. A still useful and very thorough introduction to the legal history of Spitsbergen is Geir Ulfstein, *The Svalbard*

294   S. Sörlin

Treaty: From terra nullius to Norwegian sovereignty (Oslo, 1995). Older Arctic histories tended to be national or local, or focus on the history of exploration. At the tail end of that long period of historiography we find works such as Pierre Berton, *Arctic grail: The quest for the Northwest Passage and the North Pole, 1818–1909* (NewYork, 1988). A more recent comprehensive history of the entire region, with a focus on resources, science and environment is John McCannon, *A history of the Arctic: Nature, exploration and exploitation* (London, 2012). Also wide-ranging with contributions on diplomatic history, maritime resources, cultural heritage and identity formation, particularly in the Nordic countries including Greenland but also Russia, is Sverker Sörlin, ed., *Science, geopolitics and culture in the Polar region – Norden beyond borders* (Farnham, 2013). The discussion of the Arctic as a geographical mega-project is covered by Carina Keskitalo, *Negotiating the Arctic: The construction of an international region* (New York, 2004). Two useful volumes on the Arctic Ocean as a dimension of Russian and Soviet history are John McCannon, *Red Arctic: Polar exploration and the myth of the North in the Soviet Union, 1932–1939* (Oxford, 1999), and Paul R. Josephson, *The conquest of the Russian Arctic* (Cambridge, MA, 2014). The history of science in the Arctic is one of the strands of history that is well covered by work in recent years, for example, Trevor Levere, *Science and the Canadian Arctic: A century of exploration, 1818–1918* (Cambridge, 1993), that obviously focuses on Canada; Michael T. Bravo and Sverker Sörlin, eds., *Narrating the Arctic: A cultural history of Nordic scientific practices* (Canton, MA, 2002), that covers the entire Arctic region; Ronald E. Doel, Kristine C. Harper and Matthias Heymann, eds., *Exploring Greenland: Cold War science and technology on ice* (NewYork, 2016), that focuses on Greenland. Good entry points to the history of Arctic oceanography are found in: Keith R. Benson and Helen M. Rozwadowski, eds., *Extremes: Oceanography's adventures at the Poles* (Sagamore Beach, MA, 2007); Robert Marc Friedman, 'Contexts for constructing an ocean science: The career of Harald Ulrik Sverdrup (1888–1957)', in Keith Rodney Benson and Philip F. Rehbock, eds., *Oceanographic history: The Pacific and beyond* (Seattle, WA, 2002), pp. 17–27; Simone Turchetti and Peder Roberts, eds., *The surveillance imperative: Geosciences during the cold war* (NewYork, 2014); and Julia Lajus and Anatolii Pantiulin, 'Soviet oceanography and the second International PolarYear: National achievements in the international context', in Christiane Groeben, ed., *Places, people, tools: Oceanography in the Mediterranean and beyond* (Naples, 2013), pp. 69–84. A synthetic overview of Arctic science in the twentieth century is Ronald E. Doel, Robert Marc Friedman, Julia Lajus, Sverker Sörlin

The Arctic Ocean 295

and Urban Wråkberg, 'Strategic Arctic science: National interests in building natural knowledge – interwar era through the Cold War', *Journal of Historical Geography*, 42 (2014): 60–80. A growing interest is Arctic environmental history: Dolly Jörgensen and Sverker Sörlin, eds., *Northscapes: History, technology, and the making of Northern environments* (Vancouver, BC, 2013) includes chapters ranging from the history of fossil collecting on Arctic islands to Russian Arctic industrial policy. Andrew Stuhl, *Unfreezing the Arctic: Science, colonialism, and the transformation of Inuit lands* (Chicago, IL, 2016) uses Alaska as its empirical foundation but also offers innovative approaches for how to link marine and terrestrial scientists to different communities such as indigenous populations, whalers and oil drillers. A study of the cultural and aesthetic appreciation of the Arctic and sub-Arctic, with useful observations of maritime travel and collecting, is Angela Byrne, *Geographies of the Romantic North: Science, antiquarianism, and travel, 1790–1830* (New York, 2013). There is a rich literature on impressions and images of the Arctic world, for example R. G. David, *The Arctic in British imagination 1818–1914* (Manchester, 2000). Work on historical dimensions of Arctic climate change has been growing considerably in recent years and in it there is interspersed information about sea ice, coastal communities, issues of sea-level change and other oceanic dimensions: Kirsten Hastrup and Martin Skrydstrup, eds., *The social life of climate change models: Anticipating nature* (New York, 2013); Igor Krupnik, Claudio Aporta, Shari Gearheard, Gita J. Laidler and Lene Kielsen Holm, eds., *SIKU: Knowing our ice* (Heidelberg, 2010); Miyase Christensen, Annika E. Nilsson and Nina Wormbs, eds., *Media and the politics of Arctic climate change: When the ice breaks* (New York, 2013).

11 The Southern Ocean

Alessandro Antonello

The surface waters and winds of the Southern Ocean drive constantly, without interruption by land, from the west around the Antarctic continent. The Antarctic convergence zone dramatically bounds the cold waters of the Southern Ocean at its northern edge, and encloses a marine ecosystem characterised by fewer species than warmer climes and simple, short, ecological relationships among its animal and bird inhabitants. The ocean experiences great seasonal variations, for in winter the water's surface freezes into a great extent of sea ice that substantially retreats each summer. A handful of small islands are dotted through the ocean, minuscule but essential points of passage for seals and birds. The ocean began to take on its modern structure with the slow tectonic opening of the passages between the Antarctic, South American and Australian continents between forty and twenty million years ago, which saw the establishment of the Antarctic Circumpolar Current and the thermal isolation of Antarctica leading to the slow growth of its massive ice sheet.[1]

The Southern Ocean has seen significant human activities since the eighteenth century. As recently as the 1960s and 1970s, however, 'Southern Ocean' was an uncertain and inconsistently applied name for the cold ocean that surrounds Antarctica. European explorers first began to enter into the physical zone of the ocean in the eighteenth century, and in the years since the ocean has been variously named the 'Antarctic seas', the 'Antarctic ocean', the 'southern seas', the 'southern oceans', 'The Icy Sea', or as the southerly extent of the Atlantic, Indian or Pacific Oceans. Sometimes these names for the ocean were applied to the exclusion of others, at other times alongside each other; sometimes these designations were bounded by natural features, sometimes by arbitrary latitudes and longitudes. Indeed, the Southern Ocean's name

---

[1] George A. Knox, *Biology of the Southern Ocean* (Boca Raton, FL, 2007); Beau Riffenburgh, ed., *Encyclopedia of the Antarctic* (New York and London, 2007), pp. 234–39, 344–46, 741–43 and 883–87.

The Southern Ocean

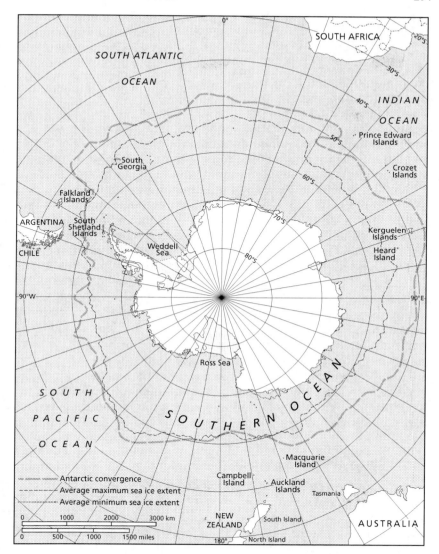

Map 11.1 The Southern Ocean

today remains contested, as it is, for example, the popular term among Australians for the waters that wash Australia's southern shores.

The shifting names of the ocean articulate more than definitional debates, but speak to its history. Since the beginning of European

298   A. Antonello

overseas expansion the 'southern oceans' have denoted a larger region, a great zone of exploration and imagination. With the rationalisation of terrestrial space through discoveries and changing politics in the modern era, there came greater demand for specificity. Since the 1970s, the cold waters surrounding the Antarctic continent, bordered to the north by the Antarctic Convergence, have generally been known as the Southern Ocean in most languages. Greater scientific certainty of biological, oceanographic and atmospheric conditions, and geopolitical developments have seen a stabilisation of the name – though there remains friction in the nomenclature between countries, and between scientific and popular usage.

As an ocean with littorals not conducive to permanent settlements, the Southern Ocean's history is perhaps less encompassing than other great and more settled basins. Though often caught up in grander imperial and geopolitical strategic projects, it has not often been central to them. Nevertheless, the ocean has been a deliberate destination, and engagement with it has been concerted and tenacious. Organised chronologically, this chapter considers the ocean's history within three major themes. First, it explores the ocean as a site of exploitation, resources and commerce, principally the waves of sealing, whaling and fishing. Second, it considers the ocean as an object of geographical, scientific and environmental thinking and sensibilities. And third, this chapter explores the persistent questions of the ocean's place in international and global order, not only in diplomatic forums but also in the less formal internationalisms of science and civil society. Each of these themes is linked, for each of the major activities in, and about, the ocean are inseparable and mutually constitutive.

Early Human Approaches

As the Southern Ocean was increasingly explored in the late eighteenth and early nineteenth centuries, it quickly became enrolled into grand ventures of exploration and empire, as well as becoming an intimate field of human labour and struggle to exploit the natural environment. As the search for southern lands – indeed, for the *terra australis incognita* of ancient and early modern thought – increasingly found wide open oceans, the promise of land receded, to be replaced by the alternative promise of the seas. The voyages of European navigators into this region, notably James Cook of England (who led the first recorded navigation below the Antarctic Circle in 1773) and Louis-Antoine de Bougainville of France (who promoted the first settlement on the Falklands between 1764 and 1767), precipitated

The Southern Ocean 299

deeper commercial interests for its marine wealth and the potential of world trade.[2] The first concerted human activities in the region were extractive and bloody, for they involved the killing of fur seals for their skins, and later of elephant seals for their oil, as well as the killing of right and sperm whales. Killing animals for furs and skins was, of course, a practice as old as humanity itself, but it had also been a practice central to early modern imperial expansion in North America and the North Pacific, developments that John Richards has called, simply, 'the world hunt'.[3]

The sealers of the Southern Ocean in the earliest times came mostly from the New England ports of North America – both before and after independence – and Britain. Through the nineteenth century, American sealers remained a constant presence, joined in smaller numbers by sealers from the colonies of Australia, New Zealand and Southern Africa. Sealers were initially tied to the whaling industry, though within a few years sealing-only voyages were embarked upon. Sealing became a more concerted industry in the south beginning at the Falkland Islands from 1775; and while whaling did occur in the Southern Ocean, at this time it was concentrated in the Arctic and warmer waters.

The sealers' movements through the Southern Ocean and the sub-Antarctic islands were opportunistic and driven by boom-and-bust exploitation. Some lucky sealers would discover beaches onto which fur or elephant seals hauled themselves to breed and moult, especially in the summer months; those lucky sealers would race to take as much as possible before a competitor also discovered the grounds; and then, having exploited the seals so ruthlessly, they would move on to another beach. And though sealers were in the vanguard of settlement and discovery, they nevertheless tended to keep their discoveries and movements secret, protecting their precious commercial advantages. Concerted sealing began at the Falklands in the mid-1770s, and proceeded in waves, moving to South Georgia after 1786, at the Juan Fernandez islands to the west of Chile after 1792, and at Macquarie, Auckland and Campbell islands south of Australia and New Zealand after about 1810. The most pronounced experience of boom-and-bust sealing occurred after the discovery of the South Shetland Islands in 1819, with the two summers

[2] Kenneth J. Bertrand, *Americans in Antarctica 1775–1948* (New York, 1971), ch. 2; David Mackay, *In the wake of Cook: Exploration, science and empire, 1780–1801* (Wellington, 1985), ch. 2; Christopher Hodson, *The Acadian diaspora: An eighteenth-century history* (New York, 2012), ch. 4.
[3] John F. Richards, *The unending frontier: An environmental history of the early modern world* (Berkeley, CA, 2003).

300   A. Antonello

in 1820 to 1822 seeing the almost complete destruction of the fur seal colonies on those islands.[4] There were two peaks of sealing after this, first at the Prince Edward Islands and the Crozets of the South Indian Ocean in the 1840s (which also saw a brief boom in the killing of southern right whales), and finally at the Kerguelen Islands and Heard Island, also in the South Indian Ocean area, in the 1850s. The early peaks of sealing activity were mainly interested in fur seals, the later peaks in the mid-nineteenth century – and continuing into the twentieth – were for elephant seals.[5] Between the 1780s and the 1830s between five and seven million seals were killed in the Southern Ocean, depending on how the figures are tabulated.[6]

The products of the seal hunt – furs, skins and oil – were sold into markets old and new. Furs and oil, of course, were old products, and found ready enough markets in North America and Europe. New ways of processing the furs to separate coarse from fine hairs were developed in the late eighteenth century, allowing for a refinement of the product and an expansion of the existing market.[7] Seal furs were also central products in opening the Chinese market to American traders after the War of Independence. From 1784 into the first decades of the nineteenth century, a constant stream of goods was sold into China – it was a necessary market as the American market had become glutted with seal products and the British market was closed to Americans. American and British domestic markets re-emerged in importance after this time.[8]

While the life of sealing and whaling in this period was bloody and testing, they were also industries with specific communities, ways of life

[4] A. G. E. Jones, 'British sealing on New South Shetland, 1819–1826, Part I', *The Great Circle*, 7 (1985): 9–20; Jones, 'British sealing on New South Shetland, 1819–1826, Part II', *The Great Circle*, 7 (1985): 74–85.

[5] Robert Headland, *A chronology of Antarctic exploration: A synopsis of events and activities from the earliest times until the International Polar Years, 2007–09* (London, 2009); A. Howard Clark, 'The Antarctic fur seal and sea elephant industries', in George Brown Goode, ed., *The fisheries and fishery industries of the United States* (Washington, DC, 1887), pp. 400–67; Rhys Richards, *Sealing in the southern oceans 1788–1833* (Wellington, NZ, 2010); Briton Cooper Busch, *The war against the seals: A history of the North American seal fishery* (Kingston, ON, 1985).

[6] The five million figure comes from Busch, *The war against the seals*; the seven million figure comes from Richards, *Sealing in the southern oceans*.

[7] Bertrand, *Americans in Antarctica*, p. 7.

[8] Bertrand, *Americans in Antarctica*; Edouard A. Stackpole, *The sea-hunters: the New England whalemen during two centuries 1635–1835* (Philadelphia, PA and New York, 1953); Edouard A. Stackpole, *Whales & destiny: The rivalry between America, France, and Britain for control of the southern whale fishery, 1785–1825* (Amherst, MA, 1972); James Kirker, *Adventures to China: Americans in the southern oceans 1792–1812* (New York, 1970).

The Southern Ocean 301

and identities. Sealers formed small and ephemeral communities on the scattered islands of the Antarctic and sub-Antarctic. If this was a world outside the reach of sovereignty and the international legal order, they were communities with connections to certain other social and economic orders. Sealers either visited briefly or established longer-term settlements on shore. Their settlements were basic constructions, using local stones, whale bones found on shore, and seal skins and sails; sometimes these constructions were free-standing, often building off caves and other local formations. Archaeological evidence suggests relatively non-hierarchical communities with heterogeneous construction styles and techniques both locally and across the whole ocean. At some islands it seems that sealers constructed their domestic and working areas separate from each other.[9]

These were temporary and extremely isolated communities, with no intention of long-term occupation or settlement. As far as is known, the settlements were occupied by men only, though women had their part in the industry in home ports or, rarely, on ships. Whatever the constraints and hardships, sealers had their own cultures and agency, bearing the maritime cultures of the time. Ben Maddison has emphasised how they were part of a 'global maritime proletariat' who, though under structures of command and with work pressures, exercised their rights and manifested their working-class cultures.[10] Indigenous peoples facing imperial expansion and colonisation also found space in the oceans and the sealing and whaling industries for themselves. Lynette Russell has traced how Aboriginal men and women in Australia 'exercised choices' in response to colonialism that included joining sealing and whaling voyages in the southern oceans.[11] If sealing and whaling were among the first global enterprises underpinning expanding markets, they also, to some extent, allowed choices and mobilities for some in changing circumstances. The southern oceans in this time, then, were complexly entangled in new imperial and capitalist expansion.

---

[9] Michael Pearson and Ruben Stehberg, 'Nineteenth century sealing sites on Rugged Island, South Shetland Islands', *Polar Record*, 42 (2006): 335–47; Andrés Zarankin and María Ximena Senatore, 'Archaeology in Antarctica: Nineteenth-century capitalism expansion strategies', *International Journal of Historical Archaeology*, 9 (2005): 43–56; Zarankin and Senatore, *Historias de un pasado en blanco: Arqueología histórica antártica* (Belo Horizonte, 2007); Angela McGowan, 'On their own: Towards an analysis of sealers' sites on Heard Island', *Papers and Proceedings of the Royal Society of Tasmania*, 133 (2000): 61–70.

[10] Ben Maddison, *Class and colonialism in Antarctic exploration, 1750–1920* (London, 2014).

[11] Lynette Russell, *Roving mariners: Australian Aboriginal whalers and sealers in the southern oceans, 1790–1870* (Albany, NY, 2012), p. 10.

302   A. Antonello

An Ocean of Whales and Whaling

After the 1850s sealing peak, a continuing though small stream of sealing and whaling voyages continued to make their way into the Southern Ocean. Around the turn of the twentieth century, as European, Australian and Japanese explorers were swiftly crossing the ocean to get to the Antarctic continent, perhaps no one quite anticipated that within a few short years a significant whaling industry would emerge – an industry that would bring great profits to a handful of companies at the cost, by mid-century, of the near-extinction of the great baleen whales. Whales had been commercial prey in the rest of the world's oceans – particularly in the Arctic seas off Greenland – for centuries, the oil from their blubber and the baleen from their great mouths put to various industrial and domestic uses. The Arctic whaling grounds had been near-exhausted by the early nineteenth century.[12] While low levels of whaling occurred in or near to the Southern Ocean during the nineteenth century, it was in the later parts of the nineteenth century that whalers began to realise the true scale of whale populations.

At the beginning of the twentieth century, it was neither given nor expected that a major whaling industry would develop and flourish for decades in the Southern Ocean. There had been boosters for Antarctic whaling in the late nineteenth century, especially in Norway and the Australian colonies, for both commercial and nationalistic reasons.[13] While whale products were certainly on the market, demand for those products around 1900 was not a promising foundation for a massive enlargement of the industry. This is precisely the problematic with which J. N. Tønnessen and A. O. Johnsen opened their magisterial and still unsurpassed history of modern whaling: whale oil prices were declining and there seemed little use for it. Even with the technological developments after the 1860s that provided the foundation of modern whaling (principally the grenade harpoon and steam-powered boats), Tønnessen suggested that in 1900 whaling was probably at its lowest levels for 300 years.[14]

---

[12] Richard Ellis, *Men and whales* (New York, 1991); Gordon Jackson, *The British whaling trade* (London, 1978).

[13] R. W. Home, Sara Maroske, A. M. Lucas and P. J. Lucas, 'Why explore Antarctica?: Australian discussions in the 1880s', *Australian Journal of Politics and History*, 38 (1992): 386–413.

[14] J. N. Tønnessen and A. O. Johnsen, *The history of modern whaling*, trans. R. I. Christophersen (Berkeley, CA, 1982), pp. 227–28 and chs. 1–2. This volume is an English translation of parts of a four-volume work in Norwegian published between 1959 and 1970. As the preface explains, apart from the sections on Finnmark whaling, the book is the work of Tønnessen.

The Southern Ocean 303

The Antarctic whaling industry began at the instigation of a very small number of people, and actually in the context of low whale oil prices.[15] The symbolic beginning of the industry came when the newly formed Compañía Argentina de Pesca – led by the Norwegian whaler Carl Anton Larsen, and funded by several foreign residents of Buenos Aires – shot its first whale off the island of South Georgia in December 1904. Within five years, several other companies had joined Pesca and oil production in the south was larger than the north.[16] Whale oil was not an overly promising product in 1904, as its price was low and no great innovations had been made to add value to it. That changed very quickly, and helped to sustain the young Southern Ocean industry. In the first decade of the twentieth century, the process of hydrogenation of fluid oils into solid fats was discovered and developed into an industrially viable technology. At the same time there was a general concern about the lack of fats in the diets of modern industrial workers. Hydrogenation allowed whale oil to be included in margarine; at first as a small percentage, then increasing with the refinement of the technology. This supplemented existing uses. Hydrogenation also allowed whale oil to become a notable international commodity – as it was cheap and could be stored without spoilage for years – in contrast to other animal fats that were often kept for domestic markets.[17]

Whaling began as a combined ocean and land-based enterprise. Ships caught whales near land (mainly around South Georgia), and then took them ashore for processing.[18] In the first decade, humpback whales were the predominant catch; from the First World War to the late 1930s blue whales were the main catch. The greatest technological change to the industry came in 1923 when the invention of the stern slipway along with other developments allowed whales to be taken on board floating factory ships and the emergence of fully pelagic whaling. By 1929, pelagic whaling was about ninety per cent of Antarctic whaling and the fleets continued to spread throughout its whole breadth.[19]

From before the First World War to the early 1930s, whaling was almost exclusively an Anglo-Norwegian concern. Norwegian and British capital funded the industry, Norwegians almost exclusively manned the

---

[15] It must be noted that, generally, the whaling industry referred to the region as the Antarctic rather than as the Southern Ocean.
[16] Tønnessen and Johnsen, *The history of modern whaling*, ch. 10; Ian. B. Hart, *Pesca: The history of the Compañía Argentina de Pesca Sociedad Anonima of Buenos Aires* (Salcombe, 2001); Wray Vamplew, *Salvesen of Leith* (Edinburgh and London, 1975).
[17] Tønnessen and Johnsen, *The history of modern whaling*, ch. 14.
[18] Robert Headland, *The island of South Georgia* (Cambridge, 1984), pp. 110–26.
[19] Tønnessen and Johnsen, *The history of modern whaling*, chs. 15 and 20–21.

304   A. Antonello

ships, the home port of those men was Sandefjord in Norway, and British scientists were the principal investigators of whales and the ocean. Yet British and Norwegian visions of the ocean were not fully coincident, as Peder Roberts has elucidated. Norwegian engagements with the ocean were commercial and industrial, led by a group of nationalist industrialists who saw a field for profit and personal aggrandisement rather than heroic exploratory endeavour.[20] It was in their pursuit of industry and profit that the Norwegians led, even forced, the British to clarify their stance towards the ocean. Before the advent of the industry, sovereignty and control over the islands of the South Atlantic sector of the Southern Ocean had been unclear and unresolved. The British imperial disposition towards this region was determined, to a great extent, by its attitudes to the Falkland Islands and the dispute over the islands with Argentineans, who refer to them as the Malvinas.[21] The British government was happy to reap the financial benefit of whaling through taxation and the leasing of land for the shore stations at South Georgia. They used these funds to 'develop' the Falkland Islands and its dependencies, including the fitting out and despatch of significant scientific voyages (discussed below).[22] By the early 1920s, some British policy-makers were concerned with the region as a whole, including the as-yet-poorly explored Antarctic continent, leading in 1926 to an Imperial policy, joined by the dominions especially Australia and New Zealand, that the whole Antarctic should be British – an aspiration that did not come to pass.[23]

Anglo-Norwegian dominance of the industry and the ocean was challenged in two ways from the late 1920s and early 1930s. In the most direct challenge, there were major new entrants to the industry. Germany, under the National Socialist government from 1933, looked to wean itself from the import of fats and re-develop its industry in pursuit of war preparations. Japan sent ships to the Southern Ocean from 1934, and within a few years had a substantial share of the oil market. And though it did not reach the Antarctic, the Soviet Union also began the development of its whaling industry.[24] In a less direct, more incipient way, growing conservation and internationalist sensibilities were also

---

[20] Peder Roberts, *The European Antarctic: Science and strategy in Scandinavia and the British Empire* (New York, 2011), ch. 3.

[21] Tønnessen and Johnsen, *The history of modern whaling*, pp. 178–82; Headland, *South Georgia*, pp. 237–41.

[22] Roberts, *The European Antarctic*, ch. 2.

[23] Peter J. Beck, 'Securing the dominant "place in the wan Antarctic sun" for the British Empire: The policy of extending British control over Antarctica', *Australian Journal of Politics and History*, 29 (1983): 448–61.

[24] Tønnessen and Johnsen, *The history of modern whaling*, ch. 23.

The Southern Ocean 305

affecting Anglo-Norwegian dominance. Through the League of Nations and the International Council for the Exploration of the Sea (ICES), the clearly emerging fact that whale stocks were being over-exploited was interpreted not only as an environmental problem but as one affecting a resource properly belonging to all peoples and that there should be international agreements to influence this.[25]

These new entrants and emerging ideas pushed whaling and the Southern Ocean into the international and diplomatic realms. The League of Nations cultivated the ICES and its whale committee (established in 1926), and work in the late 1920s led to the Geneva Convention for the Regulation of Whaling of 1931, the first international agreement on whaling.[26] Twenty-six nations signed the Convention even though Britain and Norway had ninety per cent of whaling production. An informal industry production agreement followed in 1932, which included the first use of quotas for both whales caught and barrels of oil produced.[27] These agreements, though they involved the issue of protecting whales, were still basically agreements to preserve the industry by preserving profitability. When the Geneva Convention expired in 1937, a new agreement was made, known as the London Agreement, which combined aspects of the 1931 convention and the subsequent production agreements.[28]

The most significant scientific work of the interwar years – and the first long-term, sustained research program in the Southern Ocean – was conducted by the British government in the service of whaling. Organised by a committee of the British Colonial Office, the *Discovery* Investigations deployed three ships over the period 1925 to 1939 (with a final cruise in 1950–51) to the Southern Ocean, initially concentrated in the South Atlantic sector.[29] These investigations were a mix of pure scientific research, research in aid of industry and colonial development in support of imperial strategy. They were certainly whale-focused; suggestive of this centrality was that krill, investigated closely for the first time on these voyages, was often described as 'the food of whales'. There

---

[25] Mark Cioc, *The game of conservation: International treaties to protect the world's migratory animals* (Athens, GA, 2009), pp. 126–27.

[26] Cioc, *The game of conservation*, pp. 127–29; Tønnessen and Johnsen, *The history of modern whaling*, pp. 399–400.

[27] Tønnessen and Johnsen, *The history of modern whaling*, p. 403.

[28] Cioc, *The game of conservation*, pp. 135–37.

[29] Ann Savours, *The voyages of the Discovery: The illustrated history of Scott's ship* (London, 1992), pp. 173–216; Alister Hardy, *Great waters: A voyage of natural history to study whales, plankton and the waters of the Southern Ocean in the old Royal Research Ship Discovery with the results brought up to date by the findings of the R.R.S. Discovery II* (London, 1967); John Coleman-Cooke, *Discovery II in the Antarctic: The story of British research in the southern seas* (London, 1963).

306   A. Antonello

were, to be sure, extensive investigations into physical oceanography and the biology of marine organisms. One of the effects of the investigations was to regionalise the Southern Ocean as a single and unified whole, Neil Mackintosh claiming that the layers of the ocean extended across its whole breadth – indeed, he suggested that it was 'the most important single fact demonstrated in all the work of the *Discovery II*'.[30] The whale-marking program also continued to reveal that whale populations were regionally separated. Of their long-term importance, Graham Burnett has argued that because of its 'complicity' with the industry, the *Discovery* Investigations 'trained up a generation of . . . "hip-booted cetologists"' – scientists comfortable, to some extent, with the industry and with the specimens it provided that allowed their work. For Burnett, this tradition would linger into the post-war years and the new International Whaling Commission (discussed below).[31]

The *Discovery* Investigations were also central in constituting the relationship of the British state with the ocean in the interwar years. The dispatch of scientific researchers was one strategy of showing interest and, by scale of endeavour, to crowd out other states – especially Argentina – that would seek their own deep relationship with the ocean. Adrian Howkins has categorised these strategies as 'environmental authority', the idea 'that the production of useful scientific knowledge about an environment helps to legitimate political control over that environment'.[32] Peder Roberts has looked at the ways in which the *Discovery* Investigations marked a shift in the British relationship with the Antarctic region, away from strenuous heroic efforts to wide and rational colonial development advanced with expertise.[33] In a similar way, though with less intensity, the Australian government, under the lobbying of the scientist and explorer Douglas Mawson, also engaged with the Southern Ocean, deploying expertise and science to justify presence and acquisition.[34]

The Second World War interrupted the whaling industry as it did many others. In light of demands for fats and for the redevelopment

---

[30] N. A. Mackintosh, 'The work of the *Discovery* Committee', *Proceedings of the Royal Society B*, 137 (1950): 144.

[31] D. Graham Burnett, *The sounding of the whale: Science and cetaceans in the twentieth century* (Chicago, IL, 2012) p. 29 and ch. 2.

[32] Adrian Howkins, *Frozen empires: An environmental history of the Antarctic Peninsula* (New York, 2017), p. 8.

[33] Roberts, *The European Antarctic*, ch. 2.

[34] Marie Kawaja, 'Australia in Antarctica: Realising an ambition', *The Polar Journal*, 3 (2013): 31–52; New Zealand's relationship with the Southern Ocean at this time was rather more limited, though certainly whale focused, characterised by an 'infirmity of purpose' according to Malcolm Templeton, *A wise adventure: New Zealand in Antarctica 1920–1960* (Wellington, 2000), ch. 2.

The Southern Ocean

of war-ravaged economies and industries, whaling was fully renewed post-war. Furthermore, its renewal was within a newly created diplomatic regime, the International Whaling Commission, created by the International Convention for the Regulation of Whaling, signed in 1946.[35] The 1946 Convention carried over many of the ideas and approaches of the previous international agreements, though there was an increasing sense that whales had to be more carefully protected. The push for a greater conservation focus was partly a result of the influence of the United States in both organising and dominating the negotiations. There had been significant developments in American conservation thinking in the preceding decades, and the American marine biologist Remington Kellogg was influential in official US thinking. Both Graham Burnett and Kurk Dorsey have emphasised the novelty and spirit of hope that characterised both the ICRW negotiations and the IWC's early years. With the high seas an international space, there was great hope that under the guidance of scientists the industry could be rationally managed.[36]

Throughout the 1950s it was painfully clear that whale stocks were near the brink of total collapse. The catch was consistently under the already low quotas and the industry basically uneconomical, propped up by various governmental incentives and subventions. There was little agreement about how to respond to this fact, for each whaling nation wanted to maximise its position. There was even disagreement among the scientists at the IWC. Issues of catch quotas, fleet sizes, bans on specific species being caught or protection of particular ocean areas were all part of the discussion. And in addition to the worries for the whale stocks, there was a concern that disagreement within the IWC would lead to its collapse, and a final free-for-all of whaling. The IWC's work in its first decade and a half – in both its political sense, and in the work of its scientific committee – was haunted by the spectre of a Southern Ocean stripped of its great whales. To work through issues of quota numbers, the IWC tasked its scientific committee with evaluating whale population dynamics. The final report was handed in in 1963, clearly demonstrating the decline; yet there was still no action.[37]

There has been a persistent question about the IWC, asked not only by historians but scholars from the social and biological sciences: why did it fail? One response has been that whaling demonstrates the curse of open, uncontrolled resources, in the spirit of Garrett Hardin's 'tragedy

---

[35] Cioc, *The game of conservation*, pp. 139–142.
[36] Burnett, *Sounding of the whale*, ch. 4; Kurkpatrick Dorsey, *Whales and nations: environmental diplomacy on the high seas* (Seattle, WA, 2013), ch. 3.
[37] Burnett, *Sounding of the whale*, pp. 456–503; Dorsey, *Whales and nations*, pp. 184–94.

308   A. Antonello

of the commons'. Dorsey's summation of whaling's modern history has strong overtones of this: 'Whalers recognized that they were overtaxing their resource, they tried to organize their trustworthy colleagues, and they did what they could to ruin outsiders. And in the end, they decided that they would not leave a whale behind for some other, less scrupulous, whaler.'[38] Tønnessen's answer is similar: in the 1950s, the demands of Japan, the Soviet Union and the Netherlands forestalled agreement on lower quotas (which, in any case, would still have been too high). Burnett, in his larger study of whale science and scientists, has interpreted matters differently. Reacting to the many analyses of the IWC that see a deficit of scientific knowledge as the problem, Burnett argues for an entanglement of long- and short-term developments, whereby the boundary between science and politics was mutable. In the first decade of the IWC, (most) scientists were sensitive to the politics and optimistic about the promise of scientific expertise in an international regulatory regime; they tried to cooperatively shape the industry, but in the end became disillusioned at their failure to temper it.[39] Furthermore, Burnett suggests that the difficult decisions of the IWC were passed to the scientists, so political decisions were made scientific, rather than the common idea that science was politicised. Whatever the interpretation of the IWC's failure, in a sense it was probably all too late in any case for most of the whale populations; and though whale products still sold in the global market, changing technologies were reducing demand.

Whaling began to recede from its dominant position in the human story of the Southern Ocean from the early 1960s. In 1963, more whales were killed outside the Southern Ocean, and by 1968, only the Soviets and Japanese were still whaling there.[40] One recent estimate put the number of whales taken from the Southern Ocean in the twentieth century at nearly two million individual animals.[41] The work of the IWC turned to whaling in other oceans, and a great deal of public and scientific attention was turned onto the Antarctic continent rather than the ocean. Yet, the end of whaling was not the end of the human desire to exploit the ocean. In the decades to follow, scientific, commercial and diplomatic concern turned to the Southern Ocean's other denizens.

---

[38] Dorsey, *Whales and nations*, p. 13.
[39] Burnett, *Sounding of the whale*, ch. 5.
[40] Tønnessen and Johnsen, *The history of modern whaling*, chs. 31–34.
[41] Robert C. Rocha Jr., Phillip J. Clapham and Yulia V. Ivashchenko, 'Emptying the oceans: a summary of industrial whaling catches in the 20th century', *Marine Fisheries Review*, 76 (2015): 37–48. Roche's statistic of 2,053,956 is for the whole southern hemisphere, but this number is substantially constituted by the Antarctic grounds.

The Southern Ocean   309

Contemporary Order, Protection and Management

Norwegian whalers were known to remark that below forty degrees south latitude there was no law, and that below fifty degrees there was no God, so physically demanding was the ocean.[42] While it remains as stormy as ever, the contemporary history of the Southern Ocean is one that is indeed characterised by rules and a concerted (and contested) search for international order across the whole ocean. Environmental and resource management and protection under the aegis of several international organisations and diplomatic structures are central to this order. The contemporary era of the ocean began in the 1970s (with antecedents in the 1950s) with various challenges to the international order for the oceans and global commons, new developments in scientific and environmental knowledge and a profusion of new actors from around the world. It found early expression in two major agreements in the early 1980s: the signing of the Convention on the Conservation of Antarctic Marine Living Resources (CCAMLR) in 1980 and the resultant establishment of its permanent Commission following ratification in 1982, and the moratorium placed on commercial whaling through the International Whaling Commission in 1982.[43] These developments marked a shift in the focus of diplomatic, scientific and commercial attention to the marine ecosystem, foregrounded environmental and environmentalist concerns and placed a great area of the world ocean under close management.

Concerted scientific work from the late 1950s increasingly demonstrated the extent of various fish stocks, most particularly of Antarctic krill (*Euphausia superba*), the main zooplankton of the marine ecosystem and fed hopes for new fisheries and renewed industry in the Southern Ocean. Though non-whale and non-seal fisheries had sometimes been invoked by scientists and explorers in the first half of the twentieth century, it was whaling that soaked up the capital, labour and imagination. From the early 1960s, as whaling rapidly declined, several nations, led by the Soviet Union, began seriously exploring other fisheries, through both research and at-sea trials of fishing gear and processing technologies.

---

[42] Tønnessen and Johnsen, *The history of modern whaling*, p. 158.
[43] The Falklands/Malvinas conflict between the United Kingdom and Argentina also occurred in 1982, yet its legacies are perhaps more complex, and in part less international, than the CCAMLR and IWC developments. The development of the Falkland Islands in the years following, especially in relation to fisheries, has been substantial, but still requires greater historical analysis. An important work in this regard is Klaus Dodds, *Pink ice: Britain and the South Atlantic empire* (London, 2002), chs. 8–10.

310   A. Antonello

The Soviets, followed by Japanese, Polish and East and West German researchers, saw great potential in krill and other fish.[44]

These investigations and trials occurred in several contexts which created frictions in need of resolution by both diplomats and scientists. In diplomatic terms, these new fisheries affected the balance of the Antarctic Treaty regime. The states investigating the fisheries (with the exception of West Germany at the time) were parties to the Antarctic Treaty, an agreement that had been signed by twelve states in 1959 in an effort to peacefully resolve disagreements arising from territorial claims on the continent – the Treaty 'froze' the territorial and sovereignty issues.[45] The Treaty had, in part, responded to the rhetoric of scientific internationalism that had animated the massive research effort of the International Geophysical Year of 1957–58. Though the IGY program had concentrated on the continent, the ocean was still caught up in some ways in that internationalist spirit and was enfolded into the scientific work that continued in IGY's wake. While the Treaty specifically excluded the high seas and whales, its parties were increasingly worried about developments in the Southern Ocean. They worried about continuing their peaceful relations, they questioned who would win and lose in such developments and they increasingly wondered about environmental impacts.[46]

The new potential fisheries also raised questions about the ordering of the Southern Ocean that were inescapably tied with the ordering of the world ocean at large. Developments in ideas of the 'global commons', the 'common heritage of mankind', the exploitability of the sea bed, the creation of exclusive economic zones, identification of the extended continental shelf and the negotiations towards a new and comprehensive law of the sea through the United Nations after 1973 (UNCLOS), all weighed heavily on the range of diplomatic, scientific and civil society actors engaging with the Southern Ocean.[47] The UNCLOS negotiations in particular cast into relief the limits of the international or global

---

[44] Alessandro Antonello, 'Protecting the Southern Ocean ecosystem: the environmental protection agenda of Antarctic diplomacy and science', in Wolfram Kaiser and Jan-Henrik Meyer, eds., *International organizations and environmental protection: Conservation and globalization in the twentieth century* (New York and Oxford, 2016), pp. 268–92, pp. 275–76.

[45] The twelve original signatories to the Treaty were Argentina, Australia, Belgium, Chile, France, Japan, New Zealand, Norway, South Africa, the United Kingdom, the United States and the Soviet Union.

[46] Antonello, 'Protecting the Southern Ocean ecosystem'. On the limited place of the Southern Ocean in Antarctic negotiations and diplomacy around 1959, see Alessandro Antonello, 'Nature conservation and Antarctic diplomacy, 1959–1964', *The Polar Journal*, 4 (2014): 335–53.

[47] Clyde Sanger, *Ordering the oceans: The making of the Law of the Sea* (Toronto, 1987).

The Southern Ocean

311

character of the Southern Ocean, for they pitted a collective of newly decolonised states, through the Non-Aligned Movement among others, against the much smaller group of wealthy, industrially developed states that dominated the ocean's affairs.

From an environmental and scientific perspective, the spectre of the over-hunted whales hung over these discussions. The fate of the whales was invoked in mid-1975 when the still-young Greenpeace's activities in the North Pacific confronting the Soviet whaling fleet were interpolated into Antarctic affairs by diplomats only weeks later to justify marine resource conservation.[48] The other major environmental context was the increasing salience and dominance of the 'ecosystem' idea not only in resource management, but in the broader environmental cultures emerging in global civil society. With krill seen as the most promising quarry, scientists drew attention to the fact that it is the keystone species of the Antarctic marine ecosystem, with which nearly all other animals have some very direct relationship; any over-exploitation of krill would affect other, non-exploited, species.[49]

In light of these political, economic and intellectual pressures, two developments occurred broadly. First, scientists within the overarching international architecture of the Scientific Committee on Antarctic Research (SCAR) began to create an international research framework to develop data and knowledge about the Antarctic marine ecosystem. They organised their endeavours under the title Biological Investigations of Marine Antarctic Systems and Stocks (BIOMASS). This program ran through the 1980s, generating not only new reams of data on many aspects of the ocean, but also a concerted international scientific relationship to it.[50]

The second development fed off these scientific movements, but had some independence too. The consultative parties of the Antarctic Treaty saw the problem of an absence of rules in the Southern Ocean, and began to negotiate a formal response from 1975. What was novel about their approach was that their negotiations fixed upon the ecosystem and ecological relationships between species as one of the central subjects of their agreement. In moving away from a traditional fisheries convention model that focussed on managing single fish stocks in favour of a management model that recognised fish as interconnected, the Treaty parties were making international legal history. After several rounds of negotiations, fifteen states (plus the European Economic

---

[48] Antonello, 'Protecting the Southern Ocean ecosystem', 281.
[49] Ibid., 275–76.
[50] Ibid., 277–81; G. E. Fogg, *A history of Antarctic science* (Cambridge, 1992).

312   A. Antonello

Community) signed the Convention on the Conservation of Antarctic Marine Living Resources (CCAMLR) in May 1980. The Convention was novel in international law and environmental history because of its Article II provision to hold the ecosystem at the centre of conservation actions. I have argued elsewhere that, in addition to the scientific wisdom of the provision, ecosystem-level conservation was energetically pursued by both scientists and the diplomats of certain Treaty parties, because it allowed an assertion of power and institutional dominance on both group's parts: the scientists of SCAR against the more resource-minded fisheries officials of the Food and Agriculture Organization; the Treaty parties as a collective against the New International Economic Order agenda of developing countries; and of the conservation bloc of Treaty parties against the more exploitation-minded bloc.[51]

In the years since the Convention came into force in 1982, there have been several areas of work and contention. The interests of fishing companies in the Southern Ocean have not abated, and significant catches of Patagonian and Antarctic toothfish and krill have occurred through the period. Catch limits, gear regulations, ecosystem monitoring and protection guidelines, seabird by-catch, illegal, unreported and unregulated (IUU) fishing and piracy, and marine protected areas have all animated the diplomatic and scientific efforts of parties to CCAMLR. The parties and scientists have seemingly made CCAMLR a success, certainly avoiding the fate of the whales under the early IWC.[52]

The CCAMLR structures arose out of the Antarctic Treaty regime, which had no provisions allowing discussions of whales, leaving such matters to the International Whaling Commission. From the late 1960s, given that most nations had left the whaling industry and there was irrefutable evidence of population decline, several nations and newly emerging international environmental organisations began calling for a complete ban on whaling. In a short span of years ideas and public consciousness about whales had changed dramatically; they were re-imagined from being exploitable resources to being sentient, emotional creatures nearer

---

[51] Antonello, 'Protecting the Southern Ocean ecosystem'.

[52] While some disciplines have kept a close eye on these developments, historians have not yet extensively studied this contemporary period. As a starting point, see Stuart Kaye, Marcus Haward and Rob Hall, 'Managing marine living resources, the 1970s–1990s', in Marcus Haward and Tom Griffiths, eds., *Australia and the Antarctic Treaty System: 50 years of influence* (Sydney, 2011), pp. 164–80; Andrew J. Constable, William K. de la Mare, David J. Agnew, Inigo Everson and Denzil Miller, 'Managing fisheries to conserve the Antarctic marine ecosystem: Practical implementation of the Convention on the Conservation of Antarctic Marine Living Resources (CCAMLR)', *ICES Journal of Marine Science: Journal du Conseil*, 57 (2000): 778–91.

The Southern Ocean   313

to humans, demanding complete protection.[53] The change in public perceptions, combined with developments in scientific thinking, powerfully moved several governments. Though the hunting of blue and humpback whales was banned in the 1960s, in 1972, the United States government advocated for a ten-year moratorium on all whaling in both the United Nations Conference on the Human Environment in Stockholm, and at the annual IWC meeting. After a decade of work, first in trying to reform the scientific processes for determining quotas, but then to completely ban whaling, the IWC passed an indefinite moratorium in 1982.[54] While the debates about quotas and a moratorium were concerned with whaling in all the oceans (as already noted, the majority of whaling was done outside the Southern Ocean from 1963), they nevertheless affected the Southern Ocean significantly.

Despite the commercial moratorium, from 1987 the Japanese whaling fleet continued to hunt for 'scientific purposes' in the Southern Ocean under special permit provision of the ICRW. Most Western scientists, governments and publics have been incredulous of the scientific rationale, confronting the Japanese government in several ways. Several international environmental groups have protested on the ocean itself at the very site of whaling. Greenpeace chased down Japanese whalers in the Southern Ocean in the late 1980s, manifesting a particularly robust form of 'bearing witness' that, following the Quaker faith of several of its founders, was central to the organisation's mode of activism. In so doing, Greenpeace activists drew a great deal of global attention to the Southern Ocean, and, with their physical presence, joined previously governmental and commercial activities in the ocean with an activated, not simply paper sense, of a global commons.[55] Between 2005 and 2014, the Sea Shepherd Conservation Society – founded and run by an early Greenpeace leader, Paul Watson, in 1977 – has also confronted not only Japanese whalers at sea, but also illegal fishing operations in the Southern Ocean. With a great deal of publicity – including a reality television show – Sea Shepherd manifested a further entrenchment between the anti- and pro-whaling sides of the issue in this period.

In more recent times too, other international bodies have been enrolled into the story of Southern Ocean whaling. With continuing domestic

---

[53] Dorsey, *Whales and nations*, ch. 6; Burnett, *Sounding of the whale*, ch. 6.

[54] Dorsey, *Whales and nations*, ch. 7; Tønnessen and Johnsen, *The history of modern whaling* has some details up to 1978; Michael Heazle, *Scientific uncertainty and the politics of whaling* (Seattle, WA, London and Edmonton, 2006).

[55] Stephen Knight, *Icebound* (Auckland, 1988); Paul Brown, *The last wilderness: Eighty days in Antarctica* (London, 1991). On the origins of Greenpeace, see Frank Zelko, *Make it a green peace! The rise of countercultural environmentalism* (Oxford, 2013).

314   A. Antonello

pressure, the Australian government, supported by New Zealand, applied in 2010 to the International Court of Justice to rule on the legality of Japan's 'scientific whaling'.[56] The majority of the court found that JARPA II could not be considered scientific under the convention. Much media coverage and public discussion of the judgement misinterpreted the specific focus of the case on JARPA II and painted the judgement as banning all whaling. In their way, the majority of judges of the ICJ continued a trend of privileging scientific work in the Southern Ocean at the expense of other forms of human engagement, and, as a corollary, also judging what was good science.

While the small Japanese hunt for whales in the ocean continued to gather public and governmental attention, a larger group of actors has pursued with greater intensity the other economic resources of the Southern Ocean. Tourism has also grown over the past few decades as a valuable economic activity. In addition to the Antarctic ice sheet and the region's unique wildlife, the rusting remnants of the whaling industry at South Georgia are a standard part of tourist ship itineraries. While tourists number only in the tens of thousands, the concentration of activities in the South Atlantic and Antarctic Peninsula regions brings increased chances of environmental damage, both on land and at sea. Under the watchful eye of CCAMLR, significant catches of krill and toothfish have been landed, sustaining a significant industry. Enmeshed in these economic efforts is a geopolitical push to continually refine and bolster the sense of order and power in the ocean. Furthermore, the contest between conservation and exploitation continues unabated, without clear winners – though the recent, October 2016 creation of a marine protected area in the Ross Sea suggests that a conservation-minded approach is currently ascendant, or at least diplomatically tolerable. While the victors trade the rhetoric of scientific truth and self-evident rightness of environmental protection, the contemporary historian is left to ask how long- and short-term changes and continuities have led to such outcomes, and how slowly built structures of ideas, practices and identities will shape the future.

Conclusion

Though distant from human populations, the Southern Ocean has nevertheless been a site of considerable human activity, the products

---

[56] Malgosia Fitzmaurice and Dai Tamada, eds., *Whaling the Antarctic: Significance and implications of the ICJ judgement* (Leiden, 2016).

The Southern Ocean

of which – both material and intellectual – have affected many societies, cultures and environments. If the numbers of people visiting and inhabiting the ocean have been manifestly fewer than other oceans, they have made up for it with a commercial purpose that has devastated species and had profound ecological impacts. Exploitation of natural resources is only the most obvious of the continuities through the ocean's history. Another continuity revolves around the senses of proximity and distance, in both material-spatial and temporal senses. While certain countries and communities that face the Southern Ocean have considered it local, the ocean has so often hosted visitors from distant places. The ocean has witnessed the perils and distances that we (the 'we' of modern consumer society) will allow, indeed expect, workers to endure to provide some new consumable. The products of the ocean have also very often been distanced from their source: the seal furs do not seem to have been marketed as coming from the ocean; margarines made of whale oil were not marketed as 'Antarctic' and whales were very often abstracted from their particular environments when considered by companies or diplomatic meetings; the ocean did not feature in the advertising or packaging for the Soviet krill paste that might have led to excessive harvesting; and the modern catch of Patagonian and Antarctic toothfish is relabelled and marketed as 'Chilean sea bass'. In contrast, the international community of earth scientists has, over recent decades, demonstrated the profound connections between the Southern Ocean and other parts of the Earth system. Histories and futures are also fluid in their proximity and distance. In recent environmental campaigns, the ocean has been portrayed as the 'last' ocean, relatively untouched compared to all others, a selective sense of history to be sure; the promise of the ocean has sometimes relied of strategic forgetting of the past. And the ocean's future under a changed climate seems closer than ever.

The opposition to this great, continuous exploitation has been one of the more recent changes. Since the decline of whaling beginning in the 1960s, the Southern Ocean has been increasingly contested in a variety of forums, international and diplomatic, governmental and nongovernmental, scientific and environmental. And through this contest, the ocean has been subject to constant attention and surveillance. At the heart of the contest is the question of the right way to approach the ocean. Should the ocean be emptied of its fishing vessels and preserved, or should exploitation continue?

Many elements of the stories told here are known; some are poorly known and demand continued research; and some may never be known

316   A. Antonello

because of the lack of reliable evidence. As is often the case with histories involving commercial enterprises, details associated with the making of money from natural resources can be scant or obscured – while some of the whaling ventures have left archives, few records survive of the sealing ventures and modern fishing companies seem hardly likely to open their records, if they have any at all. We must also remember to look at the ocean itself. In the past twenty years or so, the Southern Ocean has been found to be home to surprising biodiversity. And, of course, a future affected by major climate change – warming temperatures, ocean acidification, ocean freshening through the ice sheet mass loss and stormier weather – will certainly affect how we understand the past.

Further Reading

Two important reference works can be consulted for basic information about events, actors and references: Robert Headland, *A chronology of Antarctic exploration: A synopsis of events and activities from the earliest times until the International Polar Years, 2007–09* (London, 2009) and Beau Riffenburgh, ed., *Encyclopedia of the Antarctic*, 2 vols. (New York and London, 2007). Histories of the Southern Ocean and Antarctica are arguably still dominated by work that concentrates on exploratory and scientific 'firsts' and heroics. While strong in narrative, they can lack the conceptual and analytical concerns of historians. Alan Gurney's two books covering the period before 1900 are strong narratives on the major scientific and exploratory efforts: *Below the convergence: Voyages toward Antarctic, 1699–1839* (New York, 1997) and *The race to the white continent* (New York, 2000). Two classic texts in this vein worth consulting are Hugh Robert Mill, *The siege of the South Pole: The story of Antarctic exploration* (London, 1905) and E. W. Hunter Christie, *The Antarctic problem: An historical and political study* (London, 1951). Elements of the Southern Ocean's history can be found in general histories of Antarctica. See David Day, *Antarctica: A biography* (Oxford, 2012) and Tom Griffiths, *Slicing the silence: Voyaging to Antarctica* (Sydney, 2007), Griffiths' work being particular sensitive to environmental and cultural history concerns. Adrian Howkins also gives the Southern Ocean attention in the context of the polar regions and within an environmental history framework in his *The polar regions: An environmental history* (Cambridge, 2016). For a general overview of the history of science, see G. E. Fogg, *A history of Antarctic science* (Cambridge, 1992). The history of sealing is best entered through Briton Cooper Busch, *The war against the seals: A history of the North American seal*

The Southern Ocean   317

fishery (Kingston, 1985), Rhys Richards, *Sealing in the southern oceans, 1788–1833* (Wellington, NZ, 2010), and A. B. Dickinson, *Seal fisheries of the Falkland Islands and dependencies: An historical review* (St. John's, NL, 2007). Given the paucity of written materials, the archaeological literature on Antarctic sealing is also worth consulting, see Michael Pearson and Ruben Stehberg, 'Nineteenth century sealing sites on Rugged Island, South Shetland Islands', *Polar Record*, 42 (2006): 335–47. On the history of whaling in the Southern Ocean, the first stop remains the magisterial work by J. N. Tønnessen and A. O. Johnsen, *The history of modern whaling*, trans. R. I. Christophersen (Berkeley, CA, 1982), a condensed and translated version of a larger four-volume work in Norwegian. Two recent works that engage with current conceptual concerns in international history, environmental history and the history of science are D. Graham Burnett, *The sounding of the whale: Science and cetaceans in the twentieth century* (Chicago, IL, 2012) and Kurkpatrick Dorsey, *Whales and nations: Environmental diplomacy on the high seas* (Seattle, WA, 2013). On both whaling and aspects of scientific research in the interwar years, also see Peder Roberts, *The European Antarctic: Science and strategy in Scandinavia and the British Empire* (New York, 2011). The contemporary history of the ocean has, as yet, not been intensely studied by historians, though scholars from other social science disciplines have given significant attention. From an international politics perspective, though a little dated, see Peter J. Beck, *The international politics of Antarctica* (London, 1986). From a geography perspective (and more specifically, a critical geopolitics perspective), see Sanjay Chaturvedi, *The polar regions: A political geography* (Chichester, 1996) and Klaus Dodds, *Geopolitics in Antarctica: Views from the Southern Ocean rim* (Chichester, 1997). For an environmental history perspective on the recent period, see Alessandro Antonello, 'Protecting the Southern Ocean ecosystem: the environmental protection agenda of Antarctic diplomacy and science', in Wolfram Kaiser and Jan-Henrik Meyer, eds., *International organizations and environmental protection: Conservation and globalization in the twentieth century* (New York and Oxford, 2016), pp. 268–92. *Polar Record* (since 1931) and *The Polar Journal* (since 2011) are the two principal journals on polar matters, and include many specialist and detailed articles on the Southern Ocean's history – furthermore, *Polar Record* also contains a great deal of contemporaneous and primary materials on the ocean's history. The Scott Polar Research Institute, University of Cambridge, maintains a comprehensive bibliography of the polar regions, which is easily consulted. An important collection of documents relating to the government and diplomacy of the Antarctic

318   A. Antonello

and Southern Ocean is W. M. Bush, ed., *Antarctica and international law: A collection of inter-state and national documents* (London, 1982). The websites of the International Whaling Commission (www.iwc.int) and the Commission for the Conservation of Antarctic Marine Living Resources (www.ccamlr.org) are also valuable resources for primary materials, including regulations, reports, conference materials and scientific materials.

Index

Aa, Pieter van der, 185
Aboriginal Australians, 66–67, 68, 127, 301
Abu Mufarrij, 168
Adam of Bremen, 211–12
Adelman, Jeremy, 145, 146
Aden, 54, 55, 168, 171
  Gulf of, 171
Adigal, Ilango, 36
African American Monument, South Carolina, US, 10
Agatharchides of Cnidus, 167
Agnew, John, 273
agricultural exchanges, Indian Ocean, 49–50
Albert, Duke of Saxony, 212
Albrecht of Bavaria, 212
Alencastro, Luiz Felipe de, 91
Alexander III, tsar of Russia, 256
Alexander the Great, 163, 243
Al-Masudi, 168
amber, 217
Amino Yoshihiko, 187, 192
Andaman Islands, 57–59
Andaya, Barbara Watson, 49
Antarctic Circumpolar Current, 296
Antarctic Treaty, 310, 311–12
Antarctica
  see Southern Ocean
anthropology
  of Oceania, 63–66
  racial theories, 81
apprenticeship, 45
Arctic Council, 280, 291–92
Arctic Ocean, 8, 89, 105, 269–92
  as bellwether ocean, 287–91
  claims on, 272, 273, 284–85
  climate change, 277, 287–92
  crossings of, 276–77
  geography, 275–77
  prehistoric coastal settlements, 281–82
  resource extraction, 277, 284–85
  scientific research, 286–90

sea ice, 286–92
thermohaline circulation, 276
whaling, 284–85, 299, 302
Arktika, 277
Armitage, David, 171
artillery, 248
Ascension Island, 100
Ascherson, Neal, 241
Atlantic age, 22
Atlantic Charter, 93
Atlantic islands, 99–100
Atlantic Ocean, 85–108, 138
  circum-Atlantic history, 96–97
  cis-Atlantic history, 96–97
  extra-Atlantic history, 97, 105–8
  infra-Atlantic history, 97, 98–102, 108
  migration, 93, 95, 103–4, 107
  slave trade, 90–92, 93–94, 95, 104, 106
  sub-Atlantic history, 97, 102–5, 108
  sub-oceanic regions, 89–91
  trade, 106–7
  trans-Atlantic history, 96–97
Atlantis, 99
Aurobindo, Sri, 37
Azad, Abul Kalam, 57

Baekje Kingdom, Korea, 187, 188
Bailyn, Bernard, 2, 16–17, 88–89, 96
Bajau people, South China Sea, 124–27
Balhae Kingdom, Korea, 186–87, 188
Baltic Energy Market Interconnection Plan (BEMIP), 232
Baltic Sea, 89, 209–32
  artisans and artists, 222–24
  crossroads to other seas and oceans, 230–31
  Dutch and, 213, 218–24, 225, 228, 230
  English and, 225–27, 228, 229
  Hanseatic League, 215–19
  medieval and modern notions of, 209–15
  migration, 222
  model region, 231–32
  trade, 212–13, 215–22, 224–31

319

320   Index

Baltic Sea Strategy, 231–32
Balzac, Honoré de, 252
Bangudae, South Korea, 193
Banivanua Mar, Tracey, 75
Barents Sea, 274, 276, 286, 289
Barents, Willem, 276, 283, 284
Basil II, Byzantine Emperor, 245
Beaglehole, John, 62–63
Bengal, Bay of, 41
Ben-Yehoyada, Naor, 148–49, 152
Biological Investigations of Marine Antarctic
    Systems and Stocks (BIOMASS), 311
bio-prospecting, 80–81
Bin Abdul Kadir, Abdullah, 51–52
Black Death, 247
Black Sea, 89, 234–64
    ancient history, 241–44
    geography, 236–41
    Middle Ages, 244–47
    openness and enclosure, 240–41
    Ottoman Empire and, 247–50, 252,
       253–54, 256, 257
    Russia and, 250–53, 254–56, 257,
       259–60, 261–62
    trade, 239, 249, 253, 255–56
    Turkey and, 239, 257, 258–59, 260,
       261, 262
Blocke, Abraham van der, 223
Blocke, Willem van der, 223
'Blue Revolution', 15
Bolster, Jeffrey, 103
Bonaparte, Napoleon, 170
Book of Curiosities of the Sciences and
    Marvels for the Eyes, The, 34–35
Bose, Subhas Chandra, 58
Bose, Sugata, 33, 98
botanical knowledge, 49–51, 80–81
Bougainville, Louis-Antoine de, 298
Brătianu, George I., 254
Braudel, Fernand, 2, 16–17, 38, 94, 136,
    137, 158, 236–37
Browne, Samuel, 51
Brunei, 119
bubonic plague, 247
Buck, Sir Peter (Te Rangi Hiroa), 63, 67, 81
Burnett, Graham, 306, 307, 308
Byrd, Richard F., 277
Byzantine Empire, 244–46, 248, 250
Byzantium, 242
    see also Constantinople

Cabot, John, 283
Cairo Geniza letters, 166, 168
canoes, double-hulled, Pacific, 12
    see also Polynesian canoe journeys

Cape Colony, 43
Cape of Good Hope, 107
Caribbean Sea
    hurricanes, 105
    islands, 100
Carta Marina map, 283
cartography, 21
    Arctic Ocean, 279, 282, 283, 284
    Atlantic Ocean, 89–90
    Red Sea, 169
    Sea of Japan/East Sea, 184, 185, 190
castaways, Japanese fishermen, 195
Catherine the Great, Empress of
    Russia, 250
Challenger expedition, 104
Charles W. Morgan, 194
Chau Ju Kua, 117, 121
Chaudhuri, Kirti, 22, 37, 38, 39–40
Chaunu, Huguette, 94
Chaunu, Pierre, 94
Chekhov, Anton, 199–200
China
    see South China Sea
Christian IV, King of Denmark, 223
Christianity, 53–54, 79–80
circum-Atlantic history, 96–97
cis-Atlantic history, 96–97
climate change, 16, 105, 277, 287–92
coasts and beaches, Atlantic, 100–1
coerced labour
    Indian Ocean, 44–45
    Pacific Ocean, 77–78
'Coffin Ship' monument, Ireland, 10
Cold War
    Arctic Ocean, 269–70, 276
    Black Sea, 240, 258–59
    Pacific Ocean, 83
    Sea of Japan/East Sea, 191, 203–6
Collingwood, R. G., 272–73
Colombo, Sri Lanka, 55–56
Columbus, Christopher, 90, 106
commons, global, 309, 310, 313
    see also tragedy of the commons
Commonwealth of Independent States
    (CIS), 261
Congress of Vienna, 252
Coning, Jacob, 223
Conrad, C. M., 197
conservation, Southern Ocean, 304–5,
    307–8, 309–14
Constantinople (Istanbul), 239, 244, 245,
    246, 248, 250
contracted labour
    Indian Ocean, 44–45
    Pacific Ocean, 77–79

Index

321

Convention on the Conservation of Antarctic Marine Living Resources (CCAMLR), 309, 311–12, 314
convict transportation, Indian Ocean, 44–45, 58
Cook, Frederick, 277
Cook, James, 69–70, 74, 298
Cooper, Mercator, 194–95
Copenhagen, 223–24
cosmopolitanism, 54–59, 74
    Mediterranean Sea, 149–52
Cossacks, 249
Council of the Baltic Sea States (CBSS), 214–15
Crimea, 238–39, 244, 247, 248, 250, 253, 257, 258, 259, 261–62
Crimean War, 254–55
Crosby, Alfred, 76
Crusades, 139, 246
Curtin, Philip, 95

da Gama, Vasco, 39, 47, 48
d'Anville, Jean-Baptiste Bourguignon, 169
Danzig, 222, 224, 228
Das Gupta, Ashin, 38–39, 40
Davidson, Jim, 74
de Castro, João, 169
de Vries, Jan Vredeman, 222, 223, 224
de Vries, Klaas, 222
decolonisation
    Atlantic Ocean, 93–94
    Pacific Ocean, 74–75
deep-sea research, Atlantic Ocean, 104
Dening, Greg, 66, 98
deportations, Black Sea, 255, 256, 258
dhow, 49
Diderot, Denis, 249
Dircksen, Jan, 223
Discovery investigations, 305–6
diving, 104
Dorsey, Kurk, 307, 308
d'Orta, Garcia, 50
Douglas, Bronwen, 81
Douglass, Frederick, 91
Downing, George, 219–20
Drake, Francis, 8
Du Bois, W. E. B., 91, 95

Earth Summit, 1, 3
East India Company (Dutch), 43
East India Company (English), 38, 44, 50–51, 107, 123
East Korea Warm Current, 191
East Sea/Sea of Japan, 12, 182–207

abductions, 196, 203–4
migration, 12, 186–87, 201–4
naming debates, 182–86, 207
oceanic currents, 189–91, 193
refugees, 12, 202, 204
repatriations, 201–2, 203, 204
trade, 192–93
tragedy, 199–206
whaling, 193–95, 197–98
Easter Island (Rapa Nui), 67, 77–78
Eastern Roman Empire, 244–46, 248, 250
ecological histories
    see environmental and ecological histories
ecological products, South China Sea, 117, 124–27
Economic Research Institute for Northeast Asia (ERINA), 206–7
El Niño/Southern Oscillation, 72, 105
Ellemann-Jensen, Uffe, 214–15
endorheic basins, 237
Engholm, Björn, 214
England
    see Great Britain
Enlightenment
    Baltic Sea, 213
    Mediterranean Sea, 148
    Pacific Ocean, 80–81
    Red Sea, 169
environmental and ecological histories, 13–16
    Arctic Ocean, 284–92
    Atlantic Ocean, 103–5
    Indian Ocean, 46–51
    Mediterranean Sea, 136–38
    oceanic turn in, 15–16
    Pacific Ocean, 71–72, 76–77, 80–81
    Sea of Japan/East Sea, 189–99
    South China Sea, 124–27
    see also Southern Ocean.
environmental protection, Southern Ocean, 304–5, 307–8, 309–14
Ephraimson-Abt, Hans, 205
ethnic cleansing, 203, 256
European Council, 231–32
European Union, 209, 214, 215, 260, 261, 262
extra-Atlantic history, 97, 105–8

Falkland Islands, 100
famines, 257
Febvre, Lucien, 162
Findlay, Alexander George, 189–90
Findlay, Arthur, 190–91
Finland, 215, 230–31

322 Index

Finley, Moses, 137
First World War, 256–57
fisheries, 13–14
  Atlantic Ocean, 103
  Baltic Sea, 217–18, 219–20
  Southern Ocean, 309–12
fluid ontology, 18
Flynn, Dennis O., 82
fly-ship (*fluyt*), 221
Food and Agriculture Organization, 312
forced labour
  see slavery and slave trade
Fram, 276–77
Franklin, Benjamin, 90
Freeman, Donald, 68
Friedman, Thomas, 146
Frobisher, Martin, 283
Frost, Lionel, 82
Furayama Tadao, 189

Galle inscription, 35–36
Gandhi, Mahatma, 56–57
Geneva Convention for the Regulation of
  Whaling, 305
Genoa, 246–47
Genscher, Hans-Dietrich, 214–15
Ghafur, Mulla Abdul, 39
'ghost ships', 12, 204
Gietermaker, Claes Hendrickszoon, 222
Gilroy, Paul, 91
Giovanni de Pian del Carpini, 183–84
Glissant, Édouard, 102
Godechot, Jacques, 94
Gomes, Estêvão, 283
grain trade
  Baltic Sea, 217, 219, 220–21, 228
  Red Sea, 176
Grand Bassin crater lake, Mauritius, 59
Great Britain
  and Baltic Sea, 225–27, 228, 229
  and Southern Ocean, 303–6
Great Ocean Conveyor Belt, 105
Great Pacific Garbage Patch, 191
'Great Patriation of the Fatherland', 203
Greeks, ancient, 241–43
Green, Nile, 53
Greenpeace, 83, 311, 313
Grove, Richard, 50
guano mining industry, 76, 77–78
Gulf of Aden, 171
Gulf Stream, 90, 276
Guo, Li, 165, 168

Haddon, Alfred Cort, 63
hajj, 51, 52–53, 166
Hannibal, 197–98

Hanotaux, Gabriel, 162–63
Hans Sloane Herbarium, 51
Hanseatic League, 215–19
Hardin, Garrett, 307–8
Harries, Patrick, 43
Harrisson, Tom, 118
Harvey, David, 194
Haushofer, Karl, 92
Hawai'i, 71, 74
Heezen, Bruce, 104
Henry the Navigator, 9–10
Herbert, Wally, 277
Herodotus, 243, 282
Herzfeld, Michael, 145–46
Hess, Andrew, 140–41, 147–48
Hirayama Ikuo, 206
historical periodisation, 22–24
Holy League, 250
Homer, 241–42
Hondius, Willem, 222
Horden, Peregrine, 98, 136–37,
  146, 237
Hortus Malabaricus, 50
Howkins, Adrian, 306
Hsian, Fei, 120
Huber, Valeska, 166
Hudson, Henry, 284
Hult, Pieter van den, 223
hydrogenation of oils, 303
Hyphegesis Geographike, 34

Ibn al-Mujawir, 168
Ibn Battuta, 168
Ibn Jubayr, 168
Ibn Majid, Ahmad, 47–48, 49, 168
I-ching, 116
Igler, David, 70–71
imperialism
  Indian Ocean, 38–41, 43, 48
  Mediterranean Sea, 138–39,
    141–45, 150–51
  Pacific Ocean, 73–74
  Red Sea, 168–69, 170
  Sea of Japan/East Sea, 186, 201–2
  see also Black Sea
indentured labour
  Indian Ocean, 44–45
  Pacific Ocean, 77–79
India, 48, 50
Indian Ocean, 31–60, 89, 98, 105
  knowledges and environments, 46–54
  labour, 41–46
  modern formations, 54–59
  narrators of, 33–38
  Red Sea and, 156–58, 164, 171
  trade, 22, 38–42, 46, 107

Index

323

Indigenous peoples, 9, 11, 24
  Aboriginal Australians, 66–67, 68, 127, 301
  Arctic Ocean, 273–74, 275–76, 281–82
  Atlantic Ocean, 93, 99–100
  navigational knowledge, 72
  Pacific Ocean, 72, 74–75, 81–82
  Sea of Japan/East Sea, 186, 193
  South China Sea, 124–27
  Southern Ocean, 301
  whaling, 14, 193, 301
Indonesia, 49
infra-Atlantic history, 97, 98–102, 108
institution building, international, 93
Intergovernmental Oceanic Commission, 1
International Committee of the Red Cross, 203
International Convention for the Regulation of Whaling (ICRW), 307, 313
International Council for the Exploration of the Sea (ICES), 305
International Court of Justice, 313–14
International Geophysical Year, 310
International Hydrographic Organisation, 182, 184–85, 270
International Whaling Commission (IWC), 14, 306, 307–8, 309, 312, 313
Inuit, 273–74, 276, 282
Inuit Circumpolar Council, 291
Ireland, Alexander, 70
iron, 229
Islam
  Indian Ocean, 40, 52–53
  Pacific Ocean, 79
  Red Sea, 166, 168
  see also Muslim communities
Istanbul, 239, 260
  see also Constantinople

James, C. L. R., 91–92
Japan, 82–83
  see also Sea of Japan/East Sea
Japan Current, 189–91
Japan Whaling Association, 193
Jenkins, Charles Robert, 203
Jewish communities
  Black Sea, 256, 258
  Mediterranean Sea, 150, 151
  Red Sea, 166, 168
Johnsen, A. O., 302
Johnson, Charles, 144
Joint-Daguenet, Roger, 163
Jones, Ryan Tucker, 70
Journal of Pacific History, 68
Juntoku, Emperor of Japan, 200

Kafadar, Cemal, 141
Kaffa, 246, 247, 248
kamal, 47, 48
Kammerer, Albert, 161–62, 169
Kellogg, Remington, 307
Kessel, Joseph, 170
khashabat, 47
Khrushchev, Nikita, 259
kidnappings, Sea of Japan/East Sea, 196, 203–4
Knipowitsch, Nikolai, 289
Korea
  see East Sea/Sea of Japan
Korean Airlines Flight 007, 204–6
Korean War, 12, 202
Kotzebue, Otto von, 230
krill, Antarctic, 305, 309, 311, 312, 315
Krusenstern, Adam Johann von, 230
Kuroshio Current, 189–91
Kuykendall, Ralph S., 62

La Pérouse Map, 185
La Pérouse, Jean-François de Galaup, comte de, 73, 185, 190
labour
  Atlantic Ocean, 107
  Indian Ocean, 41–46
  Pacific Ocean, 77–79
  see also slavery and slave trade
labour camps, 201–2
'Lapita' culture, 67
Larsen, Carl Anton, 303
LaRue, Leonard, 202
lascars, 45–46
Latham, A. J. H., 82
law of the sea, 273, 310–11
League of Nations, 305
Lemuria, 36, 99
'Levantini', 150–51
Linnaeus, Carl, 282
Lippmann, Walter, 92–93
Livorno, 151
London Missionary Society, 80
Londres, Albert, 170

MacDonald, Ranald, 196
Mackintosh, Neil, 306
Maddison, Ben, 301
Magalhães Godinho, Vitorino, 94
Magnus, Olaus, 212, 283
Malmström, Cecilia, 231
Mamiya Rinzo, 190
Mangyongbong ferry, 202–3, 204
Manila galleons, 69, 106–7
Māori, 67

324 Index

mapping
  see cartography
Margariti, Roxani Eleni, 165, 168
marine goods, South China Sea, 124–27
marine protected areas, 314
Maritime Heritage Gallery, National
  Museum of India, 48
Marseille, 152
Matthews, Derek H., 172–73
Matvejević, Predrag, 141
Mauritius, 44, 45, 50
  Grand Bassin crater lake, 59
Mauro, Frédéric, 94
Maury, Matthew Fontaine, 90
Mawson, Douglas, 306
McKenzie, Alexander, 283
McPherson, Kenneth, 37, 47
Mediterranean Sea, 89, 98, 105, 134–53,
  234, 236–37
  Christian–Muslim division, 134–36,
    138–41, 146–49
  cosmopolitanism, 149–52
  environmental histories, 136–38
  global history and, 145–49
  naming debates, 138, 139
  Ottoman Empire and, 141–45,
    150–51
  Red Sea and, 156–58, 164
  refugees and migrants, 134, 152
  source of danger, 139–40
  trade, 147–48, 230
Meloy, John, 165
Mercator, Gerardus, 283
Mercedarians, 147–48
Meredith Victory, 12, 202
mid-Atlantic ridge, 104
migration
  Atlantic Ocean, 93, 95, 103–4, 107
  Baltic Sea, 222
  Mediterranean Sea, 134, 152
  Pacific Ocean, 63, 66–68, 77–79
  Red Sea, 177–78
  Sea of Japan/East Sea, 12, 186–87,
    201–4
Millburn, William, 123
Miller, Peter, 137
Mills, J.V., 118
'Ming Gap' thesis, 118–19
mining, 76, 79
Miran, Jonathan, 98
Mithridates VI, king of Pontus, 243
Molotov-Ribbentrop pact, 258
Mombasa, 54, 55
Moneron Island, Russia, 190
Monfreid, Henry de, 170–71
Mongols, 246

Monneron, Paul Merault, 190
monsoon systems
  Indian Ocean, 46–47, 48, 49–50
  Red Sea, 160
  South China Sea, 113, 118
Montreux Convention on the Regime of
  the Straits, 257, 260
Moon, Alexander, 50
Moresby, Robert, 170
Morgan, Nathaniel Saxton, 197–98
mother-of-pearl, 125, 175–76
mufti, 143–44
Munmu, Silla King, 188
Murai Shosuke, 188
Muslim communities
  Black Sea, 255, 256
  Indian Ocean, 41
  Mediterranean Sea, 134–36,
    138–41, 146–49
  South China Sea, 117
  see also Islam; Ottoman Empire
mutinies, *lascar*, 46

naming debates, 6–7
  Mediterranean Sea, 138, 139
  Red Sea, 161
  Sea of Japan/East Sea, 182–86, 207
  Southern Ocean, 296–98
Nansen, Fridtjof, 276–77, 279
Nanyang (South China Sea), 115, 117,
  120, 130
National Famine Monument, Ireland, 10
National Museum of India, 48
NATO, 93, 258, 260, 261
Nautilus, 277
navigational knowledge
  Atlantic Ocean, 89–90
  Baltic Sea, 222
  Indian Ocean, 47–48
  Pacific Ocean, 72
  Red Sea, 160–61, 171–72
  Sea of Japan/East Sea, 184
  South China Sea, 117–18
Nesselmann, Georg Heinrich
  Ferdinand, 213
Netherlands, and Baltic Sea, 213, 218–24,
  225, 228, 230
'New Hansa' debate, 214
'new thalassology', 2, 164
New Zealand, 67, 68, 83
nitrate pollution, 232
Nordenskiöld, Adolf Erik, 279
Norse colonisation of Arctic, 276, 282
North Korea, 12, 191–92, 202–4
North Pacific Gyre, 191
Northwest Passage, 105, 106, 283, 287

Index

nuclear facilities, 191–92
nuclear testing, 83
nuclear waste, 191
nuclear weapons, 205–6

Obeyesekere, Gananath, 74
object biographies, 58–59
Obruchev, Vladimir A., 280
Ocean Island (Banaba), 79
oceanic currents
    Arctic Ocean, 276–77
    Atlantic Ocean, 90, 91, 276
    Pacific Ocean, 72
    Sea of Japan/East Sea, 189–91, 193
    Southern Ocean, 296
Odessa, 251–52
Oki Islands, Japan, 198–99
Ottoman Empire
    and Black Sea, 247–50, 252, 253–54, 256, 257
    and Mediterranean Sea, 141–45, 150–51
    and Red Sea, 168–69
Outhwaite, Leonard, 94

'Pacific century', 22, 82–83
Pacific Ocean, 62–83, 89, 105
    chronologies, 66–68
    economic histories, 75–76
    environmental and ecological histories, 71–72, 76–77, 80–81
    geographies, 68–72
    imperial histories, 73–74
    knowledges, 79–82
    labour, 77–79
    maritime histories, 72–73
    migration, 63, 66–68, 77–79
    postcolonial histories, 74–75
    slavery and slave trade, 77–78
    temporal dimension, 82–83
    trade, 69, 75–76, 107
Pacific rim, 71
Padrão dos Descobrimentos, Portugal, 9–10
Palmer, R. R., 94
'pan Pacific' construction, 71, 82
Panama, isthmus of, 105
Parry, William, 286
Pasha of Algiers, 147–48
pearling industry, 125, 126, 175–76
Pearson, Michael, 37, 47
Peary, Robert, 277
penal colonies, 58, 199–200
periodisation, 22–24
Periplus of the Erythraean Sea, 33, 166, 167
Perry, Matthew, 196, 197–98
Persian Gulf, 41–42
Peter the Great, tsar of Russia, 250

Pétriat, Philippe, 165
petroglyphs, 193
Philippines, 69, 106–7
phosphate mining, 76, 79
Pigafetta, Antonio, 122, 126
pilgrims, 212
piracy, 35
    Black Sea, 249
    Indian Ocean, 57–58
    Mediterranean Sea, 143–44
    Sea of Japan/East Sea, 188
Pirenne thesis, 134–36, 146–47
plane crash, Sea of Japan/East Sea, 204–6
plate tectonics, 104, 296
Plato, 99
Pliny the Elder, 167
pogroms, 256
Pollock, Sheldon, 53
pollution
    Great Pacific Garbage Patch, 191
    nitrates, 232
    radioactive waste, 191
Polo, Marco, 48, 184
Polynesian canoe journeys, 63, 66–67, 68
Pomeranz, Kenneth, 127
Portman, Maurice Vidal, 59
postcoloniality, 19
Power, Timothy, 164, 166, 168
prisoners of war, 200–1
Ptolemaic dynasty, Egypt, 167
Ptolemy, 34, 35, 36
Purcell, Nicholas, 98, 136–37, 146, 237
Pytheas of Massalia, 99, 282

qiyas, 47

racial theories, 81–82
Radcliffe-Browne, A. R., 58–59
radioactive waste, 191
Rafael, Vicente, 80
Rainbow Warrior, 83
ransoming of captives, 147–48
Rapa Nui (Easter Island), 67, 77–78
Rasmussen, Knud, 279
rattan, 125
Red Sea, 89, 98, 156–79
    architectural unity, 172–73
    conceptualizing, 171–73
    geography, 159–61
    historiographic perspectives, 161–66
    identity, 178–79
    migration, 177–78
    multi-scale framework, 173–78
    naming debates, 161
    temporal framework, 166–71
    trade, 160–61, 166, 173–77

326 Index

refugees
  Black Sea, 257
  Mediterranean Sea, 134, 152
  Sea of Japan/East Sea, 12, 202, 204
religious knowledge
  Indian Ocean, 52–54
  Pacific Ocean, 79–80
relocations and resettlement
  Black Sea, 255, 256, 258
  Pacific Ocean, 79
  Sea of Japan/East Sea, 201–2, 203, 204
Rennell, James, 90
repatriations, Sea of Japan/East Sea, 201–2,
    203, 204
Réseau Océan Mondial, 1
Ricci, Matteo, 184
Ricci, Ronit, 53
Richards, John, 299
Roberts, Peder, 304, 306
Roman Empire, 243–44
  see also Eastern Roman Empire
Ross, John, 286
Ross, Sir John, 286
Rothman, Natalie, 150–51
Rothschild, Emma, 96
Rowley, Graham, 290
Russell, Lynette, 301
Russia
  and Arctic Ocean, 274, 278, 280, 289
  and Baltic Sea, 213, 227, 229, 230
  and Black Sea, 250–53, 254–56, 257,
      259–60, 261–62
  and Sea of Japan/East Sea, 190, 191,
      199–200, 201–2
  see also Soviet Union
Ruysch, Johannes, 283
Ryu Yeon-Taek, 185

Sado Island, Japan, 200–1, 203
Sahlins, Marshall, 74
Sakhalin Island, Russia, 199–200, 201
  see also Moneron Island, Russia
Sastri, Suryanarayana, 36
Schafer, Edward, 124
Schenk, Peter, the Younger, 185
Scientific Committee on Antarctic
    Research (SCAR), 311, 312
scientific research
  Arctic Ocean, 286–90
  Atlantic Ocean, 104
  Southern Ocean, 305–6, 311
  see also Enlightenment
Sclater, Philip, 36
Scoresby, William, 287
sea ice, 286–92

Sea of Azov, 238, 239, 250
Sea of Japan/East Sea, 12, 182–207
  abductions, 196, 203–4
  migration, 12, 186–87, 201–4
  naming debates, 182–86, 207
  oceanic currents, 189–91, 193
  refugees, 12, 202, 204
  repatriations, 201–2, 203, 204
  trade, 192–93
  tragedy, 199–206
  whaling, 193–95, 197–98
sea peoples, South China Sea, 124–27
Sea Shepherd Conservation Society, 313
sealing, 299–301
Second World War, 82–83, 200–1, 258
Seed, Patricia, 271
Sephardi Jews, 150, 151
Sethu Pillai, R. P., 36
settler colonialism, 93
Seven Years' War, 144, 224
sexual labour, 77
Şeyhülislam, 143–44
Shiba Kokan, 184
ship monuments, 9–10
'Ship of Miracles', 12, 202
shipping traffic, 227
ships and ship-building, 9–13
  Baltic Sea, 220, 221
  Indian Ocean, 48–49, 51–53
  steam, 51–53, 91, 170, 253
shipyards, 12
Sidebotham, Steven, 165
Silla Dynasty, Korea, 188
'Singing Ship' monument, Australia, 10
Siple, Paul A., 290
slavery and slave trade
  Atlantic Ocean, 90–92, 93–94, 95,
      104, 106
  Indian Ocean, 40, 41–45
  Mediterranean Sea, 143
  Pacific Ocean, 77–78
  ship monuments to, 10
  South China Sea, 126–27
Sloane, Hans, 104, 273–74
Smith, Bernard, 66
sonar, 104
South Atlantic Gyre, 91
South China Sea, 13, 89, 113–31
  ancient and medieval histories, 115–20
  early modern history, 120–23
  ecological histories, 124–27
  trade, 115–23, 124–30
Southern Ocean, 8, 13, 89, 105, 296–316
  Antarctic Treaty, 310, 311–12
  conservation, 304–5, 307–8, 309–14

Index

naming debates, 296–98
scientific research, 305–6, 311
sealing, 299–301
whaling, 299, 301–8, 309, 311, 312–14
Soviet Union
and Arctic Ocean, 278, 289–90
and Baltic Sea, 209, 214
and Black Sea, 240, 257–59, 260
and Sea of Japan/East Sea, 201–2, 204–5
and Southern Ocean, 309–10
see also Russia
Spate, O. H. K., 66
Spitsbergen, 284–85
Sri Lanka, 35, 36, 50
Colombo, 55–56
St Helena, 100, 107
St Petersburg, 225–26, 227, 229
Stalin, Joseph, 257–58
Stalingrad, Battle of, 258
steam shipping, 51–53, 91, 170, 253
Stefansson, Vilhjalmur, 279, 282–83
Strabo, 167
Straits of Gibraltar, 105
subaltern biography, 45
sub-Atlantic history, 97, 102–5, 108
Suez Canal, 107, 163, 166, 170
Svalbard Treaty, 272
swimming, 8–9, 104

Tagliacozzo, Eric, 41, 166
Taiwan, 124
Tamil scholars, 36
Taprobane, 35, 36
tarsh al-bahr, 179
Tatars, 247, 248, 255, 258
Te Rangi Hiroa (Sir Peter Buck),
63, 67, 81
Tharp, Marie, 104
thermohaline circulation, Arctic
Ocean, 276
Thoreau, Henry David, 101
timber and forest products, Baltic Sea,
220, 221, 228, 229
Tinker, Hugh, 44
Tokugawa shogun, 195
Tønnessen, J. N., 302, 308
tourism, Southern Ocean, 314
Toussaint, Auguste, 37
trade
Arctic Ocean, 274
Atlantic Ocean, 106–7
Baltic Sea, 212–13, 215–22, 224–31
Black Sea, 239, 249, 253, 255–56
Indian Ocean, 22, 38–42, 46, 107
Mediterranean Sea, 147–48, 230

Pacific Ocean, 69, 75–76, 107
Red Sea, 160–61, 166, 173–77
Sea of Japan/East Sea, 192–93
South China Sea, 115–23, 124–30
see also slavery and slave trade
tragedy of the commons, 307–8
trans-Atlantic history, 96–97
Trans-Atlantic Slave Trade Database, 92
transnational history-writing, 4–5
Treaty of Berlin, 256
Treaty of Lausanne, 257
Treaty of Paris (1856), 255
trepang (edible sea-cucumber), 126–27
Tristan da Cunha, 100
Trivellato, Francesca, 151
Trojan War, 241–42
Tsushima Current, 191
Tuchscherer, Michel, 163, 173
Tupaia, 69
Turkey, 239, 257, 258–59, 260, 261, 262
see also Ottoman Empire
Twain, Mark, 255

Ulleugndo Island, South Korea, 198–99
Um, Nancy, 165, 173
United Nations, 1, 16, 93, 202
United Nations Convention on the Law of
the Sea (UNCLOS), 273, 310–11
United Nations Economic, Social
and Cultural Organisation
(UNESCO), 1, 93
United States
and Arctic Ocean, 290
and Sea of Japan/East Sea, 194–99,
205–6

Valérian, Dominique, 144–45
Vallet, Eric, 165, 168
van Obberghen, Antoni, 222, 223, 224
van Rede tot Drakenstein, Hendrik, 50
van Steenwinckel, Hans, the Elder, 223
van Steenwinckel, Hans, the Younger, 223
van Steenwinckel, Lourens, 223
van Wijck, Jan, 223
Vaughan, Megan, 45
Vaugondy, Gilles Robert, 185
Venice, 143–44, 150–51, 245–46
Verne, Jules, 236
Victory, 12
Villiers, Alan, 37–38, 94

Walcott, Derek, 102
Waldseemüller, Martin, 283
Wallace line, 76
Wallerstein, Immanuel, 39

328 Index

Wang Gungwu, 117
Wang Ta-yuan, 120
war crimes, 200–1
War of Polish Succession, 224
Warren, James Francis, 127
Watson, Paul, 313
waves, 16
whale oil, 302–3
whaling, 13–14, 73
   Arctic Ocean, 284–85, 299, 302
   Atlantic Ocean, 103
   Sea of Japan/East Sea, 193–95,
     197–98
   Southern Ocean, 299, 301–8, 309, 311,
     312–14
White, John, 67, 68
White, Joshua, 143–44
Williams, Eric, 91–92
Willoughby, Hugh, 284
Winchester, Simon, 156
wind systems
   Atlantic Ocean, 91

Indian Ocean, 46–47, 48,
   49–50
Red Sea, 160–61, 171–72
Sea of Japan/East Sea, 184, 192
South China Sea, 113, 118
Wladyslaw III, King of Poland,
   247–48
women
   sexual labour, 77
   slavery, 42
World Oceans Day, 1, 3
World War I, 256–57
World War II, 82–83, 200–1, 258
Wyld, James, 185

Yokota Megumi, 203

Zanzibar, 54–55
Zeami Motokiyo, 200
Zedler, Johann Heinrich, 213
Zheng He, 35–36, 120
Zubov, Nikolai, 289